English Poetry of the Sixteenth Century

Longman Literature in English Series

General Editors: David Carroll and Michael Wheeler
University of Lancaster

For a complete list of titles see pages viii and ix

English Poetry of the Sixteenth Century

Gary Waller

Longman

London and New York

Longman Group UK Limited
Longman House, Burnt Mill, Harlow
Essex CM20 2JE, England
and Associated Companies throughout the world

*Published in the United States of America
by Longman Inc., New York*

First published 1986
Second impression 1989

BRITISH LIBRARY CATALOGUING IN PUBLICATION DATA
Waller, Gary F.
  English poetry of the sixteenth century.—
  (Longman literature in English series).
  1. English poetry—16th century—History
  and criticism
  I. Title
  821'.2'09   PR521

ISBN 0 582 49248 3csd
ISBN 0 582 49247 5 ppr

LIBRARY OF CONGRESS CATALOGING IN PUBLICATION DATA
Waller, Gary F. (Gary Fredric), 1945–
  English poetry of the sixteenth century.

  (Longman literature in English series)
  Bibliography: p.
  Includes index.
  1. English poetry—Early modern, 1500–1700—History
and criticism. I. Title. II. Series.
  PR531. W33 1986   821'.9'002   85–10959
  ISBN 0-582-49248-3
  ISBN 0-582-49247-5 (pbk.)

Set in 9½/11pt Bembo (Linotron 202)
Produced by Longman Singapore Publishers (Pte) Ltd
Printed in Singapore

English Poetry
of the
Sixteenth Century

Gary Waller

Longman

London and New York

Longman Group UK Limited
Longman House, Burnt Mill, Harlow
Essex CM20 2JE, England
and Associated Companies throughout the world

*Published in the United States of America
by Longman Inc., New York*

© Longman Group UK Limited 1986

First published 1986
Second impression 1989

BRITISH LIBRARY CATALOGUING IN PUBLICATION DATA
Waller, Gary F.
    English poetry of the sixteenth century.—
    (Longman literature in English series).
    1. English poetry—16th century—History
    and criticism
    I. Title
    821'.2'09   PR521

ISBN 0 582 49248 3csd
ISBN 0 582 49247 5ppr

LIBRARY OF CONGRESS CATALOGING IN PUBLICATION DATA
Waller, Gary F. (Gary Fredric), 1945–
    English poetry of the sixteenth century.

    (Longman literature in English series)
    Bibliography: p.
    Includes index.
    1. English poetry—Early modern, 1500–1700—History
and criticism. I. Title. II. Series.
    PR531. W33   1986   821'.9'002   85-10959
    ISBN 0-582-49248-3
    ISBN 0-582-49247-5 (pbk.)

Set in 9½/11pt Bembo (Linotron 202)
Produced by Longman Singapore Publishers (Pte) Ltd
Printed in Singapore

Contents

Editors' Preface

The multi-volume Longman Literature in English Series provides students of literature with a critical introduction to the major genres in their historical and cultural context. Each volume gives a coherent account of a clearly defined area, and the series, when complete, will offer a practical and comprehensive guide to literature written in English from Anglo-Saxon times to the present. The aim of the series as a whole is to show that the most valuable and stimulating approach to literature is that based upon an awareness of the relations between literary forms and their historical context. Thus the areas covered by most of the separate volumes are defined by period and genre. Each volume offers new informed ways of reading literary works, and provides guidance to further reading in an extensive reference section.

As well as studies on all periods of English and American literature, the series includes books on criticism and literary theory, and on the intellectual and cultural context. A comprehensive series of this kind must of course include other literature written in English, and therefore a group of volumes deals with Irish and Scottish literature, and the literatures of India, Africa, the Caribbean, Australia, and Canada. The forty-seven volumes of the series cover the following areas: pre-Renaissance English Literature, English Poetry, English Drama, English Fiction, English Prose, Criticism and Literary Theory, Intellectual and Cultural Context, American Literature, Other Literatures in English.

David Carroll
Michael Wheeler

Longman Literature in English Series

General Editors: David Carroll and Michael Wheeler
University of Lancaster

Pre-Renaissance English Literature

* English Literature before Chaucer *Michael Swanton*
  English Literature in the Age of Chaucer
* English Medieval Romance *W.R.J. Barron*

English Poetry

* English Poetry of the Sixteenth Century *Gary Waller*
* English Poetry of the Seventeenth Century *George Parfitt*
  English Poetry of the Eighteenth Century, 1700–1789
* English Poetry of the Romantic Period, 1789–1830 *J.R. Watson*
* English Poetry of the Victorian Period, 1830–1890 *Bernard Richards*
  English Poetry of the Early Modern Period, 1890–1940
  English Poetry since 1940

English Drama

  English Drama before Shakespeare
* English Drama: Shakespeare to the Restoration, 1590–1660
  Alexander Leggatt
* English Drama: Restoration and Eighteenth Century, 1660–1789
  Richard W. Bevis
  English Drama: Romantic and Victorian, 1789–1890
  English Drama of the Early Modern Period, 1890–1940
  English Drama since 1940

English Fiction

* English Fiction of the Eighteenth Century, 1700–1789 *Clive T. Probyn*
* English Fiction of the Romantic Period, 1789–1830 *Gary Kelly*
* English Fiction of the Victorian Period, 1830–1890 *Michael Wheeler*
* English Fiction of the Early Modern Period, 1890–1940 *Douglas Hewitt*

English Prose

  English Prose of the Renaissance, 1550–1700
  English Prose of the Eighteenth Century
  English Prose of the Nineteenth Century

Criticism and Literary Theory

Criticism and Literary Theory from Sidney to Johnson
Criticism and Literary Theory from Wordsworth to Arnold
Criticism and Literary Theory from 1890 to the Present

The Intellectual and Cultural Context

The Sixteenth Century
* The Seventeenth Century, 1603–1700 *Graham Parry*
* The Eighteenth Century, 1700–1789 *James Sambrook*
  The Romantic Period, 1789–1830
  The Victorian Period, 1830–1890
  The Twentieth Century: 1890 to the Present

American Literature

American Literature before 1880
American Poetry of the Twentieth Century
American Drama of the Twentieth Century
* American Fiction, 1865–1940 *Brian Lee*
  American Fiction since 1940
  Twentieth-Century American

Other Literatures

Irish Literature since 1800
Scottish Literature since 1700

Australian Literature
Indian Literature in English
African Literature in English: East and West
Southern African Literature in English
Caribbean Literature in English
* Canadian Literature in English *W.J. Keith*

* *Already published*

Author's Preface

Whether historians write history or critics criticism (even though never in the way they choose), or whether they are written by them, will never be proved by a single volume, but the process by which this volume of the Longman Literature in English series has been written certainly supports what it tries to exemplify – that the disruptive and contradictory structures that erupt within writing are the product of the interactions of many discourses, not merely the product of the will of its 'author'. As the *scriptor* of this study I recognize many intellectual debts and personal obligations while acknowledging there are many more. When Michael Wheeler, one of the General Editors of the series, asked me to undertake the volume, I had in process a study of the power of the Court over the poetry of the period. Much of that, in turn, had grown from earlier work on the Sidney Circle, and in particular from two studies of the Countess of Pembroke which convinced me (as usual, after they were published) that we needed to rethink radically our way of writing about the period. My original intention was merged into this project – and with it a cumbersome and (as I saw) increasingly archaic methodology. Over a number of years, I tried out a number of essays and conference papers and discovered further frustrations and questions. In order to let some of the answers find me, I had at times to stop reading sixteenth-century poetry, my ostensible subject, until I could find fit words by which it could speak through me. As a consequence, this study has been assembled, or assembled itself, as a process of re-education of its 'author' – as those to whom it is dedicated know (in different ways) to their cost.

My specific debts (authors may not exist, at least in the ways we once thought, but readers and friends certainly do) are many, and only the most important can be acknowledged here. As I read over the final stages of my work, I found myself drawn back to C. S. Lewis's *English Literature in the Sixteenth Century* and discovered myself agreeing, though from startlingly different perspectives, with many of his judgements: I commenced my teaching career in the rooms in which he had once taught at Magdalene College, Cambridge, and so my acknowledgement is a doubly appropriate one. His successors in the

Chair of Medieval and Renaissance Literature, the late J. A. W. Bennett and John Stevens, both helped me greatly in those early days, and later, as did other teachers and mentors, including Peter Dane, Mike Doyle, L. C. Knights, and the late J. C. Reid. More recently, I have learnt much from scholars such as the late Diane Bornstein, and Elizabeth Bieman, Ian Donaldson, Maurice Evans, A. C. Hamilton, S. K. Heninger, Jr, Alvin Kernan, Roger Kuin, Mary E. Lamb, Richard Lanham, J. C. A. Rathmell, Thomas P. Roche Jr, and Germaine Warkentin. One group of co-workers deserves particular thanks. At the MLA Convention of 1981 Leonard Tennenhouse announced breezily that I was writing what would be the first revisionist history of Renaissance literature; he, there-fore, bears a special responsibility for the work, even though I would deny that this book is quite what he described it as. But if, as I believe, there is indeed a new direction being forged in writing literary history, it is because of him and the following scholars, among others, with whom I have worked and who have contributed materially or given en-couragement to me: Kate Belsey, Marion Campbell, Jonathan Dollimore, Antony Easthope, Jonathan Goldberg, Jane Hedley, Bob Hodge, Ann Rosalind Jones, Jim Kavanagh, Jacqueline T. Miller, Louis A. Montrose, Bernard Sharratt, Alan Sinfield, Peter Stallybrass, and Frank Whigham. Among the students to whom in part this book is dedicated and with whom it was to a large extent written (in some cases giving me reason to break the Eighth Commandment): Doug Abel, Lisa Bernstein, Andrea Clough, Steven Denvir, Glen Drummond, Linda Levine, Debra Martin, Margaret McLaren, Susan Rudy Dorscht (who served as a primary research assistant and whose drafting of the Appendices is gratefully acknowledged) and – if I may simultaneously thank and acknowledge one of my General Editors – Michael Wheeler. My colleagues at Carnegie-Mellon have given me a uniquely stimulating intellectual environment. Kathleen McCormick, my col-laborator on other projects as well as a reader of some parts of this, is due especial thanks.

Research for this book has been carried out over nearly ten years, with the help of the Canada Council, and the Social Sciences and Humanities Research Council, and of short-term grants from Dalhousie and Wilfrid Laurier Universities. I wish to thank, as well, the Humanities Research Centre at the Australian National University for a fellowship which enabled me to spend four stimulating months thinking and writing in congenial surroundings in 1979. It is such necessary material support which represents, finally, the faith of one's colleagues, that often stirs the scholar into producing the most difficult, and on occasions the most tiresome, but necessary work. To all concerned, my deepest thanks.

Parts of this volume have appeared, in different form, as follows: portions of Chapter 1 in the *Dalhousie Review* (1981) and *Assays* (1982);

different parts of the material on Philip and Robert Sidney, Ralegh, and Shakespeare in *Short Fiction: Critical Views*, and *Poetry: Critical Views*, both published by Salem Press (1981 and 1982, respectively); much of the account of *Astrophil and Stella* in the special Sidney issue of *Studies in the Literary Imagination* (1982), edited by William A. Sessions, to whom special debts, personal and professional, must be acknowledged; some of the material on the Sidney Circle appeared first in *The Triumph of Death* and *Mary Sidney, Countess of Pembroke*, published by the University of Salzburg (1977, 1979); that on Petrarchanism in Chapter 3 in *Sir Philip Sidney and the Interpretation of Renaissance Culture*, edited by Gary F. Waller and Michael D. Moore (Croom Helm, 1984), and parts of the final chapter in *Silent But for the Word*, edited by Margaret Hannay (Kent State 1985). Throughout, ideas and occasional paragraphs have surfaced in editorial material in the *Sidney Newsletter*. My gratitude to its editor, Gerald A. Rubio, is enthusiastically given. In all cases, prior publication is gratefully acknowledged.

My two sons Michael and Andrew helped, as on other occasions, by allowing me to be a revisionist father. However nobody else is responsible for the final product. But then, as some of my colleagues and friends say, neither am I, since, they say, it is discourse that creates us; we do not speak, we are spoken. Nonetheless, the world of scholarship is such that I will want to accept any praise for whatever stimulation this volume may produce in its readers, so I must accept all the blame for its shortcomings.

GFW
Carnegie-Mellon University
Pittsburgh
December 1984

List of Abbreviations

The following common abbreviations of scholarly journals and series etc., have been used in this study:

ADE Bulletin	Association of Departments of English Bulletin
AUMLA	Australasian Universities Modern Languages Association
CQ	Critical Quarterly
EETS	Early English Texts Society
ELH	English Literary History
ELR	English Literary Renaissance
ES	English Studies
HLQ	Huntingdon Library Quarterly
HMC	Historical Manuscripts Commission
JEGP	Journal of English and Germanic Philosophy
JMRS	Journal of Medieval and Renaissance Studies
JWCI	Journal of the Warburg and Courtauld Institutes
KR	Kenyon Review
MLN	Modern Language Notes
MLQ	Modern Languages Quarterly
MLR	Modern Language Review
NLH	New Literary History
OLR	Oxford Literary Review
PMLA	Publications of the Modern Languages Association
PQ	Philological Quarterly
RenQ	Renaissance Quarterly
Ren and Ref	Renaissance and Reformation
RES	Review of English Studies
SEL	Studies in English Literature, 1500–1900
SLit I	Studies in the Literary Imagination
SN	Shakespeare Newsletter
SNew	Sidney Newsletter
SP	Studies in Philosophy

SpN	Spenser Newsletter
SRen	Studies in the Renaissance
TSLL	Texas Studies in Language and Literature
UTQ	University of Toronto Quarterly
YES	Yearbook of English Studies

This book is dedicated with gratitude to my colleagues and students at Magdalen, Auckland, Dalhousie, Wilfrid Laurier and Carnegie-Mellon, who have listened and argued, celebrated and criticized, and, especially, to J, K, L, M, and to S and the gang at Kalamazoo.

This booklet is offered with gratitude to my colleagues and students at Monckton ... who volunteered and tested, challenged and criticized ... K ... and to ... for the ... acknowledgements.

Chapter 1

Reading the Poetry of the Sixteenth Century

Introduction

When a modern student, even a general reader, picks up a volume of sixteenth-century poetry, what is likely to be his or her impression? When I first started teaching the poetry of Wyatt and Sidney, Shakespeare and Donne, there was a sense of their remoteness from most concerns we have in the twentieth century. Except as a kind of nostalgia, what did delicate love sonnets, songs with refrains like 'hey nonny nonny no', and seemingly artificial, conventional poems dealing with refined upper-class manners have to say to us? Even if one was interested in the history of the time – with its stirring mixture of battles, beheadings, rebellions, and religious controversies – most of the poetry seemed pale and lifeless, or else just crudely versified propaganda, monuments to dead ideas or simply the province of antiquarians. Shakespeare and Donne were, perhaps, exceptions: as F. R. Leavis put it for us, when we reach Donne after a century of dull poetry, at last we can 'read on as we read the living'.[1]

Today, all this has changed. The study of sixteenth-century poetry has become one of the most interesting fields in English literature. In part this is because of a greater liveliness in the field of literary criticism in general. In the past two decades, we have discovered so many more powerful tools with which to read our literature. In part, too, it is because we have realized just how similar, in significant ways, our age is to the sixteenth century. Despite real differences in the social, cultural, and ideological practices of the two periods, we seem to face uncannily analogous personal and collective dilemmas and obsessions.

Studying (and, for that matter, teaching) sixteenth-century poetry today can therefore be a very contemporary experience as well as intellectually challenging. Let me give one example – a poem to which I shall return in Chapter 4. My students were asked to read Sir Thomas Wyatt's best-known poem:

They flee from me that sometime did me seek
   With naked foot stalking in my chamber.
I have seen them gentle, tame, and meek
    That now are wild and do not remember
    That sometime they put themself in danger
To take bread at my hand; and now they range
Busily seeking with a continual change.

Thanked be fortune it hath been otherwise
   Twenty times better, but once in special
In thin array after a pleasant guise,
    When her loose gown from her shoulders did fall
    And she me caught in her arms long and small,
Therewithal sweetly did me kiss,
And softly said, 'Dear heart, how like you this?'

It was no dream; I lay broad waking.
   But all is turned through my gentilness
Into a strange fashion of forsaking.
    And I have leave to goo of her goodness,
    And she also to use newfangleness.
But since that I so kindly am served
I would fain know what she hath deserved.

The students were asked to write one- or two-page 'response statements' to the poem in which they described in as much detail as possible the initial effect of the text upon them – whether it was confusion, suspense, interest, indignation, or whatever. Then they were asked to try to account for why the reading had that effect. First, what was there in the nature of the *text* (its subject-matter, language, conventions, organization, themes, the gaps or indeterminacies which the reader has to fill in, and so forth)? Second, what was there in the nature of the *reader* him or (her) self that had produced that reading? How, in short, in the act of reading, had *reader* and *text* co-operated? The results were fascinating. All the men in the class felt immediate identification with the wounded male ego that is articulated in the poem – he has been rejected by a woman with whom he has unexpectedly fallen in love only to be told by her that it was all enjoyable but superficial flirtation. All the women in the class were amusedly derisive of the attitude: what, they said, about the woman's viewpoint? In such a society, and within such a philosophy of love, both so male-centred, why should a woman not get what she could out of the game of sex? Girls just want to have fun. In creating our 'readings' of the poem as a kind of amusing public argument, we were, without knowing it fully, creating something of the atmosphere of the original sixteenth-century Court itself and how such poetry might have been read. It should be added, perhaps, that this course on sixteenth-century poetry traditionally culminates in a banquet using Elizabethan recipes prepared by the students themselves, and accompanied by music and poetry readings. If we want the sixteenth-century poets to come alive, what better way than to combine poetry, music, and food!

More seriously, the students in the course were being introduced to a method of reading sixteenth-century poetry that this study will employ. The intention was to create strong readers of the poetry – readers who would bring their own most intense, often personal, questions to bear on their reading of Wyatt, or Sidney, or Shakespeare, or Donne. In particular, they were asked to read Roland Barthes's *A Lover's Discourse*, a remarkable anatomy of desire by a modern philosopher that seemed to most of the students to reflect uncannily on both the poetry they were reading *and* their own experiences. Barthes describes the lover, like the one in Wyatt's poem, remembering the love scene over and over 'in order to be unhappy/happy – not in order to understand'; and writes of how 'the ego discourses only when it is hurt'.[2] Barthes gave these student readers a powerful, contemporary vocabulary with which to articulate their questions about the text. As so often happens, the greatest enjoyment and the best criticism occur when a powerful reader encounters a powerful work.

The aim of this study is to introduce the poetry of the sixteenth century so that such confrontations, or dialogues, can occur between today's readers and the texts that come to us from the sixteenth century. To do so, we need to learn to realize that both the work and the reader have vital parts to play in producing lively, informative, effective (and affective) readings. To achieve this end, I draw on two main sources of information and insight. First, the age that produced these poems. We know so much more about the sixteenth century now – or, to put it another way, we have learnt to ask more penetrating questions about what appeared to previous ages to be a glittering and idealistic world. And, second, if the best contemporary scholarship and criticism are any guide, we have learnt to bring our own questions and concerns to bear on our reading. We ask these poems questions that arise from the world in which we read them, our world, and not only the world in which they were originally produced. We have also learnt – from psychology, philosophy, political and social sciences – to relate our readings of poetry to the wider and more vital world of non-literary concerns. Poetry, when it is *only* poetry, can easily become a marginal, spare-time diversion.

In a sense, the process I am describing is not new. Although usually without acknowledging (or perhaps even knowing) it, every age reads the poetry and other texts that come down to it from the past through its own concerns. If we look back a little further than our own time, we can see how our understanding of sixteenth-century poetry, and in particular the poetry of the two decades before 1600, has undergone interesting changes, especially in the past century. In 1861, Francis Palgrave's *Golden Treasury* established what became the basis for the modern canon of Elizabethan poetry. As well, it gave us a set of criteria for evaluating the poetry that was largely accepted for more than a century. It involved the assumption that the best poetry had an immediacy that made it easily accessible to the educated reader. While the long, public poems of the period – *A Mirror for Magistrates*, *The Faerie Queene*, Harington's translation of Ariosto – clearly required some kind of historical understanding, Palgrave's selection suggested that the Elizabethan lyricists, like Wyatt, Sidney, Spenser, Shakespeare, and Daniel could be seen as 'treasures which might lead us in higher and healthier ways than those of the world'.[3] They provided us with glimpses of an ideal order of love or harmony that the poets, all supposedly infatuated with the glories and buoyancy of the Elizabethan Age, celebrated in song just as they did in the pleasures, dances, and pageants of their lives at the Court. Even in the modern world (in this case in the middle of the nineteenth century) we could have direct access to this immediate, magical world. Such poems were delicate, immediate in their appeal, and dealt directly with universal human experiences.

Such a myth has been increasingly called into question in our century. T. S. Eliot's championing of the highly intellectual Metaphysical as opposed to the Elizabethan poets, Yvor Winters's rediscovery of a native plain-style tradition that existed alongside the dominant 'golden' or 'aureate' court lyric in the sixteenth century, C. S. Lewis's division of the century's poetry into drab and golden (terms which he vehemently asserted were not qualitative but descriptive); the articulation of the subtlety and richness of the Elizabethan poets' rhetorical training by such scholars as Richard Lanham and Rosamund Tuve – all these developments have made the amateurish *Golden Treasury* model of Elizabethan poetry less acceptable. In particular, refinements upon Winters's New Critical approach to the period have been especially influential, such as Douglas Peterson's examination of the presence of medieval rhetoric in both the plain and eloquent style and of the religious tradition of plain statement, G. K. Hunter's discussion of the division in the 1570s between moralistic, patriotic poems and courtly aestheticism, Fred Inglis's or John Williams's reinforcement of Winters's stress on the 'plain', moral-reflective, style and the claim that courtly Petrarchanism is a deviation from the main tradition. Valuable work has been done on the canon of such poets as Wyatt, Googe, and Mary and Robert Sidney; Spenser has been rescued from disfavour, and most recently, the canon has been expanded by our awareness that there is a small but significant amount of poetry written by women.

As matters stand now, the reader of sixteenth-century poetry can find diverse approaches, all of which show that it offers, in G. K. Hunter's terms, different but equal kinds of interest. A century and a quarter after Palgrave, we have come a long way. Sixteenth-century poetry is not merely the golden lyrics and delicate songs he approved. But there is one criterion of the *Golden Treasury's* praise which curiously has remained untouched in today's mainstream evaluations of sixteenth-century poetry. Palgrave praised the Elizabethan poets for their ability to unify a variety of experience, asserting that their special excellence lay rather in the whole than in the parts, in their creation of unity, harmony, and coherence.[4] Most modern criticism – including the 'New' Criticism, as well as 'Historicist' approaches that relate texts to their historical background – has taken for granted that a literary text is a unified, organic creation which 'reflects' or 'expresses' its author's views or vision, or the dominant philosophical assumptions of its age. What E. M. W. Tillyard termed the 'Elizabethan World Picture' – a philosophical conglomerate, supposedly believed by all Elizabethans, that the universe was a divinely created organism, characterized by unity, harmony, and hierarchy – has been widely seen as accepted by all educated Elizabethans. Likewise, the age's poetry is still widely seen as the expression of a buoyant society built on such order, hierarchy, and harmony, a balanced 'matching of contraries', to use a phrase of Calvin, to which I shall later return, notably in Chapter 5.

However, in the last two decades (and if one traces its philosophical sources, at least since Marx, Nietzsche, and Freud) a new paradigm has arisen in our understanding of many of the human sciences, one that is drastically affecting the way we read literature. The French philosopher Louis Althusser once suggested that our age would be looked back to as one in which the most fundamental human activities – perceiving, reading, writing – were radically revalued.[5] Perhaps not since the late eighteenth century have the roles and status of interpretation, history, reading, and writing been put so fiercely and fundamentally into question. It is now difficult to approach literary history or criticism, the teaching of language, literature, culture – even, to return to Althusser's point, the most fundamental human traits of perception and description – without being aware of a disturbing new need to ask radically different questions and to receive, however, tentatively, new and disturbing answers.

It is, however, only in recent years that such tremors have started to affect sixteenth-century studies. It was in the late 1970s that there were major signs of a stirring of what has increasingly become called a 'revisionist' literary history of the period. The Romantics and the Victorians had long been appropriated by sophisticated theoretical and practical approaches. But Michael McCanles noted, as recently as 1980, that Renaissance scholarship had still remained generally blind to the theoretical and methodological problems raised by its canonized approaches to its own material'.[6] It was about 1980 that there were signs that the ferment that had gone on in literary criticism generally had started to enter the world of Renaissance scholarship and criticism. It reflected, probably, much fine and unrecorded teaching in universities in Britain, the United States, and elsewhere, but is first seen in print in a number of books and articles published about that time. Richard McCoy's *Sir Philip Sidney: Rebellion in Arcadia* (1979), Stephen Greenblatt's *Renaissance Self-Fashioning* (1980), Jonathan Goldberg's *Endlesse Worke* (1981), Alan Sinfield's *Literature in Protestant England* (1983) all indicated that at last some of the major philosophical and cultural changes that had started to reconstruct literary criticism generally were having some impact upon sixteenth-century studies.

This study is written in the belief that the great advances in our understanding of the sixteenth century and its poetry – the work on canon, sources, traditions, rhetoric, poetics, and conventions that has occurred in the past century – will be wasted unless they are caught up into this new excitement about the *ways* we read literary and other texts. In order to make sixteenth-century poetry ours, to allow us to read it, in Leavis's words, not 'as students or as connoisseurs of anthology-pieces', but 'as we read the living', we must let it speak within the world its readers inhabit.[7] We must interrogate the poetry of the sixteenth century in our own ways, with whatever tools and methods, anxieties and affirmations, our own time affords us. In this way, we can become strong readers of sixteenth-century poetry. By beginning with what appear to be urgent questions for us, we let the poems speak to us not only of our history but also of our present. Texts are, after all, part of both our history and an account of our own place in that history.

My discussion of the texts of sixteenth-century poetry in this study is, therefore, a little different from that of conventional histories of the period. I am asking readers to concentrate on the 'dislocations' and 'disruptions' in poetic texts as well as on what they 'intend'. This advice may seem to conflict directly with notions of 'unity', 'order', and 'hierarchy' which have so long seemed inextricable from the discussions of the period's poetry and its 'world-vision'. I say 'seem' because it is, in fact, possible to interpret the sixteenth-century itself as a period of surprising upsurges and dislocations. The whole age was, after all, one of extraordinary insecurity, quite deserving the title that W. H. Auden gave to our time, the 'age of anxiety'. In other words, to insist, as I do, that the textual practices of sixteenth-century poems operate in contradiction to their own intentions may, I hope, be seen less as a demolition of them then an appropriate way into understanding and enjoying them. We are dealing with a period where there was enormous pressure upon language to grapple with new experiences, new feelings, and new social patterns. It was a time in which (as many poets themselves noted) language itself seemed to be simultaneously inadequate and overflowing. When we read sixteenth-century poetry and sense what Sidney terms its *enargeia*, we may observe not just its rhetorical power but also how much of what is going on in that poetry is not apparent. Although the poems may attempt to efface the struggle that has produced them, that struggle none the less leaves its invisible but indelible marks. What is *not* in the text is just as important as what seems to be there. As Chapter 7 will show, Shakespeare's sonnets, even (perhaps especially) the most serene of them, derive their energy from providing such a field of struggle. And they are typical of the age's poetry.

The task of criticism, therefore, becomes a very exciting one. It is that of bringing to life what has been blotted out, teasing out the conflicting discourses that fight within the text, that remain, in the words that the contemporary French philosopher Jacques Derrida has made famous, 'active and stirring, inscribed in white ink, an invisible drawing covered over in the palimpsest'.[8] We will watch, for instance, how in *The Faerie Queene* the surface text maintains an uneasy and shifting relationship with its apparent philosophical content. We will trace the movements by which a text falls short of or exceeds what it wants to say, the ways by which it is sidetracked, turned back on, or repeats itself. We will see how the period's best poems are full of eloquent silences and half-silences. We will pose the question (the writings of the few women poets of the period are excellent examples here) of what seem to be significant absences, silent or suppressed, in the texts. As Pierre Macherey, the important French critic, puts it, there are times when not only do texts *not* speak but where they *cannot* speak. There are places where a text seems unable quite to articulate what it seems to want to say. It is often in such uncertainties and disruptions where a text may speak to us most eloquently.

Does such talk of looking for 'gaps', 'disruptions', 'uncertainties', and 'absences' in texts sound strange? One of my students once likened it to what a psychoanalyst does with a patient, probing into the dark. And that is a good analogy. We are looking for the unconscious of the texts we read, not just the hidden meanings but the suppressed or repressed meanings. To mention psychoanalysis is to be modern with a vengeance, but it is interesting how some Renaissance thinkers, notably Sidney, seem to have wrestled with such issues. As I will show in Chapter 2, we may perceive in sixteenth-century theory and practice alike two contradictory views of reading. One sees texts as communicating 'messages' or 'information', a desire to extract conceptual statements from words. The other sees it as a desire to escape into the endless play and self-indulgence of language. An interesting contrast exists between Sidney and Greville, one we will see in Chapters 4 and 5. On the one hand, there is a puritanical desire to see tropes, metre and rhyme as disciplined ornament, merely means for the presentation of ideas and, in Greville's case, to be used with great reluctance. On the other hand, we can see the overflowing productivity of language, its playing off of one mode of linguistic organization against another, as a means in itself of achieving genuine knowledge.

It is interesting how some of the concerns about the untrustworthiness of language voiced in the Renaissance have surfaced in modern literacy criticism. In recent years, 'deconstruction' has become a rallying-cry (or a term of abuse) for a style of criticism that focuses on the contradictions in texts, on the radical inability of language to embody 'reality', and on the independence of texts from history. Deconstructive criticism has produced some very interesting readings of Renaissance poetry, and its contribution to our self-consciousness about language is immense. But the perspective of this study is rather different. Even if today we are all becoming used to acknowledging that a literary text does not have a fixed form, but always requires to be read, and so 'exists' only in readings throughout its history, none the less the place of the text in its history is something that we must grapple with. The study of literature is a historically situated practice, a set of changing but concrete activities that take place in educational institutions, in real historical contexts. We do not read, any more than authors wrote, in a vacuum of unlocated discourse. Therefore, while the deconstructive questions are crucial ones, I believe that it is important to try to speak of the pressure of history upon texts, that they are produced by struggles in history, that our reading of them is likewise in our own history. Often in the uncertainties, or on the edges of texts, hidden, but eloquent, we sense the pressures of history and specifically of a term I will define and develop, *ideology*.

I started off this introduction talking about the fun of reading sixteenth-century poetry, of music, food, and eager debate. And now, a few pages later, I am introducing readers to a somewhat abstract set of terms – 'deconstruction', 'absence', 'ideology'. All such terms, it might seem, take us very far from sitting back and indulging ourselves and reading Sidney's *Astrophil and Stella* or Donne's 'The Canonization'. The energy and fun of 'For God's sake, hold your tongue and let me love!' seem a far cry from such abstract matters.

But there is a real point to introducing unfamiliar, or difficult, concepts here. In any field of knowledge, as we discover we need to express or explain new experiences, we need to discover, invent, or adapt new terminology. The recent explosion in computer uses in business, home, and education has added new terms to our language which we have come (some of us reluctantly) to take for granted – *mainframe, interface, word-processor, number-crunching,* even the oxymoronic *personal computer.* Breakthroughs in any discipline are usually accompanied by the need to invent or adapt new terms. Literary criticism has been notoriously weak in developing adequate terminology, probably because of a genteel reluctance to move beyond 'appreciation' or out of an understandable desire to not offend the 'general' reader. One result has been a marginalization of literary studies among the other 'harder' human sciences, including sociology, information sciences, political theory, and philosophy.

There are, however, as today's students are discovering, real and important changes occurring in literary and associated cultural studies. And the scholarly and critical work being done in sixteenth-century literature is one shining example. As Annabel Patterson put it in 1980, 'the theorists' have at last 'got into the Renaissance'.[9] The result is that readers of this work will be given the opportunity to bring to bear some of this theoretical revolution upon their own reading. I mentioned at the start how my own students of sixteenth-century poetry were encouraged to read the poetry 'through' the work of Roland Barthes. The result was powerful, unpredictable readings, a sense of excitement and discovery. At this point I want to introduce a key term in this approach – one that has just been mentioned, *ideology*. Expert readers already accustomed to the term may be forgiven for skimming the next four paragraphs but it is important that students and general readers unfamiliar with the terminology of some of today's criticism should not be lost.

'Ideology' is a term that is sometimes associated with a simplistic Marxism. In this study the term is being used not to mean a static set of false or partial ideas which lie behind and determine the meanings of texts, but rather a complex of distinctive practices and social relations which are characteristic of any society and which are inscribed in the language of that society. 'Ideology' therefore applies to all the largely unconscious assumptions and acts by which men and women relate to their world; it is the system of images, attitudes, feelings, myths, and gestures which are peculiar to a society, which the members who make up that society habitually take for granted. All societies are held together by ideology.

In any society, especially in one as obsessed with order and control as Elizabethan England, one of the functions of ideology is, as far as possible, to define and limit the linguistic and cultural practices by which members of that society function. If, as usually happens, a society likes to think of itself as harmonious, coherent, and consensual, then it is ideology that enables this to occur. It tries to suggest the existing order of things is permanent, natural, universally acknowledged, embodying truths we would all agree with – and in so far as it persuades us that such 'truths' are not ideology (ideology, as one of my students indignantly put it, is something that *other* societies have, not ours), then it is successful. Ideology helps bind us together by giving us seemingly coherent representations and explanations of our social practices, and in particular by giving us the language by which we describe and thus try to perpetuate them. Thus ideology acts as a kind of social glue, binding us all together.

How does ideology affect literary texts? The impact of ideology upon the writings of a particular society – or, for that matter on the conventions and strategies by which *we* read those writings – is no different from the way it influences any other cultural practice. In no case, in Macherey's words, does the writer, as the producer of the text, manufacture the materials with which he works. The power of ideology is inscribed within the words, the rule-systems, and codes which constitute the text. Imagine ideology as a powerful force hovering over us as we read a text; as we read it reminds us of what is correct, commonsensical, or 'natural'. It tries, as it were, to guide both the writing and our subsequent readings of a text into coherence. When a text is written, ideology works to make some things more natural to write; when a text is read, it works to conceal struggles and repressions, to force language into conveying only those meanings reinforced by the dominant forces of our society.[10]

With much sixteenth-century poetry, the above argument will have obvious force. Clearly, some works, like *A Mirror for Magistrates* or *The Faerie Queene*, seemingly defined themselves very explicitly in relation to identifiable commonplaces of the ruling Elizabethan socio-cultural assumptions. So with such texts, it becomes our role to call the bluff of ideology to point out how it structured, or rather *constructed*, the text. To do so, we should therefore not be concerned merely with the explicit 'ideas' that are 'reflected' by a poem, but rather on how and by what means and with what distortions the text has been subjected to the power of ideology. A 'public' poem like *The Faerie Queene* is clearly vulnerable to the most obvious kinds of ideological pressure because it deals explicitly with sensitive political issues. But, as we shall see, the seemingly innocent court lyric is also the site of ceaseless ideological interrogation, inquisition, and repression. In the hands of a Surrey or a Campion, the lyric seems lightweight entertainment; with Sidney or Shakespeare it seems to become a moving articulation of a complex personality. But either way, the lyric no less than the epic occupies a place within the age's ideological struggles.

Throughout this study, however, I will be looking for ways in which the poems of the sixteenth century do not simply reflect the age's dominant ideology. It is part of our interest in reading this poetry today that we can in fact see how oppositional voices are struggling to be heard and how we can help give them voice. We can see now how even (or perhaps especially) a loyal, patriotic work like *The Faerie Queene*, which starts as a celebration of the Elizabethan monarchy, ruling class, and court ideals, ends in disillusion, in effect undermining those ideals. We can see how Wyatt's court lyrics contain scarcely veiled hints of rebellion and disgust, even (perhaps) asides about Queen Anne Boleyn. But to an extent, Spenser and Wyatt probably knew what they were voicing. That kind of opposition clearly operates on the level of very explicit ideas. But there are other kinds of opposition encoded in poetry more subtly and profoundly. One important function of the literary text – perhaps, it is often argued, what constitutes 'greatness' in a work – is that of bringing out the multiplicity, contradictions, and tensions that a dominant ideology tries to ignore or cover over. It does so not so much on the level of the explicit ideas to which a text points – but rather on the level of what my student called the text's 'unconscious', which we see both in the language and in the gaps and indeterminacies that accompany language. Poems are, after all, not ideas but words – words and spaces around words – and it is on the level of words, on the level of the signifier, that we can read the strains, oppositions, and struggles of an age. Language is the primary site of ideological struggle. It is where we locate the 'real' foundation of the poems we read. It is in language where the struggles for meaning and power took place – and where they take place in our own reading and criticism.

There have been some extremely useful refinements to this line of argument made by the important Cambridge critic, Raymond Williams. He proposes that we can use literary texts as a means of probing an age's transitional nature, looking for signs of change not so much in their explicit ideas as within what he calls a society's 'structures of feeling'. We do so in order to stress the live, ever-changing, characteristics of a culture and, in particular, the generative and regenerative part that language plays within culture. Williams writes of a society consisting of *archaic, residual,* and *emergent* experiences, values, and practices.[11] The majority of any society's practices are inevitably residual, deriving from the past and closely identified with the historically dominant class of that society. A few are always archaic, the residuum of philosophical or religious ideas from a previous age – an example in Elizabethan poetry would be the feudal structure, largely abandoned as a material practice by the end of the sixteenth century, but still very powerful in its cultural implications and as a source of ritual and familiarization for the court poets. But within the inevitable flux and contradictions of any society, new experiences and practices are always emerging, always potential, and in periods of particular stress, like the 1590s, they may start to emerge more strongly. They are usually felt before they can be put into language, because there are, as yet, Williams argues, no fully-formed structures of discourse by which they can be expressed. It is at such points of strain that certain forms of literature are most revealing. In the late sixteenth century we can look to the experimentation in the public theatre, the revival of verse satire, the unusual diversity of broken, mixed, unfinished works as indications, in Williams's words, of the sense that one often has in some of the very newest literature that it is articulating something which one already felt without words for it. He terms 'pre-emergent' those cases where the structure of feeling that is tangible in particular literary works is an articulation of an area of experience which still lies beyond us – the full significance of which may only become explicit years later as a new language becomes available. All texts, in other words, are articulation of more than they know and it is clear we must recognize that the texts we read are themselves unaware of their relation to ideology.[12]

Now let us look at the relevance of such considerations to our subject. What differences do they make to a study of poetry in the sixteenth century? They enable us to read Ralegh, Spenser, or Shakespeare in most exciting ways. There are always wider struggles going on than a writer consciously knows – contradictions rooted in the history of which he or she is a part, covered over by the comforts of ideology and only visible, perhaps, to later readers. We read not only for the obvious surface meanings but for symptomatic absences in texts and so for the signs of those ideological pressures by which it has erased or covered over. Ideology's power forces texts to remain silent about or to marginalize questions on matters that go beyond or challenge the age's orthodoxy. In the terms much favoured by older modes of criticism, the 'intentions' of a text are the ways the ideology of the text tries to mobilize certain response.[13] But the text, we can learn to see, always has other 'intentions'. A careful reader of sixteenth-century poetry, therefore, must focus not merely on what a text seems to say, or what its author seems to want to be heard to say, nor even on what it does not say, but on what it *cannot say, either at all or only with difficulty*. The text's detours, silences, omissions, absences, faults, and symptomatic dislocations are all part of what we focus on in addition to, and even at times in preference to, its surface. We look for the different languages, literary and social that hover in the vicinity of the text, trying to master and muffle it; in particular we focus on places where the seemingly unified surface of a work is contradicted or undermined, where the text 'momentarily misses a beat, thins out or loses intensity, or makes a false move – where the scars show, in the face of stress'. We ask in short not only what is there, but also what is *not* there and why, and who or what these seeming presences and omissions serve and what we, as their readers, might fill them with.[14]

The Court

This is a study of sixteenth-century poetry – and yet as I tell my students, we have to read sixteenth-century poetry *with* something, and I want them to read with as powerful a set of strategies as possible. The last few pages are, I know, difficult – I hope they repay rereading, and the discussion (here necessarily theoretical) will make much more particular sense, I hope, in ensuing chapters. They are outlining a set of strategies by which we can become more powerful readers. In investigating the poetry of court poets like Dunbar, Wyatt, Ralegh, or Greville, in Chapter 4, for instance, we shall have to look not merely to the ideas that can be abstracted from the age's commonplaces, or even those ideas of which the writer may have been aware – but to the events that have made the writer's history, and especially to ideas and feelings that play about (in the vicinity of) their writings. In many cases, the writer will have been unaware of them. They are ideas of which the subject himself may be singularly unaware, as he struggled within the complex interplay of discursive structures, symbolic formations, and ideological systems of representation that defined his cultural practices. We must try to relate the poetry we read – whether explicit public propaganda like *A Mirror for Magistrates* or seemingly innocent lyrics like Wyatt's 'Blame Not My Lute' – to the hidden interplays of power that structured the society. A collection of 'private' lyrics like Sidney's *Astrophil and Stella* no less than a massive 'public' poem like Daniel's *Civil Wars* or Spenser's *The Faerie Queene* is culturally produced, coerced, and compelled by political and wider cultural forces outside it, by networks of discourse in which it is caught or – to use Macherey's powerful metaphor – which haunt it, playing, encroaching, or teasing it from the edge of the text.[15]

Let me try to make the foregoing discussion of 'ideology' more concrete by an explicit example of how it functions. Here I draw on one of the most important modern thinkers on this subject. In his influential essay on 'Ideological State Apparatuses', Louis Althusser discusses the very concrete practices by which any society structures, even creates, the allegiances by which its members feel they 'belong' to it – the system of education, characteristic life-style, patterns of religion, family organization, and so forth. It is by means of such institutions and structures, what Althusser called 'apparatuses', that ideology functions. Except – and here we enter into a discussion of the dominant 'apparatuses' of this period – the poetry of the sixteenth century was *not* produced by 'ordinary people'. Or to put it differently, the received canon of sixteenth-century poetry is almost entirely the product of (written *for* if not always *by*) a small fraction of the population – the aristocracy, the gentry, and those aspiring members of the 'middle' classes who had some pretensions to upward mobility, what Maurice Evans terms 'a new social phenomenon', the second generation of the new bourgeoisie going to university and abandoning their fathers' professions for a life of letters. He instances Donne, Peele, Harvey, Greene, and Spenser, and points out that in fact of the major poets of the century, only Surrey belongs to the old aristocracy.[16] Some exceptions to his generalization will be discussed in later chapters, notably in chapter 8, when I comment on the poetry written by women and 'popular' poetry, but by and large it is an accurate statement.

The major institution or apparatus that dominates sixteenth-century poetry is the Court. Looking back at his youth and attempting to make sense of those years which we now recognize as one of the cataclysmic eras of English history, Edward Hyde, Earl of Clarendon, focused on the institution in which he had spent his youth. The Court, he wrote, is where 'as in a mirror, we may best see the face of that time, and the affections and temper of the people in general', for, he continued, 'the Court measured the temper and affection of the country'.[17] Throughout the sixteenth century, 'Court' was a powerful word as well as a powerful institution; it accumulated round itself ideas and feelings that were often contradictory or confusing, but always compelling. Men and women 'swarmed' to the Court (the metaphor is a favourite one) for power, gain, gossip, titles, favours, rewards, and entertainment. The Court was more than merely the seat of government, or wherever the monarch happened to be. All across Europe the *idea* of the Court, as well as its concrete existence, excited an intensity that indicates a rare concentration of power and cultural dominance. It is Gabriel Harvey's 'only mart of preferment and honour'; it is Spenser's 'seat of Courtesy and civil conversation'; it is Donne's 'bladder of Vanitie'. What powers, real or reputed, did the Court have over the destinies, tastes, and allegiances of men and women? What recurring anxieties or affirmations are associated with the Court? By whom are they voiced? With what special or covert interests? And with what degree of truth? What can they mediate to us of the Court's influence on the ongoing and deep-rooted cultural changes of the period – the complex struggles for political and social ascendancy, the fundamental changes of ideology and sensibility?

Such questions come, perhaps, down to this: how did the Court's power operate upon the particular details of life? How did the dominant ideology control the specifics of living, including the way poetry was thought of, written, and received? I stress the word 'detail' because, as Edward Said explains, 'for power to work it must be able to manage, control, even create detail: the more detail, the more real power'. Power is felt more intimately in detail – in the particulars of our everyday lives, in the particularities of poetry. It is on such domestic levels that we are deeply influenced by the dominant ideology. In the sixteenth century, the Court was one of the key places where, in the words of Michel Foucault, 'power reaches into the very grain of individuals, touches their bodies and inserts itself into their actions and attitudes, their discourses, learning processes and everyday lives'.[18] The Court produced, in all who came into contact with it, a set of expectations, anxieties, assumptions, and habits, sometimes very explicitly, sometimes by un-stated but very concrete pressures. And as we read the period's writings, we can see how writers and artists provide a kind of early-warning system; they are our most trustworthy guides to the tensions we can now look back upon.

So, then: what can the poetry of the age tell us about how it was to be exposed to, fostered by, or exploited by the Court? As Roy Strong and others have shown, throughout the Renaissance, all European Courts attempted to use the arts to control and in a very real sense create the tastes, habits, beliefs, and allegiances of their subjects. In some cases this attempt was carried out through overt state apparatuses – through control and censorship of the theatre, imprisonment of playwrights, and the patronage and protection of particular literary forms and opinions for example. Before the invention of the mechanical mass media of today', Strong writes, 'the creation of monarchs as an "image" to draw people's allegiance was the task of humanists, poets, writers and artists'.[19] Profound alliances therefore grew up between the new art forms of the Renaissance and the monarch. Around the monarch was the Court, and all over Europe, it was to the Court that intellectuals, educators, artists, architects, and poets were drawn. No less than the building of palaces or great houses, official state portraits, medallions or court fêtes, poetry was part of what Strong terms 'the politics of spectacle'. It was part of the increasing attempt – culminating in England in the reigns of James I and Charles I – to propagate a belief in the sacredness of the monarchy and the role of the Court and mobility within a ritual of power. Just as, in Strong's words, 'the world of the court fete is an ideal one in which nature, ordered and controlled, has all dangerous potential removed', and in which the Court could celebrate its wisdom and control over the world, time, and change, so poetry too became, as John Donne's friend, Sir Henry Wotton, put it, 'an in-strument of state'.[20]

In *Music and Poetry in the Early Tudor Court* (1961) John Stevens shows how the sixteenth-century lyric loses much of its point when simply read as words on a page. Court poetry, he argued, is built of 'shades and nuances of meaning' which are social rather than literary. 'What dis-tinguishes the individual from the type . . . arose from situation, not from words.'[21] Throughout the period, poetry is thought primarily of as action in and for the Court, as performance, even as production, not merely as written text. The poetry is the visible edge of a whole complex social text, the centre of which, as Puttenham's potted history of the century's poetry (probably completed by the 1580s) put it, was a firm policy of binding poetry inextricably to the Court. When he focuses on the 'new company of courtly makers' who 'sprong up' at the end of Henry VIII's reign, and 'greatly polished our rude and homely maner of vulgar Poesie', he is putting the Court's imprimatur upon not only a chosen number of poets but also upon a certain function for poetry in the Court. Briefly surveying the mid-Tudor poets, including Vaux, Sternhold, Heywood, Ferrys, Phaer, and Golding, he then culminates his history (returning to the same metaphor) by announcing the tradition continued under Elizabeth:

> And in her Majesties time that now
> is are sprong up an other crew of
> Courtly makers Noble men and
> Gentlemen of her Majesties owne
> servauntes, who have written
> excellently well as it would appeare
> if their doings could be found out and
> made publicke with the rest, of which
> number is first that noble Gentleman
> *Edward* Earle of Oxtord. *Thomas* Lord of
> Bukhurst, when he was young, *Henry*
> Lord Paget, Sir *Philip Sydney*, Sir
> *Walter Rawleigh*, Master *Edward Dyar*,
> Maister *Fulke Grevell, Gascon, Britton,
> Turberville* and a great many other
> learned Gentlemen, whose names I do
> not omit for envie, but to avoyde
> tediousnesse, and who have deserved
> no little Commendation.

Throughout his treatise Puttenham links poetry to the favour of courts and princes, repeatedly stressing the duty of the 'Civill Poet' to celebrate the values and acts of the Court in the way 'the embroderer' sets 'stone and perle or passements of gold upon the stuff of a Princely garment'.[22]

What is especially interesting about Puttenham's discussion is the way he makes poetry just another activity inseparable from the other cultural practices of the Court. While the *Arte of English Poesie* presents itself as a treatise on poetry, it is also setting out the ideal life-style of the courtier. Poetry was both an elegant accompaniment to court life, but, more important, the motivation and procedures of Court poetry and court practice are inseparable. Indirection, dissimulation (what Puttenham

terms *Beau semblant*), ornament, calculated ostentation, are all characteristics that are simultaneously those of the poet and the courtier.
Puttenham assumes that the grace displayed by poet and courtier alike is
inseperable from a training in the necessary courtly characteristics of
dissimulation and indirection. When he discusses the use of allegory by
the poet – '*Allegoria* . . . the figure of false semblant' – he describes it as
'the Courtier'; and at the conclusion of his treatise, he echoes
Castiglione's advice that the courtier should strive above all else 'to give
entertainment to Princes, Ladies of honour, Gentlewomen and Gentleman', and to do so must 'dissemble' not only his 'countenances' and
'conceits' but also, all 'his ordinary actions of behaviour . . . whereby
the better' to 'winne his purposes and good advantages'.[23] The terms are
exactly those he uses to describe the making of poetry.

The Court, then, appropriated poetry as one of the many practices by
which it tried to exercise cultural dominance. Within the Court, poetry
was seen as entertainment by and for amateur gentleman poets of the
Court; it was what Stevens calls 'idealised talk' performed and enjoyed
along with what Lewis terms 'a little music after supper'.[24] It was rarely
designed to be published. But even (or especially) if, Puttenham notes,
'many notable Gentlemen in the Court . . . have written commendably,
and suppressed it agayne, or else suffered it to be published without their
own names to it', poetry was a common means for a courtier to
construct a role for himself in the Court. It was one of the colourful
rituals by which a Ralegh or an Essex displayed his desirability (along
with dancing, music, and general self-display) and so advanced his
political fortunes. Poetry was thus one of the means by which the
courtier gained access to the monarch. Ralegh's poetry, as we shall see in
Chapter 4, was probably largely used as a key to Elizabeth's political
favour; Robert Sidney, as Chapter 5 will show, wrote most of his poetry
while in exile in the Low Countries as an expression of his desire to be
back in the centre of public affairs; while another of Puttenham's 'crew
of courtly makers',[25] the Earl of Oxford, was writing incidental verse
for over twenty years with conventional erotic subjects, and yet which
was clearly directed to his advancement in the Court.

Frank Whigham has shown how when we compare poetry with other
kinds of writing in the Court, the same cultural pattern can be observed.
The rhetoric of Elizabethan courtiers' letters shows the same hold of
ideology over language as the rhetoric of poetry, the same desire to find
a place within an already in-place discourse. The vocabulary, postures,
and assumptions of the letters of Elizabethan courtiers are, like their
poetry, essentially aimed at ceremonial display, while silently
acknowledging the anxiety and insecurity of the Court in their barely
repressed concerns with competition from other courtiers, their fears of
banishment and exclusion. Pointing out that it is such 'fictive ideologies'

which are the stuff of history, Whigham shows that it is on the linguistic and 'dramatic' level – once again, in particular details – that power and privilege are expressed.[26]

In many cases, of course, the poet is quite explicitly the spokesman for the Court – as panegyrist, as the celebrator of occasions of pageantry or of royal personages. Dunbar's 'The Thrissel and the Rois' or Ralegh's 'Praisd Be Dianas Faire and Harmles Light' are such celebrations of the Court's values and activities. On these occasions the poet finds a pattern of discourse already existing and a role waiting for him to fill. He inserts himself into it in order to establish his own place within a discursive structure that is not merely a literary one, but a whole pattern of social discourse. As such, his writing operates within a very narrow register of themes and unusual linguistic coherence on the level of both general style and particular verbal details, what linguists term the *ideologeme*. By analogy with morpheme or phoneme, the ideologeme is the verbal unit that carries ideological detail.[27] It is a useful term to stress how ideology works in the details of discourse – at the level of syntax, grammar, and vocabulary. Here Puttenham is once again our best spokesman. He writes of how the language of the poet must 'be naturall, pure, and the most usual of all of his country' and then proceeds to identify such language as 'that which is spoken in the kings Court' rather than in the 'peevish affection' of the universities let alone that spoken by the 'poore rusticall or uncivill people' or any 'of the inferiour sort' or regional speech. In short, the acceptable language of poetry is 'the usual speech of the Court, and that of London and the shires lying about london within ix myls, and not much above'.[28] By such proscriptions, poetry could be controlled by the Court. Through the ways it was written and circulated, poetry could be very precisely delimited, its language organized through both political and literary modes. It thus became one of the regime's means of social stabilization and control. As Chapters 4 and 5 will show, poets like Sir Robert Sidney and Sir Walter Ralegh record in their verse (and in ways they themselves could not have fully acknowledged) the enormous power of the Court, the ways it created and controlled its subjects by exerting pressure upon their language. The 'social' text (the events under the pressure of which the poets wrote and of which they tried to be a part) and the 'literary' text (what they made of those events) are inseparable.

If the Court is the major cultural apparatus which controlled the creation of poetry, within its activities the particular apparatus that distributed or withheld approval was the system of patronage. However suspect in our time (the pejorative associations of 'patronizing' today registering the changes that have occurred), patronage was certainly one of the major apparatuses of cultural control in pre-industrial Europe. Patronage, specifically financial support, was what all authors sought –

whether from monarch, lord, or rich man (or woman). By 'patronage', however, we should understand not simply reward of money or a position given to an author: the term covers a huge variety of activities. Much patronage, especially for poetry, operated rather in the way 'public relations' works today. A writer might be directly commissioned to produce a work. Or he might simply decide out of gratitude or in hope of advancement to dedicate a work to an influential nobleman or woman. A dedication might be initiated by the author in the hope of just getting noticed. Either way, patronage formed a network of pressure, encouragement, and exclusion, providing the powerful – and notably the monarch and the Court – with a system by which politically useful subjects could be either attached to or excluded from their presence and power.

Like today, poetry as such did not often command much reward. The cries often heard from poets about the scarcity of money and offices were numerous, poetry providing, in Ben Jonson's words, 'but a meane *Mistress*', her rewards being limited and unreliable. Directly utilitarian writing was what the sixteenth-century monarchs and Courts preferred to support. Still, there was, right through the period, even as far back as late-fifteenth-century Scotland, and, in England from the time of Henry VII and VIII, an increasingly tightly organized system of patronage that exercised power over artists, musicians, and writers, in an interaction of what Richard Green has termed 'patrons and prince pleasers'. Throughout the century, many of the poets' complaints were caused by their awareness that while support was forthcoming to writers immediately useful to patrons, it rarely seemed to percolate to poets as if, in Samuel Daniel's words, patrons did not realize 'how small/A portion' would 'turn the wheeles . . . to make their glory last'.[29]

Under Elizabeth, the patronage system in England took on a distinctive pattern. As in all late Renaissance Courts, control of the arts became increasingly oppressive – or attractive, according to one's place and achievements within the system. At the centre of the society was the Queen, around whom there was concentrated a cult of extraordinary power by which she was celebrated – as the embodiment of power, beauty, justice, the imperium, and, within the court circles, as the quintessential, unapproachable yet alluring, Petrarchan mistress. While she flirted and flaunted her sexual power among her courtiers, her portraits and personal mottoes asserted her vaunted chastity before all else. Her admirers likewise responded by praising her 'cruelty' to them in tropes derived from Petrarchanism and its Neo-platonic trappings. But hers was not merely a convenient pose to encourage courtiers to turn graceful compliments or to spend huge proportions of their incomes in bedecking themselves to attract her approval, as Ralegh for one most certainly did. Rather, it had practical and direct political importance – and especially from the late 1570s until the end of the century. Interestingly enough, Elizabeth herself spent little on patronage – certainly less than either her father Henry VIII or her successor James I. Instead, she demanded that her nobles and courtiers themselves dispensed rewards, and she used her frequent progresses through the country and visits to their great houses to encourage them to do so. In such ways, she would gain the glory while being spared the expense of the favours and perquisites that would bind her subjects more closely to her regime.

In the first twenty-five years of Elizabeth's reign, such a system worked almost exclusively to promote writers of religious, political, and generally utilitarian works. Hers was a regime that was nervous, unsure of its stability, afraid of religious and political enemies inside and out. Thus the patronage system was part of a concentrated effort by the regime to mould opinions and to direct writers to socially or politically approved goals. The tough-minded courtiers who surrounded Elizabeth – particularly Leicester and Cecil – supported writers who could be, primarily, propagandists. As Jan van Dorsten has noted, it was Sidney who was the first of Elizabeth's courtiers who was actively interested in the patronage of poetry, and it was Sidney and the Sidney Circle, especially his sister Mary, who were responsible for encouraging much of the renaissance of poetry in the last decade of the century.[30]

While patronage was the major apparatus by which the ideology of the Elizabethan Court was enforced, to glance at the typical form by which poetry circulated is to realize again the intimately detailed ways by which cultural power operated in the period. Typically, poetry was collected and disseminated during the sixteenth century not through publication (which would sometimes occur following an author's death and often without his or her family's permission, or else not at all) but rather by discrete, unpublished circulation, literally hand to hand. Poems would be copied, adapted, recopied, perhaps in a reader's own private anthologies or notebook collections or 'miscellanies'. Some of these might eventually be published but more often they remained simply the private notebooks of their compilers. Some were often not exclusively devoted to poetry, but might include a variety of fashionable poems along with useful observations on manners.

To survey some of these is to sense in most intriguing ways the silent control of the Court taste and values throughout our period. The Bodleian Library Rawlinson MS C. 813, for instance, is one from the early part of the period. Collected late in the fifteenth century, the manuscript is a typical collection of work popular and useful around the Court of Henry VII. It includes a mixture of late medieval courtly poems – medieval rhyme royal, musical lyrics, popular rhymed political prophecies, and the pseudo-Arthurian propaganda much favoured by

the early Tudors. Other early Tudor song-books which have come
down to us similarly mix love and devotional songs, popular lyrics, and
political poems.

Two slightly later miscellanies, the one published at the time, the
other remaining unpublished until the eighteenth century, stand out as
particularly significant examples. The first we know as 'Tottel's *Miscellany*'. Perhaps the most important of all the Tudor miscellanies, it was
published by William Tottel in 1557, and dedicated 'to the honor of the
Englishe tong, and for profit of the studious of Englishe eloquence'. It
not only brought together the bulk of Wyatt's and Surrey's verse; it
shows openly the process by which the Court was starting to adapt,
assimilate, and control its poetry. Most of the additional poems chosen
by Tottel seem to have been put into the collection for their ease of
imitation for the aspiring courtier, who was advised by his rhetorical
handbooks to exercise his poetic gifts according to such models. As
William Tydeman comments, it is 'hard to exaggerate the influence of
the collection'; it went through nine editions by 1587, and became part
of the courtly consciousness. It became an essential guide to the kinds
and modes of poetry that would deck out the aspiring courtier's taste.[31]
It set the pattern, as well, for many later miscellanies, some of which
were published, including *The Paradise of Dainty Devices* (1576), *The
Bowre of Daintie Delights* (1591), *The Phoenix Nest* (1593), *The Arbor of
Amorous Devises* (1597), *England's Helicon* (1601), and *A Poetical Rhapsody*
(1602).

The second comes from Scotland, a collection of almost equivalent
importance known as the Bannatyne Manuscript. It is a compilation of
poems from the reigns of James III (1460–88), James IV (1488–1513),
and Mary (1542–67). It includes work by Henryson, Douglas, Dunbar,
Lindsay, and Scott, and was put together around 1568. It reads as if it
was collected as an act of homage to a century of Scottish culture. It is a
folio of some 800 pages and, set alongside its English equivalents, even
Tottel, it shows, as W. S. Ramson and Joan Hughes note, 'not only . . .
the frivolity of English taste but its subservience to fashion'. It is
carefully organized, dividing its poems into 'ballatis' of theology,
wisdom, and morality, 'Mirry and Uther Solatius Consaittis', of love
and, finally 'Fabillis Wyiss and Sapient'. The theological poems are
mainly mediocre devotional lyrics and the 'Ballates Full of Wisdom' are
likewise conventionally didactic, like the following:

> Prayer is the maist haly devyne service
> That man heir on erth unto God may present,
> Faith with repentance is the dew and perfect device
> That withstands the divill and his cursit entent.

Lighter material includes Lindsay's play *Ane Satyre of the Thrie Estaitis*, while the love-ballads are mainly those by Alexander Scott and the fables mainly those of Henryson. The Bannatyne collection is overall a rich compendium of what its most recent editors Ramson and Hughes have called in their valuable selection from it, the 'poetry of the Stewart Court'. Its poems are characterized by a wide variety of subject and style and yet together they are 'quite remarkably of a piece, belonging to a court culture' which is 'profoundly conscious of its own traditions'.[32]

The miscellanies, published or unpublished, are thus important sources for ascertaining the Court's taste in, and control over, the development of poetry through the century. Overall, utilitarian doggerel is mixed with aureate lyrics, moral tags with political allegory, musical ditties with erotic plaints. But it is noticeable how the miscellanies later in the century show much less interest in anything but specifically courtly forms of verse. The subtle but definite class basis of the Court's demands may be seen in the ways which popular poetry – ballads, satires, folk-tales – are excluded by or assimilated to court taste. Thus it is that the canon approved by the 'courtly' readings of the age's poetry is being established.

Poetry, wrote Puttenham – for this process of the control of the canon, as in so much, a revealing spokesman – has among its most important functions, the celebration of the deeds of princes, the reinforcement of moral principles, and 'the common solace of mankind in all his travails and cares of this transitorie life'. His treatise makes quite clear the unavoidable struggle for the control and employment of poetry as one of the arts which had become 'a piece of State'.[33] Power works not only in the obvious apparatus of the State but in such seemingly marginal activities as poetry. As part of the ceremony, ritual, and pattern of court life, poetry was viewed as a decorative, essentially harmless but useful diversion, a means by which intellectuals and artists could be assimilated into the dominant class as part of the ongoing struggle to confirm and preserve the ideological structures of the Court. The 'author' is a function of the discourse which permits him to speak. Not just a 'court' poet, he is the *Court's* poet, controlled and in a real sense created by the Court. And yet although the power of the Court seemingly became irresistible, we can read, from our vantage point 400 years later, through the hesitations of the texts, the ideological struggles that were waged over language to gain such cultural ascendancy. Often, even unaware, the writings of the poets record the struggles by which they were made the Court's.

Court and poetry in England and Scotland

It is now time to try to get an overview of our topic. However differently their evaluations of sixteenth-century poetry, most modern historians of the period have generally agreed on the canonized landmarks and the main subdivisions. Later I will suggest ways we might want to look again at the canon and question the usefulness of conventional periodization, but it seems sensible at the outset to construct the residual model. Sixteenth-century poetry has generally been seen by such diverse critics as Winters, Lewis, and Evans much as follows. Coinciding with the consolidation of the English monarchy following the Wars of the Roses, the poetry of the late fifteenth and early sixteenth centuries gradually became more independent of the aureate and moralistic traditions of the later Middle Ages. By the 1530s, like English court culture generally, it became more accessible to continental, especially Italian and French, influences, notably in the work of Wyatt and Surrey, and after some thirty years of experimentation during which poetry was mainly didactic, subservient to the moral commonplaces of humanist educators, a period of splendid achievement occurred, culminating in the work of Sidney, Spenser, and (slightly apart) Shakespeare and Donne. In Scotland a similar process of continental influence and achievement occurred somewhat earlier, in the works of Henryson or Dunbar, and again in the 'Castalian' poets of the late sixteenth-century. An alternative view has highlighted a tradition of what it sees as plain, idiomatic verse, linking Skelton at the beginning of the century, Wyatt in the 1530s, and (playing down the courtly line of Sidney and Spenser and upgrading the moralistic mid-century poets) culminating in the work of Greville and, in different ways, Donne and Shakespeare. With whatever modifications or compromises, most accounts of the century's poetry today resemble one or other of these models.

The apparent strength of the 'courtly' interpretation is that it is rooted in some influential remarks made by poets and commentators late in the century, notably by Sidney and Puttenham. Sidney's *Defence of Poesie* (c. 1579) is the more important – and more readable for today's students. In particular, Sidney speaks scornfully of the state of English poetry, especially lyric poetry, marvelling that 'poesy, thus embraced in all other places, should only find in our time a hard welcome in England'. He singles out *A Mirror for Magistrates*, Surrey, and Spenser's *Shepherdes Calendar* for praise. About the same time, Puttenham was likewise trying to lay down what amounts to an authorized tradition of poetry, rejecting Skelton ('in King Henry th'eights time . . . I wot not for what great worthines . . . surnamed the Poet *Laureat*') and praising the 'new company of courtly makers', including Wyatt and Surrey, who adapted the 'sweete and stately measures and stile of the Italian Poesie', who 'greatly pollished our rude homely maner of vulgar Poesie', and who 'may justly be sayd' to be 'the first reformers of our English meetre and stile'.[34] Both readings of Elizabethan poetic history provide an ideologically partial, highly selective, reworking of social and literary texts alike. Sidney's view is that of the young Protestant aristocrat, anxious to see the Elizabethan Court dominated by his own faction; Puttenham's articulates something of the growing success of that play for power. The Sidneian literary revolution – the ideals, successes, and failures of which will be dealt with in Chapter 5 – climaxed in the 1580s and 1590s, with the spate of sonnet sequences, religious poetry, closet drama, and the publication in 1598 of the authorized edition of Sidney's own works. The *Defence* thus can be seen as an initiating manifesto of a successful literary revolution.

In 1603, with the accession of James VI of Scotland to his cousin Elizabeth's throne, the Courts of Edinburgh and Westminster were united. In the century before, the Scottish and English Courts had been quite separate with, at times, an uneasy and at times open, hostility between them. The two Courts produced, as I have briefly indicated, similar kinds of poetry. Here I want to deal in a little more detail with the differences. They are especially interesting to highlight the early sophistication of Scottish court poetry and then the brilliance of English poetry of the late sixteenth century.

While Scotland shared much of the linguistic heritage of England, through most of the fourteenth and fifteenth centuries its literary culture was generally far more sophisticated than England's. If we glance beyond our period to the mid seventeenth century, however, a strange phenomenon has occurred; the decline of Scottish aristocratic culture in the early seventeenth century is something more than the European-wide phenomenon of the ruling aristocratic caste to uphold its values and power and to adapt itself to a rapidly changing social substructure. While there are certain classical signs the English Court also suffered from, such as an increasingly exploited resource economy and labour force and the dominance of an aggressive, nascent bourgeoisie, the crucial factor is the increasing power of governmental hegemony operated by what was experienced as an imperialist power. By quite early in the seventeenth century, powerful, centralized court culture in Scotland has been dissipated as the Court has been moved to England.

Back in the fifteenth century, however, Scottish court poetry had been much more diverse and more open to European influences than its English counterpart. As Lewis comments, to move from England to Scotland at that period is to pass from 'barbarism' to 'civilization', from dullness to the liveliness and complexity of a sophisticated court society.[35] James IV of Scotland was himself an accomplished poet, and the Scots Court included such fine poets as Henryson, Douglas, and Dunbar. No English poetry of the period comes close to the variety, vigour, and insight of Henryson's *Fabillis* or (further into our period) the ease with which Dunbar's poetry shows an awareness of and uses European precedents of satire, lyric, epistle, classical translation, or the richness and technical skills of Douglas's translation of Virgil.

The major poets of the Scottish Court in the mid and late fifteenth century are often called the 'Scottish Chaucerians'. By the term is usually meant those poets who, sometime after the reign of James I of Scotland (1394–1437), wrote supposedly with the choice of a Chaucerian style in mind. James I is usually singled out as the first Middle Scots poet who showed real affinities with Chaucer, especially in *The Kingis Quair*, but the real flowering of late medieval or early Renaissance Scots poetry occurs in the reign of James III, some fifty years later. Gregory Krantzmann points out that the *Quair* is a typical court poem, one which implies that it was composed to be read aloud – in performance – as well as privately.[36] In that, it anticipated the dominant mode of sixteenth-century court poetry, both trying to speak for a whole community and yet leaving leeway for the interests, adaptations and (in a sense) rewriting by its readers. It is a Boethian treatment of a lover, imprisoned, and compensating for his captivity by dreaming of Venus, Minerva, and other deities who proffer good advice, always warning that the wheel of fortune, in love or court affairs, is unpredictable.

The most important Scots poet of the century and, after Chaucer, perhaps the most interesting English-language poet of the Middle Ages, is Robert Henryson. A lawyer, teacher, and an observer of court fashions, Henryson wrote fables, moral satire, and Chaucerian love tragedy. His *Testament of Cresseid* is a continuation and darkening of Chaucer's *Troilus and Creseyde*, and amounts to a grim moral commentary on Chaucer's handling of the story of the Trojan lovers. He takes up the question of Cressida's life among the Greek soldiers to show her moral degeneration and then her realization of her crime and guilt. She turns to warn her readers – 'Lovers be war and tak gude heid about/Quhome that ye lufe, for quohoem yet suffer paine', and blames her own 'great unstabilnes'. Though Henryson avoids any explicit Christian reference, he grimly moralizes over his heroine's behaviour. Integrity, stoicism, constraint are the values that lovers need to survive in an untrustworthy world. Henryson's other major work is *The Morall Fabillis of Esope the Phygian*, which, although often compared with *The Canterbury Tales*, is more European than English in its affinities – a characteristic of Scottish court culture in this period generally. As Krantzmann comments, there is by contrast 'no English poetry of the late fifteenth century . . . which approached the combination of stylistic variety, humour, moral rigour and intellectual control illustrated by the *Fabillis*.[37] They are witty, varied, closely observed, sensitive to speech and idiom, and shrewdly and complexly moral. They are the product of a rich and confident, if relatively small, court culture.

William Dunbar's poetry will be looked at in some detail in Chapter 4; another of the poets of the late-fifteenth-century Scots Court who justifies some attention is Gavin Douglas, a lawyer, priest, courtier, one of the Lords in Council who was pro-English and was strongly supported by Henry VIII to become Archbishop of St Andrews. Douglas's poetry includes the elaborate allegory, 'The Palace of Honour', the shorter tale 'King Hart', and a translation of the *Aeneid* into heroic couplets, or Scottish metre as the title calls it. This the first complete translation of Homer into either English or Scots, it was praised by Ezra Pound in the twentieth century as being superior to the original. That is something of an exaggeration but it is a significant rewriting of the Greek. Its main characteristic is the varied diction, which dramatically changes according to class and situation and idiom of the characters. Douglas's translation became a major influence upon Surrey's later, inferior, translation.

Surveying the Scots poets writing in the latter half of the fifteenth century, therefore, one is led to speculate on their greater sophistication, richness, and variety alongside their English counterparts. English poetry of the time is largely court doggerel, moral commonplace, and turgid political allegory. Even when we go forward fifty or more years, and exclude Wyatt, much the same observation might be made. Even during the mid sixteenth century, while English verse was labouring to find appropriate forms and vocabulary, Scottish verse was still more varied and sophisticated. In the Bannatyne manuscript, for instance, we get not only an anthology of the previous century's poetry, but also a solid body of poems of another fine Scots poet, active just a few years earlier. He is Alexander Scott, a courtier who studied in Paris, and wrote religious and erotic lyrics which, like Wyatt's or Ralegh's, are not simply, as his modern editor John MacQueen argues, expressions of a happy abandonment to the sensual power of love, 'but deeply brooding and disruptive' meditations on the self that has been created by the Court. While the traditional courtly apparatus – the Petrarchan balance of pain and pleasure, wit versus will, the 'manic-depressive alternation of rational and irrational which accompanies the passion' – are all present, there is a brittle edge to Scott's verse that reminds us of the best English poetry later in the century.[38] The freedom that love makes possible is desperately dependent on political favour; the typical experiences are those of absence, wandering, and loss, all experiences evoked in poems that can be read as simple (and superbly crafted) erotic lyrics but which have wider cultural connections. Courtly and

Petrarchan love metaphors become, as in Wyatt, the accepted language for begging political favours.

As I have implied, one of the most fascinating aspects of sixteenth-century English poetry is the socio-cultural fragility upon which its apparent confidence is built. Again a comparison with Scotland is useful here. We can sense the cultural origins of this fragility by a detailed consideration of what occurred when the Scottish Court emigrated to England in 1603–4. From the late 1580s, James built around him a group of the so-called 'Castalian' poets, who were more vitally in touch with developments in France and Italy than the English poets – as Sidney was frustratingly to admit in his pejorative remarks on the state of English poetry. When James moved south in 1603, praised by the Scots poet William Alexander for joining 'this divided Isle', he took on his new responsibilities with some relief; but in doing so, James was not just depriving Scotland of a resident Court and thereby of a centre of culture, but indirectly depriving those Scottish courtier-poets who accompanied him of much of their native cultural independence and individuality. Helena Shire asks the question which is also directly relevant to our understanding of English court poetry: on what terms could 'a phase of *Scottish Poesie* dependent upon a court culture continue to exist after the departure of the King and court?'[39] A generation of Scots poets was born and grew up in a Scotland without a Court, and Scottish literature had to wait for more than a century before a new class basis was established for a literature of a comparable quality. Once the Scots poets went south to their new, more dynamic and richer Court in England, Scottish court culture withered. Alexander's poetry, like that of his fellow Scots, relied for its appreciation on a special kind of audience; it is essentially poetry as delicate and intimate gesture, depending primarily for its impact on a knowledgeable, closely knit group of peers, one which James's Court provided in Scotland and which his protégés hoped to find in England. Such an intimate relationship between social setting and literary expectation proved to be extremely fragile. It is para-doxically both the strength and the potential self-destructiveness of court literature that it relies so heavily on such a homogenous and intimate social relationship. Scots court poetry became as peripheral as it had once been strong.

Now let us go back to England at the beginning of the century. Who are the English contemporaries of Dunbar? At times imitative of the Scots poet and, like him, looking to European models, we can find John Skelton, Stephen Hawes, and William Barclay. Lewis simply comments that most of their verse has 'no intrinsic value'. It is only a slight exaggeration. Some of Skelton's verse is probably still accessible today. He is, Krantzmann comments, 'the first truly inventive English poet since Chaucer'.[40] But the most interesting aspect of Skelton for us is the reputation that was constructed by the narrowly ideological outlook of later sixteenth-century commentators. Puttenham looked back to his work as 'rayling and scoffery', seeing his popular, seemingly disjointed, verse not merely as lacking the harmony of the court poetry he wanted to promote but, reprehensibly, allowing earthy, popular, and non-aristocratic class interests to enter it.[41] The buffoonery of his satiric 'flytings' grows out of a combination of the frank realism of popular medieval ballad with popular song. His 'Bouge of Court' reflects on the rewards and corruptions of court favour, and the three closely connected satires (1515–22), 'Colin Clout', 'Speake Parot', and 'Why Come Yet Not to Court', attack the abuses of the Church and the politicians of Henry VIII's Court. As with Dunbar, we can sense not merely a blend of traditions, but a style and political frankness antipathetic to later taste and political orthodoxy.

Other poetry written in the Court of Henry VI and early in the reign of Henry VIII that is worthy of note here includes Stephen Hawes's moral allegories *Exemple of Vertu* (1504) and *Pastyme of Pleasure* (1506), written to oppose 'vyce and the vycious to blame', by a glorification of the Christian Knight and the choice of the appropriate Christian life. Hawes was a member of Henry VII's Court, a groom of the Privy Council, who was employed (as were Skelton, Barclay, and Medwall) as a clerk and propagandist. Poetry was for him, as for other courtiers, an incidental accomplishment. His poems look back, to 'prudent Gower', 'noble Chaucer', and 'virtuouse Lydgate', as he puts it at the start of the *Exemple of Vertu*. But despite such ancestry, alongside the Scots poetry of the time his poems are weak, tedious, and rather ruminative imitations. Likewise, Thomas Heywood's epigrams and his alliterative allegory 'The Spider and the Fly' are also reworkings of tired medieval concerns written in halting diction and rhyme. George Cavendish's poems are similarly – in his own words – 'stakerying in style, onsavery in sentence'. He was a member of Wolsey's household and wrote long moralistic complaints on historical and political themes. But, as Gordon Kipling has argued, even in such limping poetry, which is typical of most of the verse of the reigns of Henry VII and the early years of Henry VIII, we can see the ways in which the Court is starting to dominate and employ the discourse of poetry. Henry VII's laureates, he suggests, 'present themselves as orators rather than poets', seeking 'to present Tudor policy in as forceful and impressive a manner as possible' in a way that is modelled on the more sophisticated Burgundian or Scottish Courts.[42]

The most compelling English poetry before the 1580s that shows us the growing presence of the Court on poetry, poet, and public and private experiences alike and which, incidentally, comes closest to the interest of the poetry written in Scotland, is that by Sir Thomas Wyatt.

Read through the printed versions first collected in Tottel's *Miscellany* (1557), Wyatt may well have seemed sufficiently sophisticated and receptive to the 'false semblant' of Petrarchan fashion to allow Puttenham to list him among the approved courtly makers. Wyatt's poetry appears hospitable to the Court's domination even though it is shot through with an uneasiness about its growing power. It asks in effect a crucial question: what language is available to the poet who, by virtue of his position and even his very existence, is tied to the Court? To be not in the Court is to be not in the world, as a character in the Jacobean play *The Revenger's Tragedy* remarks. It is interesting how Wyatt, and after him, would-be dissident courtier-poets like Ralegh and Greville, fall back on the residual language of medieval religious renunciation. It provided them with the words of an oppositional culture, as they tried to articulate emergent forces that would eventually overthrow the Court's power but for which there was as yet no language – except that of a residual and increasingly archaic social formation.

Thus, we can see from reading the poetry how a particular ideology is never totally dominant: a dominant culture, even the most powerful, always contains the potential for opposition. From 1580 to the end of the century, the period for which Puttenham is most triumphantly the spokesman, the institutions, philosophical assumptions, and systems of linguistic authority are under increasing pressure. The most interesting poetry of the whole period is written in the last twenty years of the century precisely because it is torn among conflicting ideological pressures that fracture its apparent serenity. The best poetry – that of Sidney, Greville, Ralegh, Spenser, the early Donne, Shakespeare – is that which reveals how the very act of writing itself generates forces that challenge and question the power of the dominant structures. Most of the poetry of the last twenty years of the century sets up tensions – often solved on the level of the signifier by premature closure, or seemingly unaccountable silences – between the affirmations it is being forced to make and the negation which struggle into play. The conscious allegiances of Spenser or Ralegh grant unambiguous legitimacy to the dominant ideology of the Court as they celebrate Gloriana or Cynthia, but none the less their poetry articulates more disturbing counter-discourses. The 1590s, in particular, see a struggle to establish a place for new and quite different kinds of poetry; it is a decade of frenetic experiment, the mixing of traditional genres, the attempted invention of new ones, a virulent if short-lived burst of satire, and the struggling emergence of a new class as a major consumer force. The new audiences are most radically seen in the development in the public theatres, but in poetry too – in the readership of Donne's erotic poetry and Shakespeare's sonnets – we can see the surge of new audiences and new social forces.

Struggle with and within the power of the Court, then, constitutes sixteenth-century poetry's most important characteristic. It is not one we would sense to be of primary concern if we simply read the verse of the period through the perspective that a century of criticism since Palgrave has taught us to regard as 'natural', and which has been reinforced by an explicable but misguided attempt to restore seemingly 'true' Elizabethan readings. No reading is ever innocent, and the Elizabethan poets and – even more rigorously – the structures in which they served knew this. Institutions have power only as long as the words for them to retain power and exclude alternatives from it. Hence, Elizabethan poetry tried to create not only writers but readers who were the subject of the ideology inscribed silently within the practices of textuality. But words, as Derrida puts it, are 'inaugural': they start us thinking, and writing, other (often unpredictable) words. Although they never free themselves from power, they in effect ask, 'to times in hope' as Shakespeare asserts in Sonnet 18, for future readers to understand and continue the struggles that brought them into being. This is why we, their modern readers, might well feel a real sense of responsibility for them. We can help bring their struggles into the open.

I started this introductory chapter talking about the intensity with which some of my students took over some of the strategies I am using in this book to produce involved, interesting, and individual readings of a famous Wyatt poem. They did not know they were contributing to the application of a new 'theory' of literary reading. But what came through as they read their Barthes and put it alongside the Wyatt, or later as they were introduced to Althusser, Macherey, or Williams on 'ideology' and saw just how powerful a concept it could be in probing Ralegh or Donne, was that added to the pleasure of the text, the music, the wine, and the food was the need and the excitement of using contemporary 'ways into' the poetry of the sixteenth century. After the initial enjoyment came the hard work. And, thus, greater enjoyment. And that can be true, I think, for all readers of this poetry today.

Let me conclude this opening chapter by reposing the question with which I started. From our perspective in the late twentieth century, what is our picture of the sixteenth century? Perhaps the most vivid re-creation in the popular imagination is that shown in the television series, *Elizabeth R*, starring Glenda Jackson. It is a picture that in some ways closely matches that of the poetry that will be presented in this study. It shows not a world of beauty, order, and natural (let alone supernatural) harmony, but a world of danger, intrigue, devious self-serving politicians, where the cunning and ruthless survive, and where beauty, aggression, ambition could open doors, windows, bedchamber drapes – but also lead one into the Tower or to the gallows. It was a dangerous world where personal and political fortunes changed unpredictably and were fought over by a small, interrelated class of anxious, paranoid men and women. As we watch the re-creation of this world in the comfort of our living rooms, we can romanticize the heads of traitors on pikes outside the Tower, the disease and the danger, the plots, confessions, burnings, and manipulations – just as we have romanticized the poetry. But just as the colourful swirl of robes and dances covers the conflicts and plots of Elizabethan society, so the poetry of the period, with its beauty, confidence, music, and order, covered over the same struggles, repressions, and silences. And this is where we make the period's poetry part of 'our' world. It is our privilege, as modern readers, to be able to tease out the tissues of the texts, to enjoy, to 'delight', in Sidney's term, as well as to understand something of the struggles that go into their making and remaking.

Notes

1. F. R. Leavis, *Revaluation* (London, 1936), p. 11.

2. Roland Barthes, *A Lover's Discourse*, translated by Richard Howard (New York, 1978), p. 217.

3. Francis Palgrave, *The Golden Treasury*, edited by John Press (Oxford, 1968), p. xxi.

4. G. K. Hunter, 'Drab and Golden Lyrics of the Renaissance', in *Forms of Lyric: Selected Papers from the English Institute*, edited by Reuben A. Brower (New York, 1970), pp 1–18 (p. 6); Palgrave, p. xxii.

5. Louis Althusser and Etienne Balibar, *Reading Capital*, translated by Ben Brewster (London, 1970), pp. 15–16.

6. Michael McCanles, 'The Authentic Discourse of the Renaissance', *Diacritics*, 10 (March 1980), 77–87 (p. 77); Jonathan Goldberg, 'The Politics of Renaissance Literature: A Review Essay', *ELH*, 15 (1982), 514–42 (p. 516).

7. Leavis, *Revaluation*, p. 11.

8. Jacques Derrida, 'White Mythology: Metaphor in the Text of Philosophy', *NLH*, 6 (1976), 5–74 (p. 11).

9. Annabel Patterson, 'Recent Studies in the English Renaissance', *SEL*, 20 (1980), 153–75 (p. 153).

10. The preceding three paragraphs draw on many sources. See the work already cited in n. 6, plus the following: Pierre Macherey, *A Theory of Literary Production*, translated by Geoffrey Wall (London, 1978); Raymond Williams, *Marxism and Literature* (London, 1977); Stuart Hall *et al.*, *Culture, Media, Language* (London, 1980). See also Thomas E. Lewis, 'Notes Towards a Theory of the Referent', *PMLA*, 94 (1979), 459–75; Steve Burniston and Chris Weedon, 'Ideology, Subjectivity and the Artistic Text', *Working Papers in Cultural Studies*, 10 (1977),

203–33; Thomas Metscher, 'Literature and Art as Ideological Form', *NLH*, 11 (1979), 21–40 (p. 26); Jacques Ranciere, 'On the Theory of Ideology', *Radical Philosophy*, 7 (Spring 1976), 2–15; Tony Davies, 'Education, Ideology and Literature', *Red Letters*, 7 (1978), 4–15 (pp. 3–4).

11. Williams, *Marxism and Literature*, pp. 121–27.

12. Macherey, *Literary Production*, pp. 41–42.

13. Colin Mercer, 'After Gramsci', *Screen Education*, 36 (1980), 5–15; Williams, *Marxism and Literature*, p. 112.

14. This paragraph draws on: Raymond Williams, *The Long Revolution* (London, 1961), pp. 48–71, and 'Literature in Society', in *Contemporary Approaches to English Studies*, edited by Hilda Schiff (New York, 1977), pp. 36–7; Terry Eagleton, 'Text, Ideology, Realism', in *Literature and Society: Selected Papers from the English Institute*, edited by Edward W. Said (Baltimore, 1980), p. 156; James H. Kavanagh, '"Marks of Weakness": Ideology, Science and Textual Criticism', *Praxis*, 5, no. 1 (1982), 23–38 (p. 31).

15. Macherey, *Literary Production*, pp. 79–80.

16. Maurice Evans, *English Literature in the Sixteenth Century*, (London, 1954), p. 23.

17. Edward Hyde, Earl of Clarendon, *The History of the Rebellion and Civil Wars in England* (Oxford, 1849), I, 5, 10.

18. Edward W. Said, 'Travelling Theory', *Raritan*, 1, no. 3 (1982), 41–67 (p. 62); Michael Foucault, 'Prison Talk', in *Power/Knowledge: Selected Interviews and Other Writings, 1972–77*, edited by Colin Gordon (New York, 1980), p. 39.

19. Roy Strong, *Splendour at Court* (London, 1973), pp. 19, 21.

20. Strong, pp. 19, 21, 76; Sir Henry Wotton, *The Elements of Architecture* (London, 1624), p. 6.

21. John Stevens, *Music and Poetry in the Early Tudor Court* (London, 1961), p. 208.

22. George Puttenham, *The Arte of English Poesie*, edited by Gladys Doidge Willcock and Alice Walker (Cambridge, 1936), pp. 60, 61, 50, 137–38.

23. Puttenham, pp. 186, 298–300. See Daniel Javitch, 'The Impure Modes of Elizabethan Poetry', *Genre*, 15 (1982), 225–38 (p. 225), and *Poetry and Courtliness in Renaissance England* (Princeton, 1978), p. 66.

24. Stevens, *Music and Poetry*, p. 160; C. S. Lewis, *English Literature in the Sixteenth Century Excluding Drama* (Oxford, 1954), p. 230.

25. Puttenham, p. 21.

26. Frank Whigham, 'The Rhetoric of Elizabethan Suitors' Letters', *PMLA*, 96 (1981), 864–82 (p. 882). See also the same author's longer study, *Ambition and Privilege: The Social Tropes of Elizabethan Courtesy Theory* (Berkeley, 1984).

27. Paul Zumthor, 'From the Universal to the Particular in Medieval Poetry', *MLN*, 85 (1970), 815–23 (p. 816); 'Registres Linguistiques et Poésie aux XII–XIIIe Siècles', *Cultura Neolatina*, 34 (1974), 151–61.

28. Puttenham, pp. 143–45.

29. Ben Jonson, *Discoveries*, in *Works*, edited by C. H. Herford and P. and E. Simpson, (London, 1947), VIII, 583; Richard Green, *Poets and Princepleasers*, (Toronto, 1980), p. 583; Samuel Daniel, prefatory verses to John Florio, *Queen Annas New Worlde of Words* (1611).

READING THE POETRY OF THE SIXTEENTH CENTURY 33

30. For a detailed account of the Countess of Pembroke's patronage, see Gary F. Waller, *Mary Sidney, Countess of Pembroke: A Critical Study of Her Writings and Literary Milieu* (Salzburg, 1979), chs 2, 3. For a more sceptical view, see M. E. Lamb, 'The Countess of Pembroke's Patronage', *ELR*, 12 (1982), 162–79, and 'The Myth of the Countess of Pembroke', *YES*, 11 (1981), 194–202.

31. *English Poetry 1400–1580*, edited by William Tydeman (New York, 1970), p. 240.

32. *Poetry of the Stewart Court*, edited by Joan Hughes and W. S. Ramson (Canberra, 1982), pp. 185, vii.

33. Puttenham, p. 24; Wotton, p. 27.

34. Sir Philip Sidney, *A Defence of Poetry*, in *Miscellaneous Prose of Sir Philip Sidney*, edited by Katherine Duncan-Jones and Jan van Dorsten (Oxford, 1973), pp. 110, 116; Puttenham, p. 60.

35. Lewis, *English Literature*, p. 120.

36. Gregory Krantzmann, *Anglo-Scottish Literary Relations 1430–1550* (Cambridge, 1980), p. 33.

37. Krantzmann, p. 31.

38. *Ballatis of Love*, edited by John MacQueen (Edinburgh, 1970), pp. xliv, lvi.

39. Helena M. Shire, *Song, Dance and Poetry of the Court of Scotland* (Cambridge, 1965), p. 228.

40. Lewis, *English Literature*, p. 129; Krantzmann, p. 31.

41. Puttenham, p. 62.

42. Gordon Kipling, 'Henry VIII and the Origins of Tudor Patronage', in *Patronage in the Renaissance*, edited by Guy Fitch Lytle and Stephen Orgel (Princeton, 1981), pp. 117–64 (pp. 132–3). For Hawes see A. S. G. Edwards, *Stephen Hawes* (Boston, 1983); for Cavendish, see *Metrical Visions*, edited by A. S. G. Edwards (Columbia, South Carolina, 1980).

Chapter 2

Language, the Poet, and the World

Sixteenth-century theories of poetry

Looking back at what Thomas Nashe, with typical late-sixteenth-century exuberance, called the era of 'Chaucer, Lydgate, Gower, with such like, that lived under the tyrannie of ignorance', Puttenham's *Arte of Poesie* gleefully celebrated the cultural apparatus which had become powerful enough to make many previously fashionable kinds of poetry seemingly contemptible. The barbarous ignorance of the previous age had, Puttenham asserts, neglected poesie, but now its ancient dignity was being revived by 'many notable Gentlemen in the Court'.[1] The kinds of poetry which Puttenham singles out for praise are significantly different from those that would have been familiar a century earlier, but we should remember that to consider a period's predominant genres or kinds of poetry is to focus on more than mere literary fashion. Puttenham wrote about a century after Caxton printed the *Morte d'Arthur*, and poured scorn on popular ballads and narratives, what he called 'stories of old time . . . old Romances or historical rimes, made purposely for recreation of the common people at Christmasse diners and brideales, and in taverns and alehouses, and such other places of base resort', as well as 'Carols and rounds and such light or lascivious Poemes'. All these, he scornfully concludes, 'in our courtly maker we banish . . . utterly'.[2]

Behind these changes in taste is something more than literary fashion. What kinds of poetry does Puttenham, by contrast, approve? A clue may be gained from the way he arranges both the subject-matter of poetry and its various kinds in a strict hierarchy. After the praise of the gods, the most important aim of poetry is to praise 'the worthy gests of noble Princes, the memorial and registry of all great fortunes'; this is followed by 'the praise of vertue and reproofe of vice, the instruction of morall doctrines, the revealing of sciences material and other profitable Arts, the redress of boisterous and sturdie courage'; finally, poetry is to be 'the common solace of mankind in all his travails and cares of this transitorie life.[3] Puttenham's account is strictly hierarchical, and rigidly subordinates poetry to public or, more accurately, class-specific interests. While he may talk of the 'sundry' or 'divers' forms of poetry, nonetheless he arranges them in a strict hierarchy, from heroic poetry to the epigram. His emphasis is on the public responsibility of poetry: it should praise the great, reprove vice, and 'show the mutabilities of fortune, and the just punishment of God in revenge of a vicious and evill life'. Even the lowly pastoral is rendered publicly useful by its aim 'under the vaile of homely persons and in rude speeches to insinuate and glaunce at greater matters'. 'In everie degree and sort of men', Puttenham notes, 'mens estates are unegall', and, by analogy, those kinds of poetry are preferred which serve the values and aims of the dominant power. It is a distinctively and unabashed drafting of poetry into the class struggle, the assimilation and appropriation of the 'divers' kinds of poetry into the centralizing hegemony of the Tudor Court.[4]

The theory alongside which the practice of poetry in the sixteenth century was written is far broader than what we would today label as 'literary theory'. But, nonetheless, in this Chapter I will examine something of the theory that emerges from or surrounds sixteenth-century poetry. 'Aesthetic' or 'poetic' theory, as we have understood it since Kant, was unknown to the Renaissance, although there are signs in some Italian theorists and even in Sidney that what a post-romantic perspective might term as the autonomy of art was struggling to find voice. But the issues that Renaissance poetic theorists (often with titles like 'defence' or 'apologie') raise are not often those which readers in the late twentieth century might consider seriously. Is poetry superior to history and philosophy? Does the good poet have to be a good man? Is poetry simply defined by its use of rhyme? What is the connection between poetry and oratory? Is genuine poetry inspired? Is poetry the most ancient of the arts? These may seem strange questions to us. But one reason we study the past is to become aware of alternatives to our own seemingly deterministic place in history – to be able to consider the options, possibilities, and cultural languages from which we have been cut off. By asking questions about our past, we may learn to ask more penetrating questions of our own time. But we ask such questions, necessarily, from our place in history, and from within the languages it affords us. It would, for instance, be absurdly antiquarian to try to approach Renaissance attitudes to love and sensuality and pretend that our history did not include de Sade, Nietzsche, Freud, psychoanalysis, D. H. Lawrence, or the Women's Movement, or that our understanding of the interaction of political thought and economic production, or the base of political power in the sixteenth century should rely on Hooker or Elyot and ignore Marx, Freud, or Foucault. In any case, we cannot contract out of our place in history. We ask questions of our past precisely because we inhabit a different present.

So when we read either the systematic treatises, or the incidental accounts of poetry's nature and function written by sixteenth-century writers like Puttenham, Gascoigne, or Sidney, inevitably we will encounter many issues that seem puzzlingly unimportant and irrelevant, even naïve, to us. Even sympathetic modern commentators have noted how derivative Renaissance English criticism is, or have pointed to its seemingly 'almost complete lack of historical outlook', as well as to its syncretism, its continual confusion of intellectual categories, logical contradictions, and intellectual naïvety.[5] To adapt a famous phrase of D. H. Lawrence, we should trust the poetry, not the poetics: what passes for theory seems curiously detached from the richness and unpredictability of the poetry (and the drama) written alongside it. The best theory to account for Sidney's or Donne's or Shakespeare's poetry, or Shakespeare's or Webster's dramas, is encoded in the works themselves, not in any theoretical remarks the poets or any of their contemporaries seemed to have made. As in any age, writers do not necessarily make the best readers or critics, especially of their own works. When we ask questions about what we mean by *text, reader, language, history*, or *author*, we may come up with important answers, but they are not always ones that would have occurred to the authors of sixteenth-century treatises.

One major characteristic of the poetry of the age, I have suggested, is that it was the product of many contradictions. No less is this true of the theories of poetry, and in this chapter I will attempt to tease out some of them. Earl Miner points out that Renaissance criticism is not only extraordinarily derivative but also contradictory, an ahistorical mix of 'Neoaristotelianism, Neohoratianism and Neoplatonism'.[6] S. K. Heninger, Jr, speaks of Sidney's work as marking a significant 'node in our cultural history' and of the *Defence* as 'an amalgamation of all the literary traditions known to Sidney – Biblical, Ciceronian, Platonic, Horatian, Ovidian, Aristotelian – brought not only into juxtaposition, but into mutually supportive conflation' in order to develop 'a comprehensive poetics that answered to all possible contingencies'.[7] Michel Foucault notes how, looking back, we can see that sixteenth-century learning was made up of an unstable mixture of rational knowledge, notions derived from magical practices, and the classical cultural heritage whose power and authority had been vastly increased by the rediscovery of Greek and Roman authors. It is, he continues, 'clearly structurally weak: a common ground where fidelity to the Ancients, a taste for the supernatural, and an already awakened awareness of the sovereign rationality in which we recognize ourselves, confronted one another in equal freedom'.[8]

If we take Sidney's *Defence* as one of the central theoretical documents of the century, it is clear that it brings together without questioning or reconcilement a host of contradictory views of poetry, a number of interlocking languages which continually rewrite one another. It is didactic and celebratory, Neoplatonic, Calvinist, Horatian, Ovidian, Ramist, Aristotelian – or to put it another way, it has been seen in these ways by modern scholars. In short, it is a hybrid, an interwoven tissue of the conflicts of Renaissance thought and practice. It has also, at times, something of an opaque quality, as if poetic theory were a performative discipline rather than a truth-claiming one. Sidney often seems to play with his reader as much as his concepts of poetry. At times he seems to conform closely to logic in his argument; but occasionally uses inconsistencies and contradictions, often (almost) with a self-conscious chuckle. He shifts ground – on whether rhyme and verse are essential to poetry, on whether the golden world of poetry is referential, on the place of rules, on the truth-value of poetry. Ronald Levao has argued persuasively that a central part of Sidney's argument is that it is 'feigned', that it is 'deliberately tangled and ambivalent', and that the discussion of poetic inspiration is 'at best metaphorical' and, more importantly (a point to which I will return) less a description of the poet's art than an account of its effect on the reader. Sidney, by this argument, is really interested in poetry's work in the world, its practical manifestations; so his uses of neoplatonic cliché or philosophical commonplace are carefully chosen rhetorical devices to develop a theory of fiction that will be persuasive rather than 'truthful'. Levao argues that the treatise is thus 'one of the most daring documents of Renaissance criticism', suggesting that the creative power of the mind tries to make order of a world that lacks inherent rationality and coherence, and inspires men towards practical action not fixed 'truths'.[9]

Didacticism and social utility

But the most obvious characteristic of sixteenth-century treatises on poetry is nothing so sophisticated. It is rather their blatant didacticism. Although later commentators have seen Sidney's *Defence* as based upon a distinction between 'fact' and 'fiction', none the less the great Romantic narrowing of literature to 'creative' or 'imaginative' writing had not yet been institutionalized. Only in the late eighteenth century is there what Terry Eagleton calls a 'new division and demarcation of discourses'. In writing the *Defence*, Sidney was instead attempting to justify poetry as a valuable activity within a Protestant society. Alan Sinfield terms the *Defence* 'the most fully developed attempt to establish a puritan–humanist aesthetic', one insisting on the didactic function of poetry to 'move men to take goodness in hand'.[10]

The social utility of poetry was an assumption that was widely taken for granted. The dominant literary theory of the late Middle Ages, as Robert Montgomery puts it, 'seeks to explain or defend the value of fiction primarily in terms of the ends it gains in the mind of the reader and ultimately in his moral behaviour'.[11] In the sixteenth century, most arguments on poetry follow along these lines. All writers agreed that poetry's universal and ancient status is conceded by the best authorities, that because of its divine origins and social nature, poetry could (despite objections from some Protestants) be a moral force, and that it mixed didactic truth with a delight that enhanced its power to change men's lives. Sidney's formulation is typical here: poets, he writes, 'do merely make to imitate, and imitate both to delight and teach; and delight, to move men to take that goodness in hand, without which delight they would fly as from a stranger, and teach, to make them know that goodness whereunto they are moved'. The conclusion of the *Defence* likewise stresses that poetry is not 'an art of lies, but of true doctrine', and 'full of virtue-breeding delightfulness'. From a post-Kantian perspective, are there the beginnings of an 'aesthetic' approach to poetry, hints of the treasured Romantic and modernist notion of the autonomy of the work of art? Some may be found in Sidney's *Defence* and in some earlier Italian theorists, but such elements are always found alongside the more obvious moralizing or utilitarian sentiments. Sidney writes of the poet's 'high flying liberty of conceit', the 'vigour' of the poet's 'invention', and in one half of the most famous aphorism of the *Defence*, he asserts that 'our erected wit maketh us know what perfection is'. But this ecstatic, Neoplatonic celebration is then immediately countermanded by the other half of the same sentence, that, none the less, 'our infected will keepeth us from reaching unto it'.[12] 'Erected wit' and 'infected will': in those great opposites are epitomized the contradictory languages of sixteenth-century poetry.

Regardless of the kinds of poetry, then, didactive assumptions dominate most of the century's poetry. In the early part of the period, we see that the bulk of the work of the early Tudor humanist poets, like More, Barclay, or Hawes, even the more lively poetry written by Skelton, is stolidly didactic, and eminently painful to wade through. At best, Barclay brings to his *Ship of Fools* some rough plainness as he attacks court corruption; while Hawes's *Example of Vertu* and the *Pastyme of Pleasure* dimly anticipate *The Faerie Queene's* combination of chivalric romance, dream vision, and religious didacticism. But most early and mid-century English poetry, with the notable exception of Wyatt's, seems similarly utilitarian and pedantic. It is abstract and moralizing, epitomized in *A Mirror for Magistrates* (1559 and subsequent editions) or in what was the century's most popular verse, Sternhold and Hopkins's versions of the Psalms. It seems to be worlds apart from the delicate sophistication and seeming individuality of later poets like Sidney or Shakespeare. So too is most of the poetry in the Scottish Court. Indeed, a modern reader's impression of most British poetry between 1480 and 1580, with the exception of Dunbar and Wyatt, is not likely to be favourable. It is, overall, as Yvor Winters put it, 'astonishingly poor'.[13] In short, writing in the *Defence* of the stolidness of English poetry before about 1580, Sidney seems to be making an accurate judgement.

C. S. Lewis unabashedly blames the bulk of 'earnest, heavy-handed, commonplace' poetry on humanism, arguing that the pious, sober-minded educationalists of the first seventy years of the century saw poetry as requiring heavy moralizing, encyclopaedic scope and heavy-handed allegory, thus continuing the worst of medieval solemnity in its epigrammatic, halting, moral commonplaces, precepts, and saws. 'All the facts', he argues, 'seem consistent with the view that the great literature of the fifteen-eighties and nineties was something which humanism, with its unities and *Gorboduc* and English hexameters, would have prevented if it could, but failed to prevent because the high tide of native talent was then too strong for it.'[14] But it is a view of poetry that does not disappear in the last decades of the century. Moralistic poetry is as strong in the 1590s, in the work of Greville or Chapman, as it had been earlier in the century.

Such moralizing poets as Googe or Turberville certainly saw poetry, as Lewis implies, as the natural outcome of the principles of humanist education. A poem for them is typically a well-modulated collection of *sententiae*. It is designed to show the universality of the human lot and, more particularly, the moral and civic principles of the Tudor establishment. These poets writing in mid century were by and large highly trained, public-minded statesmen, lawyers, scholars, concerned with the pacification and reform of society and they directed their poetry (which was very much a minor part of their lives) towards a readership of similar men. They shared the belief that poetry should inculcate an obedience to authority, the recognition of civic order, and reinforce doctrinal and moral stability. When we read it today, we might well ask what kind of 'self' does it ask for? What role is the reader asked to occupy? It is that of a sober, primarily male, citizen, a member of a community linked together by unchanging moral virtues. The best of this poetry – some of Googe's or Gascoigne's – is distinguished by sonority, directness, and a stubborn dedication to the educational and moral ideals of humanism. Occasionally something more struggles to the surface. Gascoigne's poetry, undoubtedly the most interesting written in England between Wyatt and Sidney, is more distinctive because it starts to articulate a little of the bind in which his poetry has been put as it wrestles to express something through, but not confined to, the moral commonplaces of the society. A typical eager seeker for court preferment, the speaker of Gascoigne's verse remains moralistic, and in fact his choice of the complaint curiously medieval; none the less some of the contradictions characteristic of the age's most interesting poetry are starting to come through these serious lines.

Before the last decades of the century – indeed the age's most ambitious poetical work before *The Faerie Queene* – the quintessential didactic work of poetry, which combined both the general moralistic caste of late medieval public poetry and the distinctive role of the new Protestant regime, was *A Mirror for Magistrates*. This was a collection of versified tragic tales taken from English history, first compiled by Thomas Baldwin under the reign of Mary, but not printed until 1559. It shows exactly how traditional, civic-minded moralistic poetry was both reinforced by and yet in significant ways undercut by Protestantism. It was very popular – perhaps the second most popular work of poetry (after Sternhold and Hopkins's lugubrious versifications of the *Psalms* (1559) of the century. It went through nine editions by 1610, most with newly added tragedies 'all to be oftener reade, and the better re-membered' by 'the learned (for such all Magistrates are or should be)'. In the 1563 edition, an Introduction was added, and the chronicle of tragedies taken as far as the War of the Roses. In the 1587 edition, the editor, Thomas Blenerhasset, included a tale of Uther Pendragon and in his introduction described the additions as covering historical events 'from the conquest of Caeser unto the comying of Duke William the Conqueror'. Its authors included prominent nobles and courtiers, and the combination of medieval allegory, solemn moralistic tragedy, and public responsibility (all reinforced in the successive additions) served the Elizabethan regime as a continually adapted reinforcement of its political aims. In the Introduction, written by one of Elizabeth's leading courtiers, Thomas Sackville, Earl of Dorset, the figure of Sorrow appears and invites the reader to 'leave the playning, and the byter bale/ of worthy men, by Fortune overthrowe', and after introducing a pageant of allegorical figures like Remorse, Maladie, and Warre, the first of those whose tales are to be told in the ensuing tragedies is introduced. The *Mirror* thus continues the fifteenth-century English taste for en-cyclopaedic, moralistic poetry. It adapts the patterns of Boccaccio, or Lydgate's *Fall of Princes*, to present a compendium of the dominant Tudor reading of English political history. It was a secular equivalent of the homilies, giving detailed applications of its lessons, providing a 'mirror' for princes, governors, and soldiers. The collection was widely imitated, its basic formula adapted to other material, its political intent reinforced by many similar works.[15]

It is worth underlining both the popularity and typicality of such works. Despite our preference today for the period's lyrics, the bulk of the poetry extant from at least the first three-quarters of the sixteenth century is unremitting in the way it subordinated itself to the public needs of the regime. The poetry before 1580 is mainly such versified Protestant and civic propaganda – moral commonplaces, precepts, *encomia*, epitaphs, expostulations on patriotism, exposures of moral dangers, or on social evils, the dangers of life in Court, the shortness of life in general. It sets out the rules for responsible behaviour, usually reinforced by stern moralizations of theological commonplace, like Googe's:

> Behold this fleeting world, how all things fade,
> How every thing doth pass and wear away;
> Each state of life, by common course and trade,
> Abides no time, but hath a passing day.

Such verse, as William E. Sheidley comments on Googe (one of its most indefatigable producers), was designed to advance the general programme of the new regime, which included 'purging the realm of vice, papistry, and dissension, while educating the populace to the need for civil order, obedience, and a patriotism focused on the crown'.[16] Even the period's satiric verse, such as Gascoigne's *The Steele Glas* (a typical continuation of the *Mirror* fashion), is designed to point out the social ills of the time, to purge them so that the Court might become more like the pattern given, so the assumption was, by the Queen herself. Typical targets are the frivolity of modern courtiers and the corruption of foreign, especially Italian, influences. It is poetry firmly in line with Ascham's requirement in *The Scholemaster* that literature 'gather examples' and 'give light and understanding' to good precepts.[17]

Most of the century is dominated by such utilitarian poetry, and it would be a mistake to see such lugubrious verse as being transcended, as Lewis for one was wont to do, by an upsurge of aureate, sophisticated courtly lyrics from 1570 on. The utilitarian emphasis continues. Its most triumphant creation is unquestionably Spenser's *The Faerie Queene* (1590–96), which is perhaps the clearest and richest example of how the Elizabethan regime advanced its ideals through poetry. Political allegory, whether the clumsy moralization of the *Mirror* or the rich polyphony of *The Faerie Queene*, is built on a desire to subdue language to power, to make signification transparent to meaning and to paralyse the potential promiscuity of language into fetish and shibboleth.[18] Ironically, as we watch the intellectual (though decidedly not the poetic) disintegration of Spenser's masterpiece in its final books, we can see even the most confident hegemony contains within itself, even in repressed form, oppositional forces and the inevitability of its own transformation.

A strongly didactic theory of the public responsibility of the poet, then, is emphatically not an aberration that dies out in the last quarter of the century. In fact, it gains strength as Elizabeth's reign proceeds and later is reinforced by the Stuart monarchy. This is, as Alan Sinfield points out, the poetry of a one-party State.[19]

To what extent to modern histories of sixteenth-century poetry see it in such explicitly political terms? To modern liberal readers, such stentorian views as Puttenham's may seem more associated with Soviet censorship or the poetry of post-1948 China. Sinfield has, in fact, suggested that the closest parallels we find in our own time with both the theory and use of poetry in the sixteenth century are with Stalinist Russia, pointing out the uncanny parallels between Sidney's sentiments and Leonid Brezhnev's address to the XXVI Congress of the Soviet Communist Party where it is argued the 'vivid images of our contemporaries move people, prompt debates, and make people think of the present and the future' by presenting a heroic ideal so that 'the reader or the viewer sees his own thoughts and feelings, and the embodiment of the finest qualities' of the national character. As Sinfield comments, 'some of the same virtues are absolutized in the *Defence*, and the same exemplary role is assigned to literature', thus covering up, 'in the interest of a particular view of culture and society', the range of possibilities poetry might and does, in fact, produce.[20]

To draw such a parallel is a startling reminder of the socio-cultural realities encoded in most Elizabethan poetry. Modern critics have, however, shied away from such comparisons. Most modern scholars, whether they are advocates of the golden poetry of Sidney or Spenser, or the 'native' or 'plain' style of Wyatt, Greville, or Ralegh, agree upon a clear distinction between 'public' poetry, like *The Faerie Queene* or *A Mirror for Magistrates* where the values and ideals of the Elizabethan political regime are foregrounded, and the shorter, 'private', occasional lyrics, such as the Petrarchan sonnet, the madrigal, or song. One is clearly acknowledged as didactic even when, as with *The Faerie Queene*, much more is going on in the poem; the other is usually seen as the outgrowth of an autonomous tradition of a lyric utterance, either diversionary or meditative, expressing escapism, doubt, love, joy, anguish, acting as Puttenham's 'common solace of mankind',[21] and thus to be read, with appropriate allowances for diction or ethos, as lyrics of personal, even confessional, utterances or else simply as rhetorical exercises on commonplace themes.

We will return to this argument about the modern preference for the lyric in Chapter 3. The lyric is one of Puttenham's meaner kinds of poetry. Another lowly kind, the pastoral, is patently used by sixteenth-century poets as part of their public roles and responsibilities. '*Eclogues*', Puttenham writes, are poems which 'in base and humble stile . . . uttered the private and familiar talke of the meanest sort of men', using 'the vaile of homely persons to insinuate and glaunce matters'.[22] The mystification of the pastoral is yet another cultural practice of the late sixteenth century which shows the inseparability of 'literary' and 'social' texts. The propagandist intent of a didactic poem like the *Mirror* is clear enough; much more discrete and yet as revealing is the use to which the Court put the seemingly harmless escapism of the pastoral eclogue and a range of poetry in which the pastoral mode permeated – the prose romances, romantic drama, and (eventually, especially in the Jacobean Court) the court masque. To study the pastoral is, once again, to see how social tensions and ideological pressures operated in poetry. We may see this by concentrating precisely on a major absence 'in' the pastoral. Ironically, what is *not* found in court pastorals are the real conditions of Elizabethan country life, which was, especially from mid century on, passing through disruptive and painful transitions as land was appropriated and exploited by such great families as the Sidneys and the Herberts. In the placid, sophisticated world of Elizabethan pastoral no such disturbances occur. As Louis Montrose comments, the pastoral's origins and connections are made presentable for service in the Court, and the shepherd-poet's plaints, however disguised, are the loyal expression of political aspirations. This is the case even when the pastoral is used for satire. In Spenser's *Colin Clouts Come Home Again* (1591), the poet attacks court corruption, while praising the Queen and the noble ladies around her; within what he terms 'this simple pastorall' both sycophantic praise and stern moral satire coexist, and in this uneasy juxtaposition of flattery and satire we encounter pleas for personal advancement along with condemnation of those who seek 'with malice and with strife/To thrust downe other' and himselfe to raise'. Returning to his plantation in Ireland, Spenser is looking back at England, and sternly rebukes and seemingly rejects the Court, but the whole poem is motivated by his desire to advance by means of its influence.[23] Such tensions, and the unacknowledged gaps and repressions of the poem, are among those that typically dislocate much of the poetry of the 1590s including, most importantly, the final books of Spenser's own great epic.

Didacticism, then, and of a distinctively civic and moral kind, is the predominant note of sixteenth-century theory, and it is borne out in the poetical practices of the age. Whether the emphases are Boethian, Augustinian, Horatian, or Calvinist, most Renaissance pronouncements on poetry insist on the social, educational, and moral responsibility of the poet. They also emphasize that poetry's role is to be subordinate to what they saw as the given meanings of the world – whether they were conceived as given by God's Word, the order of Nature, or the need for civic responsibility. The commonplace formula was that poetry both taught and pleased. Poetry was justified as supporting the establishment of the godly State. Poetry can help reform man's will: 'no learning is so good as that which teacheth and moveth to virtue', as Sidney writes.[24]

Poetry is not only a moral teacher, but it is the supreme moral teacher among the other arts. It combines the conceptual advantages of philosophy with the concrete instances of history. Poetry will entice men into virtuous actions by imitating real virtue, not false illusion – by its imitation of what Sidney calls the 'golden' world, a world of moral inspiration of what may and should be. The poet, Sidney argues, 'doth grown in effect another nature, in making things either better than nature bringeth forth, or, quite anew, forms such as never were in nature'. 'Poetry', therefore, he asserts, 'is an art of imitation, for so Aristotle termeth it in his word *mimesis*', not by simply reproducing the given world but by 'a representing, counterfeiting, or figuring forth to speak metaphorically'.[25] The main emphasis here is on metaphor as the primary way of speaking which brings about the effects of imitation – and thus affecting the mind and the senses of the readers. Readers of poetry will thus be enticed towards the emulation of moral excellence by the power of poetry's *mimesis*, as it creates speaking pictures of how Nature might fulfil its potential. Even in the discussion of metaphor, in short, the final test of poetry is always in *praxis* – how it contributes to the moral improvement of its readers and to the wider society.

But it would be a peculiarly partial reading of Sidney's *Defence* or of the entire thinking about poetry in the period to see didacticism as totally dominant. It may be true, as Sinfield argues, that Sidney handles the central issues of his treatise in distinctively Protestant ways and that we cannot understand him unless we see him as 'part of a faction committed to reinforcing the influence of Protestantism within the cultural apparatus and the state generally'.[26] But the *Defence*, and indeed the period's other treatises on poetry, are less absolute than Sinfield's argument suggests. Like poetry, even a prose treatise brings into play contradictions and tensions it would consciously like to exclude. The *Defence* combines many contradictory strands which tend to unravel the hard-line Protestantism of parts of its argument, and I shall now proceed to tease out some of them.

Neoplatonism

The first we shall glance at is neoplatonism, a suggestive accretion of ideas derived, at some distance, from Plato and remixed, from the late fifteenth century onwards, by such thinkers as Ficino and Pico della Mirandola – and subsequently popularized in such works as Castiglione's *Il Cortegiano*. According to the Neoplatonist model, through his God-given power the poet creates 'another world' analogous to the way God himself created the world. The world is a rational universe created by a rational Creator who, in Heninger's words, followed the precepts of the Book of Wisdom, making the universe 'according to number, weight, and measure'.[27] As usual, Sidney's is the most elegant English formulation of the poetical application of such an optimistic doctrine. Although his idea that the poet creates a new Nature is not original – it is derived from the Neoplatonic view of the artist as the vehicle of the Divine Ideas, popularized by such Italian critics as Landino or Scaliger – it is a most intriguing expression:

> Only the poet, disdaining to be tied to any such subjection, lifted up with the vigour of his own invention, doth grow in effect another nature, in making things either better than nature bringeth forth, or, quite anew, forms such as never were in nature . . . so as he goeth hand in hand with nature, not enclosed within the narrow warrant of her gifts, but freely ranging only within the zodiac of his own wit.

Here the poet is celebrated as an autonomous maker. He takes the miraculous creation of the world by God, the divine poet, as his model, and draws down the magical powers of the universe into his own mind, 'the zodiac of his own wit'. The superiority of the poet's world is unabashedly celebrated in such a formulation since Nature's 'world is brazen, the poets only deliver a golden'. The poet's greatness is de-pendent on aspiring to encapsulate in his poem that beauty and splendour that shine in all natural things, and thus continuing God's divine creativity in his work. He is

> . . . set . . . beyond and over all the works of that second nature: which in nothing he showeth so much as in poetry, when with the force of a divine breath he bringeth things forth surpassing her doings – with no small argument to the credulous of that first accursed fall of Adam, since our erected wit maketh us know what perfection is, and yet our infected will keepeth us from reaching unto it.[28]

It is fascinating that here, at the end of his ecstatic sentence, Sidney comes right back to didacticism, and most particularly, in the Calvinist emphasis of the 'infected will', to man's radical inability to embody in

action what poetry inspires him to perform. Yet is not poetry as well
infected by such radical imperfections? How did Renaissance writers
reconcile such oppositions? How can the erected wit, and the infected
will coexist? These are contradictions that (as we shall see in Ch. 5)
surface in Sidney's poetry as well.

The general Neoplatonic caste of the so-called Elizabethan world-
picture is a particularly interesting phenomenon – and most relevant for
the way poetry and poetic theory were rewritten by other cultural codes
and so assimilated into the dominant understanding of cosmic and
political order. As Jon Quitslund has shown, most Elizabethan poets'
interest in Platonism is little more than a reverent and convenient lip-
service, a 'dilution of serious thought', but it gave their work a distinctively aesthetic aura which undermines the otherwise ubiquitous
grey utilitarianism.[29] Their primary interest was in raiding
Neoplatonism for compliments to the beauty of a mistress, or to express
the ennobling power by which men might perceive God, or perhaps to
make claims for the status of the poet as a prophetic articulator of truth –
in Sidney's case, as against the historian or philosopher or practical man
of affairs. The poet is thus a creator, mediating between the world of
transcendent forms and the brazen world of Nature. Spenser's
articulation of such a theory in the October Eclogue of the *Shepheardes
Calender* or *The Tears of the Muses* combines Neoplatonism and
traditional Horatianism along with a Christian emphasis on divine inspiration. Another assimilation of Neoplatonism found commonly in
sixteenth-century discussions of poetry is the numerical coherence between the individual poem and that of the created world. It is often
expressed by means of a musical analogy. Sidney mentions how the
'same exquisite observing of number and measure of words' has a
'divine force' in it, and thus introduces the close relationship of music to
poetry. He speaks further of the 'planet-like music of Poetry'. 'Music'
here includes far more than the modern term suggests. As Heninger
argues, behind the phrase is the Boethian philosophy of the intercon-
nection of the divinely ordained harmony of the universe (*the musica
mundana*), the individual man's harmony (*the musica humana*) and the
expression of universal harmony in instrumental music (*the musica in-
strumentalis*). Sidney typically gives this theory a practical application:
poetry's echo of the *musica mundana* leads to a therapeutic reorganization
of the psyche towards cosmic harmony.[30]

What kinds of poetry would this slightly less didactic theory favour?
One kind, clearly, would attempt to unite its audience almost as a
community of believers and so would subordinate irony or ethical
conflict to the overall effect of participatory delight. 'It is the right
harmony of lyric', asserts Dowland, which 'stirs men up to admiration
and delight'; such effects are achieved by aspiring to the incantatory

effects of music, with syntax and idea conceived of as parts of a musical whole, representing not so much a precise emotion as the morphology of emotion – not describing feeling so much as what it feels like to feel. To *hear* (always, we should remember, an important experience for a modern student of the Elizabethan lyric) Dowland's setting of 'My Thoughts Are Winged with Hopes' or Sidney's 'Who Is It that this Darke Night' would be, according to such a theory, to enter into an atmosphere of lyrical harmony and thereby to participate in an order that was not simply superficial pleasure nor direct and vulgar moralization. Such poems rarely attempt to arrest or obstruct the verse's flow to create a dislocation between sense and movement; the words are chosen to please the ear, to soothe the senses. There is, they seem to assert, no need to know anything more than the shimmering surface – to foreground any ambiguity, tension, or urgent personal voice would dislocate the pattern. Light, harmony, proportion, and grace are meant to constitute the experience which the poem opens up in its readers, and it is our recognition of the poem's aptness, and our participation in its pattern of rich harmony, that Sidney includes in his key Neoplatonic term, 'delight'. That, too, it is asserted, is a kind of knowledge. As Ralegh's celebration of the Queen and the virtues of the regime puts it:

> In heaven Queene she is among the spheares;
> In ay she Mistres like makes all things pure,
> Eternitie in hir oft chaunge she beares;
> She beautie is, by hir the faire endure.

The Queen is not *like* Beauty; she *is* Beauty: she is above time, beyond criticism, and the courtiers around her do not question this. They just *know* it:

> A knowledge pure it is hir worth to kno,
> With Circles let them dwell that thinke not so.

Anyone doubting that this is the case is cursed; more, is clearly sub-human. Such knowledge is 'natural': or, more accurately as we might now say, is ideology! Poems like this, or Campion's 'Rose-cheekt Lawra' or 'Come, O Come, my life's delight' attempt to create the experience of participating in a timeless world. Even given the necessarily sequential pattern of lines and stanzas, such poems try to fix us in a stasis, without any relation to the passing of time in the mutable world outside the experience of reading or hearing the poem. They are concerned with celebration not discovery; they aim to be experiences of healing and restoration, not of alienation or stringent self-discovery. They aspire to what Sidney terms a 'conveniency to nature'.[31]

Such a world is very different from our own. As Foucault has argued, such an 'order of things' depends on the belief that the universe was held together by resemblance and similitude. It implies that the universe of discourse, too, is likewise held together by a semantic repertoire the most important features of which are hierarchy, similitude, analogy, the general sympathy of word to thing. And it is the particular gift of the poet to discover such order in language, to make explicit what was essentially implicit in all the signatures and signs of the visible and invisible universe. The interplay of resemblance could be found in every aspect of the world; men could be assured that nothing could escape connection, and that the invisible world of metaphysical forms was inextricably linked to the little worlds of man and society.[32]

For a modern reader of sixteenth-century poetry, such a theory – more than a theory, since it was part of the ingrained assumptions of the age and so should be treated as part of the sixteenth-century's dominant ideological structures – can be pieced apart to show it merely to be an unstable accumulation of empirical observation, superstition, pseudo-magical practices. political obfuscation, and ancient authority. But because such connections also affect the realm of language we must ask both how poetry fitted into the overall structure of discourse, and what effects the breakdown of the whole scheme from the late sixteenth century onwards had on poetry. As Foucault argues, until the end of the sixteenth century, 'the value of language lay in the fact that it was the sign of things. There is no difference between the visible marks that God has stamped upon the surface of the earth, so that we may know its inner secrets, and the legible words that the Scriptures, or the sages of Antiquity, have set down in the books preserved for us by tradition.'[33] Nature, the texts of antiquity, the Bible, society, men's individual natures were all linked, and the poet above all else was asked to relate and restore the invisible but unbroken links between men and things. As this particular order broke down, the disruption and dislocation are mediated through the poetry. As part of a whole new division of discourse, we get a new poetry, and a new poetic theory.

Rhetorical theory

Didacticism and Neoplatonic resemblance, then, are two major ingredients of the Renaissance pot-pourri of poetic theory; another was a broad and increasing strain of Aristotelianism, which broadens as the century goes on to become the next century's dominant neo-classical formalism. As the works of classical philosophers and poets became available in England, many of the questions which had, much earlier, been raised in Italy and other parts of Europe came to interest and eventually to dominate English criticism – the debate over the status of the vernacular, the moral defence of poetry, the development of the all-encompassing category of 'convention' against 'nature', and the emergence of neo-classical rules, thus adding to the forces that were relocating reality from an ontology based on a Platonic or Christian world of being to one based in the phenomena of physical nature. Texts like Cicero's *De Inventione*, the *Rhetorica ad Herennium,* Horace's *Ars Poetica*, and, especially, Aristotle's *Poetics* became increasingly quoted (often from Italian translations and commentaries) and discussed. As well, more specifically focused rhetorical handbooks like Cicero's *De Oratore*, Quintilian's *Institute of Oratory* and, especially powerful late in the century, Ramus's works, brought about major changes in the understanding of rhetoric. Poetry was put under increasing pressure by a new movement of humanist educators who, as Nashe put it late in the century, 'repurged the errors of Arte, expelled from their puritie, and set before our eyes a more perfect method of studie'.[34]

Despite its appropriation by sophisticated theoreticians of communications and university writing programmes, 'rhetoric' is still a suspect word today. Like 'ideology', it carries with it unnecessary connotations. Yet as Terry Eagleton points out, rhetoric is the earliest kind of literary criticism.[35] Throughout the Middle Ages, the study of rhetoric was a training in discourse theory, the theory of the pragmatic and highly ideological uses of language in concrete social practices. During the sixteenth century, we can trace particular changes in the theory and practice of rhetoric which are illuminating for our understanding of the poetry – in particular the gradual separation of 'invention' and logic from decoration or rhetoric. What became seen as 'eloquence' became criticized as an unnecessary intrusion between the speaker of 'truth' and its reception. Throughout the sixteenth century, in fact, two rival views of rhetoric coexist uneasily and by the end are breaking into clear conflict. There is, on the one hand, what Richard Lanham has termed *homo rhetoricus*, the man who plays freely with language, devising rather than merely discovering truth, indulging in the copiousness and richness of rhetoric; on the other hand, there is *homo seriosus*, seen in the Protestant or Ramist view of language, whereby rhetoric is seen merely as appropriately chosen devices of persuasion.[36] Is logic an inventive process or merely the mirror of what nature provides? Where Erasmus, following Quintilian, argues for the variety and pleasure of *copia*, with logic and rhetoric in equal balance, both Ramism and Protestantism were suspicious of the self-indulgence of the humanist exaltation of language. Logic is aligned with nature, rhetoric with convention, artifice, and embellishment. By the end of the century, ornament is increasingly suspect, moderation and clarity becoming admired for both prose and poetry. In particular, by rigidly separating logic from rhetoric, Ramism implied that the 'truth' was a matter of the given objects-in-nature which were to be 'discovered' not 'invented', while the arts of language were merely the necessary clothing of those truths. 'More matter and less art' asks Shakespeare's Ramist Queen Gertrude in *Hamlet*. As Eagleton summarizes the process, 'a vigorous division of labour was gradually instituted between thought and speech, language and discourse, science and poetry'.[37]

If 'rhetoric' was at issue in the sixteenth century, so too was the key Aristotelian term *mimesis*, or 'imitation'. Every art, argues Sidney, has 'the works of nature for his principal object' and poetry is to be defined as 'an art of imitation', and the poet by 'that feigning' of 'notable images of virtues, vices, or what else'. The poet 'imitates' to teach and delight. One of the questions Sidney raises is: what is the object of *mimesis*? What does the poet imitate? In his *Republic*, Plato has attacked the arts as being based on deception, merely counterfeiting the appearances of things; later works like *Timaeus* and *Sophist* modify the harshness of his criticism, but it was left to Aristotle to redefine *mimesis* as a presentation of the universal or characteristic mode of existence, the 'conveniency to nature' as Sidney puts it.[38] During the Renaissance, the varied and contradictory interpretations of the concept included the Neoplatonic valorization of the poets' access to the world of forms, an adaptation of Aristotelian 'universals' into the reproduction of local particularities, and a pedagogical view, as the careful, even mechanical following of a literary model. If we glance ahead, too, early in the next century, for Ben Jonson 'imitation' has become simply the reasoned, judicious use of the thoughts, words, and examples of approved authors.[39] Jonson's difference from Sidney is important here. For Sidney, the essence of the poetic act was the art of 'figuring forth to speake Metaphorically'. Metaphor is conceived of as a means of extending knowledge by means of the vital use of words to make visual (not merely conceptual) its meanings: 'it is that feigning notable images . . . which must be the right describing note to know a poet by'. It is a process best charac-terized by *enargeia*, force, power, not merely by a mere manipulation of words. As Heninger notes, when Sidney is writing the *Defence* '"metaphor" is still a prominent term in the critical lexicon with a rich history and wide applicability'.[40] But for Jonson, as for Bacon or Hobbes, metaphor is merely ornamentation, a device to be used to illustrate pre-existent matter, and the imagination a faculty to be used with some caution. From Sidney to Jonson is merely one generation, but the difference in poetic theory and the whole understanding of language and/as reality is immense.

Discussions of such issues, as with so many issues important to the period's poetry, should not be oversimplified or too quickly harmonized. Sixteenth-century views of 'imitation' betray the century's conflicts as surely as the rest of the cultural apparatus. Too often, as Jacqueline Miller has shown, modern accounts of imitation in the Renaissance try to show that just as that which is 'imitated' is supposed to be transformed into a new creation, so the heterogeneity of the various writings that are woven together in the theory can be harmonized. She points out that Sidney's virtuoso performance in the *Defence* is a barely disguised acknowledgement of the contradictions with which he is working. One interesting example she discusses is the bee metaphor used by theorists from Petrarch on: 'we should write as the bees make sweetness, not storing up the flowers but turning them into honey, thus making one thing of many various ones, but different and better'. It is a comparison that occurs repeatedly, uneasily and contradictorily, throughout the period. When Renaissance theorists deal with it, they generally seem unable to provide a coherent programme for achieving this elusive goal. Even more interestingly, the various theories proposed do not only contradict those proposed by others, but are internally contradictory as well. Sidney's account is, as usual, instructive, a temporary coincidence of two discordant voices. On the one hand, he argues, the poets are different from arithmeticians or philosophers who follow Nature, or grammarians and rhetoricians who follow rules, since 'only the poet . . . doth grown in effect another nature . . . not enclosed within the narrow warrant of her gifts'.[41] Yet, on the other hand, he repeatedly stresses the need to follow artificial rules, models, and ancient masters. It is not only the disparity between such views, but the attempt to pair such recognizably discordant ideas that seems to be most representative of the period's thinking about poetry. Inherently contradictory concepts are brought together, held only by the writer's desire, and not by any kind of achieved harmony. It is left to the next century to attempt to sort out the contradictions.[42]

In speaking of poetry as an art of *mimesis*, the art of 'figuring forth to speak metaphorically', Sidney is voicing the commonplace that the poet is closely allied to the orator. His remark combines a description of the orator as he who masters the figures of rhetoric, and the poet as he who imitates the actions of men. Both share the same goal of persuasion. The Ciceronian and Horatian emphasis on the teaching function of poetry and the humanist emphasis on language's persuasion, together produced the assumption that certain tropes would produce certain effects on an audience. Erasmus's *De Copia*, widely used as a school text, concentrated on the orator's effects on an audience and inculcated a view of poetry as an art of conscious choice and calculated effect. The recovery of and commentaries on Cicero or Quintilian, the influence of Ramus late in the century, all reinforced the close association of poetry and oratory. Gradually, native English handbooks were written to translate into English the precepts of classical oratory. These included Leonard Cox's *The Arte or Crafte of Rhethoryke* (1528), Thomas Wilson's *Art of Rhetoric* (1553), and Abraham Fraunce's *Arcadian Rhetoric* (1589). Parts of Puttenham's treatise are also in this vein.

From such works, all dealing in immense detail with grammar, rhetoric, and logic, we can piece together an extremely complicated system of language as persuasion, one that was to be acquired by 'studie & discipline or exercise' in schools and universities, and then applied to the various arts of discourse, including poetry. It involved the selecting and developing of a subject (invention) and then elaborating or amplifying it according to approved structures and illustrations by schemes and tropes. Many sixteenth-century poems read as if they are handbook exercises, which indeed they often are; others, more subtle and complex, like Sidney's, can none the less equally be rooted firmly in the same training and assumptions. The seemingly endless exercises in translation, imitation, and adaptation focused the poet's skill upon the appropriate rhetorical devices. Lanham's *homo seriosus* and *homo rhetoricus* were thus both served by such study. The former, like most poets of the mid-century period, saw the goal of poetry as communicating given truths. Language must therefore be chosen to be transparent, self-effacing, and to highlight the apparent referential reality. The latter saw language itself as central, not the truths to which it purportedly points – thus the poet conceived of himself as a player, as a master of roles, in effect what Plato had sternly rejected as sophistry and what the rhetorically inclined Elizabethans lauded as the production of *copia*, copious matter. The 'method' (otherwise called 'disposition' or 'arrangement') of the organization of a poem or poetic sequence would be chosen in order to influence the anticipated reader response most effectively – for instance, in Ramus's influential scheme, by simplicity and directness (the 'natural' disposition), or by digression and complication (the 'prudential').[43] Poets wishing to instruct their audiences would be likely to choose the former; poets seeking display, entertainment, or provocation, the latter – although it is fair to point out that in the most interesting poems of the period, the characteristics of the so-called plain and eloquent styles are inevitably mixed to complement or challenge each other.

The mid-century period is best seen as a muddled but finally useful time of experiments in finding ways by which words could be used to serve poetic eloquence of many kinds. Tottel's *Miscellany* may be seen as Shakespeare's Slender saw it – as a model handbook of rhetorical exercises, giving subsequent poets models for their own verse, 'a fullscale attempt', as Peterson puts it, 'to extend the possibilities of the short poem by adapting the various themes and modes of *dispositio* that are outlined and illustrated in the handbooks of rhetoric currently in the use of schools'.[44] Poets were encouraged to note such models, to consult rhetorical handbooks, and to model their work on examples in the miscellanies of verse, whether published or simply privately circulated. The poets of the mid century carefully followed and experimented with the resources their models provided them. Turberville is obviously and carefully following handbook patterns in his verse, and Gascoigne's best poems adapt a decorously plain style straight from the models provided by the rhetorical handbooks. As Ringler points out, the most valuable part of Sidney's training was the thorough grounding he received in logic and rhetoric, and by the time he wrote, the lessons of the period of experiment in mid century had been absorbed.[45]

Puttenham's *Arte* is, on this as on much else, an important treatise. The assumption that poetry and oratory are closely linked is paramount throughout the *Arte*, which on one level is an orthodox textbook of rhetoric. After a first book which deals with poetry in general, and raises questions about the status of the vernacular, the ancient authority of poetry, the place of rhyme, and the subjects and forms of poetry, Puttenham devotes book two to 'proportion poeticall'. The art of writing poetry, he argues, 'is a skill to speake and write harmonically.' Poetry is a kind of 'Musicall utterance', its harmony based on stanzaic form, metre, rhyme, and figure. The third book is 'of ornament poeticall' and in twenty-five chapters he, like many others, treats of the 'figures and figurative speaches' of rhetoric, 'which be the flowers . . . and colours that a Poet setteth upon his language by arte, as the embroderer doth his stone and perle, or passements of gold upon the stuffe of a Princely garment'. As Marion Trousdale has noted, the discussion of ornament, 'which by us may be deemed irrelevant if not intrusive, is essential to the Elizabethans, not as the expression of meaning, but as the pleasure of art'. Poetry and oratory are throughout intermingled in Puttenham's discussion: 'figures,' he asserts, are 'the instruments of ornament in every language'. He then gives an exhaustive description of the tropes and figures, concluding that 'in all things' the poet must 'use decorum' or a 'lovely conformitie, or proportion, or conveniencie between the sense and the sensible' which 'nature her self' observes in her own works.[46]

Sidney too is most conscious of the need to exploit poetry's closeness to oratory. In his work, we can see how a successful poem had to have a sense of audience in the way that an oration or formal address did. And at this point we discover a vital part of sixteenth-century poetical theory which is far more congenial, perhaps, to modern taste than the seeming artificiality of rhetorical handbooks. It is that much Elizabethan poetry is intensely reader-oriented. When modern authorities discuss the interaction of poetry and rhetoric, by and large they have assumed a writer-oriented perspective. What has been often overlooked is that part of the poet's training was always to have his readers in mind, continually to be aware that the power of poetry resided in the forcefulness to a reader of the image that was presented to what Cicero termed the mind's eye. Sidney's *Defence* emphasizes how poetry aims to produce visible images in order to move his audience in the way that an orator does. Henry Peacham's *Garden of Eloquence* (1577) sets out in a rigid hierarchy the appropriate rhetorical figures, beginning with metaphor, and emphasizes how the reader or hearer must seem to see 'a lyvely image . . . then a reporte expressed with the tongue'.[47]

The writer-centred theory of poetry, whether 'imitative' or 'inspirational', was, in other words, complemented by a strongly affective theory. The true poet, writes Sidney, 'holdeth children from play, and old men from the chimney corner'; he adds that poetry was a more effective teacher than history or philosophy because its power is rooted in the will of its readers. Typically, Earl Miner notes, Renaissance theorists try to 'join mimesis and affectivism into a whole . . . unaware that they are espousing two different critical propositions that have no necessary connections with each other'. But we can see how rhetoric becomes, at best, a means of relating a poem to its audiences in order to manipulate, persuade, or cajole, to urge participation or debate – in short, to 'move', in Sidney's key term. True poets, he asserts, 'imitate both to delight and teach' and, he goes on, 'delight, to move men to take that goodness in hand, which without delight they would fly as from a stranger; and teach, to make them know that goodness whereunto they are moved'. Here the discussion of *mimesis* is joined with the standard Horatian formula of delighting and teaching, pleasure and profit, interrupted by a Protestant insistence that knowledge alone is never sufficient to change the will and produce effective action. 'Delight' captivates a reader; 'moving' produces an effect on the will, since, Sidney argues, switching back to an Aristotelian dictum, 'as Aristotle saith', it is not *gnosis* but *praxis* which 'must be the fruit' of teaching.[48]

Sidney's concern with the interrelation of poetic discipline and audience response is couched in terms of moral awareness and practical application. But his fusion of the inspirational or writer-centred view and the affective or reader-centred view is not just an aside in his main argument. He goes on to talk further of the poet's powers to move readers by arguing that 'truly I have known men that even with reading *Amadis de Gaule* . . . have found their hearts moved to the exercise of courtesy, liberality, and especially courage'.[49] It might be suggested that such statements still preserve the determinative nature of the writer's intention – that the 'great' poet, say, is he who communicates his 'message' to an essentially passive audience. But in fact something much more interesting is going on here.

I would ask readers at this point to recall the opening pages of this study where I talked about how one modern class of students was encouraged to develop 'strong' responses to Wyatt's 'They Flee from Me'. Such an encouragement to read a poem *against* its apparent intention seems justifiable only with the help of modern theories of the autonomy of the reader, and the need to bring contemporary issues and questions into the reading process. But in fact Sidney also deals with the question. He confesses, for instance, that poetry's ability to move its readers is not predictable or automatic; men may not be moved at all, or may not translate vision into praxis. Critics have traditionally provided reductive glosses on Sidney here by reference to the mechanistic working of faculty psychology, but Sidney, as A. Leigh Deneef points out, is not naïve on this matter: 'because his entire defence rests upon the correct perceptions of the reader, reading poetry becomes as central an issue as writing it'. Poetic power may be, as Margaret W. Ferguson has argued, 'viewed as a circuit of energy which goes from author to work to reader', and that energy can be diverted, adapted, or resisted, as well as used for illumination. When Sidney contemplates English poetry, he continually points to the way poetry directs us to self-study; poetry opens to us the possibility of discovering virtue in ourselves, in becoming the way we might extend or explore the self. When we read, we temporarily adopt a new 'self', one suggested by the poem and our experience of reading it. The play between that flickering self, the self with which we started to read the poem, and the reconstituted self we have when we finish reading the poem is, it has been suggested, part of the essential value of reading poetry – perhaps even of reading in general.[50]

Sidney's interest, however indirect, in the unpredictable interaction of text and reader is shared by a number of late-sixteenth-century writers. In his essay 'Of Experience', Montaigne is also interested in the means by which reading changes a reader and he seems, as Sidney does, to oscillate between a belief that the reader is essentially passive in the reading process and an acceptance that the reader is creative. And, like Sidney, Montaigne is also fascinated by how reading of his *Essaies* might lead to a reading of the self.

If reading and introspection are closely linked in some theoretical discussions, they are certainly prominent in the poetry. In *Astrophil and Stella*, for instance, we are watching the early stages in England of what is to become the striking 'open form' of baroque art – dynamic, stressing indeterminacy of effect, disruption and broken surfaces, dilated space, illusory and relativistic effects, inducing the spectator to shift viewpoint continually, thus emphasizing how the work's meanings are partial, kinetic, and continually metamorphosing. The emphasis is increasingly on the active inventive role of the spectator who becomes an actor, a participant in the work's meanings. The result, as Barthes puts it, is to make the reader no longer merely a consumer, but 'a producer' of the text.[51]

The best poetry of this whole period is characterized by this kind of rich and subtle sense of audience. Dunbar's poems to the Queen of Scotland play to and with his anticipated primary audience of her court ladies and their aristocratic friends. Wyatt's 'Who So List to Hunt' creates a world where love and its uneasy place in Court are self-consciously described in general terms, with the poem inviting its audience to see their own individual and collective experiences alluded to:

> Whoso list to hunt, I know where is an hind,
> But as for me, helas, I may no more.
> The vain travail hath wearied me so sore,
> I am of them that farthest cometh behind.[52]

In the typical court lyric of the time, love is not primarily a private pursuit, or a therapeutic exercise. Typically, such poems are filled with references to other texts, literary and social, and in the case of Wyatt's poem, to one special 'other' whose threatening if marginal presence gives his poem its particular shape – King Henry VIII himself.

It has often been argued that one of the major technological breakthroughs of the Renaissance was the printing press. Speech was accorded an apparent permanence and audiences given an accessibility to writing in ways that revolutionized the spread of ideas and the comprehension of writing. Yet, for all its obvious manifestations such as the encouragement to poets to publish rather than have their works circulate in manuscript, the printing of poetry only gradually changed the ways poets thought about language itself. Part of the strength of sixteenth-century poetry remains its closeness to the oracular tradition. A major problem of teaching sixteenth-century poetry today is the need to stress that we are not dealing with monumentalized texts but with texts (even scripts) for performance, not with an authoritative authorial voice but with performative writing. Writing is inaugural, open, and therefore often (in the eyes of *homo seriosus*, like Fulke Greville) dangerous. This is something of which the editor of Tottel's *Miscellany* seems to have been aware when he created, by his limiting and repressing titles, the persona of 'the lover' through whose authorized words we are meant by Tottel to read the poems. As Kamholtz notes, 'the very act of titling – asserting the presence of a speaker and frequently proposing moral *sententiae* – imposes some distinction on the courtly lyrics, as does the change from manuscript to printed word. The printed poem belongs to a different political context and a different literary tradition.'[53] The oral-acoustic primacy of language, marked in the closeness of poetry and oratory, does gradually become replaced by a more intentionalist and instrumentalist view based on the primacy of authorial will and directed vision, but it is a transition that does not take place overnight and, indeed, perhaps has never been fully completed in that the strongest modern poetry remains closest to the speaking voice. And it is perhaps only in recent years that we have once again started to take seriously a reader-centred understanding of literary cognition. Now we know that when we read we assimilate information and make associations in relation to an already existing and always changing view of the world. It is the reader's cognitive processes that create the reading, not the author's intentions. Even though sixteenth-century poets were indeed worried about that realization – someone like Greville, for instance, would have viewed it as one more instance of man's sinfulness – they were, oddly enough, more aware of the issues involved in reading than any theorists before the twentieth century. In developing a reader-centred cognitive model or pedagogy, today's theorists are returning to something of which the sixteenth-century poets were, at least, dimly aware.

Our discussion of the close and fruitful connections between poetry and oratory, intention and reception, has brought another important issue into sight. The very power of language was becoming at once a matter of celebration and a matter of fear. Many Elizabethan theorists praised language that was copious; *copia*, the ability to create multiple meaning from language, was seen as one of its distinctive features. The various possibilities of language differentiated it from the 'brazen' world of Nature in that language's central characteristic was its multiplicity. Poetry, Puttenham argues, is more admirable than prose because it is 'a maner of utterance more eloquent and rethoricall'; it is capable of infinite production. Its pleasure was in variation, copiousness, in the transgressions of daily speech. As Marion Trousdale points out, essential to such definitions of language and poetry is the assumption that 'reality', what Sidney termed the world of Nature over which history or philosophy might claim some dominion, was different from the world of language. We do not turn, he argues, to poetry for its philosophical or historical 'truth'. Although paraphrase, or *periphrasis*, was one of the rhetorical devices by which a poem might be composed, what a modern student might present as a 'paraphrase' was certainly not seen as identical with the poem. One of the defining characteristics of the rhetorical mode of writing was that 'one fable could not only yield many glosses, but that it was expected to do so'. Words generated other words and other matter; language was plural, copious, overflowing.[54]

Such theoretical observations seemed justified by the mixture of celebration and anxiety Elizabethan scholars and educators showed towards their language. Some complained that the Latin and Greek languages were too 'copious and plentiful' or criticized their 'inkhorn terms', just as they did dialect or archaism. Yet other writers perceived that the inrush of new experiences in the age meant, in Ralph Lever's plaintive but revealing phrase, that there were 'more things, then there are words to expresse things by', or in Richard Mulcaster's more reasoned judgement, that 'new occasions' bring 'furth new words'.[55] Such a bountiful overflowing of new language had immense consequences for poetry. But there was often a sense of alarm that language's multiplicity might get out of hand, and a desire that it should be disciplined and controlled, and so cleansed, as Nashe put it, 'from barbarisme'. To make the language 'gorgeous and delectable' was one thing; to make it a hodgepodge was plainly unacceptable, especially in a society where political and cultural control was paramount. Language, in the words of Tottel's preface, should be 'to the honor of the Englishe tong, and for profit of the studious of Englishe eloquence'.[56] Social order might well be threatened by a language run riot. It is not merely a literary argument when Puttenham insists that the language of poetry is that of the Court and its environs.

In short, once again, we distort the significance of poetry and poetical theory if we isolate them from the socio-cultural pressures which produced them. As Eagleton has pointed out, the systematic literary and rhetorical treatises of the age are merged with what we would today term discourse theory: they analyse not merely the 'literary' value of figures and schemes, tropes and arrangement, but the material effects of particular use of language within broader cultural contexts. What we call 'criticism' or 'literary theory', they called 'rhetoric' and saw it explicitly as the instrument of training the governors and members of the ruling class in the techniques of political domination. Puttenham's book is, as Javitch, Montrose, and others have shown, a guide to the procedures of gaining and maintaining political power, by means of controlling language. As Eagleton goes on, 'rhetoric emerged as a discourse theory utterly inseparable from the social relations' of the Elizabethan ruling class, the members of which, orator, poet, and courtier alike, shared not only common political but stylistic characteristics. The decorum of which Puttenham and others repeatedly speak is consistently identified with proper conduct, a sense of disciplined grace in social situations, in which 'the good maker or poet . . . ought to know the comeliness of an action as well as of a word'. Puttenham's discussion of rhetorical figures concentrates on what he terms 'sensible' figures, which 'alter and affect the mind by alteration of sense', and in particular the quintessential court figure, *ALLEGORIA*, 'which is when we speake one thing and thinke another'. Any poet or courtier who cannot skilfully employ such a 'figure of *false semblant* or dissimulation' is 'sure never or seldome to thrive and prosper in the world'.[57]

Some modern scholars of the period have written of the contradictions of the period's practices of language as if they were, in principle, reconcilable. But language is always a site of struggles that are never resolved, even though the struggles may be overlaid with others. None the less it is tempting to try to see some unity or direction in the sixteenth century's struggles over language. Lawrence Manley, for example, has argued that the contradictions and struggles we have seen may be highlighted by seeing a shift in the object of poetic imitation from 'nature' to 'convention'. The increasing popularity of Ramist rhetoric and neo-classical instrumentalism were certainly confronting users of language generally with a crucial philosophical conflict. The arts of speech and language 'were called upon to mediate between the nature and structure of reality, on the one hand, and the changing expectations, habits and shared assumptions of men on the other'. Manley has further argued that over the course of the sixteenth century, there was a gradual displacement of the criterion of 'natural' fitness by the idea of the 'conventional'. It was based on a developing contradiction between 'norms rationally derived from nature and norms conventionally received from tradition or prudentially derived from historical and contemporary circumstance'. Where 'conveniency to Nature', in Sidney's phrase, had long remained a 'universal and transcendent test of fitness', Puttenham speaks of the poet as a dissembler, a 'counterfeiter', and relates the different kinds of poetry to social practices and court rituals, what Spenser calls 'the use of these days'.[58]

The argument between 'nature' and 'convention' deserves to be placed in a wider cultural context. The movement Manley describes is part of a larger and more general revision not merely of 'aesthetic theory' but the whole ordering of discourse – from knowledge conceived as relating all the languages of Nature to one another, thus restoring, in Foucault's words', 'the great unbroken plain of words and things' and making everything speak, to 'an immense reorganization of culture' in the classical age. In this transition the place of language, including the language of poetry, becomes dissociated from 'Nature'. Henceforth language has value not as reality, but as the art of signifying, naming, and organizing things by means of complex sets of rules and conventions. Writing ceases 'to be the prose of the world; resemblances and signs have dissolved their former alliance; similitudes have become deceptive' so that things 'are no longer anything but what they are', and words are only the instruments by which we represent things.[59]

Metre, vernacular, language

I have looked at some of the diverse traditions of thought that feed into the sixteenth-century discussions of poetry. I want now to illustrate one or two particular issues that preoccupied theorists and poets during the century – issues which inevitably brought out the differing sources, allegiances, and fashions by which poetry and poetic theory were being formed as sites of struggle. The incipient classicism of English criticism which did not fully emerge until Jonson, can none the less be seen in stray remarks by Erasmus or Ascham or Wilson as they puzzled over the questions of decorum or argued whether classical prosody might be adapted into English verse. Similarly, more is at stake in the (to us, perhaps, silly) controversies over whether English as opposed to Latin or Greek, was fit for poetry.

The question of the appropriateness of the vernacular, for instance, was raised much earlier by poets and politicians in the Courts of Italy and France, and by the English from about the middle of the century onwards. Puttenham's aim that 'there may be an Art of our English Poesie, as well as there is of the Latine and Greeke'[60] is a belated echo of Dante and Petrarch, Boccaccio or Ariosto, and was reinforced by a strong strain of nationalism that grew up in sixteenth-century English educational theory. 'Our national tong is rude . . . our language is so rusty' bewailed Skelton, early in the century; in English, unlike Latin and Greek, everything is expressed in 'a manner so meanly, bothe for the matter and handelynge, that no man can do worse', is Ascham's similar opinion fifty years later. In *The Elementarie* (1582), Mulcaster asks that the English develop 'the verie same treasur in our own tung', noting 'I love the *Latin* but I worship the *English*'. The doubts about English were partly caused by its supposed lack of dignity. It was 'symple and rude', lacking the 'gaye termes of rethoryk', Caxton noted late in the previous century. And there were seemingly practical considerations. There was no standard form of English. Where Latin was the language of the learned, the vernacular was, seemingly, subject to change, variation, and vulgar usage. Many writers felt acutely that English lacked an aureate diction suitable for ceremonial or complimentary poetry since, as Hawes put it in *The Pastyme of Pleasure*, 'elocucyon/doth ryght wel clarify/The dulcet speche/frome the language rude', thereby making explicit the class bias of courtly diction. Nationalistic, political, and religious pressures over the century brought more and more educationists and writers to try to improve the language – by adopting archaisms, dialect words, or by imitating classical or Italian syntax – in short by augmenting vocabulary and syntax to make English more dignified or adaptable than, in Caxton's words, 'the

comyn termes that be dayli used'. Should the language of the common
people be used by poets? Should English poetry imitate the syntactical
patterns of Latin or Greek? Was dialect acceptable in courtly poetry?
Were archaisms, revived (or invented) by poets like Spenser, merely 'the
rude skill of common ears', as Tottel scornfully put it?[61]
     Such questions proccupied English poets for the whole century. In-
deed, most poetry of the century may be seen as a workshop in which
the poets fumbled, under socio-cultural pressures they did not fully
comprehend, for acceptable language and forms for poetry. Wyatt's
innovations in adapting Petrarchan modes are less important than his
struggles in forging a flexible syntax and a sparse, effective vocabulary;
Grimald's verse, which was also collected by Tottel, was written in part
to see whether latinisms, archaisms, and compounds could augment the
vocabulary. An increasing number of systematic and theoretical treatises
that grappled with such questions were written; and the age abounds in
handbooks in which commonplaces, rhetorical tropes and schemes were
collected. However dull much mid-century poetry seems – consider E.
K.'s protest against the 'rakehellye route of our ragged rhymers' and the
attacks on those who have 'made our English tongue a gallimaufray or
hodgepodge of all other speeches'[62] – for fifty and more years, English
was buoyantly expanded, polished, augmented, and thus (often despite
the improvers themselves) made more flexible by the work of the
'workshop' poetics of the period and the collectors of rhetorical techniques.
     Two other developments, one short-lived and (as it turned out)
retrogressive, the other profoundly important for all subsequent poetry
until our own century, will likewise illustrate the contradictions and
variety of sixteenth-century theory and practice alike. The first is the
attempt, made largely by academics and a few members of the Sidney
Circle, to adapt classical metres into English. Classically trained scholars
found syllabic and rhyming verse barbarous; Spenser noted that Sidney
had devised a set of rules and observations on the principles of the art.
But although Sidney, the Countess of Pembroke, Fraunce, Campion,
and others produced workmanlike examples, the rapid changes in
spelling, idiom, and flexibility that English was undergoing would
simply not conform to any academic's desire to discipline a living
language. In the *Defence* Sidney had argued that 'ryming and versing'
did not make a poet, and in the *Arcadia*, the shepherds Dicus and Lalus
argued along lines that would have been familiar to Sidney and his
Circle. Dicus speaks of the 'secret music' and constant variety of poetry
which can be achieved by appropriately measured words; Lalus, on the
other hand, argues that poetry must appeal to the intellect as well as to
the musical sense and 'he that rhymes observes something the measure
but much the rhyme, whereas the other attends only measure without

all respect of rhyme; besides the accent which the rhymer regardeth, of which the former hath little or none'. As A. C. Hamilton comments, 'the history of English poetry shows that Lalus wins the debate. Quantitative verse failed because the English language is strongly and stubbornly stressed.' Sidney himself had said as much, commenting on English verse, that 'though we doo not observe quantitie, yet wee observe the Accent verie precisely'.[63]

Like Senecan closet drama, a literary experiment that the Sidneys also supported, quantitative verse was one of the dead ends of late Elizabethan cultural development. Yet in the 1570s and through the 1590s, quantitative experimentation was widely seen as one possible way of creating an independent and learned literature in England. As part of the humanists' reforms, Elizabethan schoolchildren were brought up to accept and respond to quantity in scanning classical verse, to recognize the harmony of quantitative metres from the way a poet manipulated the lines' oral qualities. From Ascham onwards, pedagogues and poets attempted to wrestle the uncooperative vernacular into quantitative verse, finding, as classically trained scholars, the mere counting of syllables and the barbarity of rhyme somewhat simple alongside the sophistication of Latin verse, which appealed to the learned mind because of its difficulty and the technical skills required for its composition. Consequently, as Derek Attridge remarks in the most comprehensive and sympathetic recent treatment of the Elizabethan Quantifiers, 'the experiments were the natural result of the attitudes to verse and metre inculcated by the grammar schools', and were thus a typical expression of the age's beliefs in the value of education.[64] Classical versification was one of the major interests of the European humanist movement, and Sturm, Ramus, Baïf, Estienne, and Lipsius, among others, had written quantitative verse. Given the distinctly pedagogical orientation of English humanism, it was an experiment that was inevitably going to be made, even if, with rare exceptions, it turned out to be a dead end. It also, one might suppose charitably, represents the willingness to experiment that characterizes the whole Elizabethan literary revolution.

In October 1579 Spenser wrote to Harvey that 'the twoo worthy Gentlemen, Master SIDNEY and Master DYER' have proclaimed 'a generall surceasing and silence of balde Rymers . . . in steade whereof, they have, by autho[ri]tie of their whole Senate, prescribed certaine Lawes and rules of Quantities of English sillables for English Verse'. Later the same month he writes again requesting these 'Rules and Precepts of Arte' which Harvey has devised, or requesting his friend to 'followe mine, that M. Philip Sidney gave me, being the very same which M. Drant devised, but enlarged with M. Sidneys own judgement, and augmented with my Observations'. As the correspondence proceeded, Spenser came to have more doubts on the practicality of the scheme. The document to which Spenser referred is preserved in the St John's College, Cambridge, manuscript of the *Old Arcadia*. It is a brief guide to the determination of English syllabic quantities, based upon recognizable classical rules, while attempting throughout to allow for the idiom of ordinary English speech. In his own verse, too, Sidney seems to have followed the general rule of a prosody modelled on Latin but, as far as possible, considering common English pronunciation. Many of the eclogues in the *Arcadia* use quantitative verse, phaleuciacs for instance, in 'Reason, tell me thy mind, if here be reason' and irregular asclepiads in 'O sweet woods the delight of solitariness' (Eclogues 33 and 34). A number of contributors to Davison's *Poetical Rhapsody* used phaleuciacs; and Campion's triumphant 'Rose-cheeked Laura' is probably the one acknowledged masterpiece of the movement.[65]

What were the Quantifiers attempting to do? The fundamental metrical pattern of classical scansion is based upon the duration of syllables, which were divided into short and long, and which were combined in different measures. The basic problem for the experimenters in England – as in Italy or France – was to adapt fixed syllabic rules to a language without established punctuation or spelling. Another crucial problem involved the adaptation of the movement of a line to ensure forceful and idiomatic movement. Hence the caesura was crucial in the handling of a line, permitting rhythmical breaks in the quantitative structure. The successful versifier thus had to be extraordinarily sensitive not only to a highly intellectual structure but to the cadence of his lines, as Campion clearly is:

> Rose-cheekt *Lawra*, come,
> Sing thou smoothly with thy beawties
> Silent musick, either other
>   Sweetely gracing.
>   Lovely formes do flowe
> From conceit devinely framed;
> Heav'n is musick, and thy beawties
>   Birth is heavenly.
>   These dull notes we sing
> Discords neede for helps to grace them;
> Only beawty purely loving
>   Knowes no discord:
>   But still mooves delight,
> Like cleare springs renu'd by flowing,
> Ever perfect, ever in them-
>   selves eternall.

Campion comments that ditties and odes may be 'compounded' in 'simple numbers' and yet still maintain the rules of scansion. But Campion, Walter R. Davis notes, is 'the last champion of that Quixotic attempt Sidney had inaugerated . . . to adapt the accentual language to the quantitative scansion and verse forms of Latin poetry'.[66]

Directly contrary to the quantifying movement was the movement towards the gradual regularization and developing cultural dominance of the iambic pentameter. Antony Easthope likens the development of pentameter to that of linear perspective in art and harmony in music; it is a historical creation, naturalized by the buoyant court culture of the century as the dominant metre of English poetry. It is well established by the time of Tottel's *Miscellany* and Puttenham's praise of Wyatt and Surrey as the first reformers of English verse is the culmination of a deliberate cultural movement to discriminate, in Easthope's terms, 'the "properly" poetic from the "improperly" poetic, poetry from verse'. The significance of the pentameter line lies not in its form, so much as the way it became identified with a single, personal voice, a poetic form seemingly transparent to the poet's 'real voice'. Pentameter works to 'disavow its own metricality', disclaiming 'the voice speaking in the poem in favour of the voice represented in the poem.'[67] It is the form which becomes identified with the 'I' of Elizabethan ideology, inter-pellating a reader who identifies with the poem's voice, and thus laying the basis for what readers in our century have seen as the 'living' voice of the poet.

These observations are supported by some work by John Stevens on the conflict between metre and music in the century's poetry. Medieval poetry, Stevens argues, is rare in metaphorical sound, with the relationship between words and metre being, as he puts it, 'better called metaphysical than physical'. During the sixteenth century, a change occurs which establishes a particular kind of artificial metrical correlation with sound as the dominant one. What he terms the 'old' sound was imitative of speech, without special supplementary self-consciously 'poetic' devices; what he terms the new is 'characterized by verbal individualism'. He sees Tottel and *A Mirror for Magistrates* as crucial in this conflict: both were fascinated by what they termed 'the stateliness of the stile removed from the rude skill of common ears', and encouraged a sonorous, full, emphatic verse-line. The result was 'a metrical revolution' in the middle of the century. Over twenty or thirty years, the poets found new possibilities in a regularly measured, accentual-syllabic iambic verse based upon a philosophy which Stevens describes as the 'liberation of English verse from the bondage of speech'. Words were liberated from their traditional sound-patterns, syntactical normality was broken, and above all, what Stevens calls 'the voice of performance' is created by a flexible relationship between speech and metre. The result is 'a great opening-up of the metaphorical resources of sound' where 'the "old" sound was the sound of speech, its poetry the poetry of speech', the 'new' sound 'is an artifact, and more highly wrought'. It marks, Stevens concludes, 'the "Tottelization" of English metre'.[68]

It is an intriguing and important argument, one that gives some credence to the views that first, sixteenth-century poetry is inseparable from the Court's power, and second, that beneath the sparkling and seemingly serene surface of court poetry, there is a sullen undercurrent of counter-dominance. I have spoken of the poetry as a site of cultural struggle, but it is so not simply on the levels of poetics, metrics, or music. What we perceived in the disjunctions of the age's thinking about and practice of poetry points to an irreconcilable broader cultural struggle. On the one hand, as William Kerrigan puts it, the period was a 'culture of imagemakers' in which 'homo ludens devoted immense imaginative energy to the symbolizing and resymbolizing of his own coherence'. In pageantry, emblems, gardens, and buildings, as well as in prose and poetry, it is a culture of the promiscuous spreading of signs. It is a word-drunk culture: a running riot of loquacity, as verbal effects, rhetorical flourishes, literary experimentation, all constitute a powerful logophilia. If, in Brian Vickers's words, 'the great inspiring force was rhetoric, that unlimited repertoire of linguistic expression and literary form', rhetoric is not simply or primarily a literary manifestation.[69] Language reigned, promiscuously spreading, interweaving signs and things in a common space reconstituting the very order of the universe as writing – multiple, active, continually disseminated.

As we have noted, textuality in the period lives by *copia*, by the infinite flow of commentary which focuses and expands upon the infinite grammatical and rhetorical resources it contains within itself. Renaissance discussions of writing frequently see textuality as cornucopian, characterized by fullness, inexhaustibility, and discursive richness. Copiousness is a God-given mark of writing's self-conscious/self-multiplication, to scatter meaning. Renaissance texts are 'characteristically reflexive, dialogic, open-ended . . . they proliferate in order to question themselves and to lay bare their own mechanisms'.[70] Those mechanisms are often deconstructive, gleefully laying bare the contradictions within their own logic, calling attention to the rhetorical nature of all writing, just as Sidney does in the very style of the *Defence*, and thereby undermining what a later age would see as intellectual cogency by the distraction and randomness of his rhetoric. Foucault quotes Montaigne's saying that 'there is more work in interpreting interpretations than in interpreting things; and more books about books than on any other subject; we do nothing but write glosses on one another' and then comments that 'these words are not a statement of the bankruptcy of a culture buried beneath its own monuments; they are a definition of the inevitable relation that language maintained with itself in the sixteenth century'. He continues with an observation crucial to our understanding of sixteenth-century poetry: the relations language 'maintained with itself' enabled language 'to accumulate to infinity, since it never ceased to develop, to revise itself and to lay its successive forms one over another. Perhaps for the first time in Western culture, we find revealed the absolutely open dimension of a language no longer able to halt itself', because, never being enclosed in a definite statement, it can express its truth only in some future discourse which 'does not have the power to halt the progression, and what it says is enclosed within it like a promise, a bequest to yet another discourse'.[71]

But then, on the other hand, alongside such celebration of textuality, we must note as well the growing tide of hostility to Renaissance logophilia. The promiscuity of language is continually confronted by an anxiety to find ways of limiting its meanings and power. The tireless repetition of commonplaces, the search for gnomic utterance, the popularity of emblem and referential allusion in allegory are also features of the age. It is as if a plethora of expression were constantly being bullied into knots of meaning, much in the way that the Protestant propagandist marked the margins of his own text by 'Mark ye this, ye hogges and dogges' or 'Here be sound doctrine'. What is at stake in Protestant attacks on poetry, romance, images, is ultimately a deep suspicion of writing. Words let loose meaning, and as Protestantism tended to read the Bible, the word, preached, proclaimed and valorized in the authorized Word of the living God is acceptable only in that it is (if received by the Elect) unvarying and closed. But human words, over-flowing in the materiality of signs into history let loose a promiscuity of writing that ends in damnation. By what miracle can words, black marks on a white page, become bearers of meaning? It is a question that haunts Protestant intellectuals and poets, like Spenser and Greville. In *Caelica* and *The Faerie Queene* there is a problematic relationship between words and meaning, writing and representation, such that every attempt to approximate truth is necessary yet feared because it will inevitably dissolve into an infinity of random signifiers.

It is often argued that it is out of the sixteenth century's anxiety about writing that the first signs of the autonomy of fiction arises, in Sidney's *Defence* in particular. As we have seen, the conventional defences of poetry – that it is ancient art praised by the greatest authorities, that it has a moral force more powerful than related arts – point to an un-easiness about the intersection between language and history. Where Protestants insisted that human powers be accorded as little access to truth as possible, Sidney insists that the poet, 'freely ranging only within the zodiac of his own wit' creates his own world. Yet, uneasily, contradictorily, he none the less insists on the power of poetry to refer to and influence our world. He argues that 'the poet . . . nothing affirms, and therefore never lieth'; he 'never affirmeth . . . never maketh any circles about your imagination, to conjure you to believe for true what he writes'. If the essential feature of poetry is its 'feigning', then its cultural site is a distinctive one, neither referential like history nor abstract and disconnected from the particular, like philosophy. As Levao argues, there is something unsettling about Sidney's argument in that he does not explicitly argue for 'fiction' over 'fact'; but instead he suggests that any attempt to make sense out of the world is necessarily based on illusion, and that poetry is thus a special instance of the fictionality that pervades all discourse.[72] Thus man's only access to understanding is through fiction and enigma, and through his participation as an active reader, whether of the universe or of poetry. It is this *copia*, this open-endedness of both writing and reading, which Sidney's friend Fulke Greville so distrusted, which constitutes one essential characteristic of poetry in the *Defence*.

As the sixteenth century ended, and with the impact of neo-classicism being felt increasingly, a new order of language is starting to emerge. This process meant a gradual but immense reorientation of human culture as older kinds of writing became repressed, disciplined, or marginalized. Language became seen as an instrument of mediation and description, a sign-system not a symbolic system, capable of being systematized, made transparent to essential truths which could be communicated, with as little ambiguity as possible. It became, in short, a means by which the human psyche could be controlled, disciplined, and ordered. Gradually the promiscuous riot of *écriture* which so enlivens sixteenth-century poetry, Thomas Nashe's 'gallimaufrey of language', became an object of study, regulation, and control. Seventeenth-century poetry marks a process of a slow but gradual and inevitable limitation, as poetry takes its place, marginalized and restricted, in a new order of discourse.

Notes

1. Thomas Nashe, 'Preface to Greene's *Menaphon*', in *Elizabethan Critical Essays*, edited by G. Gregory Smith, 2 vols (Oxford, 1904), I, 318; George Puttenham, *The Arte of English Poesie*, edited by Gladys Doidge Willcock and Alice Walker (Cambridge, 1936), p. 21.

2. Compare Fredric Jameson: Genres are complex 'sociosymbolic messages or

narrative constructs imbued with the (ideological) charge of a lived reality'. See *The Political Unconscious* (Princeton, 1980), p. 40.

3. Puttenham, p. 24.

4. Puttenham, pp. 25, 38, 42.

5. Earl Miner, 'Assaying the Golden World of English Renaissance Poetics', *Centrum*, 4 (1976), 5–20 (p. 7).

6. Miner, 'Assaying the Golden World', p. 7.

7. S. K. Heninger, Jr, 'Speaking Pictures: Sidney's Rapprochement between Poetry and Painting', in *Sir Philip Sidney and the Interpretation of Renaissance Culture*, edited by Gary F. Waller and Michael D. Moore (London, 1984), pp. 3–16 (p. 15); and '"Metaphor" and Sidney's *Defence of Poesie*', *John Donne Journal*, 1 (1982), 117–49 (p. 119).

8. Michel Foucault, *The Order of Things* (New York, 1970), p. 32.

9. Ronald Levao, 'Sidney's Feigned Apology,' *PMLA*, 94 (1979), 223–33 (pp. 223, 232).

10. Terry Eagleton, *Literary Theory: An Introduction* (Oxford, 1983), p. 18; Alan Sinfield, *Literature in Protestant England* (London, 1983), pp. 23, 270.

11. Robert Montgomery, *The Reader's Eye: Studies in Didactic Literary Theory from Dante to Tasso* (Berkeley, 1979), p. 1.

12. Sidney, *A Defence of Poetry*, in *Miscellaneous Prose of Sir Philip Sidney*, edited by Katherine Duncan-Jones and Jan van Dorsten (Oxford, 1973), pp. 81, 109, 120, 77, 78, 79.

13. Yvor Winters, *Forms of Discovery* (Chicago, 1967), p. 1.

14. C. S. Lewis, *English Literature in the Sixteenth Century excluding Drama* (Oxford, 1954), pp. 1, 2, 20, 28, 19.

15. For the *Mirror*, see *The Mirror for Magistrates*, edited by Lily B. Campbell (Cambridge, 1938).

16. Barnabe Googe, 'An Epitaph on the Death of Nicholas Grimald', in *English Renaissance Poetry*, edited by John Williams (New York, 1963), p. 96; William E. Sheidley, *Barnabe Googe* (Boston, 1981), p. 18.

17. Roger Ascham, *The Scholemaster*, in *Elizabethan Critical Essays*, I, 20.

18. Terry Eagleton, *Walter Benjamin or Towards a Revolutionary Criticism* (London, 1981), p. 5.

19. Sinfield, *Literature in Protestant England*, p. 3.

20. Sinfield, 'The Cultural Politics of the *Defence of Poetry*', in Waller and Moore, pp. 124–43 (p. 140).

21. Puttenham, p. 24.

22. Puttenham, pp. 26, 38.

23. Edmund Spenser, 'Colin Clouts Come Home Again', in *Spenser's Minor Poems*, edited by Ernest de Selincourt (Oxford, 1910), pp. 308, 327; Louis Adrian Montrose, 'Of Gentlemen and Shepherds: The Politics of Elizabethan Pastoral Form', *ELH* 50 (1983), 415.

24. Sidney, *Defence*, p. 102.

25. Sidney, *Defence*, pp. 78, 79–80. Here I have, following Heninger, preferred Ponsonby's reading of 'imitation'; see '"Metaphor"', pp. 120–29.

26. Sinfield, 'Cultural Politics', p. 127.

27. S. K. Heninger, Jr, *Touches of Sweet Harmony: Pythagorean Cosmology and Renaissance Poetics* (San Marino, 1974), p. 382.

28. Sidney, *Defence*, pp. 78, 79.

29. Jon A. Quitslund, 'Spenser's *Amoretti* VIII and Platonic Commentaries on Petrarch', *JWCI*, 36 (1973), 256–76 (p. 258).

30. Sidney, *Defence*, pp. 109, 119, 121; Heninger, 'Speaking Pictures', p. 9.

31. Sidney, *Defence*, p. 92. This paragraph draws on Gary F. Waller, Critical Puritanism and the Elizabethan Lyric Poets', *English*, 21 (1972), 83–8.

32. Foucault, *Order of Things*, pp. 17, 25; Heninger, 'Speaking Pictures' shows how such a theory permeates Sidney's thought.

33. Foucault, *Order of Things*, p. 33.

34. Heninger, 'Speaking Pictures', p. 3, Thomas Nashe, *Works*, edited by R. B. McKerrow, revised by F. P. Wilson and W. W. Greg (revised edition, Oxford, 1958), 5 vols, III, 307.

35. Eagleton, *Benjamin*, p. 101.

36. Richard Lanham, *Motives of Eloquence: Literary Rhetoric in the Renaissance* (New Haven, 1976), p. 4.

37. Eagleton, *Benjamin*, p. 105.

38. Sidney, *Defence*, pp. 78, 81, 92.

39. Richard S. Peterson, *Imitation and Praise in the Poems of Ben Jonson* (New Haven, 1981), p. 4.

40. Heninger, '"Metaphor"', p. 144.

41. Sidney, *Defence*, p. 78. See also O. B. Hardison, Jr, 'The Two Voices of Sidney's *Apologie for Poetrie*', *ELR*, 2 (1972), 83–99 (p. 97).

42. Jacqueline T. Miller, 'New Readings of Sidney', *SNew*, 3, no. 2 (1982), 12–15.

43. John Webster, '"The Methode of a Poet": An Inquiry into Tudor Conceptions of Poetic Sequence', *ELR*, 11 (1981), 22–43.

44. Douglas L. Peterson, *The English Lyric from Wyatt to Donne* (Princeton, 1967), p. 51.

45. *The Poems of Sir Philip Sidney*, edited by William A. Ringler Jr (Oxford, 1962), p. xix.

46. Puttenham, pp. 64, 137–38, 262; Marion Trousdale, *Shakespeare and the Rhetoricians* (London, 1982), p. 94.

47. Henry Peacham, *The Garden of Eloquence* (London, 1577); sig. A3.

48. Sidney, *Defence*, pp. 92, 81, 91; Miner, 'Assaying the Golden World', p. 13.

49. Sidney, *Defence*, p. 92.

50. A. Leigh DeNeef, 'Rereading Sidney's *Apology*', *JMRS*, 10 (1980), 155–91 (p. 186); Margaret W. Ferguson, *Trials of Desire* (New Haven, 1983), p. 146; Bernard Sharratt, *Reading Relations* (London, 1983), pp. 16–24.

51. Cathleen M. Bauschatz, 'Montaigne's Conception of Reading in the Context of

Renaissance Poetics and Modern Criticism', in *The Reader in the Text*, edited by Susan R. Suleiman and Inge Crosman (Princeton, 1980), pp. 266–91; Roland Barthes, *S/Z*, translated by Richard Miller (New York, 1974), pp. 15–16.

52. Sir Thomas Wyatt, 'Whose List to Hunt', *Complete Poems*, edited by R. A. Rebholz (New Haven, 1981), p. 77.

53. Jerome Z. Kamholtz, 'Thomas Wyatt's Poetry: The Politics of Love', *Criticism, 20 (1978), 349–65 (p. 351)*.

54. Puttenham, p. 8; Trousdale, pp. 117, 125.

55. Ralph Lever, *The Arte of Reason* (London, 1573), foreword; Richard Mulcaster, *The First Part of the Elementarie*, edited by E. T. Campagnac (London, 1925), p. 172.

56. Nashe, *Works*, ii, p.61; Francis Meres, in Smith, *Elizabethan Critical Essays*, ii, 310; Richard Foster Jones, *The Triumph of the English Language* (Stanford, 1953), p. 5; *Tottel's Miscellany*, edited by Hyder Edward Rollins, revised edition (Cambridge, Mass., 1965), p. 28.

57. Eagleton, *Benjamin*, p. 101; Puttenham, pp. 276, 186.

58. Lawrence Manley, *Convention: 1500–1750* (Cambridge, Mass., 1980), pp. 137, 19, 107; Sidney, *Defence*, p. 92; Puttenham, pp. 3, 298; Edmund Spenser, 'A Letter of the Authors', *The Faerie Queene*, edited by A. C. Hamilton (London, 1977), p. 737.

59. Foucault, *Order of Things*, pp. 40, 43, 47–48.

60. Puttenham, p. 4.

61. John Skelton, 'Phyllyp Sparrow', *The Complete English Poems*, edited by John Scattergood (Harmondsworth, 1983), p. 91; Roger Ascham, Preface to *Toxophilus*, edited by Edward Asker (Westminster, 1895), p. 14; William Caxton, quoted by Vere L. Rubel, *Poetic Diction in the English Renaissance from Skelton through Spenser* (New York, 1941), p. 1; William Hawes, *The Pastyme of Pleasure*, edited W. E. Mead, EETS, 6, s. 73 (London, 1928), pp. 917–18; *English Poetry 1400–1580*, edited by William Tydeman (New York, 1970), p. 5; Tottel, p. 2.

62. Spenser, *Minor Poems*, pp. 5, 6.

63. Sidney, *Works*, iii, 10; *The Countess of Pembroke's Arcadia (the Old Arcadia)*, edited by Jean Robertson (Oxford, 1973), pp. 189, 90; Hamilton, *Sidney*, p. 63; Sidney, *Works*, iii, 44.

64. Derek Attridge, *Well-Weighed Syllables: Elizabethan Verse in Classical Metres* (Cambridge, 1974), p. 113.

65. *Elizabethan Critical Essays*, i, 89, 99. For more detailed discussion, see G. L. Hendrickson, 'Elizabethan Quantitative Hexameters', *PQ*, 28 (1949), 237–60; Mary E. I. Underdown, 'Sir Philip Sidney's "Arcadian" *Eclogues*: A Study of his Quantitative Verse' (unpublished doctoral dissertation, Yale, 1961); William A. Ringler, Jr, 'Master Drant's Rules', *PQ*, 29 (1950), 70–74. The paragraphs on quantitative verse are adapted from my study, *Mary Sidney Countess of Pembroke* (Salzburg, 1979), pp. 121–28.

66. *The Works of Thomas Campion*, edited by Walter R. Davis (London, 1969), pp. 309–10, xix.

67. Anthony Easthope, *Poetry as Discourse* (London, 1983), pp. 65, 74.

68. John Stevens, *The Old Sound and The New* (Cambridge, 1982), pp. 11, 15, 16, 17.

69. William Kerrigan, 'The Articulation of the Ego in the English Renaissance', in *The Literary Freud: Mechanisms of Defense and Poetic Will*, edited by Joseph H. Smith (New Haven, 1980), pp. 261–308 (p. 266); Brian Vickers, 'Approaches to Elizabethan Literature', *Queen's Quarterly*, 85 (1978), 308–14 (p. 308).

70. Terence Cave, *The Cornucopian Text: Problems of Writing in the French Renaissance* (London, 1979), p. 82.

71. Foucault, *Order of Things*, pp. 38, 40.

72. Lewis, p. 319; Sidney, *Defence*, pp. 78, 102; Levao, p. 28.

Chapter 3
Erected Wit and Infected Will: Cultural Contradiction in the Lyric

The lyric

Right at the bottom of Puttenham's hierarchy of poetical kinds is the poetry today we find most characteristic of and interesting in the sixteenth century. We may want to describe it in less florid ways than Palgrave, but nonetheless of all the poetry that has come down to us from the period, it is Puttenham's 'meanest sort' which is to be 'used for recreation only' that has most excited readers and commentators on this period over the last century or more. When Puttenham writes of how such poetry deals with 'the common solace of mankind in all his travails and cares of this transitorie life', he is referring to what we have come to see as perceptive, moving, 'individual' lyrics – the poetry, especially the love poems and songs and sonnets, of Wyatt, Sidney, Shakespeare, and Donne. In particular, we usually think of the so-called 'golden' poetry of the last twenty years of the century. When we browse through an anthology of the age's poetry, we may note its musicality, vivacity, melancholy, or anguish, and find ourselves agreeing with Puttenham when he writes of how love 'of all other humane affections is the most puissant and passionate, and most general to all sortes and ages of men and women'. To be effective, Puttenham goes on, such a subject re-quires 'a Poesie variable, inconstant, curious, and most witty of any others', whereby the 'many moodes and pangs of lovers' might 'thoroughly . . . be discovered'.[1] Here at last, we may surmise, is the stuff real poetry is made of: it is, conventional literary history has argued, predominantly in the short love lyric that the age's most dis-tinctive characteristics are shown – most especially in the last twenty years of the century.

The reasons for the twentieth century's preference for the lyric are less a conscious repudiation of Elizabethan presuppositions than our own dominant literary and broader cultural ideologies. In particular, Practical Criticism, and New Critical modes in general, are demonstrably most successful with the short lyric which can (seemingly) easily be detached from history and established as an autonomous structure and subjected to formalist analysis. The enormous prestige since the Romantics of the short lyric as the apparent revelation of sincere personal feeling (Wordsworth's 'spontaneous overflow of powerful feelings') helps modern readers to respond enthusiastically to lyrics. Thus Sidney's, Shakespeare's, or Donne's lyrics can be all too easily read as (naturally) expressing direct personal feelings. Any teacher who has tried to disentangle the ideological strands from, say, Ralegh's or Donne's lyrics, knows the scepticism or disappointment of students indoctrinated with the potent if contradictory combination of New Critical formalism and naïve Romanticism. Why should they be asked to look at what is 'not' there? Why not just enjoy (or laugh at) Astrophil and his rehearsing of 'poore Petrarch's long deceased woes'? Why not simply indulge ourselves voyeuristically with Donne and his devious seductions of diverse women? Or Marlowe's gleeful self-indulgence:

> Come live with me, and be my love,
> And we will all the pleasures prove
> That valleys, groves, hills and fields,
> Woods, or steepy mountain yields.

Elizabethan lyric verse offers us a seemingly spontaneous experience of what Sidney called 'delight', although a more accurate description of the pleasure we may feel is Roland Barthes's *jouissance*. Such poetry seems to resist what Richard Howard calls 'the prudency of ideological analysis'. It creates a 'site of bliss', not of contradiction. It is the '*brio* of the text'; its '*will to bliss*', where we are claimed or desired, it seems, by this bliss (how strange that the master semiotician of our time can sound, seemingly, so close to Palgrave) which reaches us 'across the centuries, out of certain texts that were nonetheless written to the glory of the dreariest, of the most sinister, philosophy'. Such poems seem to speak to us of 'all the pleasures which societies object to or renounce'. In the words of Barthes's conclusion to his luxuriant celebration of textual pleasure, 'it granulates, it crackles, it caresses, it grates, it cuts, it comes: that is bliss'.[2]

That is an experience that an enthusiastic and sensitive teacher today can easily encourage in students of sixteenth-century lyric poetry – and it is a quality which should not be missed by any reader. The poetry invites its readers to enter into such sensual appreciation of word, sound, and many kinds of suggestiveness. The best love poems of the age – Wyatt's 'They flee from Me', many of Sidney's lyrics, most of Shakespeare's or Donne's – offer us manifold pleasures that go beyond mere consumption or dry academic analysis. It is a blissful experience indeed to look up from the final lines of *Astrophil and Stella*, Sonnet 108 –

So strangely (alas) thy works in me prevaile,
That in my woes for thee thou art my joy,
And in my joyes for thee my only annoy.

– and recognize that we have been there; we have wept with Astrophil, and laughed with Sidney; we see the conflicts and contradictions of love in our own experiences.

Yet, clearly, the lyric poems of the period were not always intended to be taken as seriously as we take them. Many critics accord Shakespeare's sonnets the status of philosophical treatises – they offer us deep, penetrating insights into our dilemmas; we recognize ourselves in the lacerations of Sonnet 129 or the complexity of prevarication and self-deception in the 'dark lady' sonnets. Or we may see in 'They Flee from Me' the seemingly universal anguish of a man or woman caught between conflicting emotional allegiances, not knowing what social and sexual roles to take up, and failing in all. Life, we may say, is often like that, and it is the function of poetry to illuminate that for us. The lyric seems to do so much more easily than *The Faerie Queene*, if only because a lyric is easier to read, or at least takes a shorter time. Thus we have made the lyric, Puttenham's least poetical kind, our central kind, the one by which we most appreciate sixteenth-century poetry.

Now, it is not my desire to do anything but enhance the pleasure we get from reading sixteenth-century poetry. C. S. Lewis once remarked that 'if we are ever to enter into the life of our ancestors we must try to appreciate the *Arcadia* as well as the *Astrophil and Stella*', as if somehow we could 'enter into the life of our ancestors'.[3] Modern readers (the present writer among them) can indeed come to admire, enjoy (even in Barthes's sense) the *Arcadia* and *The Faerie Queene*, although it is difficult to imagine *A Mirror for Magistrates* producing bliss except in the most sado-masochistic circumstances. But there is, in fact, a strong case to be made for the cultural centrality of the short poem in our understanding as well as our admiration of the sixteenth century; and it is a case that can be made precisely because the lyric is Puttenham's least regarded form of poetry. But it is not the case which has traditionally been made. It must start by conceding that this lowly kind of poetry is clearly less significant in the public world than the celebration of the deeds of kings, the death of great men, and the moral virtues of public servants which Puttenham argues are the prime duties of poets to write about. Moreover, despite the growing professionalization of writing towards the end of the century, much of the typical lyric poetry of the age is the work of amateurs, of part-time poets. Primarily courtiers or statesmen, they wrote occasionally, merely as a pastime, sometimes as relaxation, and always as part of the plumage of being a courtier. They wrote disparaging the work for which we revere them.

Yet it is because sixteenth-century poets did not see their roles as poets as serious that their lyrics can be seen as central to the age. They were self-consciously the upholders of the regime in which they struggled for place, employment, even for survival. So we can ask about how their public roles in fact overflowed into their poetry. Did it represent an escape for them from the pressures of the public world? Was it therapy? Private revelation? Does it aspire to, simply, being self-indulgence? If the poetry seems often deliberately to exclude the public role of the poet, what is the significance of that exclusion? Are Sidney or Ralegh pre-Romantics, acknowledging that the world is 'too much with us'? Certainly some poems in *Astrophil and Stella* and in other lyric collections do seem to be asserting that love is a private refuge, an escape from pressure and anguish. Such a view is taken to its extreme in the songs of the period, where a timeless world of music and harmony is evoked, where the individual human experience becomes uplifted into a realm of ideal celebration and beauty. It is seen quintessentially in the work of the poet-musicians John Dowland or Thomas Campion:

> Free beauty is not bound
> To one unmoved clime:
> She visits ev'ry ground,
> And favours ev'ry time
> Let the old loves with mine compare
> My sov'raigne is as sweet, and fayre.[4]

This is the lyric seemingly pure and simple. A melodious combination of sound and atmosphere, calling, even as we read it, for the sound of the lute, the swirl of court ladies' dresses, and the polite ripple of civilized courtly conversation. It is the lyric that one of my students described as 'upper-class musak'.

But, as Marvell was to write in the middle of the next century, 'at my back, I always hear/Time's winged chariot hurrying near'. Why, we might ask, is history, the material conditions of real existence, so politely (though no less ruthlessly for that) excluded from such poems? To what extent does the seeming absence of the historical distort or limit our readings of a seemingly innocuous lyric apparently written for sheer enjoyment? In fact – and here we begin the construction of a different case for the centrality of the short poem – the poet can be seen as a demystifier of the public order he serves precisely because of that innocuousness. He works on the seemingly innocent boundary between private and public languages, caught between conflicting cultural discourses which we can see struggling and rewriting one another. Because loss or absence, ostensibly of the beloved, seems to be the primary subject of the lyric, the form with all its variations and possibilities was superbly placed to articulate loss or absence of other kinds. Despite its apparent superficiality and seemingly marginal social role the court lyric was uncannily able to articulate the significance of the complex relations between language and power, literary text and social text.

What gives the sixteenth-century lyric its particular importance is the way in which even a literary kind which seems so culturally peripheral becomes a site of intense cultural struggle. To demonstrate this, in this chapter I am going to tease out two major discursive structures which wrestle within both the literary and wider cultural texts of the age. They are Petrarchanism and Protestantism. They are not the only structures of discourse which we can locate in the poetry, but they provide us with a fascinating and far-reaching set of interactions and contradictions which are very useful for understanding, and enjoying, the poetry of the age. In particular, they allow us to read the poetry put into play by and within the Court in extremely powerful ways. By focusing on the ways the poetry was produced, bringing out the '*difference* within the work',[5] the unevenness within textuality, and insisting on the diversity not the apparent harmony of the lyrics, we shall learn much about the way poetry, and its readers, are culturally produced – and (if we think about the way we read today) not just in the sixteenth century.

The Englishing of Petrarch

'O Petrarke hed and prince of Poets all'[6]: thus Tottel's *Miscellany* intro-duces what for the whole period, especially in the last quarter of the century, became an increasingly powerful literary space. The sixteenth-century poets saw themselves both admiring and battling with one of European literature's most dominant and authoritative father-figures. English lyric poetry in the sixteenth century is made up of the traces and struggles of many texts. But the single name that stands above them all is that of Petrarch, who gave not just Renaissance poetry, but Western discourse, one of the most hospitable conceptual schemes by which we have discussed sexual desire and its relationship with language. Francesco Petrarch (1304–74) remains one of the Western Europe's seminal figures. His poetry had, as Charles Trinkaus puts it, a very 'special relationship to the new mode of philosophical con-sciousness that was emerging in the Renaissance'.[7] Although regarded in his lifetime primarily as a historian, humanist, and general man of letters, it is through his vernacular poetry, the *Trionfi*, and in particular, his lyric poetry, the *Canzoniere*, that Petrarch's impact was transmitted to later centuries. His collection of lyric poems, written to Laura, was started in the 1340s and given a definite shape almost twenty years later, a decade after the death (6 April 1348) of the lady whom Petrarch incidentally probably only knew slightly. By his death the collection had undergone further modifications, finally consisting of 366 sonnets, divided in two parts: 1–263 before Laura's death, 264–366 afterwards.

For three centuries the emergence of what Foucault has termed writing 'the truth of man's sex'[8] was mediated through Petrarch – or, more accurately, through what became known as Petrarchanism. Generations of commentators and imitators elaborated a collective (mis)reading of his poetry of such power that it was impossible to locate oneself within the discourse of writing sexuality into poetry (or court society) outside the complex and inclusive code of Petrarchanism. Commentaries on the *Canzonieri* abounded throughout the fifteenth century; major imitations of the poems were appearing in Italian at the same time, in Spanish in the late fifteenth century, and in French shortly after. As Robert M. Durling comments, 'all over Europe the very emergence of Renaissance style was inseparable from the influence of the *Rime sparse* and the *Trionfi*'.[9]

The first characteristic of Petrarchanism that made it such a powerful collective text, encouraging and requiring continual rereading and interpretation, was its adaptability. By the time the English poets started to read him seriously, Petrarch had been mediated to them by nearly 200 years of imitators, commentators, and adaptors. It was inserted into the complex social text of a courtly society that retained many of the trappings of the uneasily feudal society from which Petrarch himself wrote and which, as it changed, changed Petrarchanism. As read and rewritten by English poets from Wyatt to Donne, Petrarch's poems provided a discursive space in which rhetoric, theatricality, individual and socio-cultural codes were mingled, and explored. For 200 years and more Petrarch was rewritten variously – as writing a diary of sexual desire, as compiling a handbook of rhetorical ornamentation, as a systematic expositor of love, as Neoplatonist, Stoic, Ovidian, Christian, and Aristotelian. The surprising opaqueness of the verbal registers in the *Canzonieri* helped make his work uncannily adaptable to a huge variety of readings and provide us with yet another instance of the reader-centred nature of the period's poetry. Petrarchan poetry could be solemn, witty, or blasphemous; Petrarch could be imitated slavishly or scurrilously mocked. What modern commentators have termed 'anti-petrarchist' sentiments are also as much a part of the Petrarchan mode as the more obviously serious poems where Petrarch is revered as philosopher, psychologist, and master rhetorician. Shakespeare's seemingly anti-Petrarchan Sonnet 130 is a dramatic tribute to the power of Petrarchan commonplaces as the inevitable language within which poet and lover alike necessarily had to struggle:

> My mistress' eyes are nothing like the sun –
> Coral is far more red than her lips' red –
> If snow be white, why then her breasts are dun –
> If hairs be wires, black wires grow on her head.

Donne's 'The Canonization' stands out in English Petrarchan poetry for its bravado and irreverence towards Petrarchan conventions, but it is not at all unusual alongside Italian poems of more than a century before which parade their irreverent wit with similar panache. Laura herself could be interpreted by Neoplatonist commentators as an earthly love drawing the soul towards Good, or towards God (as in Spenser's *Amoretti*); she could be presented as an erotically enticing yet tantalizing frustrating court lady to be wooed, complained at, and scorned, as in many of Wyatt's poems or in this sonnet by Drayton:

> Since ther's no helpe, come let us kisse and part,
> Nay, I have done: you get no more of me,
> And I am glad, yea glad with all my heart
> That thus so cleanly, I my selfe can free,
> Shake hands for ever, cancell all our vowes . . .[10]

Even when, as in these lines, the Petrarchan characteristics of paradox and balanced desire and frustration are not foregrounded, they are what gives the thought its tension. Most of the love poetry of the age operates within the Petrarchan framework. Petrarchanism seemed to be infinitely hospitable, even to attitudes that seemed to undermine it. Donne's 'The Flea', heavily overlaying Ovidian elements on a Petrarchan base, no less pays homage to Petrarch's poems on Laura's affection for her pets than Sidney's more gentle seventy-third sonnet, with its characteristic mix of desire and frustration in the final lines.

Let us first, then, look at Petrarchanism as a flexible rhetoric of erotic desire. It rests on a series, even a system, of conventions about love. It sees love as a frustrating though inspiring experience, characterized by a melancholy yet obsessive balance between desire and hopelessness, possibility and frustration. Its fundamental characteristic is conflict, usually expressed as a balance of powerful opposites, forces within or outside the lover which simultaneously move him on and hold him back. As Leonard Forster explains, 'later generations were less interested in the balance than in the antitheses' and it is 'this elaboration and exploitation which is the essence of Petrarchanism'. The exploitation produced a rich and complex idiom of love – the obligatory language of love for over 200 years. While Forster warns us against describing petrarchist poets as being conscious of working within a system – it was 'for them a natural mode of conventional utterance and conventional behaviour in certain circumstances'[11] – none the less, from our perspective, we can see Petrarchanism as just that: an intriguing, systematic ordering of the discourse of erotic desire. Today, even when we recognize frustration and contradiction as recurring parts of love, we none the less see Petrarchanism as artificial, and finally even destructive. But that it seemed natural in the sixteenth century only goes to show how ideology, the social glue of a particular culture, works.

But Petrarchanism was more than a poetic rhetoric. It was adapted – outside as well as inside poetry – to very precise political purposes, especially in England, where the fact of a Virgin Queen on the throne produced an extraordinary transference of the Petrarchan manner to politics. Elizabeth systematically encouraged her (male) courtiers to relate to her in the role of Petrarchan lovers, always in hope, caught between desire for advancement and fear of losing their places, single-mindedly devoted to the hopeless attainment of her favour, and grateful for any token. So Petrarchanism was not simply a charming and sophisticated fashion for court entertainment or for fictionalizing love affairs. It became, especially in the last twenty years of the century, part of public policy. There is a vast literature of minor verse written to Elizabeth, or to an unnamed but obvious royal lady, and to other courtly ladies, that are transparently pleas not for sexual but political favours. We will see some examples when we look in detail at the poetry of Sir Walter Ralegh (Ch. 4) and Sir Robert Sidney (Ch. 5). This adaptation of a poetic style to political goals was not new. In Petrarch's own work, the relationship between the poet and his beloved seems to reflect the uneasy reorganization of feudal class relations: Laura is the suzerain, her poet a vassal, eager to follow her yet aware of his un-worthiness and the hopelessness of attaining her. In the same way, the political relations of the Elizabethan Court were articulated through Petrarchanism. The system engendered an infinitely extendable and enormously flexible system, at once psychological, rhetorical, and socio-cultural – in short a system of discourse that encouraged participation and assimilation.

'Always historicize' is Fredric Jameson's stern advice on reading the past. It is a warning not to speak loosely of 'universal' themes in poetry, but to insist on the particular, on the 'priority of the political interpre-tation of literary texts' and on the material reality of history as 'the absolute horizon of all reading and all interpretation'. In one sense, it is easy to see all sixteenth-century poetry – what I have loosely termed 'public' and 'private' poetry alike – as closely tied to the history that produced it. No poem in this (or any other) period is simply a free-floating object in its own right. But we should be careful here. These poems become less interesting if we read them as merely 'reflecting' Elizabethan commonplaces, however much the lyrics often look like a collection of elegantly expressed clichés. Each lyric must be carefully 'refocused' in Jameson's words, 'as a *parole*, or individual utterance, of that vaster system, or *langue*' of the dominant class discourse.[12] The Queen's use of Petrarchan trappings is a clear instance of the blatant political manipulation of language in the interests of a dominant ideology. As Forster notes, inheriting the shakiest throne in Europe, with a populace divided by religion, faced with a 'ruling class composed of energetic, violent and ruthless men', Elizabeth turned her position as a woman to advantage by encouraging her courtiers to adopt the Petrarchan roles of 'men irresistibly attracted, preferring the light of her eyes and her favour' to other, lesser and less dangerous lights. Poetry became assimilated into an iconic ritual whereby Elizabeth was worshipped as 'the Faery Queene'. But even these obvious compliments can be sentimentalized if the praises are not seen for what they dare not say they are – pleas for political favour not erotic satisfaction.[13]

Now to the particulars of the Petrarchan system. From thousands of poems, a composite mistress can be readily composed, her physical parts anatomized or modestly alluded to. She might have, in the conventional conceits of Ralegh's 'Nature that washt her hands in milk', such features as 'eyes of light', 'violet breath', 'lips of jelly'; typically her hairs would be likened to wires, 'crisped', in the words of another Ralegh poem, her breasts compared to young does, and so forth. Such charms would often be set forth, either rapturously or satirically, in a blazon, a catalogue-poem listing the ravishing physical characteristics of the Petrarchan mistress, with her 'fayre golden hayres', her doe-like breasts, rosy cheeks, and other physical charms.[14] But the most crucial characteristic is the contrast between her fair outside and her icy or stony heart which inevitably causes the lover suffering. In the words of Ralegh's poem:

> At Loves entreaty, such a one
>   Nature made, but with her beauty
> She hath framed a heart of stone,
>   So as love by ill destiny
> Must dye for her whom nature gave him
> Because her darling would not save him.

But what Petrarchanism focuses on is not these physical charac-teristics *per se*, but their effect on the lover. Typically, it is expressed as masochism – as cruelty, disease, distress, and pain. The lady's effects upon the lover are like fire, ice, blindness, mischief, instability, and yet the lover is inevitably drawn to her, puzzled over his self-torture. And, in particular, it is the combination of such effects which characterizes the peculiar impasse of Petrarchan love. Sexual desire is at once repetition (and thus frustration) and transcendence (and thus hope). It is, together, frustration balanced by hope, the love of God by the love of the world, time by fame, passivity by restlessness, public by private, coldness and ice by fire. Achievement, consummation – indeed, even presence – are rare in such poetry. Absence is a seeming necessity; presence is not conducive to poetry. There would be no need to write at all if presence were attained. In short, despite the apparent transcendence of the beloved, she is in fact focussed upon only as the inspirer of the male protagonist's words and the occasion for his enjoyably miserable feelings. She is notable primarily for her absence. She is absent, in a sense, in order that the poetry can be written at all. Words arise only in absence and if the hoped for correspondence between word and desire occurs, usually the sequence closes.[15]

In describing the Petrarchan mistress and the love relationship thus, it can be seen how the mistress is entirely the product of the discourse in which she is placed. The second major characteristic of Petrarchanism is therefore that it is, in fact, not simply a rhetoric for declaring passionate yet frustrated love. It seems to focus on the depicting and idealizing of the beloved and to offer her patient, unrewarded service, but in fact it provides a discourse of control and domination. While the lover idealizes his beloved he is intent on controlling her and what she stands for. Laura is the unapproachable medieval lady, her lover spurred on by his suffering. But in Petrarchan poetry, she is not only a woman desired, loved, worshipped, but the muse, the precursor of divine love, and in particular the excuse for the poet to display his rhetorical skills in depicting the sufferings of the dominant male lover-poet. The poet-lover's shifting desires and projections make a Petrarchan love poem into a theatre of his desires, not hers, one in which the poet takes the active role and in which the woman is assigned silent, iconic functions. As an object of desire she is inserted into a discursive structure already and seemingly always in place, an apparently natural language of sexuality and sexual difference which can provide her visibility only within the poet's powers. She is the subject of his anguish, manipulation, and struggles of conscience. What does Petrarch's Laura reply to her beloved? What does Stella reply to Astrophil's earnest self-regarding pleas for favour? We are told occasionally, but her words are given to her by the poet:

> '*Astrophil*' sayd she, 'my love
> Cease in these effects to prove:
> Now be still, yet still beleeve me,
> Thy griefe more than death would grieve me.'

When, as in *Astrophil and Stella*, lover and beloved are dramatic characters outside which the poet stands, the structures in which they operate are further controlled by a male-centred discourse:

> Therewithall away she went,
> Leaving him so passion rent
> With what she had done and spoken
> That therewith my song is broken.
> (*Astrophil and Stella*, Song 8)

Is the woman's silence the repression of the poet? Or of the dominant male character? Or, in fact, of the discourse itself? Her alluring unapproachability, the icy fire of her own passion, allow her only to locate herself within a discourse in which women are given the role of being a focus of gaze, the object of men's obsessions and insecurities. As Larysa Mykyta comments, the female 'makes up for, somehow compensates for, an original deficiency in the wholeness of the male, therefore putting into question that wholeness of the male, therefore putting into question that wholeness and its concomitant power'.[16] In short, the Petrarchan mistress is less the subject of eroticization than of power.

The Petrarchan poet, then, could focus on the beloved's external beauties, her surroundings, even on the object of fetishization like her favourite pet, her handkerchief, or other accoutrements; or her spiritual qualities of chastity, unapproachability, wisdom, virtue could be the objects of similar obsession. But the real focus is on her effects on the poet himself; she is the means by which his autonomy and identity can be established. All the mistress's characteristics, and the events of their relationship, appear in a state of deliciously anxious fluidity which forms a rhetoric for the construction of a remarkably fluid self: love at first sight (or its alternative, Astrophil's 'with a dribbed shot' (Sonnet 2), the lover's obsessive, yearnings, the stimulation of frustration and rejection, the intensity of insecurity and occasional brief achievements. The world of Petrarchan love is claustrophobic, self-conscious, and introverted, obsessed with the contradiction between external image and internal effect:

> Desyrous for to win,
> And loth for to forgo,
> Or new change to begin.
> How may all this be so?

The incomprehensive changeability of the self and its insecurity and lack of fixed identity in the world are the real object of fascination.

Thus, thirdly, as the examples we have glanced at show, Petrarchanism finds its natural expression in the paradox:

> Amid my Bale I bath in blisse,
> I swim in heaven, I sinke in hell:
> I find amends for every misse,
> And yet my moane no tongue can tell.[17]

The delicate balance of opposites, precarious and ever-endangered, is presented as a psychological schema, as if language were transparent of the actual movements of the mind and erotic relationships. Thus love is the icy fire, the pleasant pain (or poison), the illuminating darkness, joyful despair, even (in Sidney's anticipation of Derrida or Althusser) the 'absent presence' (*Astrophil and Stella*, Sonnet 104). In the words of Wyatt's workshop translation of Petrarch's *Rime*, CLXXXIX:

> I find no peace and all my war is done.
> I fear and hope, I burn and freeze like ice.
> I fly above the wind yet can I not arise.
> And naught I have and all the world I seize on.

All the Petrarchan clichés, it seems, are in this poem: living–dying, imprisonment–freedom, sorrow–laughter, death–life. And the inevitable blame is self-directed in the typical masochism of the mode:

> Likewise displeaseth me both death and life,
> And my delight is causer of this strife.[18]

The Petrarchan paradox could thus very easily become a slick rhetorical trick. Yet there is built into it a claim to be a psychology which uncannily takes it beyond schoolbook rhetoric and which raises the fundamental question of the 'self' which Petrarchanism tries to create for its readers. The very nature of the paradox is such that closure is always undermined even while it is being asserted, just as the sonnet form often seems to repress (especially if there is a final, Shakespearian, couplet) what the body of the sonnet attempts to force into consciousness, thus creating an emotional dislocation between the sonnet's overall structure and the individual units which make it up. Incidents, surroundings, events are disciplined and internalized and then resolved by devices of closure – the combination producing and pointing forward to further repression and frustration. The result is that resolution, even 'meaning', is always questioned, identity always decentred. In the same way paradox represents an acknowledgement of failure, that nothing can be asserted without a supplement being also as true. Such a discovery is then projected back on to the psychosexual situation the poem purports to evoke. The Petrarchan paradox looks therefore as if it is a psychological code, especially when the poem's 'I' claims to represent or interpret 'actual' experience. The typical claim of the I of the Petrarchan poem is that the poetic act derives from description of personal experience, not merely literary conventions (like other, less, or less inspired poets). It is a view echoed by modern critics who read Sidney's *Astrophil and Stella* as being 'about' Sidney's love for Penelope Devereux and the main subject his own complex personality.[19] Certainly, many Renaissance commentators on Petrarch read his lyrics as biographical confessions, as written directly to or about Laura.[20]

Thus the lyric is seen as a version of confession. Like a confession, the poem is a ritual whereby the subject that speaks is also the subject under investigation. Like a confession, the poem is articulated in the presence of an eavesdropper, its readers, who variously listen, judge, intervene, or forgive. Both poem and confession, too, are cast within a ritual of difficulty, where words well up as obligatory, 'halting', as Sidney puts it in *Astrophil and Stella's* opening poem, even though they may be profuse. Foucault, from whom I adapt this description, applies it to the confessional, but it applies equally well to the Petrarchan sonnet. Both are ways of putting desire into discourse. Each provides a mechanism not for the revealing of a pre-existent 'self' so much as for the creation of that 'self'. Simultaneously burning and freezing, suspended in delicious pain and alluring frustration – these terms of Petrarchanism, no less than the formulae of the confession, made up a language of the psyche by which the sixteenth-century poet could structure the language of the self given to him.

We have moved into a discussion of the next major characteristic of Petrarchanism. The 'self' in sixteenth-century poetry is an especially problematic category. Perhaps, as many modern philosophers, from Nietzsche to Lacan argue, it is always in question. But in the highly artificial world of the sixteenth-century Court, the 'self' of the courtier, blown this way and that by the winds of fortune, is not a given, but rather created by conflicting codes of behaviour and action.[21] In the words of one of Gascoigne's sonnets:

> In haste poste haste, when first my wandring minde,
> Behelde the glistring Courte with gazing eye,
> Such deep delightes I seemde therin to finde,
> As might beguile a graver guest than I.
> The stately pompe of Princes and their peeres,
> Did seem to swimme in flouddes of beaten goulde,
> The wanton world of yong delightfull yeeres,
> Was not unlyke a heaven for to beholude.

This is the Court, that 'haplesse haven' in which 'waves of wanhope' 'tost me to and fro'.[22] Even from such moralistic verse, we may see why

Petrarchanism provided a perfect language for the aspiring courtier and how it created a discourse in which his restless anxious 'self' could be located. Stephen Greenblatt has written of the 'self-fashioning' of the Renaissance courtier, but the phrase perhaps implies too much conscious control, as if the courtier could choose to make a self, as if he were in control of that choice. The subject who speaks is, instead, a montage of languages that speak him, and part of the power of the Petrarchan code was that it asks us to adopt a continually decentred self, always under attack, unstable, and changeable, aware both of the power of memory, the pull of impossible futures, indelible pasts. A basic theme of Petrarch's own poetry is, as Forster notes, the incomprehensible changeability of the self in love, which is so violent as to call its very identity into question.[23]

Such a discovery is especially disruptive because of the clash with the residual belief in the stability of a person's inner spiritual and moral self, traditionally isolated as the soul. The Petrarchan 'I' is a device that looks as if it is stable, but in fact puts into discourse a radically decentred self that finds its only recourse in language. By 'self' here, of course, we should not understand the comfortable eighteenth-century belief in a real, stable 'self' with an autonomous inner life. As Anne Ferry points out, the terms available to sixteenth-century poets to discuss such issues were crude but none the less revealing. Such phrases as 'the closet of the heart', 'secrets', the juxtaposition of 'inward' and 'outward', Polonius's 'to thine own self be true' and so forth point to the grappling with a phenomenon that the poetry bears out – that the received language and its residual philosophical contexts were being outstripped by the mediations of experience we can perceive and highlight in the poetry. As we follow through a collection of Petrarchan lyrics (or, for that matter, if we look ahead and see Donne's or Herbert's adaptions of the sonnet to religious ends) we discover that the self that writes is continually re-written and the more it writes, the more words interpose themselves as frustration, as negative mediations between the desperate subject and its object of desire, or between, in Eugene Vance's words, 'the spoken signifier and its signified, dispossessing both into a centerless, unending productivity' that remains textual. Hence the longer the self of the Petrarchan sequence pursues its goals the less likely it will be materialized – 'the less its signifiers point to some expressive or referential context: they point, instead, only to the discourse in which they begin and end'.[24] The desired object in Petrarchanism, it has often been observed, constantly recedes: its primary function is merely to frustrate the final, unreachable, guarantee of the identity of the self which pursues it.

When we also consider the larger structure of the sonnet sequence, the way it is organized by the poet or editor, the same unresolvability presents itself. The sonnet form accretes obsessively minute and random details. We come to the unresolved end of one sonnet and then are pressured to go on. Many readers attempt to deal with this impasse by looking for narrative continuity to provide a comforting unity. This raises an interesting question often faced by a modern reader – especially one used to sequential narrative, as in the novel. Should a sonnet sequence be read as a narrative? That is, cumulatively rather than randomly? The temptation is certainly to see it written or arranged by the author or the editor as a story. The method of the composition used in the typical collection makes each poem a variation on a conventional theme, and often making reference to earlier collections (notably, of course, Petrarch's). John Freccero has shown how the *Canzoniere* may be seen as 'fragments strung together like pearls on an invisible strand', discontinuous, open to a multiplicity of juxtapositions and combinations, always insisting upon a self that is fragmented, dislocated, self-questioning. Many linkages may be suggested by the poet, or the lover, even (at times) the lady, but such hints of a plot are invited rather than imposed. The sequential cross-references provide the poet with opportunities for rhetorical display to provide multiple perspectives on the situations and dilemmas of love. Carol Neely has argued that in a typical Petrarchan collection fragmentary composition, reflecting the randomness and unpredictability of the experiences being wrestled with, might well be followed by a careful rearrangement by author or editor to suggest the outlines of a general sequence. Thus a common arrangement would be an introductory sonnet, setting forth the starting-point, praising the beloved, and often discussing the need or problem to write poetry, and often a set of concluding poems. She argues that English sequences typically show this pattern, with the central sonnets declaring and analysing the experience of love. Some sequences (e.g. Drayton's *Idea*, with its six very distinct editions) changed radically over their lifetime, with each new arrangement allowing for modifications of the sequence.[25]

But even when a general 'story' is suggested by such arranging, do we have to regulate our own readings thus? The author or editor should be seen rather as yet one more 'reader', giving one possible interpretation of what might have been originally a more random collection and, like any reading, subject to revision. It embodies, at best, an authorial hope, an attempt to impose a reassuringly continuous narrative and closure upon what may more significantly be seen as random and disruptive. What makes a sonnet collection hang together is its openness to different readings – its excitement lies in unpredictability operating within a determined set of limits. Germaine Warkentin notes that the unity or 'collectivity' of Petrarchan sonnet sequences is built on the concept of *varatio*, variety, 'a simple but flexible structural concept: that of a work exhibiting the variety of the moods of the lover, set forth in *rime sparse* or separate lyrics', a principle which, she adds, English sixteenth-century poets tended to imitate more and more loosely.[26]

Petrarchanism, then, offered both authors and readers an intensely complex discursive space in which to play. It afforded a suggestively anxious mixture of poetic workshop and psychological encounter session. It provided a space in which the poet could experiment, trying out figure and form; it offered a psycho-erotic model in which ideological and social tensions were acted out. The sonnet itself is such a model space – a *stanza*, a small room, like those no doubt of study or closet in which it would be written or read, 'much excellentcie ordred in a small room' as Daniel put it.[27] It is play, we should not forget, however, that is dependent primarily on performance, on the communal roles of both writer and reader or hearer. A Petrarchan sonnet, or collection of sonnets, typically presents itself for production – appealing not only to its audience's collective codes, but also inviting interpretations of a more apparently private kind.

Throughout the elaboration of Petrarchanism over three centuries, a fundamental challenge was to combine sharp particularity of metaphorical power with open-ended generality to encourage greater access and application for readers.[28] Thus, the sonnet evoked the concrete and the circumstantial, but it still defined itself in relation to an audience's expectations and to public referents rather than by the writer's biographical or subjective feelings. The poet is thus less the originator than the articulator of his culture's valorization of a particular reading of love. We read these poems today in much the same way, thinking of them in relation to our love experiences, to our dilemmas and problems. And we put a narrative structure upon a collection of sonnets in part because we habitually project our encounters with love upon the future, compare them with the past, and brood over the present. The Petrarchan collections offer us suggestive possibilities for understanding ourselves, but as in any reading situation, interpretation consists in part of what we bring to the act of reading and in part what the work brings.

As I shall show with *Astrophil and Stella* in Chapter 5, the Petrarchan rhetoric worked by a remarkably keen sense of its readers' participation in the concretization of poems. As William J. Kennedy has argued, if we study the many commentaries on Petrarch, not only can we construct a highly valuable history of the reception of his poetry, but we can develop a model of the fundamental norms of reading at the time. Kennedy sees, in particular, the introduction of printing as crucial: it brought about a shift in rhetorical strategies from oral performance to private reading, a shift he sees especially clearly demonstrated by the early sixteenth century. Looking at English Petrarchan (and other lyric) poetry, his argument can be extended. From Wyatt on, there is a tendency to become more aware of varied audiences, to adopt rhetorical strategies which would involve different kinds of readers and readings – by means of dramatic personae, heightening the effect of 'individual' voices, asking for response or for the participation of different audiences, often by direct address. This process, slowly developing throughout the first three-quarters of the century, reaches its high point in Sidney, Shakespeare, and Donne.[29]

One distinctive note of these collections of poetry is the emphasis, then, on self-examination – seen in the continual insistence on the inner experience of the lover, and hence of the reader. There we have an interesting difference between the sixteenth-century English court poet, writing and acting within this hospitable literary and social discourse, and his medieval predecessors. The interaction of poems with their audiences was not new. But the medieval court poet's most significant role was that of announcer or spokesman for the Court's values, 'as indispensable to the state of the herald', as Zumthor puts it. The poet's role, whether as storyteller or *jongleur*, was strongly defined and circumscribed by the models of reality he had culturally and linguistically available to him, including – in his social role – the horizon of expectation of the public he wrote for, whether it was the monarch, the patron, or the demands of the social life of the Court. It is easy to put the explicitly didactic and propagandist role of the professional court writer within such a model, but as John Stevens and others have shown, it also fits the seemingly value-free functions of the court love poet. For the medieval courtly maker poetry was part of a social game which expressed the Court's sense of collective identity. The poet's writings were contributions not to a self-contained autonomous category of 'literature' but primarily to 'social life and, especially, to the delicate fiction of courtly love which helped to sustain the life and interest of social relations'.[29] The relationship between this kind of poetry and the social reality that lay within the Court and beyond is an extremely problematic one. Rather than providing a direct mirror of social realities, medieval court poetry is distinctive in that it is unusually self-referential – a subtle arrangement of words, topics, tropes from a narrow range of possibility. Moreover, what we have noticed as being so important in the sixteenth century, what Zumthor terms the 'je du poète' (i.e. the notion of individual voice mediated through the language and structure of the poem) is less pronounced than it became in the later period. 'Although creation as such is indubitably individual', he argues, it is true of all medieval literary works that they appear 'less as individual creation . . . than as a mimetic activity, derived from a need for collective participation, comparable to choral song or dance'.[30] What differentiates this medieval structure from that characteristic of the sixteenth century is the increasing complexity of the codes within which courtier and poet had to work. In particular, what develops is an increasing sensitivity to and uneasiness about the nature of the 'self', the 'individual', and the 'individual voice' of the poet within the discourse that spoke through him. Petrarchanism provided a repertoire which allowed a reader to move around in the dialectic between his 'own' experience and that of the sonneteer and their shared cultural codes.

The characteristics of Petrarchanism I have isolated have presented a period of almost 250 years of cultural history as if it were ahistorical and unchanging. Discursive structures may aspire to be read synchronically, but they are always experienced diachronically. We should not conclude that Petrarchanism was monolithic or unchanging; that would be to dehistoricize what was a historical phenomenon. And so we should next ask: what distinctive changes, adaptations, omissions, what strong or weak misreadings, can we perceive in the English appropriation of Petrarchanism?

It has been influentially argued, notably by J. W. Lever, that there is a distinctive English adaptation of Petrarchanism. It is seen most especially in Wyatt's or Sidney's emphasis on the moral dilemmas of erotic experience, and in the relative neglect of the spiritual allegory of Petrarch's love for Laura. What might also be commented upon as well is the relative lateness of the English interest in Petrarch. Indeed, George Watson has argued persuasively that 'in Renaissance England Petrarch was a name rather than a book', that what Petrarchan influence can be perceived from Wyatt onward is largely indirect, responding primarily to ideas and tropes that were most naturally adapted to what was perceived as native English interests.[31]

Part of the distinctive characteristics of the 'Englishing' of Petrarch lies in the contrasting socio-cultural contexts in which Petrarch and the English poets of the sixteenth century wrote. Petrarch's poet-lover is more meditative than his English descendants, more obsessed with a tangle of secular and religious conflicts. What the English poets seized upon particularly was the mechanism of the Petrarchan conceit, and such techniques as the isolation of the oxymoron, the employment of natural or landscape settings as representational of the movements of the mind, and specifically concrete courtly settings and activities such as the hunt, battlefield, public roles and responsibilities. One of the earliest Petrarchan pieces in England is Wyatt's workshop poem, 'I Find No Peace', where the poet can be perceived as simply experimenting, attempting to reproduce mechanically the tricks of his original. Closely based on Petrarch's 'Pace non trove e non o da far guerra', with its easily imitable oxymoron of peace/war, this poem provided a model for more than a dozen sixteenth-century English poets to try their hand at the techniques. The play on the logical impossibilities codified in the war and peace oxymoron, like the equally ubiquitous fire and ice paradox, show one especially important way the Elizabethans perceived Petrarchanism: as what Gabriel Harvey termed 'a tablet of rare conceits', a rhetorical master-text, adaptable to the increasingly self-conscious rhetorical world of the Elizabethan Court, where show, display, self-aggrandizement were, seemingly inevitably, associated with becoming humility, and thus the means of acquiring place and, if not power, at least the possibility of power.

The first major impact on English poetry of Petrarchanism, then, comes with Wyatt and Surrey. Wyatt was experimenting in the Petrarchan manner probably by the late 1520s, and his poems were published in Tottel's *Miscellany*. Therafter, we can trace increasing interest in the ensuing decades, until in the last twenty years of the century Sidney, Watson and a host of other poets like Daniel, Barnes, Lodge, Robert Sidney, Smith, Drayton, Greville, and others took up the fashion; then Donne and Shakespeare, late in the century, modified the mode to produce (at least by English standards) some startling transformations. Such, it should be said, is the conventional outline of Petrarchan 'influence' in England, but it is a travesty of the complex process by which Petrarchanism inserted itself into the literary and social texts of the age. Petrarchanism is so criss-crossed and continually re-written by other discourses, most notably by Protestantism, but also by Neoplatonism, Aristotelianism, and various other classical philosophical strains, not to forget the material practices of the Court itself, as to make any such discussion simplistic.

What of the supposed start of this assimilation? J. W. Lever claims that Wyatt was 'deliberately breaking new ground in a direction where he could expect no guidance from the literary past of his own country'.[32] Puttenham certainly saw Wyatt as a forerunner of Elizabethan court poetry; what he ignores (as he does in his account of Skelton) is Wyatt's strong sense of the popular lyric. The Wyatt of Puttenham's account is the smooth courtier, not the satirist. In fact, what contributes to the distinctiveness of English Petrarchanism is its integration, or struggle with, the continuing native courtly lyric and with the popular song. Another is the sense – very strong in Wyatt, as it is in later poets – of the painful particularities of the poet's cultural situation. With Wyatt, it emerges typically as a dislocation between the requirements of the courtly code and the unease of the courtly self which finds itself written and structured in ways it finds uncomfortable or strange. The first nineteen sonnets of Wyatt's in the Egerton Manuscript, his own private book, are translations or adaptations of Petrarch, and they are distinguished by their struggle to achieve a distinctive voice. 'I Know an Hind', for instance, is transformed from Petrarch's original to a more meditative ironic poem, full of self-pity, bitterness, and disenchantment about the vulnerability of the self in a dangerous society. 'Some Fowls There Be' is also much less reasonable, and also without the emphasis on religion, than the Petrarchan original. Throughout what stands out in Wyatt's Petrarchan poems is the unease about his own position in the Court.

One important problem faced by Wyatt and his follower, Henry Howard, Earl of Surrey, was the problem of adapting the sonnet, the main form in Petrarch's *Rime*, to English. Not all Petrarchan poems are sonnets, just as not all sonnets are Petrarchan. But 'Petrarchan' and 'sonnet' became if not synonymous, at least intimately associated. Lewis speaks of Wyatt as 'a man who was escaping from the late medieval swamp',[33] and his technical achievements are less impressive than Surrey's. Wyatt's basic technical challenge was to get the Petrarchan sonnet to fit the English iambic pattern. He breaks the Petrarchan sonnet into two uneven units, octave and sextet, and then struggles to find enough rhymes in English to match the flexibility and flow of Italian. The English sonnet eventually becomes much more structured and logical than its Italian model and it was in fact Surrey who introduced the most important technical innovation – the so-called Shakespearean sonnet form, consisting of three quatrains and a concluding couplet. Later in the century Thomas Watson wrote some eighteen-line 'sonnets', three quatrains each followed by a couplet, and later too, we find the so-called Spenserian sonnet, with the three quatrains linked by internal couplets and a concluding couplet. These metrical experiments make the later English Petrarchan sonnet a more flexible and idiomatic poetic unit than the form of some of Wyatt's experiments, and than the muddle and controversy over English verse forms in the mid-century decades might have promised.

When in 1557 Tottel published his collection of Wyatt's and Surrey's poetry, along with some other verses by various other poets, the most influential collection of secular verse before the 1580s was available for five decades of readers. Tottel's *Miscellany* went through nine editions by 1587 and its part in forming the consciousness of aristocrats and those aspiring to gentility alike may be grasped by Shallow's reference in *Merry Wives of Windsor* (i.1. 205–6) to his constant need for his 'book of songs and sonnets'. It is also interesting to see the particular way Petrarchanism was assimilated during the mid-century decades. While Sidney found, in his *Defence*, little to praise in his immediate predecessors, it is obvious he had read them carefully. There are a significant number of mid-Tudor collections which use Tottel or Petrarch's *Canzoniere* as models of eloquence, but consistently stressing the moral and civic virtues rather than metaphyisical or psychological aspects. They were intended, as Turberville puts it, to warn us 'to flee that fonde and filthie affection of poysoned unlawful love'. As Germaine

Warkentin shows, they combine the Petrarchan rhetoric with the medieval *Mirror* tradition and the moralistic public poem. Such collections include Turberville's *Epitaphes, Epigrams, Songs and Sonets* (published 1567), Googe's *Eglogs Epytaphes and Sonnettes* (1563), and Gascoigne's *A Hundredth Sundrie Flowres* (1573). These mid-Tudor poets with their determinedly utilitarian view of the public responsibility of poetry, were suspicious of the frivolity evoked by many Petrarchan sonnets and songs. As Panofsky puts it, they seemed to have read Petrarchan verse as 'texts containing facts, arguments, and examples, not as aesthetic objects but as compendia'.[34]

Their collections of poems are much closer to the medieval *speculum morale* than to Petrarch. They used their poetry primarily to display their humanist ideals and oratorical capacities in the hope they would find court employment. Turberville writes love lyrics as if they were a frivolous task, purportedly for others who indulge themselves in vanities. Posturing as one who 'never came where any beautie lay', his role is that of the unwilling hired servant: 'I had my hire, so he mought purchase grace.' In the preface to his poems, he argues against 'any youthlie head' following 'such fragile affections' as the 'meere fiction of these Fantasies'. Only Gascoigne, writing in the 1570s, attempts to create an atmosphere of levity, indulgence, and play and a rhetoric to match it. Like Sidney, he also wrote a treatise on poetry in which he attacks the 'playne and simple maner of writing . . . we are fallen into', and in his own poetry brings a sense of dramatic situation and an awareness of audience into the lyric that had been lost since Wyatt.[35]

To explain the changes that we can see coming over the short courtly lyric in the 1570s and, in particular, the seemingly sudden upsurge of Petrarchan love sonnets in the 1580s, simply as a discovery or revival of Petrarchanism is far too simple. To ask the traditional literary history questions – to what extent English lyric poetry of the 1580s and 1590s is best seen in the Petrarchan mode? or whether Petrarchanism is an aberration, a swerving from the native plain style transition? – is to raise not so much improper but inadequately and incompletely formulated questions. Petrarchanism was rewritten by too many conflicting, subverting, and modifying discourses for us to accept such simplistic questions. One such complicating factor is the life of the Court itself. The growing rhetorical flexibility and prestige of the vernacular, the Court's new-found role for poetry as a method of control, as an instrument of hegemony, and the simultaneous sense of possibility and frustration experienced by an ambitious, highly educated generation of men like Sidney, Greville, Dyer, Ralegh, Essex – all are major factors in the so-called 'renaissance' of the 1580s which Sidney and Puttenham praise so highly.

The year 1579, the date of publication of Spenser's *Shepheardes*

Calender, the likely date when Sidney was writing the *Defence* and starting the *Arcadia* and also contemplating what later became *Certain Sonnets* and *Astrophil and Stella,* coincided closely with the date when his sister the Countess of Pembroke was settled into Wilton House, later the centre of an attempt to continue her dead brother's literary, political and broader cultural ideals. The last four years of the 1570s are then a landmark of fundamental importance. As Brian Vickers comments, 'before *Astrophil and Stella* English poetry was a desert; before the *Defence* there is hardly any criticism worth reading . . . one can hardly over-estimate Sidney's significance as a pioneer and prodigious experimenter'.[36] The 1580s and 1590s see an explosion of literary experiments, among which are conventionally listed the increased number of Petrarchan sonnet sequences – by Daniel, Smith, Tofte, Drayton, Spenser, Lodge, Philip and Robert Sidney, Barnes, Percy, Barnfield. There is also an increase in the publication of miscellanies of verse – most especially *The Phoenix Nest* (1593), and, perhaps the most representative collection, *A Poetical Rhapsody* (1602). This is what we have usually seen as the so-called golden age of Elizabethan poetry. It is the era of Sir Walter Ralegh's gallantry, Sidney's noble death, Spenser's celebration of Gloriana, Marlowe's celebration of sensuality, Donne's buoyant flippancy, Southwell's Catholic meditations, the mellifluous sensitivity of Shakespeare's sonnets, the easy-flowing melancholy of Drayton or Daniel of whose sequence Lewis aptly remarked it has 'no ideas, no psychology, and of course no story: it is simply a masterpiece of phrasing and melody'.[37]

But it is not a simple transition from lugubrious, halting moralistic verse by earnest civic-minded fumbling poets like Googe or Turberville to the sophisticated aestheticism of a Sidney or Daniel. There is no such great change. The amount and energy of the poetry increase dramatically, but there is no abandonment of the 'drab' style and its replacement by a 'golden'. The tradition of moralistic verse continues – in Spenser's Christianized Petrarchan collection the *Amoretti,* in Greville, Ralegh, and others. Even Sidney's *Astrophil and Stella,* supposedly the zenith of the 'golden' style, is deeply concerned with moral questions – specifically those raised by Protestantism.

Protestantism

In the final section of this chapter, therefore, I want to introduce the major disruptive discursive structure of the age – one that did not only invade Petrarchanism but the whole socio-cultural framework. It is one, moreover, with great power today even if its rivalry with Catholicism has largely died down. Indeed, one way of engaging the interests of some contemporary students of the sixteenth century may be with the socio-cultural as well as the theological roots of the religious beliefs they profess or have been brought up with. It is often a revelation to see either the fierce, intellectual rigour of Calvin, the revolutionary writings and acts of an Archbishop of Canterbury like Cranmer, or to realize how like the more bizarre reaches of American evangelism some of the theology of the sixteenth century sounds.

Like most successful revolutionary movements, Protestantism combined an impatient élitism with a deep-rooted populism. Moreover, it articulated not just intellectual changes, but complex, deep-rooted shifts in the whole social formation. It is therefore too simple to speak of the 'influence' of Protestantism upon Petrarchan poetry: we are dealing with a situation of overdetermination, a complex interaction of too many cultural codes to be reduced to one or two. As Alan Sinfield puts it, 'we know that thought and behaviour are in practice criss-crossed by assumptions of which we are only half-aware and which, if pressed, would prove radically divergent'. Any social structure, however hierarchical and repressive, is always layered and crossed by contradiction and we need to read, Sinfield goes on, 'very carefully, the mediating practices through which meaning is constructed' in the literary forms of the period.[38]

An Englishman (or woman) born in the reign of Henry VIII could, with some affluence and a lot of good luck, have lived through the reign of five other monarchs – and five changes in official religion. Between the 1540s and the 1620s, such a person would have seen the last stages of the Henrican reformation, the uneasy Protestantism of the Edwardian protectorate, the short-lived radical Protestantism of the abortive reign of Lady Jane Grey, the about-face of Marian Catholicism with its burnings of Protestants, well publicized by Foxe and later controversialists like Thomas Beard, the return to a deviously politic Protestantism under Elizabeth, the growing religious split of the 1580s and 1590s which saw both a Catholic revival and the growing disaffection of separatist sects, and finally, (beyond our period) the highly theocratic, aristocratic Anglicanism which developed under James and was intensified under his son. Religious controversy was, arguably, the most prolific literary form of the whole age: More against Tyndale, the Genevan exiles under Mary, Catholic and dissenting controversialists, Hooker and his great adversary Perkins, and a huge number of popular controversialists including those who produced the so-called Marprelate Tracts of the late 1580s.

What was a revolutionary allegiance for many young radicals of the

1540s and 1550s became a conventional set of assumptions for the generation of intellectuals, courtiers, and poets born (as were Sidney, Greville, and Shakespeare) in the 1550s and 1560s. Calvinism, usually in a moderate, hazily doctrinal, version, provided the dynamic of much sixteenth-century poetry and hardly any major literary figure is untouched by its power. The Calvinist doctrine of God's Providence struck a deep chord in the lives of sixteenth-century men and women. Poets as diverse as Sidney, Wyatt, Spenser, Ralegh, and Marlowe were allured by its sternness and deterministic certainty. Much Elizabethan writing, Sinfield has argued, represents 'a confident and elaborate attempt to render coherent, persuasive and effective' a set of doctrines which are for the most part alien to us today. He argues that 'strong Protestantism' (i.e. Calvinism) was 'hardly disputed in the English Church before 1600' and, however, remote from modern experience it may be, 'if we are to comprehend the literature written during the period of its dominance we must attempt to see why many found it helpful and comforting at the time'.[39]

Traditional Renaissance scholarship has generally agreed that Protestantism 'defined the first problem of English criticism' by making poets and poetic theorists justify or 'defend' poetry.[40] In recent years Barbara Lewalski, Sinfield, and others have shown that the Protestant reformers themselves were neither exclusively negative nor monolithic in their views of poetry, and that whatever contradictions the idea of a 'Protestant poetic' may contain, it none the less provided a major aspect of the theory and practice of poetry from the Reformation to the time of Milton. It is clear that writers like Puttenham, Harington, Webbe, and Sidney found a need to defend poetry against certain 'Puritans' because of the earnest, angry, or well-intentioned zeal of Protestant (mainly, though not exclusively, Puritan) polemicists. But such moralistic defences of poetry against even more moralistic Puritans are not really the central issue. Most of the poets of the century were, in any case, themselves pious Protestants. In fact, from Protestant theology, devotional practices, and biblical commentaries, we can piece together what Lewalski terms 'a substantial and complex poetics',[41] which we can see articulated in an interesting phenomenon developing from the middle of the century – a body of Protestant devotional poetry.

For Protestants of the sixteenth century, poetry was not something that could be separated from the godly pursuit of a Protestant State. As part of the Reformation dynamic, there grew up a body of devotional, propagandist, and polemical writing that helped spread the theological arguments that were the intellectual meat of the movement. What Protestant poetry there was was fiercely utilitarian. Under Edward VI, for instance, there was a strong biblical poetry movement, whose authors combined reverence for biblical themes and what they perceived as

an appropriately unadorned populist poetic style. John N. King terms
the poetic theory implied by this movement a 'major shift in mimetic
theory', and points out how the prolific 'gospellers' who wrote on
biblical or devotional subjects in a variety of popular forms – ballads,
fourteeners, poulter's measure – were deliberately rejecting the
Italianate courtly forms like the sonnet and *ottava rima*.[42] He argues that
the Protestant Court of Edward VI was thus far more eclectic than
under Elizabeth in that 'Italianate' and 'native' forms and fashions
coexisted. Such a division is to oversimplify the way the court poetry
itself was permeated by Protestantism. The miscellanies from this
period jam together contradictory strands of taste and allegiance.
Perhaps the most accessible for a modern reader is the Arundel
Harington Manuscript, which was begun by John Harington the elder
in the 1550s, and then continued until late in the century by his son,
the Elizabethan courtier, John Harington the younger.[43] It includes
some Petrarchan lyrics, but (at least from this early period) more brief,
moralistic lyrics on fortune, penitence, sin, and other Protestant
themes. If we look at Scotland, we can see how the Bannatyne
Manuscript, collected in 1568, puts together the taste of the Catholic
Stuart Courts of Scotland; and in the same way the Harington Manuscript collects a representative selection of the Tudor (and Protestant)
Courts of England.

The poets King singles out as important in this early Protestant
poetry are hardly household (or even lecture-room) names: Luke
Shepherd, a popular gospeller and satirist, who wrote in rough
Skeltonic verses and rambling alliterative verse, and Robert Crowley, a
printer and propagandist, who saw Langland's *Piers Plowman* (which he
printed) as prophetic of the religious and social revolution of the time.
His own verse is awkward and rough, as in 'The Voyce of the Last
Trumpet' which in thumping doggerel admonishes the godly:

> Give easy awhyle
> And marke my style
> You that hath wyt in stove
> For wyth wordes bare
> I wyll declare
> Thyngs done long time before.[44]

In addition to such examples we should not forget the age's most
popular work of poetry, the versification of the Psalms prepared for
use in church by Sternhold and Hopkins, often known as the Old
Version, the most famous of which is still to be heard in churches:

Oh God our help in ages past
   Our help in years to come:
Our shelter from the stormy blast
And our eternal home.
                   (Psalm 100)

In thumping broken-backed adaptations of fourteeners (alternating lines of eight and six syllables) the delicacy and emotional riches of the Psalms are hammered into unmemorable (though memorizable!) shape. As Cobrun Freer puts it, 'the Sternhold–Hopkins psalter was a public joke as poetry' and the chief problem in discussing it is to keep it 'from seeming a comic anthology'. Its syntax is wrenched, its idioms distorted, and its rhymes forced, in such masterpieces of bad taste as:

Leave off therefore (saythe he) and know
   I am a God most stout:
Among the heathen hye and low,
   and all the earth throughout.
                   (Psalm 46)[45]

With such poetry to choose from, it is not difficult to see why Protestant poetry, at least that written before the end of the century, has been neglected by modern readers. Its outstanding products do not appear until the seventeenth century in the devotional verse of Donne, Herbert, Vaughan, or Traherne. In our period, the one minor masterpiece of the movement is the Sidney *Psalms*, which will be looked at in Chapter 5.

But Protestantism did far more than produce a quantity of mediocre verse. Its most important impact can, in fact, be seen in the poetry it scorned – the poetry of the Court. First, it provided a model of both poetry – those parts of the Bible which were seen as poetic, notably the Psalms – and of the poet. Sidney, following Calvin, Beza, and others, describes King David as the approved mirror of the Christian poet:

. . . he maketh you, as it were, see God coming in His majesty, his telling of the beasts' joyfulness and hills leaping, [is nothing else] but a heavenly poesy, wherein almost he showeth himself a passionate lover of that unspeakable and everlasting beauty to be seen by the eyes of the mind, only cleared by faith.[46]

When we penetrate beneath both the thundering attacks on the vanity of poetry and the pomposity of the pious arguments about the use of poetry by Crowley or Sternhold, many intriguing implications emerge. In their theological treatises, when the Reformers discussed the nature of man, they thought little of what we would term the faculty of imagination, but they were eager to defend artifice or images if truth was served. Hence much sixteenth-century Protestant discussion of art and poetry focuses on the means of discriminating between true and false images. We see it, for instance, in the vivid way Spenser deals with the question in the first book of *The Faerie Queene*, where Red Cross cannot distinguish between Una and the dream produced by the malevolent Archimago, the 'source of images'. At stake is the question that, as we shall see in succeeding chapters, all the poets of the age who professed strong religious allegiances – Sidney, Spenser, Donne, Greville, in particular – had to face: how can one trust the products of the distorting human mind? Is not, to use Sidney's famous phrase, the 'erected wit' always undercut by the degraded and irredeemable 'infected will'? How can a poet at once embrace Calvin and Castiglione? These are the contradictions which, as we shall see, create much of the energy in the poetry of Sidney (Ch. 5) and Spenser (Ch. 6).

Second, Protestantism set up a series of challenges to sixteenth-century men and women, not least to poets. As Sinfield notes, it created a universe of strife and tension, it demanded total allegiance in every aspect of life; it challenged the humanist belief in the educability of man; it created a stern, wrathful, and determining god whose power reached into every moment of a man's life; and it focused relentlessly upon the inner coherence (or disparateness) of a person's sense of 'self'.

Protestantism reinforced what we have already noted as a major anxiety of Petrarchanism – the uneasiness about the relationship of the 'I' of a poem and the 'I' of the poem's author. To what extent and through what mediating structures does language articulate private, individualistic feelings or thoughts? To what extent is poetry mimetic of the poet's inner states of feeling or of its readers? And what is the relationship between the state of salvation of the poet and the poem's 'truth' or integrity? Must the poet be a good man? One of the most powerful contradictions thrown up by Protestantism is the privilege extended to the subject on the one hand and the precariousness of that subject before God on the other. Whether chosen or rejected, saved or reprobate, the individual is isolated before God. He was constantly exhorted to look at the signs of salvation within, while he knew that his inward nature was evil. He was constantly called upon to witness to God's truth while his very nature was totally corrupt. He called upon God with his innermost being, while knowing that inner voice was able to call on God only by God's grace. Alongside such paradoxes and contradictions, the Petrarchan paradoxes of ice and fire, war and peace, seem petty and pathetic.

When the Protestant turned to poetry, then, especially given its use in the Bible, and most notably in the Psalms, he could find a powerful model for articulating the paradoxes of the created self. The Protestant self, curiously analogous to the Petrarchan self, is always in flux, always changing even while it articulates an ideal of stasis. So the Protestant poet, whether he was as obsessive as Greville or as ambitious as Spenser, would inevitably find himself writing out his contradictions and anguish into his poetry, at once fascinated by words and aware of their untrustworthiness and suspicious of their promiscuous materiality. It is an issue fundamental to Sidney's poetry as it is to Donne's.

A third issue also has curious affinities with one special trait of Petrarchanism. It concerns the Protestant concern with language – specifically the relationship between God's Word and men's words, between divine intentionality and the medium of expression. In the work of Greville, especially, a matter central to the Protestant poetic becomes the extent to which the black marks on a white page of a written text can become bearers of meaning. For Greville, and with other Protestant poets such as Spenser, there is a problematic and (given that a man's salvation, not merely his literary reputation, was at stake) fearful question of the relationship between word and representation, when it is perceived that every attempt at representing meaning might dissolve into an infinity of random signifiers. Half a century later, Milton was to deal with the problem by imperiously invoking the Holy Spirit as his muse; Greville is more tentative and anguished; Spenser, as *The Faerie Queene* becomes more and more beyond his capacities to finish, is increasingly more despairing until he rejects his own poetic creation as an example of the mistrustful promiscuity of worldly signification.

With all of these issues, it can be seen how the dominant drives of Protestant theology and devotion variously overlap with, contradict, or reinforce the merely 'literary' structures of Petrarchanism. In particular, what this potent combination brought under scrutiny in the sixteenth century was the issue I have just mentioned – the overlapping concepts of 'self,' 'individual', and 'personality'.

Fredric Jameson points out that ideological struggles are always fought out within a shared code that may disguise the real issues at stake. These struggles inevitably operate within residual rather than emergent terms, and so in order to find out exactly what was going on, it is important not to be trapped into describing it strictly within the commonplace terms of the age. As Macherey puts it, 'the act of knowing is . . . the articulation of a silence', since 'what can be said *of* the work can never be confused with what the work itself is saying'.[47] Renaissance individualism is an especially complex phenomenon. It was picked out by Jacob Burckhardt a century ago as the central focus of the period – and that is a view that remains largely unchallenged. But we have tended to understand it within the philosophical commonplaces of the Renaissance without a sense of how those commonplaces were contradictory and blind to their own place in history. Thus we have learned to describe the godlike man evoked by Pico Mirandola's *Oration on the Dignity of Man*, and the anxious self-obsessed searches for signs of salvation interpellated by Protestantism as compelling examples. Or we have seen the sixteenth century as developing a gradual differentiation of the notion of the 'individual' from that of the community, whether conceived of as a church or a political or social group.

It is relevant at this point to glance at another closely related expression of the age's anxieties. It is one we find widespread in poetry – a concern with time and mutability. Time is, on the one hand, an abstract category of experience, as when Sidney's friend, the Huguenot theologian Philippe de Mornay, writes, 'what greater contraries can there be, than time and eternitie', thus pointing to the residual medieval view by which time is created by and ultimately guided by God.[48] On the other hand, there is time experienced by the self, as the passing of moments, the experience the Elizabethans characteristically described as 'mutability'. It is evoked in Spenser's 'Mutability' Cantos or in Shakespeare's Sonnet 60: 'Like as the waves makes towards the pebbled shore,/So do our minutes hasten to their end'.

The terms which this issue is expressed are highly instructive. For most sixteenth-century writers, time is still a religious notion, marked by the transience of human life, the inevitability of death, the transcendent eternity of God and His constant guiding of time towards His own mysterious ends. But what is interestingly observable in late-sixteenth-century poetry is a growing uneasiness about the traditional understanding of, and language for, time. Where the scholastic doctrine of God's providential control of time stressed what John Veron called the 'general ruledom' of God, Protestant theologians saw time much more in terms of God's intervention in particular moments of time. Calvinist theology and popular devotion are distinctive for their simultaneous avoidance of a general doctrine of Providence and yet a rejection of any possible fortuitousness. The result is a view of time that is under God's control and yet is, from the human viewpoint, absolutely unpredictable. 'What if this present were the world's last night?' is the way one of Donne's religious sonnets opens – and it is a common cry of anxiety. Before each moment lies, for all we know, the abyss. The overall control of our lives may be in God's hand, but we cannot see, from moment to moment, where that control will take us. Each moment of human existence is therefore radically dependent on God: 'every yere, moneth and day is governed by a new and speciall Providence of God', wrote Calvin. Donne's sermons are full of such emphases. 'Upon every minute of this life, depend millions of years in the next', he writes and is echoed in many religious writers.[49] A recurring phase in the sermons and tracts of the age is the Pauline exhortation to 'redeem the time', to seize each moment's opportunity. A widespread nervousness about the discrete moments of man's life permeates the writing of the age.

A century later, Descartes provides us with a revealing perspective on such concerns. 'From the fact that we are now', he writes, 'it does not necessarily follow that we shall be a moment afterwards.' George Poulet has observed that 'the religions of the seventh century are all religions of *continued grace*', in the sense that God is felt to be holding up each moment of each man's life.[50]

Now let us put these two issues together – the Renaissance concern with the 'individual', and the obsession with time. How does our awareness of the sixteenth century's apprehension of time help us into the age's sense of the 'self'? The self that is created by Reformation theology and devotion and in the everyday religious practices of Protestants, including Sidney, Greville, Spenser, and even Donne, takes a most distinctive form. The Protestant self is one that is anxious, obsessed with its own state of salvation. It is the self that is created by the reading of the Geneva Bible, the pouring over handbooks of self-knowledge, of searching for signs of election. It is the self that is created by the massive works of Perkins, Ames, or Downame, and by the crude propaganda of Foxe or Beard. It is the decentred self of Greville's or Donne's religious poems. Greville asserted that we should see 'God's revenging as put upon every particular sin, to the despair, or confusion of morality'[51]; the pious believer was exhorted to look inwards, to look in his heart and write, to adapt Sidney's phrase – to see if there were signs of belonging to the covenant of grace. The self that is found is one radically subject to time. In each changing moment there might be new signs, as well as new opportunities for temptation, sin, and damnation. Or it might provide unpredictably, the opportunity for God's grace arbitrarily to appear. In the words of Greville's *Caelica*, 'down in the depth of mine iniquity'

> Depriv'd of human graces, and divine,
> Even there appears this saving God of mine.

Always there is, however, the fear that in the words of the 'chorus sacerdotum' from Greville's *Mustapha*:

> . . . when each of us, in his own heart looks,
> He finds the God there, far unlike his books.

The Protestant 'I', like the Petrarchan 'I', then, is an anxious, self-obsessed, confessional, and above all time-bound 'I'. Its poetry is 'self'-obsessed and that obsession often emerges in a concern with time, mutability, and flux – as we will in particular see with Shakespeare's sonnets in Chapter 7. The Reformation world is what Foucault terms a 'confessing society',[52] one obsessed with self-examination and with developing means to produce some fixed truth about the self.

The problematic nature of the self and its languages is thus not only a central concern in the age's secular poetry – it is a concern into which the age's theological contradictions feed. We can see the curious phenomenon of conflicting discursive structures – here, Protestantism and Petrarchanism – crossing and rewriting each other. And it is fascinating seeing the contradictions between the official language – of theology or philosophy – with the articulated experience in writing. While the assumption of a unifying, fixed self remains fundamental to the religious and philosophical commonplaces of the age, the poetry continually exposes the fragility of the self – its artificiality, its temporality and vulnerability, its uneasy place within the age's ideological struggles. Throughout the age's poetry, we can see how the world of the sixteenth-century self is one of arbitrary events, unpredictable moments. It is a world dominated by changes, chances, and unpredictability. Shakespeare's sonnets are perhaps the greatest articulation of the inescapable determinism of time in the language:

> Since brass, nor stone, nor earth, nor boundless sea,
> But sad mortality o'ersways their power,
> How with this rage shall beauty hold a plea,
> Whose action is no stronger than a flower?
> O how shall summer's honey breath hold out
> Against the wrackful siege of batt'ring days,
> When rocks impregnable are not so stout,
> Nor gates of steel so strong, but time decays?
>
> (Sonnet 65)

But the presence of time the destroyer, the corrupter, the dislocating power that continually disrupts love, beauty, the security of the self, saturates late-sixteenth-century verse.

Why were the late Elizabethans so obsessed with time? Another, more pertinent, way of putting that question is to ask what was this residual language – time, mutability, decay – really getting at? Are there any senses that such a vocabulary was adequate? Are there signs of an alternative discourse arising?

There were, in fact, a few signs in the late sixteenth century especially that some writers are indeed sensing that the residual vocabulary was inadequate. Shakespeare, we have traditionally thought, was one. But Shakespeare's discursive radicalism comes through as we shall see in Chapter 7, with wonderfully subtle indirection. An especially important

figure is the Italian philosopher Giordano Bruno, who spent two years
at Oxford (1583–85), published six books in England, had close contacts
with the Sidney Circle, and dedicated his sonnet sequence *gli heroici
furore* to Sidney. Among Bruno's many heretical philosophical
speculations – he saw God as a variable being, inseparable from the
created universe, speculated on the infinitude of the universe, and saw
Fortune, not Providence, as the highest power of the world – was a
rapturous celebration of the mutability of the self. Typically he couches
it in metaphysical terms, but often as if reaching towards some future
epistemology. The typical sixteenth-century attitude to temporality is
one of anxiety, with the self uncertainly caught between a desire for
permanence and a fear of change. For Spenser, for instance, the principle
against which the undeniable unpredictability of the world must be
measured is that of God's eternity. Time's destructiveness must be
subsumed into a larger, eternal purpose which

>   . . . is contrayr to *Mutabilitie*:
> For, all that moveth, doth in *Change* delight:
> But thence-forth all shall rest eternally
> With Him that is the God of Sabbaoth hight.
>
> (*The Faerie Queene*, vii, 8. 2)

But for Bruno – and there are, as we shall see, intriguing echoes in some
of Shakespeare's and Donne's sonnets – the self is defined precisely by its
changeableness. Men, Bruno writes, 'are fools' if they 'dread the menace
of death and of destiny, for all things in the stream of Time are subject to
change and are unconquered by it; and this thy body, neither as a whole
nor in its parts, is identical with yesterday'. In the ever-changing world,
the self is always decentred: 'if in bodies, matter and entity there were
not mutation, variety and vicissitude, there would be nothing agreeable,
nothing good, nothing pleasurable'. In a spirit very different from
traditional Christian theologians and preachers he exhorts his readers to
accept their destiny as mutable beings and not to 'waste time, whose
speed is infinite, on things superfluous and vain; for with astonishing
speed the present slips by and the future approaches with equal
rapidity'.[53] Montaigne, widely read in England – not least by
Shakespeare and Donne – was another writer obsessed by the mystery of
the self and its dissolving. 'I describe not the essence,' he exclaims, 'but
the passage', and 'not a passage from age to age . . . but from day to
day, from minute to minute'. Because, he argues, man's life is 'but a
twinkling in the infinit course of an eternall night', men must 'tooth and
naile retaine this use of this lives pleasure, which our yeares snatch from
us, one after another'.[54]
    The Petrarchan interpellation of the lyric 'I', which is so intimately

bound up with the major transition from classical thought to the
self-conscious subjectivity of the Renaissance thinking; the Protestant
obsession with the self decomposing before eternity or held together only
in each new moment by God's grace; the emergent strains of speculative
libertine philosophy like Bruno's or Montaigne's; the powerful insistence
in the Court on *beau semblant*; and interacting with all, the last stage of the
breakdown of the feudal mode of production – all these interacting and
conflicting systems leave their marks on the poetry of the age. The lyric 'I'
is invested with a keen anxiety about identity, a longing for a stable
centre; it is what Paul Zumthor speaks of as a 'hollow I', needing to be
filled and yet never satisfied. Neither theological certainties, nor the ritual
of the Court, nor even the willed physical presence of the beloved can
satisfy this anxiety. As Greenblatt has argued, a desperate faith in such a
central core informs Wyatt's poetry, but what emerges is the artificiality
and constraints with which the self is constructed. A mobility and
restlessness of desire likewise haunts the poetry of Sidney, Ralegh,
Donne, and Shakespeare and – observable in the stern way by which it is
repressed – in Spenser's and Greville's. What Greenblatt has termed
'unresolved and continuing conflict'[55] is a distinctive characteristic of the
age's poetry and of much of its richly complex and problematic life. It is
time now to turn to the details of some of that poetry.

Notes

1. George Puttenham, *The Arte of English Poesie*, edited by Gladys Doidge Willcock
   and Alice Walker (Cambridge, 1936), pp. 24, 45.

2. Christopher Marlowe, *The Complete Poems and Translations*, edited by Stephen
   Orgel (Harmondsworth, 1971), p. 209. Roland Barthes, *The Pleasure of the Text*,
   translated by Richard Howard (New York, 1975), pp. vii, 7, 39, 46, 67.

3. C. S. Lewis, *English Literature in the Sixteenth Century, excluding Drama* (Oxford,
   1954), p. 380.

4. *The Anchor Anthology of Sixteenth Century Verse*, edited by Richard S. Silvester
   (New York, 1974), p. 538.

5. Pierre Macherey, *A Theory of Literary Production*, translated by Geoffrey Wall
   (London, 1978), p. 5.

6. *Tottel's Miscellany*, edited by Hyder Edward Rollins, revised edition (Cambridge,
   Mass., 1965), p. 28.

7. Charles Trinkaus, *The Poet as Philosopher* (New Haven, 1979), p. 2.

8. Michel Foucault, 'The History of Sexuality: Interview', *OLR*, 4, no. 2 (1980), 3–14
   (p. 3).

9. *Petrarch's Lyric Poems*, translated and edited by Robert M. Durling (Cambridge, Mass., 1976), p. vii.

10. Michael Drayton, *Poems of Michael Drayton*, edited by John Buxton (London, 1953), I, 176.

11. Leonard Forster, *The Icy Fire* (Cambridge, 1969), pp. 4, 5, 22.

12. Fredric Jameson, *The Political Unconscious* (Princeton, 1980), pp. 9, 17, 38, 85.

13. Forster, pp. 128, 131–32.

14. Spenser, *Amoretti*, 81, in *Spenser's Minor Poems,* edited by Ernest de Selincourt (Oxford, 1980), p. 412; *The Poems of Sir Walter Ralegh*, edited by Agnes M. C. Latham (London, 1951), p. 21.

15. Compare William Shullenburger, 'Lacan and the Play of Desire in Poetry', *Massachusetts Studies in English*, 7 (1978), 33–40 (pp. 34–35).

16. Larysa Mykyta, 'The Obscuring Clarity of Reason', *Society for Critical Exchange Reports* (Spring 1982), 68–87 (p. 79).

17. Sylvester, pp. 213, 248.

18. Forster, p. 4; Sir Thomas Wyatt, 'Whose List to Hunt', *Complete Poems*, edited by R. A. Rebholz (New Haven, 1981).

19. J. W. Lever, *Elizabethan Love Sonnets*, second edition (London, 1966), p. 71.

20. See Donald L. Guss, 'Renaissance Practical Criticism – a Polemical Survey', *PMASAL*, 52 (1967), 337–44 (p. 342).

21. Forster, p. 27.

22. Sylvester, pp. 258–59.

23. Stephen Greenblatt, *Renaissance Self-Fashioning* (New Haven, 1980); Forster, pp. 3–4, 14–23.

24. Anne Ferry, *The 'Inward' Language: Sonnets of Wyatt, Sidney, Shakespeare, Donne* (Chicago, 1983); Eugene Vance, 'Love's Concordance: The Poetics of Desire and Joy of the Text', *Diacritics*, 5 (Spring 1975), 40–52 (p. 49).

25. John Freccero, 'The Fig Tree and the Laurel: Petrarch's Poetics', *Diacritics*, 5 (Spring 1975), 34–40 (p. 34). See also Germaine Warkentin, 'The Meeting of the Muses: Sidney and the Mid-Tudor Poets', in *Sir Philip Sidney and the Interpretation of Renaissance Culture*, edited by Gary F. Waller and Michael D. Moore (London, 1984), pp. 17–33 (p. 18); Carol Thomas Neely, 'The Structure of English Renaissance Sonnet Sequences', *ELH*, 45 (1978), 359–89.

26. Germaine Warkentin, '"Love's Sweetest Part, Variety": Petrarch and the Curious Frame of the Renaissance Sonnet Sequence', *Ren. and Ref.*, 11 (1975), 14–23. See also Charles Altieri, 'Rhetorics, Rhetoricity and the Sonnet as Performance', *Tennessee Studies in Literature*, 25 (1980), 1–23 (p. 7).

27. Samuel Daniel, 'A Defence of Rhyme', in *Elizabethan Critical Essays*, edited by G. Gregory Smith (Oxford, 1904), II, 366.

28. Trinkaus, pp. 2, 40.

29. William J. Kennedy, 'Petrarchan Audiences and Print Technology', *JMRS*, 14 (1984), 1–20 (pp. 2, 6, 18).

30. Paul Zumthor, 'From Hi(story) or the Paths of the Pun: The Grand Rhetoriquers

of Fifteenth-Century France', *NLH*, 10 (1979), 231–65; 'From the Universal to the Particular in Medieval Poetry', *MLN*, 85 (1970), 816; *Essai de Poétique Médiévale* (Paris, 1972), p. 189f; John Stevens, *Music and Poetry in the Early Tudor Court*, (London, 1961), p. 206.

31. George Watson, *The English Petrarchans: A Critical Bibliography of the Canzoniere* (London, 1967), pp. 2–3.

32. Lever, p. 15.

33. Lewis, p. 225.

34. Warkentin, 'Meeting of the Muses', p. 21; Richard J. Panofsky, 'A Descriptive Study of English Mid-Tudor Short Poetry, 1557–1577 (unpublished Ph.D. dissertation, University of California, Santa Barbara, 1975), p. 182.

35. George Turberville, *Epitaphs, Epigrams, Songs and Sonnets (1567)* and *Epitaphes and Sonnettes (1576)*, edited by Richard J. Panofsky (New York, 1977), pp. ix, 119; George Gascoigne, *Certayne Notes on Instruction*, in *Elizabethan Critical Essays*, I, 150.

36. Brian Vickers, 'Approaches to Elizabethan Literature' *Queen's Quarterly*, 85 (1978), 308–14, p. 312.

37. Lewis, p. 49.

38. Alan Sinfield, *Literature in Protestant England* (London, 1983), pp. 3, 5.

39. Sinfield, *Literature in Protestant England*, pp. 14, 19.

40. *Elizabethan Critical Essays*, I, xiv.

41. Barbara K. Lewalski, *Protestant Poetics and the Seventeenth Century Religious Lyric* (Princeton, 1979), p. ix.

42. John N. King, *English Reformation Literature: The Tudor Origins of the Protestant Tradition* (Princeton, 1982), pp. 16, 209.

43. See Ruth Hughey, *John Harington of Stepney, Tudor Gentleman: His Life and Works* (Columbus, 1971).

44. King, p. 319.

45. Coburn Freer, *Music for a King: George Herbert's Style and the Metrical Psalms* (Baltimore, 1972), p. 60.

46. Sidney, *A Defence of Poetry*, in *Miscellaneous Prose of Sir Philip Sidney*, edited by Katherine Duncan-Jones and Jan van Dorsten (Oxford, 1973), p. 77.

47. Jameson, *Political Unconscious*, p. 84; Macherey, pp. 6–7.

48. Philippe de Mornay, *A Worke Concerning the Trueness of the Christian Religion*, translated by Sir Philip Sidney and Arthur Golding (London, 1587), p. 139.

49. John Veron, *A Fruteful Treatise of Predestination* (London, 1563), fol. 85; John Calvin, *The Institutes of the Christian Religion*, translated by Thomas Norton (London, 1561), I, xvi, 4; John Donne, *The Sermons of John Donne*, edited by G. R. Potter and Evelyn M. Simpson (Berkeley, 1953–62), III, 288.

50. René Descartes, *Principles of Philosophy, A Discourse on Method*, etc., translated by John Veitch (London, 1912), p. 173; George Poulet, *Studies in Human Time*, translated by Elliott Coleman (Baltimore, 1956), p. 18.

51. 'An Edition of Fulke Greville's Life of Sir Philip Sidney', edited by J. C. Kuhn (unpublished doctoral dissertation, Yale University, 1973), p. 163.

52. Michel Foucault, *The History of Sexuality*, Volume i, *An Introduction*, translated by Robert Hurley (New York, 1978), p. 59.

53. Giordano Bruno, *The Expulsion of the Triumphant Beast*, translated by Arthur D. Imerti (New Brunswick, 1964), p. 89; *Giordano Bruno's The Heroic Frenzies*, translated by P. E. Memmo, Jr (Chapel Hill, 1966), pp. 175, 219–20. The material in this and succeeding paragraphs is adapted from Gary F. Waller, *The Strong Necessity of Time* (The Hague, 1976), pp. 39–40.

54. The *Essays of Michael Lord of Montaigne*, translated by John Florio, introduced by A. R. Waller (London, 1910), ii, 232; i, 261, 25.

55. Zumthor, 'From the Universal', p. 816; Greenblatt, *Renaissance Self-Fashioning*, p. 8.

Chapter 4
A Century of Court Poets: Dunbar, Wyatt, Ralegh, Greville

Poets and audiences

Every age has its dominant cultural apparatuses which both control and make possible the characteristic cultural forms, including poetry. For the sixteenth century it was the Court. The Court nurtured, encouraged (or discouraged) particular kinds of poetry, provided support, audiences and in many less obvious ways produced the distinctive characteristics of the age's poetry. In this chapter we will examine the poetry of four poets whose careers, covering over 150 years, were moulded and defined by the Court. The first, William Dunbar, was a Scots poet of the Courts of James IV and V, in the late fifteenth century. The second is Sir Thomas Wyatt whose poetry was seen by Sidney, fifty years after, as marking a radical breakthrough in the development of the whole age's poetry. From the Court of Henry VIII we will go forward to two contrasting figures who wrote under Elizabeth and later her 'cousin of Scotland', James I and VI under whose reign the crowns and Courts of England and Scotland were united: Sir Walter Ralegh, the most flamboyant of Elizabethan courtiers, and Fulke Greville, second Lord Brooke, and a close friend of Sidney.

With all four, we shall see how the poetic texts they wrote and the social texts by which they were in a real sense written are inseparable. All were taken into the Court's attempt to control poetry as a means of articulating its values, to make it an 'art of state'. For all four, poetry was something incidental, merely a small part of their public careers. All of these poets were glittering public successes and yet also experienced failure, frustration, and (in two, almost three, cases) execution. All four used poetry as part of the equipment of becoming noticed at Court – to entertain, advance a cause, to cope with political defeat or disillusion.[1]

The Court provided all these poets with their primary audience and at this point it is worth stressing in less theoretical terms than were possible in Chapter 2, the way 'audience' is important in our understanding of sixteenth-century poetry. There are some poems in this period written primarily for their authors, like entries in a diary – many of Greville's *Caelica* poems, for instance. But most of the poetry, whether public, epic poetry like *The Faerie Queene* or seemingly more private lyric poems, are directed out to a multiplicity of audiences. They were, after all, often read and performed, among audiences of friends, especially at Court. In the life of the Court, many of the love poems of the period must have meant very different things according to different audiences. Even (perhaps especially) those poems written as expressions of devotion or love were no doubt adapted to different occasions (or women!), and were variously understood by different members of their audiences. Some very particular references – to black eyes, or boating on the Thames, or special tokens or words – may have acted as a kind of secret, even confessional, code, but in general the court poems are deliberately designed to be as indeterminate as possible, so that different audiences could relate to them. As we read or listen to them, we fill in the gaps and indeterminacies we encounter in the text: we bring our own experiences to bear on the poems and so in a real sense their meanings become ours.

We can very readily deduce the multiplicity of audiences from the poems of the period – in the rhetorical techniques, in the way the 'I' of the lyric poem invites a reader or hearer to become part of the poem's experience for a time. Part of the 'delight' of poetry, to use Sidney's term, is the way that when we read we become part of the 'suture' effect, as we oscillate between the 'self' the poem asks us to participate in as we read and the 'self' we (think we) are. As Bernard Sharratt explains it, it is as if '"I" were both present and absent, looking over my own shoulder rather than simply identified with myself, yet unable to be seen even in the mirror I hold up to myself'. The 'mirror' of course is the poem: the particular *frisson* we get from the poem is the experience of reading, rather like the participation we get from love, and as Sharratt puts it nicely, 'the "primal scene" of literature is always an act of a reader rather than a mysterious attribute of a text'.[2] It is we – the successive 'I's of the poem's readings – who make the poem's meanings.

Such considerations are sometimes a little disconcerting to modern readers. We read much contemporary poetry as 'confessional', somehow articulating the intimacies of the poet's self sorting out the complexities of his or her experience. But the 'self' of contemporary poetry is likewise made up of a tissue of languages, and a number of modern philosophers have argued that our age will be looked back to as one when the notion of the 'self' was finally dissolved (after 400 years of trying!) back into the languages which make it up. *Die Sprache spricht*, wrote Heidegger: language itself is the speaking subject. Just as Einstein saw the notion of an 'object' as 'one of the most primitive concepts' of human thinking, so the notion of a fixed 'I' is less the guarantee of our identity than a figure or metaphor whereby we focus our desires upon the world.[3]

But what about the poet's 'intention'? Did he not have a special audience or even a special meaning in mind? Often a special audience is named, as we shall see in a moment with Dunbar. But there are many, perhaps most, poems where the audience is left indeterminate. And there are occasions when even the primary audience is changed, as a poet might decide to change the colour of the eyes of the lady 'in' his poems as a compliment to his new-found love – or else to disguise that fact! There is at least one example of a sixteenth-century poet commenting on his own poems in this way. In his *Autobiography*, the (extremely) minor poet Thomas Whythorne explained how in an exchange of love verses with a noble lady by whom he was employed, he deliberately left his verses ambiguous and open-ended so that his audiences, both the lady and other later readers, might fill out the lines with their own meanings. 'A man', he writes, 'cannott alway speak in prynt' and so, he says, 'I mad this song sumwhat dark and dowtfull of sens bekawz I know not serteinly how shee wold tak it, nor to whoz handz it miht kumen after that she had read it'. His own interpretation of the poems he prints in the autobiography is, to say the least, ambiguous, as if the friend he is addressing needs to have the whole affair explained away! Poets not only change their minds about poems; they change their minds about love. To adopt the ironical advice of Greville's *Caelica*, 22, 'no man' should 'print a kiss, lines may deceive'.[4]

With such considerations about audience and the performative nature of sixteenth-century poetry in mind, let us turn to a sample of four court poets, and first to Dunbar and Wyatt.

Dunbar and Wyatt

Dunbar's poetry shows the relative backwardness of the English Renaissance – something that Sidney was to comment upon in the *Defence*. It shows, moreover, that long before the English monarchy had consolidated its power and started to use poetry as an instrument of State, the Scottish Court, especially under James III and IV, was showing the peculiar hold over poetry and poets exercised by the age's dominant institutional structure. Even more than Sidney's or Ralegh's a century later, Dunbar's poetry shows how confident he is in his inheritance of both a native Scots tradition of courtly poetry and a whole European tradition, from which English poetry at the time and for much later was relatively isolated. Dunbar is self-consciously the servant and the panegyrist of a system upon which his living depends. 'The Thrissell and the Rois', for instance, is a typical public court poem, an epithalamion celebrating the marriage of James IV and Margaret Tudor. Written in rhyme royal and taking the form of a dream allegory, it presents an idealized picture of the Court and the monarch on whom its life centres as models of stability, much as a Ralegh's 'Praisd Be Dianas Faire and Harmless Light' does nearly a century later.

Indeed, Dunbar's verse has a confidence in its significant place in its society, conveyed in part in a lightness of touch not found in England before Sidney. The Court presents itself as harmonious and sophisticated, the embodiment of a golden age as replete and aureate as the language in which its celebrations are expressed. Like many of Ralegh's, Dunbar's poems are essentially pieces of reassuring pro-paganda, full of stylized and dehistoricized landscapes decked out in courtly garments – the May morning, rose gardens, birds singing, ladies dreaming, and goddesses visiting the humble poet, who then wakes and tries to tell his vision. In such poems, Dunbar is flattering, light, even occasionally lascivious and flirtatious. As Tom Scott notes, there is often a 'homeliness' about his poems, 'almost a cosiness as of the pater-familias at his own fireside'. In 'Of a Dance in the Quenis Chalmer', there is a warm, idealized picture of the Queen's room. It is a place of good company, cheerfulness, a place where the poet is welcomed as an entertainer and even encouraged to be an occasional and helpful critic.

Dunbar has a particularly strong sense of his audience, most of whom were probably such court ladies. His idealized pictures of them create an atmosphere of dignity, hierarchy, and order in such poems as 'The Goldyn Targe' while a similarly situated poem, 'Sweet Rois of Vertew and of Gentilnes', is one of the most moving lyrics in the period, a celebration of sensitivity and beauty as fine as most of Wyatt's fifty years later. Likewise, 'Of a Dance in the Quenis Chalmer' is the confident work of a courtier favoured for his skill and usefulness to the Court, slyly adding sexual innuendo to the traditional role of court wit and favourite. In such poems, using the pose of the speaking bard, Dunbar's verse is notable for its confident dramatization of a multiplicity of court voices. He will address his audience collectively or individually and will sometimes include their possible responses in the poems, which seem to be designed to evoke a distinctively congenial, communal, atmosphere. In 'Tua mariit Wemen and the Wedo' he presents a witty account of three shrews' different views of men, and invites his audience to choose among them, putting the question 'Quhilk wald ye waill to you wif, gif ye suld wed one?' It is a nice device to include his courtly audience in the poem. Similarly with 'Of a Dance' where the fun and harmony are paramount: the poem is a light-hearted account of how the lead dancer can never keep his feet in time, and so sets the pattern for the rest of the dancers:

> Than cam in Maistir Robert Scha,
> He leuket as he culd lern tham a;
>   Bot ay his ane futt did waver,
>   He stackeret lyk ane strummall aver
>   That hopscchackellt war aboin the kne:
>   To seik fra Sterling to Stranaver,
>   A mirrear daunce mycht na man see.[5]

The 'man' who stands out (apart, that is, from the women) is 'Dunbar the Mackar' himself, who leaps about in the 'dirrye dantoun' so enthusiastically that he loses a shoe.

Such poems – often enlivened by some fairly coarse humour – show the place of poetry in the life-style of the late-fifteenth-century Scottish Court. In them poet and audience are clearly in harmony. But Dunbar's poetry also introduces us to a darker side of court poetry – to the power relationship between poetry and Court. The Court of James IV of Scotland generated a myth of itself much like that of the Court of Elizabeth I of England – that it was a golden age of harmony, stasis, and order. But even in Dunbar's most apparently celebratory verse there emerge hints of a darker side, incongruities that occur on the level of idiom or syntax, and that suggest the strain and dislocation of subduing poetry to the Court. More explicitly in the long poem 'The Flyting of Dunbar and Kennedie', a satiric account of a sustained argument between poets (which, of course, Dunbar wins), the genial tone and the comic invective cannot hide a darker insecurity over status, not only of the person of the poet, but of poetry itself.

In short, reading Dunbar – situated as he is as a late 'Scottish Chaucerian' at the beginning of our period, we become aware not just of his skill as a 'makar' but of the rich and powerful court culture, for which he is the spokesman and panegyrist, and yet of which he is also the product and victim. Not unlike Wyatt's or Ralegh's, Dunbar's poems reveal a darker underside than the light-hearted courtly game or witty flytings.

For his world is inherently fragmentary. As Scott comments, 'disintegrated and bitty, its proper form (is) the short poem, for there is no wholeness to sustain a long one'. That is a remark worth pondering with all these 'occasional' poets. Perhaps the short poem predominated throughout the age not just because it usually took less time to write but because it was the best record of the felt fragmentariness and arbitrariness of court life. Certainly in Dunbar's short lyrics, beneath the

dominant fantasy of the Court's benevolent and harmonious power, is a
sense of it as watchful, plotting, controlling. In 'Schir, Ye Have Mony
Servitouris' we see the typical anxious self produced by the Court: we
sense it as a world of time-serving professional entertainers, divines,
and anxious courtiers, all surrounding and dependent upon the King.
Celebration is undercut by what it tries to exorcize – the anxiety of
separate selves created by and at the mercy of the Court. Dunbar, Scott
suggests persuasively, is a 'poet of revolution before the time for revolution is ripe'.[6] His poetry articulates a frustration through and despite the Court's language, the energy of his verse beating against the
Court's desire to master it. This is an anxiety that as yet has not found
alternate language; it emerges, therefore, as a coarseness or an intrusion
of moral outrage or frustration in the way a century later it erupts into
the poetry of Ralegh or Robert Sidney.

The second of our four poets in this chapter is Sir Thomas Wyatt.
Like Sidney, fifty years later, Wyatt has some claim to be seen as an all-
round Renaissance man. He was a soldier, statesman, diplomat, linguist,
and courtier. Although later in the century his reputation as a poet fell
below that of the Earl of Surrey, in our time he has been generally seen
as by far the more interesting. The reason is largely because of what is
perceived as his anticipations of the vigorous, idiomatic, and dramatic
style of Donne, as in the opening of the sonnet 'Farewell love and all thy
laws forever/thy baited hooks shall tangle me no more'. Wyatt was, like
Sidney, born into a court family. His father, Sir Henry Wyatt, was a
Privy Councillor, and before he was twenty, Wyatt was active at Court.
His life – the probability of an affair with Ann Boleyn, daring diplomatic missions, an interest in Italian fashions and poetry – was, as David
Starkey puts it, 'though dramatic . . . in no way unusual. Every major
aspect of it could be paralleled in the biographies of a dozen or more of
his contemporaries at the court of Henry VIII.'[7] He was a flamboyant,
but not unusual, courtier-poet, at least in the style of his life.

What sets him apart is his poetry. Wyatt's is certainly the most
compelling English poetry written before the 1580s. For us, it articulates
brilliantly the growing pressures of an increasingly centralized Court
upon poetry and poet, upon public and private experiences alike. First
collected after his death in Tottel's *Miscellany*, Wyatt seemed, forty years
later, to be sufficiently sophisticated and attuned to the 'false semblant'
of Petrarchan fashion to allow Puttenham to list him among the 'new
company of courtly makers'. But struggling to be heard in his poetry are
various other contradictory voices – those of the puzzled or indignant
lover, the frustrated or anxious courtier, and that of a humanist moralist
whose wisdom was rooted in a tradition to which the ostentatious,
paranoid Court of Henry VIII was at once paying lip-service and
ignoring. Raymond Southall writes that Wyatt was a member of 'the

last English Court to participate in a living courtly tradition', but what emerges in the gaps, absences, and repression of his verse are more the strains of a late medieval moralist adrift in a new, seemingly amoral world which is intent on using traditional moral commonplaces to justify a ruthless *realpolitik*. Caught among these contradictory discourses, Wyatt's poetry articulates a losing battle against an enormously powerful collective power determined to control access to and forbid participation in the dominant discourse except on terms dictated by itself.[8]

As with Dunbar, when we look at his life, Wyatt is a typical courtly 'maker'. He was not only a prominent diplomat and a fortunate courtier – in that he was the only one of five courtiers accused of adultery with Queen Anne Boleyn in 1536 to escape execution – but he was also an accomplished court entertainer. Most of his poetry is conventionally elegant, clear, impersonal, speaking with the voice of the collective, directed at his audience rather than to his own experiences. It is largely occasional verse, simply elegant dramatizations of courtly values, contributions to the games of love, preferment, and intrigue in the Court. It is poetry (as John Stevens puts it) as stylized talk, but it is unusually intelligent, taking advantage of the new interest in humanist rhetorical theory, especially the Ciceronian ideals of directness and concentrating on the emotional effects of language upon an audience.[9] Stephen Greenblatt has argued that the court lyric in Wyatt's circle was like the diplomatic mission, 'sent forth to perform the bidding of its creator, to manifest and enhance his power at the expense of someone else'. Just as 'Wyatt was sent, on behalf of Henry VIII, to entice, to threaten, to complain of ingratitude, to circumvent attack, so Wyatt's own lyrics circulated through the court on their author's behalf.'[9]

What makes Wyatt's poetry different is the vigour and flexibility of the voice. Unlike the verse of his contemporaries, there is little aureate diction, and although, read together, Wyatt's poetry tends to be monolithic in tone, when he starts to experiment by adapting the complex use of the verse paragraph as a unit of argument, Wyatt's courtly songs become delicate and evocative, like the haunting and quietly witty 'Blame Not My Lute' which opens:

> Blame not my lute for he must sound
> Of this or that as liketh me.
> For lack of wit the lute is bound
> To give such tunes as pleaseth me.
> Though my songs be somewhat strange
> And speaks such words as touch thy change
>   Blame not my lute.

Such poems use the strength of the late medieval court poetry – a plain, muscular line, a direct voice, a sense of a shared community which will take part in the poem's performance. In other poems, some of the less felicitous characteristics of late medieval verse can be seen: lumbering, broken, heavily end-stopped lines, the hints of aureate diction, heavy allegory. But alongside the bulk of earlier sixteenth-century verse, Wyatt's poetry makes a marked movement away from the copious, aureate diction towards the plainer lyric which was becoming popular in the song-books.

But Wyatt is of more interest to us than as a rather belated Petrarchan experimenter. His is the first substantial body of work in the period in England through which the power of the Court speaks as the controller and creator not only of the dominant discourse but of alternatives to it, which however dimly apprehended and unable to find a place within it except by negation, none the less radically disrupt it. Poetry is thus linked not merely to courtly dalliance or personal desire, but to the increasingly ruthless and desperate need to find a place within power. Referring to John Stevens's remarks, that poetry in Henry's Court was 'a little music after supper', Greenblatt comments ironically, 'I tend to think of it more as a little small talk with Stalin.'[10]

Wyatt's satires have frequently been seen in such a context but as we saw with Dunbar, and will see with Ralegh, where a writer is *deliberately* attacking the Court, his arguments tend to be archaic and moralistic. The court poets look in vain for a newer language by which to reject the social structure which sustains and controls them. Alternative ideologies exist only in the strains and gaps of the text. But speaking through the poetry, where it is, as it were, off its guard, are the fragments of alternative discourses. As always, the emergence of cultural alternatives and, eventually, a whole new social formation is always uneven and outpaces the available discursive structures. Wyatt's satires, however stringent, still operate within the dominant discourse. In his third satire, addressed to Sir Francis Brian, a fellow flamboyant and outspoken courtier, for example, he ironically considers the principles by which courtly success is determined. One manuscript is submitted: 'How to Use the Court . . .':

> Thou know'st well, first whoso can seek to please
> Shall purchase friends where truth shall but offend.

It is vigorous but finally commonplace satire, nothing but sound moral advice without hope of shaking what already in Wyatt's time was seeingly unshakeable, the power of the Court itself. Wyatt's other two long verse epistles also satirize, in similar medieval moralizing manner, the abuses of the Court, where one must learn 'to cloak alway the vice' and 'press the virtue that it may not rise'. But nowhere is there the means explicitly to call into question the structure that holds the whole together. Wyatt may raise the question of where the honest man finds succour at Court – but it is the typical question of one who has lost, or is anxious about losing, his place and is not able to conceive of cultural alternatives.

Something more interesting goes on in the poems found in Wyatt's personal manuscript, known as the Devonshire Manuscript. There we find poems that, ostensibly less political, provide more subtle, indirect references to the ways in which the Court created and controlled its members. Many adapt for political ends as well as erotic ones – for the first time in any extensive way in English – the Petrarchan conventions of love's secrecy, its paradoxes, and in doing so articulate the cultural anxiety of the dangerously brittle conditions of life at Court. In origin, these poems look like *vers de société*, pleas designed to titillate and amuse, their author the self-effacing spokesman for a closely knit yet nervously anxious social group. But many of these poems are disrupted by a discomfort with the game that is more than conventional erotic disillusion. Even songs like 'My Lute, Awake!' and 'My Pen, Take Pain', as Jonathan Z. Kamholtz comments, 'hint at an artistic mode on the verge of collapse, for they are lyrics which end symbolically in the silence of the court artist'.[11] In other poems, the fear behind this repression becomes very specific – at least as some of the poems might have been read by Wyatt himself. 'Ye old Mule' is in origin, perhaps, a 'private joke' at Anne Boleyn[12]; 'Whoso List to Hunt' is a fine piece of wistful irony, a graceful withdrawal from erotic and political entanglements. But although such poems may have had specific erotic occasions, and however much they look like conventional love poetry, they are less erotic than political lyrics: their 'I' is written not merely by literary languages but by the language of political power. So paradox – 'I my self my self always to hate' – becomes a language of cultural paralysis; the repeated 'I' is insistent, urgent, yet somehow still controlled by the codes in which it must function even while it struggles unsuccessfully to articulate something beyond them. New modes of articulation, 'active and pressing but not yet fully articulated', in Raymond Williams's terms, are crying out to be heard, but there are as yet no words for them.[13]

Wyatt's most celebrated lyric – the one with which this study opened – 'They flee from me that sometime did me seek', may stand as a prime example not just of the complexity, verbal sensitivity, and increasing metrical dexterity of Wyatt's poetry (as it is conventionally seen) but also of the multiple anxieties articulated by his poems and about the power that both brings them into existence *and* controls them. In Chapter 1, I mentioned the variety of readings the poem can provide today. It can certainly be read as a fictional dramatization of erotic anguish, or (if we put it back within sixteenth-century society) within the Renaissance tradition of debating questions about love, here raising specifically the question of fickleness ('new fangleness') and desert ('what she hath deserved'). It is thus a communal lyric: the 'you' in the final lines contains a genuine question, as the speaker turns to his audience in puzzlement: 'But since that I so kindly am served,/ I would fain know what she hath deserved.' But the puzzlement which looks for an audience's responses is more than a sophisticated plea for sympathy by the hurt male ego. It is the product of conflicting discursive structures by which the poem is disrupted throughout. The undecidability of 'kindly' comes from its meanings as 'according to kind', 'with kindness'. But which kind? The lover has carefully played by the rules of the courtly game, only to find them undermined by a disturbing and unique experience of love, 'once in special', for which his training as a courtier in 'fals semblant' has not prepared him, but with which the lady in question remains content. She might even (if my gleeful women students today are to be believed) gloat over it: girls just want to have fun.

Thomas Whythorne, occupying a similar role in relation to his lady, writes that 'her joy waz to hav men to bee in loov with her, and to brag sumtyms how shee kowld handl such az wer so, az how shee kowld fetch them in, and then how shee kould with a frown mak them look pal, and how with a mery look shee kowld mak them to joy again'. He also gives the male members of Wyatt's audience a possible answer: 'to dissembull with A dissembler waz no dissimulasion, and to play with her az the hunter doth, who hunteth A har, asmuch to see her subtyl skips and leaps az for to get her karkas'.[14] In such remarks we come very close to the texture of the Renaissance Court and to poetry's place in it. But Wyatt's lover cannot yet perhaps rise to such bravado. Ostracized by those he once hunted, whether women or all those who, like timid and eager animals, hunt and are hunted in the Court, the poem's speaker cannot choose which language – courtly, political, individualistic – deals best with his emotional complications, and his 'gentleness' (like 'kindness', a key undecidable word, torn apart by the conflicting discursive systems that float and eddy around it) has proved inadequate before this new complexity.

And what (as my students insisted) about the woman? Can we imagine that she has a voice in such a world? In Dunbar's poetry, the women are reduced to an admiring audience, to be praised, flattered, idealized, and – in certain genres – reviled as sexually voracious. All these roles are part of a courtly game. Can the same be said of Wyatt's poem? It is clear that it can be read as embodying a typical male fantasy, wanting, even with the best, most idealistic intentions, to fix a woman as a possession – tamed, overcome, part of what as a male and a courtier, he deserved. But what *political* force does that taming try to repress?

The hurt and puzzlement of this poem, evocative and perplexing, contain, therefore, more than just the anxiety produced by the conflicting codes of erotic desire. Greenblatt points out parallels in the language of diplomatic dispatches, including Wyatt's own, to the language of love poetry, and his point can be extended. Political power is expressed in terms of personal allegiance and pressure; erotic power is expressed in the codes of political domination. What is at issue in the relationship is simply (or complexly) power, the same preoccupation with domination and submission, in which 'the options are to enforce submission or to submit, to be the aggressor or to be the victim'.[15] The pain of a poem like 'They Flee from Me' arises not only from thwarted power but from an inability to formulate any more creative alternative to that permitted by the Court, either on the erotic or the political level. To take a wider perspective, such poetry shows how cultural forms are being put under pressure by what Williams terms emergent 'structures of feeling'. They articulate socio-cultural experiences which do not, at least for the writer, have words in which they can be voiced.

Ralegh

For the third and fourth examples of court poets in this chapter, we move forward some fifty years or more where, in the poetry of the last twenty years of the century, we can see emerging much more noticeably the conflicts that haunt Dunbar's and Wyatt's. Part of the greatness of late-sixteenth-century poetry arises from the way we can see the increasing emergence of alternatives to the power that brought it into being.

Let us start by looking back from the very end of the era. The succession of Elizabeth by her 'cousin of Scotland' in 1603 was chiefly manoeuvred by a man whose family had manipulated many of the routine aspects of English politics for four decades, Sir Robert Cecil. In the anxious shuffling for court influence and position that accompanied James's accession two other men's careers were thwarted by Cecil's craft and power. Each had served the Queen, although in very different roles; each was an occasional, though exceptionally fine, poet; and a comparison of their careers shows both the lure and unpredictability of the power of the Court and the place of poetry within it. The two poets are Sir Walter Ralegh and Fulke Greville, later first Baron Brooke.

In 1601, Ralegh and Greville were associated, probably for the only time in their careers, in their joint arrest of some of the followers of the Earl of Essex who had supposedly plotted to overthrow the Queen. Greville had long been a cautious supporter of Essex, and in the 1601 crisis fought carefully to save the Earl's life while always maintaining his overall loyalty to the Queen. Ralegh had, for a decade, made no secrecy of his jealousy of Essex, the man with whom he had fought for the favours of the ageing Elizabeth. Over twenty years earlier, both men had entered the Court without spectacular advantages: the flamboyant Ralegh became a favourite of the Queen; Greville later recalled his own 'misplaced endeavours'[16] in Elizabeth's Court but his caution and circumspection earned him a series of responsible positions. The fall of Ralegh in 1603 and his sentence to death for treason, were spectacular events, as was his eventual execution in 1617; the fall of Greville, as part of Cecil's prudent policy of eliminating supporters of Essex, went virtually unnoticed. In 1615 Greville, an embittered sixty-year-old, returned to high public office; in 1617, after a fruitless voyage to find the supposedly fabulous wealth of El Dorado, Ralegh perished on the scaffold. During their years of exclusion, each wrote a major work which meditated on the monarch and the Court in which they had served: in Greville's case, a life of the man whose memory and friendship he carried to the grave, Sir Philip Sidney; in Ralegh's, what belies its title by being one of the most revealingly subjective works of the age, the great unfinished *History of the World*. Greville, hiding his revulsion from the Jacobean Court, never published his work; Ralegh brazenly published his as an affront to James and his Court.

Ralegh accepted and chose to live out the myth of the Elizabethan Court, conceiving his life as a flamboyant epic, and his handful of poems are part of that myth. As one lyric puts it, its naked request for favour appropriately disguised in the gentility of Petrarchan plaint: 'Then must I needes advaunce my self by Skyll/And lyve to serve, in hope of your goodwyll' (Sweete ar the thoughtes). Advancing himself by skill meant, in Ralegh's case, accepting the Court as an arena of self-assertion, or (in another of the metaphors that recurs in his work) as a new world to be conquered. Both are recurring metaphors. In Thomas Pynchon's metaphor he 'yo-yos' between the roles of the courtier, politician, explorer, free-thinker, poet, amateur philosopher, and lover. Greenblatt has suggested that Ralegh saw his life as a work of art, and that the Court was, in another of his favourite metaphors, a great theatre in which the boldest actor was the most successful. He argues that Ralegh's role-playing incorporates two contradictory Renaissance traditions, one seeing life as a series of required roles, the other seeing life itself as a play that is empty, futile, and unreal.[17] But was Ralegh that much in control of his roles? Was the multiplicity of his life the product of his personal autonomy? It is true that if he was to succeed in the glittering and dangerous world of the Elizabethan Court, he needed to take on and excel at whatever roles the Court thrust upon him. But they are all roles given him by the Court. Unlike someone like Sidney, who was a courtier by birth and privilege, Ralegh was one because his survival depended upon it. He has to commit himself absolutely to each role forced upon him and in a world that was dangerous, unpredictable, and changing; the wonder was that he survived so brilliantly for so long. The roles he played, including that of poet, were like the explorations, the 'discoveries' he made, short, tactical essays, opportunistic and pragmatic, quick impositions of his will-power over the world into which he found himself thrust.

What makes Ralegh so interesting for us is, first, that the 'selves' he lived out were not, in fact, self-created; and second, that his. poetry registers his struggle to accept his position in the Court's discourse of power. Unlike Dunbar and Wyatt, he was a poet because poetry was a distinctively effective way of advancing himself. Puttenham mentions Ralegh as one of the 'crew of Courtly makers, Noble men and Gentlemen' of the Court. 'Blown this way and that (and sometimes lifted into real poetry)', as C. S. Lewis rather condescendingly put it (the parentheses revealing his own ideological positioning), Ralegh's poetry (and, indeed, his life) articulate for us with fearful clarity not merely the gaudy surface of the late-sixteenth-century Court, but something of the process by which the subjects of the Court were moulded.[18]

So Ralegh's career as a poet and a courtier (the two are almost inseparable, literary and social text repeatedly writing and rewriting each other throughout his life) should not be simply seen as the daring, wilful assertion of the gentleman adventurer who strode into the Queen's favour with a graceful and opportune sweep of his cloak and who wrote a handful of charming lyrics. That would be to take at least some of his poems and the power they hoped to participate in too much for granted. Ralegh's poetry is put into play both by and in power. It demonstrates, probably more clearly than that of any other Elizabethan poet, the unconscious workings of power upon discourse. Specifically it shows how power works upon the language, which it controlled, selected, organized, and distributed through approved and determined procedures, delimiting as far as possible the emergence of oppositional forces and experiences. As we have seen, the Elizabethan Court used poetry and poets alike as one of its means of stabilization and control. To confirm its preferred values, it tried to restrict poet and poem as far as possible to the dominant discourses of a colourful, adventurous world but in Ralegh's case only at the cost of a frustrating and finally despairing powerlessness.

Much of Ralegh's poetry looks like typical Petrarchan love poetry. It can be, and no doubt was by many members of his original audiences, read as such. For those wanting to register the *frisson* of noble language and unrequited love, 'As You Came from the Holy Land' and 'The Nymph's Reply to the Shepherd' read marvellously in a modern classroom. With the stanzas read alternatively by 'lover' and 'pilgrim' the former, in particular, conveys the dialogic nature of the poetry, drawing its audience into the debate, especially in the final stanzas (who exactly speaks them is debatable; they can be made to work well in different ways) about the nature, even the possibility, of 'true' love. Skimming over the surface of Ralegh's verse, we encounter the typical paraphernalia of the Petrarchan lyric – hope and despair, pleasure and fortune, false love, frail beauty, fond shepherds, coy mistresses, deceitful time. 'As You Came from the Holy Land' can be read not only as a superbly melancholy love affirmation, one of the most moving love lyrics of the language, but also as a political poem, praising the impossibly inaccessible ideal offered the courtiers by the Queen. 'Nature that washt her hands in milke' takes the reader through a witty blazon of the perfect mistress's charms, her outside made of 'snow and silke', her 'inside . . . only of wantonesse and witt'. But like all Petrarchan mistresses, she has 'a heart of stone' and so the lover is poised, in perpetual frustration, before his ideal. Then in the second half of the poem, Ralegh ruthlessly tears down all of the ideals he has built. What gives the poem its power is the unusually savage use of the Elizabethan commonplace of Time the destroyer or the thief – ravaging, lying, rusting, and annihilating as Time 'turnes snow, and silke, and milke to dust'. What was to the lover the 'food of Joyes' is ceaselessly fed into the maw of death by the mistress and her wantonness is rendered dry and repulsive.

Likewise, the ruthlessly demystifying reply to Marlowe's delicate 'The Passionate Shepherd' (if, as well, it *is* by Ralegh) is an impressively terse expression of the *carpe diem* motif. What is stressed in the solemn, logical, emphatic brooding over moral wisdom, not the light, celebratory escapism of the court idyll:

> The flowers doe fade, and wanton fieldes,
> To wayward winter reckoning yeeldes,
> A honny tongue, a hart of gall,
> In fancies spring, but sorrowes fall.
>
> Thy gownes, thy shooes, thy beds of Roses,
> Thy cap, thy kirtle, and thy poesies,
> Soone breake, soone wither, soone forgotten:
> In follie ripe, in reason rotten.
>
> ('The Nimphs Reply to the Sheepheard')

Typically, Ralegh's poetry has superb control of mood, movement, voice modulation, and an appropriately direct rhetoric. Like Wyatt, he pares down the ornate tropes of the courtly tradition, chooses syntactical and logical patterns which emphasize rationality and urgent, emphatic movements of mind. Ralegh's poems are quintessentially those of the gifted amateur: a seemingly casual compliment, occasional verses typically dropped, as the manuscript title of another poem possibly by him has it, 'Into My Lady Laiton's Pocket'. But Ralegh's poetry does more than put sexuality into discourse: inevitably the language of erotic compliment and complaint is inseparable from the language of power. Despite their seemingly trivial, light, or occasional nature – epitaphs on Sidney's death, 'A Farewell to False Love', dedicatory poems to works by Gascoigne or Spenser, poems directly or indirectly written to the Queen – their significance reverberates far beyond their apparently replete surface configurations of stock metaphor and gracefully logical structure.

It will have been noted how I am continually using 'possibly' about the authorship of many of Ralegh's poems. We do not in fact know whether many of the poems attributed to him in the manuscripts and miscellanies in which Elizabethan court poetry typically appears are, in fact, his. Although we have access to more autograph writing for Ralegh than for any other major Elizabethan poet except Wyatt and Robert Sidney, we can only speculate about the authorship of many of the best poems attributed to him. In one important sense, however, it does not matter: Elizabethan court poetry often speaks with the voice of a collectivity and its authors are *scriptors* or spokesmen for the values of a dominant class and its ideology. An author's relationship to the languages that traverse him are much more complex than allowed for by the sentimental nineteenth-century biographical criticism which has held sway in Ralegh scholarship until very recently. In any court lyric, there is an illimitable series of pre-texts, subtexts, and post-texts which call into question any concept of its author as a free, autonomous individual. Like those by other court poets, Ralegh's poems, like those of Sidney or Spenser, are sites of struggle, attempts by Ralegh (or whatever court poet may have written them) to write himself into the world. Hence there is a sense in which we should almost speak of 'Ralegh' and 'his' poems alike as texts, requiring always to be read against what they seem to articulate, often speaking out in their silences, in what they cannot or dare not say but none the less manage to speak.

Some of the poems are, however, very explicit about their ideological allegiances. They are quite simply propagandist art. 'Praisd Be Dianas Faire and Harmles Light' is a poem (again only possibly by Ralegh) which reifies the ideals of the Court in a hymn of celebration, demanding absolute allegiance to the magical, timeless world of the Elizabethan Court in which no challenge to the replete atmosphere can be admitted and in which the readers are permitted to share only so long as they acknowledge the beauty of the goddess the poem celebrates:

Praisd be Dianas faire and harmles light,
Praisd be the dewes, wherwith she moists the ground;
Praisd be hir beames, the glorie of the night,
Praisd be hir powre, by which all powres abound.

The poem's atmosphere is incantatory, its movement designed, like court music, to inculcate unquestioning reverence and subordination. Only the subhuman (presumably any reader foolish, or treasonous enough to dissent from its vision) are excluded from the charm and the power it celebrates: 'A knowledge pure it is hir worth to know,/With Circes let them dwell that thinke not so.'

Puttenham mentions Ralegh's poetry approvingly as 'most lofty, insolent and passionate', and by the mid 1580s, Ralegh already had the reputation of a fine craftsman and thus is listed among Puttenham's 'crew of Courtly makers, noblemen and gentlemen' of Elizabeth's Court. 'The course and quality of men's lives serving in the court is of all others the most uncertain and dangerous', wrote Ralegh,[19] and like every courtier-poet of the age he used his verse as one of the means by which he clambered for position. He is the lover, poor in words, but rich in affection; his passions are likened to 'floudes and stremes'; the lover prays 'in vayne' to 'blinde fortune' and resolves none the less 'but love, farewell, thoughe fortune conquer thee,/No fortune base nor frayle shall alter mee'.

The typical pose is that of the worshipper, devoted to the unapproachable mistress or of the idealizing devotee with the Queen as the wavering star, the chaste goddess, the imperial embodiment of justice, the timeless principle on which the universe turns. In the way that Ben Jonson's masques were later to embody the dominant ideology of the Jacobean Court, Ralegh's poems evoke the collective fantasy of the Elizabethan – a world that is harmonious, static, and from which all change has been exorcized. However seemingly depoliticized, these poems are the product of the allurement and dominance of the Court, their confidence less that of the poet himself than of the power of the structures in which he struggled to locate himself.

As well as this miscellany (sometimes startlingly evocative, invariably competent and provoking) of poems, there are four closely connected and important poems, all undoubtedly Ralegh's, which are found in his own handwriting among the Cecil Papers in Hatfield House, north of London, the family home of Ralegh's great enemy Robert Cecil. They are 'If Synthia be a Queene, a Princes, and Supreame', 'My Boddy in the Walls Captived', 'Sufficeth it to Yow, My Joyes Interred', and 'My Dayes Delights . . .'. The third of these, a poem of 522 lines, is headed 'The 11th: and last booke of the Ocean to Scinthia' and the fourth is headed 'The end of the bookes, of the Oceans love to Scinthia and the beginninge of the 12 Boock, entreatinge of Sorrow'. The existence of one or more closely connected poems written to the Queen and entitled something like *Cynthia* seems to be mentioned by Spenser in *The Faerie Queene*, and is usually identified with these two poems.

The second, usually called 'Ocean to Scinthia', is the most important of the group. It appears to be the barely revised draft of an appeal, if not to the Queen herself, at least to that part of Ralegh's mind he knew to be occupied by her power. It lacks many narrative links; its four-line stanzas are often imperfect, with repetitions and gaps which presumably might have been revised later. But its unfinished state makes it not only a fascinating revelation of Ralegh's personal and poetic anguish; in its very fragmentariness it is perhaps the clearest example in Elizabethan court poetry of the way the dynamics and the contradictions of power speak through a text. Indeed, nowhere in Elizabethan poetry is a poem so obviously constitutive of ideological struggle. 'Ocean to Scinthia' repeatedly deconstructs the philosophy to which it gives allegiance: its incoherences, gaps, uncertainties, and repetitions at once affirm the dominant Elizabethan court ideology and articulate a desire to oppose it. What in Ralegh's other poems is simply ignored or repressed is here starting to emerge in the fractures and symptomatic maladjustments of the text.

The poem is addressed to a patently transparent female figure, who has withdrawn her favour from the faithful lover. Ralegh projects himself as a despairing lover fearful (and fearfully) aware that his service has been swept into oblivion, simultaneously acknowledging that honours inevitably corrupt and yet that he cannot withdraw from pursuing them. The 'love' he has seemingly won includes favours that open doors to glory, but also to ruin and death. Yet even knowing this, it is as if he cannot help himself. He must 'seeke new worlds, for golde, for prayse, for glory', with the tragic result that he bewails:

> Twelve yeares intire I wasted in this warr,
> Twelve yeares of my most happy younger dayes,
> Butt I in them, and they now wasted ar,
> Of all which past the sorrow only stayes.

The result of his 'twelve yeares' dedication has been imprisonment and disgrace. Yet he is helpless before his own ability to abandon the glories of office. 'Trew reason' shows power to be worthless. Yet even while he knows that 'all droopes, all dyes, all troden under dust', he knows also that the only stability in the world of power is the necessity of instability and emulation.

The Petrarchan commonplace with which the successful courtier has played so effectively, almost on demand – the helpless lover wooing the unapproachable mistress who is the unattainable goal of desire – has suddenly and savagely been literalized. The role Ralegh has played has become actualized in a way that explodes his habitual adaptability. He cannot protest that the game of the despairing lover is only a game; it has now become real. In 1592 he wrote to Cecil: 'My heart was never broken till this day, that I hear the Queen goes away so far off – whom I have followed so many years with so great love and desire, in so many journeys, and am now left behind her in a great prison alone.'[20] The letter is an obvious echo of the lines from Ralegh's adaptation of the Walsingham ballad, 'As You Came from the Holy Land':

> She hath lefte me here all alone,
>   All allone as unknowne,
> Who somtymes did me lead with her selfe,
>   And me lovde as her owne.

Whether Ralegh wrote these haunting lines is almost beside the point: the courtly game to which they gesture, and yet transcend, is that played by and through all courtiers. But in Ralegh's life the contradictions which were now given voice had been repressed and silenced. Now they are revealed as terrifyingly real. Ralegh himself has ceased to play Elizabeth's game by marrying; he has thus found the role of masochistic victim he cast himself in for political advantage has been taken literally and he has become an outcast. 'Ocean to Scinthia' expresses the agony of a man whose choices and commitments have been built on the myth of a changeless past in an ever-moving power struggle. The very unfinished quality of Ralegh's fragment is the perfect formal expression of the disruptiveness that has overwhelmed him.

We are fortunate that another key poem of this period is among the Hatfield Manuscripts. 'The Lie' is an ejaculation of explicit rage, a struggle to find form for deep frustration in finding no alternative to renunciation and repulsion. It is a statement of deeply felt impotence, written, it is often suggested, after Ralegh's release from prison in 1592, but before he was restored to favour. Ralegh's poem is seemingly total in its rejection of the ideology by which he has lived: natural law, universal harmony, love, court artifice are all rejected in a mood of total condemnation. And yet Ralegh's poem is neither philosophically nihilis- tic nor politically radical: his revulsion from the court does not allow for any alternative to it. What 'dies' is the I of the poem, as he gives the lie to the world, and takes refuge in a savage *contemptus mundi*. 'The Lie' is an explosion of the frustration that throughout the century has underlain the Court's ideological confidence. In such poems the ideology of the Elizabethan Court is betrayed by the very writing it controlled: the poem constantly releases an anxiety for realities which challenges the surface harmonies, even if the struggle cannot be heard against the dominant language of the court poetic mode. Ralegh's characteristic melancholic formulation of the persistence of 'woe' or pain as the very mark of human self-consciousness is the special tell-tale sign of his texts as sites of struggle and repression. 'The life expires, the woe remains' is a refrain echoed elsewhere as in 'Of all which past, the sorrowe onely staies' ('like truthless dreams'); it is also echoed in phrases throughout the History. Such recurring motifs create more than a characteristic tone to Ralegh's verse. They point to the thwarted insurrection of subjugated experience struggling to find expression, knowing that there are no words permitted or seemingly possible for it.

Ralegh's poems, then, are haunted by what they try to exorcize. The fragility and uncertainties of court life in the 1580s and 1590s undermine his poetry's announced role as the spokesman of a replete court ideology. Despite their confident surfaces, his poems are less celebrations of the power of the Queen and Court than a conspiracy to remain within its protection. The Petrarchan clichés of 'Like truthless dreams, so are my joys expired' or (if we accept it as Ralegh's) the Neoplatonic commonplaces of the Walsingham ballad become desperate pleas for favour, projections into lyric poems of political machinations. 'Conceipt begotten by the eyes' (if it *is* Ralegh's) also starts out as a stereotypical contrast between 'desire' and 'woe', and emerges as a poignant ejaculation of radical insecurity – a powerless acknowledgement that the self of the court poet is a creation of the discourses he has uneasily inhabited and from which he now feels expelled. Above all, the Hatfield poems show us with wonderful clarity what all Elizabethan court poetry tries to repress, that however the poet asserts his autonomy, he is constituted through ideology, that he has no existence outside the social formation and the signifying practices legitimized by the power of the Court. Ralegh, like every other poet who wrestled within the Court, does not speak so much as he is spoken.

More than twenty years after his fall from favour and after ten years of imprisonment under James, Ralegh published his incomplete History. Pious in intention, the work (like so much of Ralegh's poetry) articulates a philosophy that radically undercuts its intentions. It reveals a view of history with no final eschatological goal, no ultimate consummation. History consists only of the continual vengeance of an angry God until 'the long day of mankind . . . and the world's Tragedie and time near at an end'. A few years later, on the eve of his execution, Ralegh took up the last lines of one of his early lyrics:

Even such is tyme which takes in trust
Our yowth, our Joyes, and all we have,
And payes us butt with age and dust:
Who in the darke and silent grave
When we have wandred all our wayes
Shutts up the storye of our dayes.

– and appended to it, in two new lines, the only hope he could conceive of, a *deus ex machina* to rescue him, in a way neither Queen nor King had, from the grip of time's power: 'And from which earth and grave and dust/The Lord shall rayse me up I trust.' It is a cry of desperation, not a transformation of 'the consuming disease of time', as he puts it in the *History*.[21] What is finally triumphant over Ralegh is the power of that world in which his handful of poems are an extraordinarily moving acknowledgement and testament.

Ralegh's importance, then, belies the slimness of his poetic output. The author of perhaps two dozen extant poems, mostly short lyrics, plus a number of brief verse translations in the *History*, he is none the less one of the most important of the Elizabethan courtly makers, articulating with fearful clarity not merely the gaudy surface and fashions of the late Elizabethan age, but much of the felt pressure of the Court upon the lives and sensibilities of those caught in it. Ralegh described himself towards the end of his life as 'a sea-faring man, a Souldior and a Courtier', and his poetry articulates much of what drove him to those vocations. He knew, deeply and bitterly that, as he puts it in the *History*, there is nothing more 'becoming a wise man' than 'to retire himself from the Court'. Yet the Court was his stage and it was, he wrote, where he 'exercised in the service of the world'.[22] The achievement of his poetry is that it gives reverberating words to the struggles of those who lived in and were controlled by the Elizabethan Court. Most of his poems look, on the surface, like delicate, even trivial, songs, complaints, or compliments typical of the most superficial kind of Petrarchanism. In fact they are constituted as rich, confused, responses to the complex and powerful set of discourses, symbolic formations, and systems of representation that made up the Elizabethan Court. They try to carve out a private space in a public world and find only that privacy is in turn produced by the very public structures it tries to exclude. Ralegh's poems thus offer us a unique way into the interplay between the social text of Elizabethan society – the events that made Ralegh's history – and the literary text – the poems that he made of those events. Ralegh is, in many ways, the quintessential court poet of the Elizabethan period in that his poems are determined by, and finally silenced by, the power of the Court.

Greville

Ralegh's poetry articulates, at a pre-formative stage, something of the oppositional cultural forces that were already challenging the hegemony of the Court. Of course, as well, he is an alluringly tragic figure and his boldness and defiance make a fascinating contrast with Greville's more sombre and calculated career. More clear-sightedly than Ralegh, Greville brooded over the nature of the Court that he entered along with the man he admired all his life, Philip Sidney. One of Greville's later contemporaries wrote that he had 'the longest lease and the smoothest time without rub', of any of 'the Queen's favorites', and in that alone can be seen how Greville's achievements were very different from Ralegh's. The substance of his remark in 1598 – 'she in her princely nature knoweth that I have commanded mine own genius, and left all courses in the world that advance other men, only for her sake'[23] – could have been spoken by Ralegh, but like all of Greville's achievements at Court, it is more prudent. It also contains, characteristically, a deep pessimism about his ability to change the course of events in Court. Under Elizabeth, he achieved some modest advancement: he held a series of minor positions as a courtier and a soldier including, in 1598, Treasurer of the Navy. During the Essex crisis of 1599–1601, he seems to have been unable to commit himself absolutely either way, perhaps seeing Essex in some way as the inheritor of Sidney's ideals and yet disturbed by the flamboyance of the Earl's methods. His caution and fear endeared him to neither faction but he managed to survive and was, probably, on the verge of becoming a Privy Councillor when the Queen died.

Like Wyatt and Ralegh, Greville was a courtier before he was a poet, but his poetry was kept at a greater distance from his life at Court. Greville's earliest poems are known to have circulated among members of the Sidney Circle from the 1570s on. Puttenham mentions him, as well, as one of his 'crew of Courtly makers', but though some of the *Caelica* poems were set to music later in the seventeenth century, none was published in his lifetime and very few are found in manuscript collections. What we now know as *Caelica*, a collection of 108 sonnets and songs, was kept and continually revised by Greville in a manuscript and only published some thirty years after his death in 1628. *Caelica* is therefore even more miscellaneous than most collections of sixteenth-century lyrics: although many are addressed to a mistress, named variously as Caelica, Myra, or Cynthia, there are no narrative links, and their most insistent focus is not on love so much as politics and theology. They are often tortuously compressed and crammed with tight philosophical argument. Throughout, Greville is grappling to overcome the affective seductiveness of Sidney's rhetoric, trying to pare it down, attempting to get it closer to what he sees as truth. The obscurity of his poetry is a consequence of a deep-seated and probably increasing scepticism about court poetry and its place in a culture which he found degraded, alien, and corrupt but to which he could conceive no alternative. He tries to use poetry as a weapon against all that it had evolved to do – and especially what his friend Sidney had achieved so well. Germaine Warkentin also argues that the poems 'reveal Greville's boredom with the intense focus on the self of the poet which marks all the vernacular amorous poetry from the twelfth century onward'.[24] That is particularly the case with the later, explicitly religious poems. Very often, he seems to write poetry as a man who distrusts it, and his distrust spreads beyond the surface rhetoric to the world of which it is an expression. The impact of many of the poems, therefore, is to call into question not merely a poetic style, but a whole style of life. There are a few that Greville would presumably have felt safe about circulating at Court. Some are moralistic, grimmer versions of Wyatt's satires: Sonnets 91 and 92 are conventional attacks on false nobility, 81 praises Elizabeth triumphing over Fortune, and 83 is a plea for favour which uses the conventional motifs of being exiled from paradise, withering in anguish and loneliness. It concludes with an effective but disarming play on his own name: 'Let no man ask my name, nor what else I should be;/For *Greiv-Ill*, paine, forlorn estate do best decipher me.'

More interesting, however, are the poems where he broods over the ways the Court creates (or, in Greville's eyes, exalts and so corrupts) the self. In the early poems, Greville may start from the conventional Petrarchist stance, but he injects it with an unusual bitterness, as in 5:

> Who trusts for trust, or hopes of love for love,
> Or who belov'd in *Cupids* lawes doth glory;
> Or joyes in vowes, or vowes not to remove,
> Who by this light God, hath not beene made sorry;
>   Let him see me eclipsed from my Sunne,
>   With shadowes of an Earth quite over-runne.

To hope for access to any kind of reality through the conventional courtly paraphernalia, to 'trust for trust', or to seek divine love through human agency is not merely rhetorical affectation – it is self-deceptive folly. The poems in *Caelica* often take as their starting-point the commonplace stance of the courtly lover which, as we saw, Ralegh took so seriously, that the forlorn lover is the required rhetorical role of the courtier. Such a role, in Greville's view, is appropriate for men only because their nature, like the courtier's, is 'restlesse', 'wandring', and basically self-deceptive. In Sonnet 10, the lover, 'invited' to see 'Vertues and beauties' in the 'glory of those faire eyes', may view his mistress as a divine goddess, but the poem tries to get its readers to reject such theologizing as fraudulent, self-deceptive, and irrational. The poem asks an ironical question – 'Then tell me *Love*, what glory you divine/Your selfe can find within this soule of mine?' – which not only demands an inevitable negative reply, but also undermines any possibility of courtly idealizations being anything but unreal and self-deceptive. Throughout *Caelica*, such terms as 'love', 'delight', 'beauties riches', 'glory', 'hope', 'desires affinity' – all the talismanic phrases of the courtly poet – are invested not with their felt sense of security, but with fragility. They are all evidence of man's fall into self-deception. *Caelica*, Sonnet 22, paints the whole courtly game of love as a self-deceptive farce; 24 goes further and depicts courtly art, 'painting, the *eloquence of* dumbe conceipt', as deception; 49, with grim facetiousness, makes very explicit Greville's rejection of the deceptiveness of courtly love, courtly rhetoric, and the court ethos. Some poems, especially Sonnets 1 and 3, do assert a belief in the transcendence of one, singular, figure – some idealized mistress, perhaps the Queen – but even here (presumably when Greville is writing most under the influence of Sidney) a deep scepticism enters. If love, delight, virtue, and reason 'are from the world by Natures power bereft', and only in 'one' creature, 'for her glory, left' (Sonnet 1), then the possibility of even greater disillusion occurs should such an ideal fail.

Dunbar's poems are the product of a Court that is still essentially feudal; Wyatt's of a buoyant if paranoid Renaissance Court; Ralegh's poems are part of a campaign for an impossible autonomy within a Court that had evolved into a complex cultural machine. But all are the products of similar struggles and of the repression of alternatives to the ideology that has brought them into being. Greville's are slightly different. Because they are deliberately cast as private meditations, his poems seem to allow a scepticism about the Court to appear more clearly than the others. When we compare his more public poetry, the verse-treatises and poetic dramas, we can see him brooding cryptically over the great issues of the years after Sidney's death and being able to give a more explicit treatment of the issues. *Mustapha* was written in the 1590s, and includes a series of debates on matters Greville must have thought much over at the time of Essex's fall. *Alaham* and the early drafts of the Treatise on *Monarchy* were probably written at the end of the 1590s: their dominant political philosophy is one of non-resistance, even to a tyrannical monarch, and when we consider them alongside the deep-rooted scepticism of *Caelica*, a fascinating paradox is revealed. Unlike Ralegh, who was told at his final trial that 'he had lived like a star, and like a star he must fall, when it troubled the firmament', Greville made no attempt to blaze forth his rebellion. Yet it is clear that his rejection of the Court and its values was much more radical and clear-sighted than Ralegh's. There is more than what recent biographers have seen as circumspection or caution. He sees the courtier called by God to a passivity before the unrelieved evil around him, observing how 'when evill strives, the worst have greatest name . . . Those mischiefes prosper that exceed the rest.' The Court and its politics show that it is, indeed, the tyrants, atheists, and the ruthless who triumph, 'as if the earth . . . were to the worst left free'. In *Mustapha*, the question 'is Providence of no . . . use to power?' seems to be necessarily given a disturbingly negative answer. What the faithful courtier must do, it seems, is to accept a grim Calvinist paradox – that while man's salvation depends not on his works but only on God's predestinate will, yet his election is nevertheless tested by his activity within the world where he must survive in ways his creed abhors. The courtier must accept the secular ethic that he must 'first judge your Ends, and then your Meanes', leaving judgement 'to His will that governs the blind prosperities of Chance; and so works out His own ends by the erring frailties of human reason and affection'. In Greville's grim Calvinist scheme, there seems to be no way of knowing the divine will since 'when each of us, in his owne heart lookes/He finds the God there, fame unlike his Bookes'.

A similar dualism characterizes Greville's meditations on public policy elsewhere: 'The world doth built without, our God within;/He traffiques goodnesse, and she traffiques sinne' or 'Fly unto God: For in humanity/Hope there is none' are typical sentiments. True fame may be afforded to the elect, whereas those – presumably like Ralegh, whom Greville referred to as being possessed by 'pride' in 1603 – who seek earthly fame

> Make Men their God, *Fortune*, and *Time* their worth,
>   Forme, but reforme not; meer hypocrisie,
>   By shadowes, only shadowes, bringing forth.

What differentiates Greville's from Dunbar's, Wyatt's, and Ralegh's poetry – and it is an indication of how the strains of late-sixteenth-century court poetry are becoming more evident – is his deeply engrained Calvinist pessimism. The increasing power of Calvinism is a major factor in changing the tenor of sixteenth-century poetry. Dunbar was a Catholic, Wyatt an uneasy Protestant, but in different ways Ralegh and Greville are deeply scarred by the Protestant dynamic. Yet where Ralegh took refuge in a deterministic scepticism, Greville's radical Protestantism produces something much more disruptive.

The contradictions involved in holding together Protestant and courtly, Calvin and Petrarch, that we will see Sidney struggle with, are also what give Greville's poetry its distinctive strength. His work is situated at the intersection of vast contradictory cultural claims which

132 ENGLISH POETRY OF THE SIXTEENTH CENTURY

are all the more powerful because Greville struggles to be as rational and as untouched by sin as he can, even while he believes that rationality and truth are denied him.

Greville's starting-point seems invariably to be his observations of the society around him. Like the other three poets we have considered in this chapter, he gained first-hand insight into the workings of power and his picture of society is a grim one. The virtuous man must either opt out of society, or else accept the necessity of craft and policy as the 'base instrument of humane frailtie' (*A Treatise of Monarchy*, 284). Protestant activism makes the first of these alternatives unacceptable. Greville praised Sidney as 'a man fit for conquest, Plantation, Reformation, or what action soever is greatest and hardest among men'; a noble nature like Sidney's could not escape the responsibility of public duty, even in an unredeemable world. It followed from the Calvinist ethic that man's salvation depends not on his works but on God's predestinate will and yet, paradoxically, continual activity in the world is still stressed to be the test of a man's election. So, argues Greville, even the godly must employ the very means they abhor, since God, as he puts it, 'made all for use'.[25]

Among some late-sixteenth-century Calvinists politics come to be regarded as the consequence of man's fall. Yet although secular life is outside the realm of grace, it is none the less, necessary for the proper ordering and disciplining of men. The Christian must still live in these two spheres of life, and so his life will necessarily be contadictory and tragically corrupt. In special cases of remarkable virtue, like Sidney, some limited achievement seems possible – though one might sense in Greville's praise of Sidney a belief that his ideals were never adequately tested. But the Christian is forced by his own sinfulness to acknowledge that craft, deviousness, and seeking advantage are the means of survival in society. To face up to one's inner corruptiion means that one learns 'first judge your Ends, and then your Means', leaving the outcome 'to His will that governs the blind prosperities of chance'.[26]

Coming through Greville's writings is a deeply troubled awareness of contradiction – God cannot err and yet events seem to display only the triumph of evil. In *Mustapha* he asks 'is Providence of no . . . use to power?' His faith answers yes, his experience of politics, no. *Alaham* echoes Greville's troubled scepticism when he writes 'that God of whom you crave/Is deaf, and only gives men what they have'.

Compelling in their logic, Greville's poetic dramas mull over such questions. His poetry seems continually to be torn apart by irreconcilable contradictions in his faith. He, of course, blames man's depraved nature, seeing men, as the first chorus in *Mustapha* puts it, as 'a crazed soule, unfix'd'; or, in the grim lines of the 'chorus sacerdotum' of Mustapha: 'when each of us, in his owne heart lookes/he finds the God there, farre unlike his Bookes'. Man is 'borne under one Law, to another bound:/Vainely begot, and yet forbidden vanity'. In the end only Eternity can redeem the inadequacies of time: 'Fly unto God: For in humanity/Hope there is none', argues Alaham (Act IV).

There are some experiences which look as if they offer hope within the world. Greville is acutely conscious that his friend Sidney saw human love at least tantalizing us with that possibility. But Greville's stern Calvinism dares not accept any state less than perfect, and the disillusion inherent in man's idealizations of love is a pressing theme in *Caelica*. Greville constantly stresses both the transience of love, and its underlying cause: 'For lest Man should thinke flesh a seat of blisse,/God workes that his joy mixt with sorrow is' (*Caelica*, 94). In love, as in politics, Greville looks for God's approval in vain in the world and in himself, and concludes in *A Treatise of Religion*, 7, that 'Nature contains him not, Art cannot show him.' The world is merely a testing-gound for men's perseverance. The faithful can only combine their determination to obey with a humble awareness of the ultimate incompatibility of the world which is 'made for use', whereas God is made only 'for love' (*A Treatise of Religion*, 114).

Calvinism seems to have given Greville a rigorous context to settle many of the issues that haunted him. Nevertheless, a frustrated idealism keeps forcing its way through the surface of his poetry. As opposed to Sidney, whose idealism seems to have fed on the disillusions and failures it perceived in love – witness the seventh song of *Astrophil and Stella* – Greville works through a kind of *realpolitik* of love. Love and human aspiration seem inevitably associated with guilt and mistrust, which is projected on to the formerly peerless mistress, and love itself thereby corrupted:

> Whence I conceav'd you of some heavenly mould,
> Since Love, and Vertue, noble Fame and Pleasure,
> Containe in one no earthly metall could,
> Such enemies are flesh, and blood to measure.

The disillusion in the last line is strongly wrought through the concrete, agonized imagery, and then is put into the inevitable theological context:

> And since my fall, through I now onely see
> Youre backe, while all the world beholds your face,
> This shadow still shewes miracles to me,
> And still I thinke your heart a heavenly place:
>   For what before was fill'd by me alone,
>   I now discerne hath roome for every one.
>
>   (*Caelica*, 64)

The mistress is still the desired paradise: but the limitations and jealous demands of fallen men have corrupted the vision so that the largess of heaven becomes equated with the hell of promiscuity.

The later sonnets show Greville fleeing the show of earthly love, but he is grimly aware that he cannot escape the bonds of earthly existence. Even man's deepest, most sincere, cries for salvation are interwoven with guilt and sin. Some of the most striking of the later sonnets show Greville looking within his own guilt and depravity, and finding in his deepest isolation, the presence of God as in *Caelica*, 99:

> And in this fatall mirrour of transgression,
> Shewes man as fruit of his degeneration,
> The errours ugly infinite impression,
> Which beares the faithlesse down to desperation;
> Depriv'd of humane graces and divine,
> Even there appeares this *saving God* of mine.

The last phrase is an oddly grasping one, the product of a faith that demands that the believer look for certain signs of assurance and yet denies the possibility of finding such signs. The strength of Greville's best poetry is that it articulates the struggle to accept what is clearly antipathetic to much of his life. As Thom Gunn finely puts it, 'the body cries out in pain at the rejections it is forced to make, and in the note of the cry we recognize the very humanity it is a cry against'.[27]

Greville's poetry is clearly distinct from the other court poets we have looked at in its foregrounding of Calvinist theology and the contradictions it raised for courtier and poet alike. It is fortunate, therefore, that we have a document of his – the life of Sidney – written at the end of the first decade of the new century, as he looks back at his youth and maturity in the Court. He chooses his dead friend as the focus of his own frustrations. He sees Sidney as the embodiment of ideals the Court has abandoned. 'I am', he says, 'enforced to bringe poignant evidences from the dead, amongst whom I have founde more liberall contribution to the honor of true worthe, then amongst those which now live.' Greville's *Life of Sidney* is thus a key document in our understanding of the ways in which the Court and its power operated. Greville is able to look at the Court he has been rejected by. He sees it from the perspective of a man who remembers nostalgically how the Court had once promoted virtue, piety, and goodness. He presents himself as an admirer of the man who in his 'too short scene of his life' exemplified a phoenix-like 'greatness of heart'.[28]

Greville's admiration for Sidney was something from which he never wavered. But writing the *Life*, and revising it, was a process that brought out more and more contradictions in his own commitments to the Court. Whenever Greville points to a characteristic of Elizabeth's Court or policies, he does so in order to criticize James and his Court. Elizabeth, he notes, was opposed to extra-parliamentary proclamations of new taxes; she saw how the 'Court it selfe' might become 'like a farm'. He points to James's 'monopolouse use of Favourites', and the endangering by royal power by what he calls 'selfe-prerogatives' such as the selling of honours. Where Elizabeth 'kept awe stirring over all her Countes and other chiefe imployments', James's lackadaisical manners, his 'Princely licentiousnesse in behaviour' is blamed as a 'fashioner of Atheisme among . . . Subjects'.[29] In such remarks, we sense Greville's total distaste for the manners and entertainments of the Stuart Court. Even though he sought employment under James he must have found the characteristic life-style of that Court most disagreeable. From *A Treaties of Monarchy* it is clear that he regarded the use of illusionistic art in masques and pageants as dangerous and self-deceiving; in the *Life* he is similarly derisive of Kings who 'suffer or rather force their Wives and daughters to descende from the inequallitie and reservedness of Princely education into the contemptible familiarity' of shepherds and pastoral disguises. Like the thrones they support, the courtiers of the Jacobean Court live by pride and self-ignorant deception.[30]

Such observations clearly constitute a radical revulsion from the Jacobean Court, from its policies, its ethos, its use of art as propaganda, and its degeneration from the Elizabethan era. Yet Greville's strong belief in non-resistance, even to tyrants, puts him into further contradiction. In Chapter 6, we shall see how Spenser tried to disassociate Elizabeth from the corruption he perceived in her Court; so Greville uneasily disassociates James from the criticism he makes. He describes James as 'that chief and best of *Princes*' and 'amongst the most eminent Monarchs of that tyme'. What he focuses upon is, most significantly, 'the Courte it selfe', the institution and commitments which he himself had entered with such hopes and served with such faithfulness. He sees it, from his exile, 'becoming like a farme, manured by drawing up not the sweate but even the brows of the humble subjects'. What, like the most virulent anti-court satirist of the 1590s, he terms 'the catching Court ayres' are the sign of an infection that is destroying England.[31] His is as wholesale a rejection of the Court as any by Webster, or Tourneur, or Shakespeare, and all the more significant because it was voiced by a man who like Dunbar, More, Wyatt, and Ralegh, knew the Court intimately not merely as an ideal but from years of service.

Yet there is another aspect of Greville's condemnation of the Court in the *Life* which helps us see how his poetry is distinctive. Feeling for the difference between Sidney and the new world of 1610, Greville predictably sees it in Sidney's piety. Unlike the Jacobean courtiers, Greville argues, Sidney combined his exemplary 'image of quiet and action' with a sense of his own unworthiness before God. Yet Greville must face an awkward question here. While he praises Sidney's greatness of mind, he cannot but ponder the 'secret judgements' of God who 'cut off this Gentleman's life, and so much of our hope'. He is uneasily aware that the God Sidney served chose to permit his death, and that the ideals Sidney represented had failed. Sidney had been called to a life in the world – he was 'a man fit for Conquest, Plantation, Reformation, or what action soever is greatest and hardest among men' – yet even he was merely the sinful instrument of God's will. All men, even Sidney, must accept 'what our owne creation bindes us to' – the absolute incompatibility of man's actions with God's will.[32] Greville's Calvinism reads Sidney's death as God's harsh but just judgement on England. Indeed, as Greville revised the *Life*, an increasing scepticism about his own memories of Sidney's ideals came through. As Greville, the exponent of Calvinist *realpolitik*, contemplates the world before him, more and more his friend's idealism receded into self-delusion.

In this chapter I have looked at four poets whose commitments to their vocation were formed by the pressures and demands of their being situated in or subject to the court. Each struggled to locate his writing within the complex socio-cultural text of his society; each articulated both the excitement and the anxiety of living, entertaining, and striving for prestige in the Court. By placing them together, we can see certain apparent continuities in the dominant mode of sixteenth-century poetry. But we can also see, as we try to account for some of the differences among the four poets, more than the usual factors that are traditionally ascribed to the 'maturity' or 'continuity' of sixteenth-century poetry, like the impact of Petrarchanism, growing stylistic sophistication, and so forth. What emerges are the growing ideological strains within the court hegemony. In particular, as Greville's poems show, there is the richly disruptive presence within the court poetry of Protestantism.

It has been persuasively argued by Alan Sinfield that a fundamental strand of literature in England between 1550 and 1650 is the working out of the contradictions inherent in Protestantism, so that cultural practices seemingly impossible early in the sixteenth century were increasingly able to find space and plausibility and eventually to transform the whole society.[33] What we can observe in the four court poets studied in this chapter is something of the first phase of this process. All four are marked by a frustrated search for oppositional or counter-dominant voices. They are all court poets committed to the values and practices of an increasingly powerful ideology which held them seemingly totally, reinforced their bondage with religious, moral, and material practices, and yet frustrated their search for any alternative. For Dunbar, the buoyancy and hierarchical order the Court embodies cannot hide the uneasiness and dislocations of experience for which he and his fellows had, as yet, no words to express. For Wyatt, the lack of an alternative voice is also seen in his falling back on medieval moral commonplaces, or on the puzzled silences of some of his lyrics. For Ralegh, fifty years later, such frustration is expressed in bitterness, revulsion, and once again a recourse to increasingly archaic moralism. With Greville, what had been a part of the dynamic of the early-sixteenth-century Court has become a plausible alternative to it. As Protestantism gradually rewrote the languages of the Court, while, as it were, Calvin and Castiglione battled in the discourse of Elizabethan poetry, gradually alternative models of poetry, court behaviour, and wider social practices became possible. The poet whose work, life, and reputation best illustrate this process is the major subject of Chapter 5.

Notes

1. Arthur Marotti, 'John Donne and the Rewards of Patronage', in *Patronage in the Renaissance*, edited by Guy Fitch Lytle and Stephen Orgel (Princetown, 1981), p. 220.

2. Bernard Sharratt, *Reading Relations* (London , 1983), p. 31.

3. Gary Waller, 'I and Ideology: Demystifying the Self of Contemporary Poetry', *Denver Quarterly*, 18, no. 3 (Autumn 1983), 123–38 (p. 125).

4. *The Autobiography of Thomas Whythorne*, edited by James M. Osborn (Oxford, 1961), pp. 3, 41. I owe this reference to Dr Bernard Sharratt of the University of Kent at Canterbury.

5. Tom Scott, *Dunbar: A Critical Exposition of the Poems* (Edinburgh, 1966), p. 160. Quotations from Dunbar's poems are taken from *The Poems of William Dunbar*, edited by James Kinsley (Oxford, 1959).

6. Scott, pp. 19, 210.

7. David Starkey, 'The Age of the Household: Politics, Society and the Arts *c.* 1350–*c.* 1550', in *The Later Middle Ages*, edited by Stephen Medcalf (New York, 1981), p. 278. Quotations from Wyatt's poems are taken from *Collected Poems*, edited by Richard Rebholz (1978).

8. George Puttenham, *The Arte of English Poesie*, edited by Gladys Doidge Willcock and Alice Walker (Cambridge, 1936) p. 61; Raymond Southall, *The Courtly Maker* (London, 1964), p. 23.

9. John Stevens, *Music and Poetry in the Early Tudor Court* (London, 1961), ch. 9; H. A. Mason, *Humanism and Poetry in the Early Tudor Period: An Essay* (London, 1959), p. 171; Stephen Greenblatt, 'The Resonance of Renaissance Poetry', *ADE Bulletin*, 64 (May 1980), 7–10 (p. 8).

10. Greenblatt, 'Resonance', p. 9.

11. Jerome K. Kamholtz, 'Thomas Wyatt's Poetry: The Politics of Love', *Criticism*, 20 (1978), 349–65 (p. 354).

12. Raymond Southall, 'Wyatt's "Ye Old Mule"', *ELN* (1967), 5–11 (p. 5).

13. Raymond Williams, *Marxism and Literature* (London, 1977), p. 126.

14. *Autobiography of Whythorne*, pp. 36, 40.

15. Greenblatt, 'Resonance', pp. 8, 9.

16. Greville, *Life*, p. 127.

17. Stephen Greenblatt, *Sir Walter Ralegh: The Renaissance Man and his Roles* (New Haven, 1973), p. 44. Quotations from Ralegh's poems are taken from *The Poems of Sir Walter Ralegh*, edited by Agnes Latham (London, 1952). See, however, the more rigorous though still unpublished edition by Michael Rudick, 'The Poems of Sir Walter Ralegh: An Edition' (unpublished doctoral dissertation, University of Chicago, 1970).

18. Puttenham, p. 61; C. S. Lewis, *English Literature in the Sixteenth Century excluding Drama* (Oxford, 1954), p. 519.

19. Sir Walter Ralegh, *The Cabinet Council*, in *Works* (London, 1829), 8 vols, VIII, pp. 113–14.

20. HMC, *Salisbury*, IV, 220.

21. Ralegh, *History*, II, vi, 9, in *Works*, II, 97; *Poems*, p. 72.

22. Quoted by Greenblatt, *Ralegh*, p. ix; Ralegh, *Works*, VIII, 114; *History*, Preface, in *Works*, II, xxxii.

23. Sir Robert Naunton, *Fragmenta Regalia* (London, 1641), p. 50. Quotations from Greville's poems are taken from *Poems and Dramas of Fulke Greville, Lord Brooke*, edited by Geoffrey Bullough (Edinburgh, 1938–39).

24. Charles Larsen, *Fulke Greville* (Boston, 1980), p.31; Germaine Warkentin, 'Greville's *Caelica* and the Fullness of Time', *English Studies in Canada*, 6 (1980), 398–408 (p. 400).

25. Greville, *Works*, edited by A. B. Grosart (London, 1870), IV, pp. 37, 32.

26. Greville, *Works*, IV, 32.

27. *Selected Poems of Fulke Greville*, introduced by Thom Gunn (London, 1968), p. 61.

28. Greville, *Life*, pp. 119, 116.

29. Greville, *Life*, pp. 177, 161, 160, 171, 46.

30. Greville, *Life*, pp. 28, 177, 139.

31. Greville, *Life*, pp. 131, 105, 29.

32. Greville, *Life*, pp. 105, 126, 2, 198, 98, 45.

33. Alan Sinfield, *Literature in Protestant England* (London, 1983), pp. 129, 134.

Chapter 5

Three Sidneys – Philip, Mary, and Robert

Philip Sidney

One of the most powerful myths of the period, one that has lasted to the present day, concerns the courtier, politician, and poet Sir Philip Sidney. Sidney is not the most prolific poet of the age, but his career and place in sixteenth-century culture are central to our understanding of the age and its poetry. He was, indeed, the focus of many myths. One we have alluded to while discussing Greville – the lost leader, whose tragic death signalled the death of Elizabethan idealism. Part of Sidney's fascination has been the ways both his own and succeeding ages have appropriated him: as the lost leader of the golden Elizabethan age to Greville and other Jacobeans, and later the Victorian gentleman, anguished Edwardian, committed existentialist, apolitical quietist, even (most recently) a member of the Moral Majority. Like all great writers, Sidney and his works have been continually rewritten by successive ages, his poems and his life alike inscribed into different literary, political, and cultural discourses. As recent scholars have become more attuned to both the linguistic and ideological complexity of Renaissance literature generally and to the new possibilities of reading it by means of contemporary critical methods, Sidney's writing has been seen, both in its seemingly replete presence and its symptomatic gaps and absences, as central to our understanding of Elizabethan poetry and culture. The 1970s and 1980s are seeing a major re-evaluation of Sidney.

How did Sidney's contemporaries see his poetry? In the words of one perceptive courtier, he was 'our English *Petrarke*' who 'often conforteth him selfe in his sonnets of Stella, though dispairing to attain his desire . . .'. Thus Sir John Harington in 1591, and generations of readers have similarly sighed and sympathized with Astrophil's tragi-comic enactment of 'poor Petrarch's long deceased woes' and have often likewise identified Astrophil with Sidney himself. The question of auto-biography will be discussed later on. As depicted in conventional literary history, *Astrophil and Stella* marks a poetical revolution no less than Wordsworth's *Lyrical Ballads* or Eliot's *The Waste Land*: a young, ambitious poet, brilliantly acting upon his impatience with the poetry he criticized in his poetic manifesto, the *Defence of Poesie*, to produce a masterpiece. 'Poetry almost have we none', he wrote, 'but that lyrical kind of songs and sonnets', which 'if I were a mistress, would never persuade me they were in love'.[1] His poems were written to remedy this situation. Typically, none of them were published in his lifetime; along with his other writings, they circulated among a small but important coterie of family and court acquaintances during the 1580s. Sidney's vocations were those of courtier, statesman, Protestant aristocrat, and patriot before that of a poet, yet his poetry was clearly a major commitment for him. Sidney's writings often served, as A. C. Hamilton argues, as the outlet for frustrated political ambition and forced inactivity.[2]

Sidney's major poetic work, *Astrophil and Stella*, marks the triumphant maturity of Elizabethan poetry and as well, the first full, belated but spectacular, adaptation of Petrarchanism to English aristocratic culture. It remains today one of the most moving, delightful, and provocative collections of love poems in the language, all the more powerful in its impact because of the variety of discourses that strain within it for articulation – erotic, poetic, political, religious, cultural. We may read it, as Harington did, as the articulation of thwarted, obsessive love; but it opens itself to much richer readings, which reinforce Sidney's position as the central literary and cultural figure in the English Renaissance before Shakespeare. Sidney is also important in our construction of a history of sixteenth-century poetry in that he was the central figure in what is termed the 'Sidney Circle', a loosely linked group of late-sixteenth-century courtiers, poets, divines, and educators who were dedicated, before and after his death, to his ideals for the reform of poetry and to the values of the Elizabethan Court. They included Philip's sister, Mary Sidney, Countess of Pembroke, and his younger brother, Robert, later Earl of Leicester; as well, the Circle at various times included such poets as Spenser, Dyer, Greville, Breton, Daniel, Fraunce, and Lok.

Sidney was educated to embrace an unusual degree of political, religious, and cultural responsibility. Both the *Defence* and *Astrophil and Stella* are manifestos not only of poetic commitments but of broader cultural practices. For Sidney, poetry and its social uses were inseparable. Like other Elizabethan court poets, Sidney's poetry is put into play within a structure of power, and it tries to carve out a discursive space under ideological pressures which attempted to control it. The Court was more than a visible institution for Sidney and his contemporaries: poetry was both an articulation of the power of the Court and a means of participating in that power. But where a poem like

Ralegh's 'Praisd Be Dianas Faire and Harmles Light' shows the Court contemplating its own idealized image and compelling allegiance, Sidney's poetry has a more uneasy relation to the Court's power. Although on the surface, his writing appears to embody in Terry Eagleton's words, a 'moment of ideological buoyancy, an achieved synthesis'[3] of courtly values, the significance of Sidney's position in the Court makes his poetry an unusually revealing instance of the struggles and tensions beneath the seemingly replete surface of Court and court poetry alike.

More than that of any of his contemporaries before Donne and Shakespeare, Sidney's poetry evokes a felt world of bustling activity, psychosocial pressure, and cultural demand – in short, both the everyday detail of court life and, beneath, the workings of power upon literary and historical discourse. In *Astrophil and Stella* the institutions that shape the poetry – the Court, its household arrangements, its religious and political controversies – are evoked in the tournaments (Sonnet 41), the gossip of 'curious wits' (Sonnet 23), and the 'courtly nymphs' (Sonnet 54). But what distinguishes Sidney's poetry is the forceful way more than just the glittering surface of the Court energizes it. Despite his posthumous reputation as the perfect Renaissance courtier, Sidney's public career was one of political disappointment and humiliation; he seems to have been increasingly torn between public duty and private desire, much in the way the hero of his sonnet sequence is. As Richard McCoy has shown, all of Sidney's works are permeated with the problem of authority and submission. Like himself, all his heroes (including Astrophil) are young, noble, well educated and well intentioned, but as they become aware of the complexities and ambiguities of the world, they become diverted or confused, and it is as if Sidney finds himself caught between compassion and condemnation of their activities.[4] In the *Arcadia*, Sidney attempted to solve in fiction many of the tensions he was beset with in his life, and *Astrophil and Stella* similarly served as an outlet for political and social frustration. In the romance, Sidney's narrative irresolution and (in the *Old Arcadia*) premature and repressive closure reveals deep and unsettling doubts. In the ambivalences and hesitations, the shifting distance between poet and character, the divided responses to intellectual and emotional demands in *Astrophil and Stella*, Sidney's ambivalent roles within the Court are similarly articulated. In the *Defence*, literature is depicted as a potent ideological instrument for inculcating those virtues appropriate to the class of which he is a spokesman, but inevitably it is the incomplete, uncertain, or dislocated work that is a sign that the writer is grasping to find expression for new emergent realities, dimly perceived but increasingly influential in the lived experience of his society.

What gives Sidney's life and poetry alike their particular caste is

Protestantism. An insistent piety continually challenges and contradicts the courtly values in Sidney's work, and also sets up contradictions in his life which helped to make him, politically at least, a failure. In his political career, Sidney was a hotheaded Protestant aristocrat; in his poetry, in A. C. Hamilton's phrase, Sidney is 'a Protestant English Petrarch'.[5] The development of Protestant poetry seen in the gospellers and slightly more sophisticated poets like Turberville, culminates in Sidney and his Circle. But although the members of Sidney Circle were, in Andrew Weiner's phrase, 'godly aristocrats',[6] actively promoting the Protestant cause in Europe and supporting the Calvinist reformers at home, none the less Sidney's Protestant poetic is much less overtly didactic. His ideological configuration is more a *bricolage*, an assemblage of different fragments, and it is that characteristic which makes him the central poet of the whole age. For, unlike his friend Fulke Greville, for whom a radical Protestant suspicion of metaphor and writing itself constantly undermines poetry's value, Sidney tries to hold together what in the *Defence* he terms man's 'erected wit' and 'infected will'.[7] As such, his poetic can be seen as central to the poetry of the whole century: intensifying its focus on intellectual contradictions, wanting to be both militantly Protestant and courtly. Indeed, what Sidney uniquely brought to the Petrarchan lyric was a self-conscious anxiety about the dislocation of courtly celebration and Protestant inwardness, between the persuasiveness of rhetoric and the self doubt of sinful man, between the insecurity of man's word and the absolute claims of God's Word.

The tension in Sidney's poetry between the courtly and the pious, between Calvin and Castiglione, disrupts *Astrophil and Stella* in rich and energetic ways and constitutes the basis for its varied and continuing appeal. Its contradictions open up the possibility of powerful and varied readings. Sidney's own theory sees poetry focusing on the reformation of the will, on praxis, and thus it is possible to read the poems as an *exemplum* of the perils of erotic love – in Alan Sinfield's words, of 'the errors of ungoverned passion'.[8] Sidney, by this reading, displays Astrophil deliberately rejecting virtue, and treating Stella as a deity in an open repudiation of Christian morality. Astrophil's cleverness consists of trying to avoid or repel the claims of reason and virtue, and the outcome of the sequence is the inevitable end of self-deception – or, in a popular current reading, self-realization by Astrophil and a determination to reform. The final sonnets, 107 and 108, are a crux in such a reading, and critics have even seen one of Sidney's earlier *Certain Sonnets* as the appropriate moralistic conclusion to the later collection:

Leave me ô Love, which reachest but to dust,
And thou my mind aspire to higher things:
Grow rich in that which never taken rust:
What ever fades, but fading pleasure brings.

But such a narrow closure emphasizes only one of the languages which are operating in *Astrophil and Stella*. The inwardness of the poems – not necessarily, it should be noted, their supposed autobiographical dimension, but their concern with Astrophil's self-conciousness, even self-centredness as lover, poet, courtier and, through Astrophil, with the 'self' we take on when we read – is a blend of Protestant and Petrarchan self-obsession. It is one which points to a distinctive late-sixteenth-century strain within the inherited vocabulary and rhetoric of the poet in his role in the Court, in particular between the pragmatic demands of the Court and the demand that poetry advance the cause of Protestantism. Sidney is at the centre of this battle, determined to follow his friend Hubert Languet's advice that his talents should be at the service of 'his country, and of all good men; since you are only the stewart of this gift, you will wrong Him who conferred such a great benefit on you if you prove to have abused it'.[9]

   Travelling in Europe, Sidney had discovered sophisticated Protestant Courts where poets, scholars, and musicians were encouraged more than they were in England. Shortly after his return, his sister Mary became the Countess of Pembroke and established at Wilton what one of her followers was to term a 'little Court',[10] dedicated, both before and after his death, to the renaissance of English courtly culture. We look back to Wilton and its earnest group of poets, theologians, and philosophers and see their dedication to the Sidneian ideals. What we can also see in the 'little Court' are the forces which, identified in the 1620s and 1630s, would challenge and eventually overwhelm the hegemony of the Court. In other words, in the very movement that was attempting to establish and glorify the domination of what were perceived as traditional courtly values lay the elements that were to challenge and shatter it. Even in Sidney's 'first and only work as a courtier-poet',[11] as A. C. Hamilton describes *The Lady of May* (1579), we can see Sidney's unease with his role as a court poet. It shows Sidney's unwillingness to be effaced in the traditional courtly manner; he asks for participation and discrimination from the Queen, but not for an authoritarian intervention. However, when at the end of the work's performance, she chooses the 'wrong' side of the argument, her intervention can be read as not only a rejection of the political argument Sidney is advancing on behalf of the Leicester Circle, but also of his attempt to assert a prophetic role for the court poet rather than the residual, essentially feudal, role of entertainer and panegyrist. Sidney's literary career was a frustrated attempt to realize a new role for the court poet, one based upon the integrity and responsibility of values which he was unable to embody in his public life, and which more and more he poured into his writing. His remark to the Earl of Leicester during the French marriage crisis that he was kept 'from the courte since my only service is speeche and that is stopped'[12] has wider application than to its occasion. It articulates a frustration towards the traditional subservience of poet to the Court, a stubborn insistence on forging a distinctive role for the poet.

Sidney has often been characterized as balancing opposite ideological, rhetorical, or vocational demands, holding together what Calvin termed a 'matching of contraries'.[13] In the *Defence* and *Astrophil and Stella* the elements of such a balance can certainly be found. Poetry is at once a fervent reaching for the sublime and yet bound inseparably with man's 'infected will', just as Astrophil is at once inspired by and degraded by his love for Stella. Throughout his writing, the claims of rhetoric and truth, humanism and piety, Calvin and Castiglione, make their claims on Sidney and it is clear that he wrestles to hold them together satisfactorily. But he did so in desire not in actuality – and perhaps his fascination for later ages and his centrality for understanding sixteenth-century poetry is grounded in such contradictions. 'Unresolved and continuing conflict', in Stephen Greenblatt's phrase, is a distinctive mark of Renaissance culture and Sidney's is a central place in that culture.[14]

Where we first see this *bricolage* of conflicting discourses in Sidney's poetry is in the versifications of the Psalms, started by him about 1579, and revised and completed by his sister the Countess of Pembroke after his death. The Sidney *Psalms* are the first post-Reformation religious lyrics that combine the rich emotional and spiritual life of Protestantism with the new rhetorical riches of the secular lyric. Even in Sidney's forty-three Psalms (generally inferior to those of his sister), contradictions are clearly seen. There are distinctive Protestant notes – a strong stress on election in Psalm 43, echoing Beza's and Calvin's glosses rather than the original text, for instance. Then there are other Psalms where a strain of courtly Neoplatonism is highlighted, notably in Psalm 8 which presents man as a privileged, glorious creation, 'attended' by God, an 'owner' of regal status and 'crowning honour'. Man emerges as a free and wondrous being, 'freely raunging within the zodiack of his owne wit', a phrase from the *Defence* in which Sidney typically juxtaposes, without integrating, the great contraries of his age.[15]

About the same time he was experimenting with the Psalms, Sidney was working over a variety of other poems – pastoral dialogues, songs, experiments in quantitative metres – which he inserted into the *Arcadia*, and a collection of miscellaneous love sonnets and songs. What we now know as the *Certain Sonnets* looks like many other collections of the 1560s and 1570s, based on the model provided by Tottel's *Miscellany* and working through the common mid-century poetic modes of blazons, songs, moralistic poems, and rhetorical experiments. But as Germaine Warkentin has pointed out, through the *Certain Sonnets* is emerging a new poetic – one based on the use of vividly dramatic voices, and one starting to exploit more fully than before in English poetry the psychology and eloquence of Petrarchanism. Out of the *Certain Sonnets* grew *Astrophil and Stella*. Sidney was tinkering with the earlier poems during 1581–82 and abandoned them the next summer to write what became the first major Petrarchan collection of the English Renaissance.[16]

This sequence of 108 sonnets and 11 songs anatomizes the love of a young, restless, self-conscious courtier, Astrophil, for a court lady, Stella. The collection's aim is set out in the opening sonnet where, he claims 'I sought fit words to paint the blackest face of woe/Studying inventions fine, her wits to entertaine.' We are taken into the familiar world of Petrarchan convention and cliché: Astrophil is the doubting, self-consciously aggressive lover, Stella the golden-haired, black-eyed, chaste, and (usually) distant, and (finally) unobtainable. The landscape is familiar – Hope and Absence, frustrated desire alleviated temporarily by writing, the beautiful woman with the icy heart who pitilessly resists siege and yet encourages her admirer, and the final misery of the lover who ends his plaints in anguish at her 'absent presence' (Sonnet 104). Earlier Petrarchan poets like Wyatt had tried to achieve urgency or conversational informality, but read as a whole, English poetry had not, since Chaucer, been distinguished by such continual conflict and energy in a concentrated, closely knit collection.

Modern critics, reacting against earlier impressionistic Romantic readers of the collection, have shown how the energy and variety of Sidney's poetry rest on a thorough exploitation of the riches of Renaissance rhetoric – through use of apostrophe, dialogue, irony, shifts in decorum, modulations of voice. To the humanist education he received at Shrewsbury School and Oxford, Sidney added a thorough study of continental and English poetry. It is seen especially in the various ways he tries to loosen the rhythmical movement of English line. By his familiarity with the conventional techniques of Renaissance love verse, which he parodies in Sonnets 6, 9, or 15, Sidney uses his poems as workshops to try to improve what he saw as the inadequacy of English poetry.

Above all, he tries continually to combine the demands of formal verse with an immediacy of idiom, providing a voice that will involve his reader in the often tortuous movements of his character's broodings, arguments, and self-deceptions. Especially notable is the lightness and wit with which even Astrophil's most tortured self-examination is presented. Parody and the continual exaggerated use of erotic or literary clichés and puns are obvious enough, but the whole sequence is characterized by a sophisticated playfulness – for instance the outrageous puns on 'touch' in Sonnet 9 leading to the self-pity (Astrophil's, not Sidney's) of the last line:

> The windows now through which this heav'nly guest
> Looks over the world, and can find nothing such,
> Which dare claime from those lights the name of best,
> Of touch they are that without touch doth touch,
> Which *Cupid's* selfe from Beautie's myne did draw:
> Of touch they are, and poore I am their straw.

The pun is on physical and emotional touching and the glossy black of Stella's eyes: 'touch' was a shiny black stone like coal which could attract by a kind of magnetism or static. The poor lover ('*poor* Astrophil' we are constantly tempted to say, laughingly) is helpless, and explodes into flame, like straw before a spark. Similarly sophisticated and yet often just plain fun are the tongue-in-cheek anguish of the sonnets on Cupid, or the usually delicate uproariousness of some of the erotic sonnets, in which Sidney invites his readers to share his enjoyment at the varied follies and complexities of human love. We laugh with him; we laugh at or are sympathetic with poor Astrophil.

But what of Stella? Does she share in the fun? We should not forget how firmly *Astrophil and Stella* is encoded within a male-dominated discourse. Stella is, like other Petrarchan mistresses, reduced to a disconnected set of characteristics, acknowledged only as she is manipulated by or impinges on her lover's conciousness. She is entirely the product of her poet-lover's desires. Sidney's sonnets provide a theatre of desire in which the man has all the active roles, and in which the woman is silent or merely iconic, most present when she refuses him or is absent. Astrophil does not want us – although it is arguable that Sidney might – to call into question the power of his anguish or the centrality of his struggles of conscience. Yet it seems legitimate to ask what Stella might reply to Astrophil's earnest self-regarding pleas for favour. Even if her replies are not in most of the poems (and where they are, as in Song 8, they are, we should note, reported to us through Astrophil's words), what might she say? Is her silence the repression of the character? Or is it, more directly, that of Sidney? Or of a whole cultural blindness that fixed women as objects of gaze and analysis within a discourse they did not invent and could not control? When we consider in these ways how the dynamics of Sidney's text function, once again what is found are literary and cultural texts that are interactive, their languages rewriting each other with continual contradictions.

An older criticism faced (or perhaps avoided) these issues by focusing on the biographical origins of the sequence. In part as an outcome of the Romantic valorization of poetry as the overflow of 'sincerity' or 'genuine' experience, earlier critics sentimentalized the obvious connections between Sidney's life and the fiction of Astrophil's love for Stella into a poetic *roman-à-clé*. Yet as Germaine Warkentin has pointed out, the story of Sidney's poems is common to many mid-century sonnet collections. Undoubtedly, Sidney plays with his readers' curiosity about some kind of identification between himself and Astrophil and between Stella and Lady Penelope Rich (née Devereux) for whom Sidney was once suggested as a husband. Sidney also builds into his sequence references to his career, to his father, contemporary politics, to his friends and – of most interest to the curious – to Lady Rich's name in two sonnets (24, 37) which were omitted from the first publication of the collection. But the relationship between Sidney and his characters and between the events of his life and those seemingly within his poems should not be simplified. Sinfield argues that 'the hints of Sidney in the poem' are made deliberately ambiguous by bringing the poet to the surface of the poems alongside and in a shifting relationship to the lover so that any desire to see Astrophil unambiguously 'as a fiction or as Sidney', or as 'a stable compound' of both 'is frustrated'.[17] And just as Sidney manages simultaneously to have much in common with Astrophil, be sympathetic with him, and yet to criticize or laugh at him, so the gap between Stella and the historical Lady Rich is even wider and always shifting – at best one can regard some of the references as sly or wistful fantasies. Whether Sidney and Lady Rich were sexually involved, *Astrophil and Stella* gives us no firm evidence on the subject.

As we saw in Chapter 3, one of the distinctive possibilities of Petrarchanism was to set the traditional debate on the nature of love in terms of what appeared to be a lover's psychology and was in fact a complex and subtle rhetoric. Part of the fascination Petrarch had for English poets in the late sixteenth century was a puzzlement about how Petrarchan conventions might fit 'real' experiences. Typically, Sidney's poems open themselves to many readings. Whether they are seen as a collection of discrete lyrics or whether we choose to read them as a sequence, thus allowing for connection, juxtaposition, or qualification, the poems in *Astrophil and Stella* focus our attention on the 'thrownness' of love – on the lover finding himself within a pre-existing structuring of experience, a 'race' that 'hath neither stop nor start' (23), one which continually disrupts his sense of a stable, controlling self. But the self that is put into question in *Astrophil and Stella* is not, or not primarily, that of Sidney.

We are dealing here with poems which require an unusually active involvement from their readers, and which produce meanings only within the changing encounters between poem and readers. The poet offers his poems to an audience of sympathetic listeners as a mirror less of his experiences than of theirs. Sidney's poems work upon their readers, suggesting, manipulating, but never compelling, meanings. As we have seen, the Petrarchan lyric is typically inaugural, requiring its completion in its audience's experiences and responses. The continual isolation of the 'I', especially as it is focused in Astrophil's obsession with the self, directs us continually to our own self-consciousness – literally so if the poems are read aloud, and *we* are forced to speak all the 'I's in a sonnet like 'Because I Breathe Not Love to Everie One'. What Rudenstine calls Sidney's style, 'the outward sign of a particular style of life',[18] refers less to Sidney than to his audiences. One such audience is other lover-poets: in Sonnet 6, for instance, where Astrophil distinguishes his own 'trembling voice' and the sincerity of his love from those of other lovers and so thereby provokes them to respond by praising their own mistress or talents. At times his suffering hero will ostensibly address another, rather special, named audience – 'I *Stella's* ears assayll, invade her eares', he says in Sonnet 61. Or he (or Sidney) will address a friend (as in Sonnet 14) or even, occasionally, himself (as in Sonnet 30). But always the most important audiences are the ones unnamed, those of us who, through the poems' history, will read them, meditate upon, and act out their drama. Such readers are addressed variously – as friends, fellow victims of love, or fellow poets. In Sonnet 28, such an audience is appealed to directly: 'You that with allegorie's curious frame,/Of other's children changelings use to make. . . .' Similarly the 'fooles' chided in Sonnet 104 constitute an audience outside, although (it is hoped) sympathetically open to, the conflicts the poem dramatizes.

Sonnet 37, one of the two 'Rich' sonnets, where references to Lord and Lady Rich seem to be directly made, is especially effective because of the witty complexity of its appeal to a multiplicity of audiences. It starts as a therapeutic exercise: 'My mouth doth water, and my breast doth swell' – a disease which, since we are invited to overhear, can be cured, oddly enough, only by being talked about to others. It next seems to become a personal confession – again, we should note, therapy witnessed – and then, in the final line, turns outward to an audience which knows, or now knows, or at least may have become curious about, the identification of Stella with Lady Rich. Could we imagine Penelope Devereux Rich herself in the original audience? Would she have been embarrassed or amused? Either would be possible – just as other listeners' and readers' reactions, and therefore their readings of the poem, could have varied from indignation to titillation, puzzlement to disapproval. We should even consider Sidney himself as part of such an audience. As with any writer, however, we invite him to *our* readings as a guest, not as a master of ceremonies: long before he purged himself on his death-bed of 'vanity' of 'my Lady Rich' which haunted his mind, he may well have become embarrassed by or disapproved of his own poems in ways that his enthusiastic readers ever since would politely, but firmly, reject.[19]

Another place where the inevitable diversity of a specifically courtly audience's involvement is requested can be seen in the series of questions in the sestet of Sonnet 31, 'With How Sad Steps, O Moon'. There the lover is displayed as being overwhelmed by passion, anguish, and self-division, so that an audience is invited implicitly to help him in his choice:

> Then ev'n of fellowship, ô Moone, tell me
> Is constant *Love* deem'd there but want of wit?
> Are Beauties there as proud as here they be?
> Do they above love to be lov'd, and yet
> Those Lovers scorne whom that *Love* doth possesse?
> Do they call *Vertue* there ungratefulnesse?

Interestingly enough, such questions may be seen as rhetorical only if, as indeed well we might be, we are sympathetic with Astrophil. But if we see Astrophil's self-obsessive melancholy as misguided, then we can enter into a different kind of discussion with the sonnets, responding to them as if we were in a debate on the nature of love's demands upon us. Indeed, within the courtly group among whom Sidney wrote, the poems must have variously tempted, seduced, stimulated, pleased, annoyed, even (we must admit) bored. The poems in *Astrophil and Stella* placed their original readers at the focal point of a network of traditionally learnt expectations and demands. They invited all their readers to bring their own experiences into the struggles and problems of Astrophil's woes, and to participate in the calculated, sophisticated poise and grace with which Sidney presents them. And whatever meanings they disclose now, they show us that they cannot be treated as texts that are complete and closed unless we ignore that they demand performance not passivity. To adapt some phrases of Barthes, Sidney's texts are not lines of words realizing a single message; they are 'multi-dimensional' spaces in which 'a variety of writings', including those of his readers, 'blend and clash'. We can enter the texts by any of several routes, none of which we are forced to accept as the authentic one – however strongly Astrophil, or even Sidney, may try to persuade us. As Barthes puts it, we enter 'a galaxy of signifiers, not a structure of signifieds'. We play within a ludic space, and the codes thereby mobilized will 'extend as far as the eye can reach, they are interminable', or at least will extend through the work's history.[20]

When we look, too, at Sidney's own delightfully self-conscious rhetoric, we can see how the stylistic strategies of *Astrophil and Stella* place inordinate emphasis on language that aims to open meanings in the reader's experience. One particularly successful feature is the exploitation of the gap between Astrophil's anguish or seriousness and Sidney's own enjoyment of his hero's fumbling enactment of 'poore *Petrarch's* long deceased woes' (Sonnet 15). Sonnet 5, 'It is most true, that eyes are form'd to serve/The inward light', conveys simultaneously a brooding, self-obsessive solemnity on Astrophil's part and a sympathetic though amused delight on Sidney's – a combination seen in the lightness of movement counterpointing the solemnity of Astrophil's slightly exaggerated argument. In Sonnet 10, likewise, we witness a sympathetic dramatization by Sidney of a struggle within Astrophil. As J. P. Castley notes, 'behind the straight face . . . behind the apparent self-depreciation' of such poems, 'the smile is all the time playing'.[21] The straight face is Astrophil's and in so far as we are lovers, we may sympathize or criticize; the smile is Sidney's and in so far as we respond to witty, sophisticated dramatizations of human emotional conflicts in subtle verse, we are probably delighted. In such poems, the more serious the philosophical brooding by the lover, the more it is undercut by the tone of the verse which looks out, almost with a wink, to the audience, inviting our amusement as well as our sympathy. At the end of Sonnet 57, for example, as Astrophil turns for sympathy to his audience, so Sidney turns to prompt *his* audience towards amusement at his hero's sufferings:

> A prety case! I hoped her to bring
>   To feele my griefes, and she with face and voice
>   So sweets my paines, that my paines me rejoyce.

Sonnet 20, 'Fly, Fly My Friends', is another obvious example where the sophisticated poise of the poet places him among his audience, watching, describing, and inviting discussion of (perhaps even disapproval of) his hero's antics and agonies. Such a process is encouraged even where the poem's speaker expresses a desire for privacy. The 'trembling voice' of Sonnet 6 which displays 'the Map' of Astrophil's 'state' is evoked in poetry that is hardly 'trembling'.

Sonnet 54, 'Because I Breathe Not Love to Everie One', is an especially interesting case. The poem starts as a monologue, articulating Astrophil's humble claim that nothing matters except that 'Stella know my mind'. An even more blatant (and marvellous) contradiction is the last line. Asserting 'I breathe not love to everie one', he none the less is heard by everyone – 'They love indeed, who quake to say they love.' Astrophil may, indeed, quake, but Sidney's brilliantly vivid rhetoric hardly quakes. Furthermore, between the poem's quiet opening and dignified (though amusing) conclusion, monologue has turned to drama, and we overhear the argument of the 'courtly nymphs' of Astrophil's audience with him:

> . . . acquainted with the mone
> Of them, who in their lips *Love's* standerd beare;
> 'What he?' say they of me, 'now I dare sweare,
> He cannot love: no, no, let him alone.'

When the poem turns outward, directly to the courtly nymphs themselves, we can imagine them as part of the original audience:

> Professe in deed I do not *Cupid's* art;
> But you faire maides, at length this true shall find,
> That his right badge is but worne in the hart.

This primary audience, the 'courtly nymphs', is rebuked – and then the poem turns from mocking them to a wider, more sympathetic, audience, which, of course, includes us. The result is that we become aware of a clear division between Sidney and his character – we sympathize with (or criticize) Astrophil in his silence, and we are delighted with Sidney in his eloquence. We become aware of ourselves as lovers of poetry and as lovers of love. Sidney's sonnets, in short, require us to respond – and in complex, unpredictable ways – to the viewpoints they provoke us to produce.

Astrophil and Stella is therefore what Barthes terms a playful text, i.e. one that depends strongly on its audience.[22] It invites our participation both to reproduce the process, intellectual and emotional, by which the poem's struggles come to be verbalized but also to go beyond them, adding our own. It has a capacity to invade us, to direct and inform our responses, but as well, to open us to an awareness that it functions only through a process of deliberate reciprocity. As readers or lovers or poets (or all three) we put ourselves at risk, inveigled as we may be into a state of sympathy and vulnerability by the text.

Scholars have often pointed to the cross-fertilization at the end of the sixteenth century between the lyric poem and the increasingly dominant literary form of the age, the drama. As Chapter 7 will suggest, Shakespeare's sonnets and Donne's *Songs and Sonets* are more frequently mentioned in this way, but *Astrophil and Stella* also has some claims to be seen as dramatic. Above all other literary forms, drama is open-ended, subject to misreading, to adaptation by directors, actors, or spectators. As Michael Goldman puts it, we are 'engaged' by a play through its 'unique emphasis on the body'. It may rise in the dramatist's imagination, 'but it takes place between two sets of bodies, ours and the actors'.[23] We respond, we debate, we walk out of the theatre with those responses and that debate in a real sense becoming a part of our changed and changing lives. Something of this open-endedness, the literary form as script, eliciting response and action, is shared by *Astrophil and Stella*. When we read Sidney's poems, we are encouraged not merely to consume them, but to enter them, as into a theatre where, in a sense, it is we who produce their meanings. Having read *Astrophil and Stella*, whether in Sidney's intimate circle of friends, relaxing at Wilton or Westminster, or in our classes, studies, or jetliners today we are fulfilling his desire for his own poems *only* if we integrate his skills and delight in his creation and Astrophil's woes with our own. To adapt another of Barthes's suggestive metaphors, Sidney's sonnets are a 'stereographic space'[24] where *scriptor* and reader are, equally, performers.

What then, of any attempt (like Harington's, or many modern critics) to see a definitive 'story' in *Astrophil and Stella*? Surveying the history of Sidney criticism, especially in the past forty years, one discovers a curious anxiety to find a coherent, sequential organization not merely made possible by the poems, but as a required means of reading them. *Astrophil and Stella* is thus often read as if it were a poetic novel. C. S. Lewis cautions against treating the Petrarchan sequence as if it were 'a way of telling a story'; *Astrophil and Stella* is, he says, 'not a love story but an anatomy of love'; Max Putzel speaks of the poems' 'careful disorder'; but on the other hand and more typically, A. C. Hamilton argues that the sonnets are organized into a sequence or 'one larger poem' with a unifying structure, and other critics have written of what they see as careful structure and sequence.[25] In Hamilton's scheme, Sonnets 1–12 form an introduction, 13–30 concentrate on Astrophil's isolation, with 41–68 concerned with his moral rebellion, 71–85 with his attempt at seduction, and the final poems with his failure. The songs serve especially well to highlight the wish-fulfilment of Astrophil's love – his frustration, his self-involvement, his wistful fantasies. Song 8 is especially moving in its culmination as Sidney cleverly breaks down the distance between narrator and character in the final line where he confesses that 'my' song is broken:

> Therewithall away she went,
> Leaving him so passion rent,
> With what she had done and spoken,
> That therewith my song is broken.

In the collection's later poems, if it is read according to this narrative structure, Astrophil's fantasies seem less and less realizable. His self-pity intensifies, occasional realism breaks in, and there is acceptance of the conventional Petrarchan stasis, vacillating between joy and pain, optimism and despair. As Hamilton points out, the mutability of human love, which haunts so many Elizabethan sonnet sequences, enters Sidney's only indirectly, but as the sequence ends, Astrophil is shown 'forever subject to love's tyranny, a victim of *chronos* forever caught in time's endless linear succession'. The melancholy hopelessness of the sequence's final lines points to the stasis of despair and hope finally and frustratingly balanced between woe and joy.[26] Such a narrative constructs *Astrophil and Stella* as a moral *exemplum*.

But other divisions have been proposed – and clearly for readers who wish to find a narrative development from the initial onset of love to a final (ir)resolution rather than read the poems as exercises in love's variety, then *Astrophil and Stella* is open to such a reading. Ann Rosalind Jones has argued that it is possible (and peculiarly satisfying) to see Astrophil as undergoing a gradual disintegration and loss of control. But Jones also points out that Sidney's sequence does not use the linking devices of other poets, like Dante or Scève, which might more strongly encourage a sequential reading of the collection. So that when and if we construct a sequence, it is necessarily selective or, if we insist on including all or most of the poems, it will necessarily be characterized by an unstable, eddy movement, 'dramatically *dis*ordered', as Jones argues. 'Even at the end of his experience', Astrophil 'can predict the course of his writing no better than the course of his love', and so each sonnet becomes a new starting-place. In short, while *Astrophil and Stella* allows for a linear development, it does not force one upon a reader and encourages us just as readily to view Astrophil's experience as unpredictable and random.[27]

So far, I have taken *Astrophil and Stella* pretty much at face value – as a collection of love poems. But bearing in mind the socio-cultural context for the period's poetry, a rewarding approach is to note how, though ostensibly about love, Sidney's poems are none the less traversed by a variety of overlapping and contradictory discourses – most particularly those of court politics and Protestant theology.

One recurring contradiction is between the demands of what the poems wish us to see as the 'public' world of political responsibility and the 'private' world of erotic desire. In many sonnets, Astrophil presents his love in terms of a debate between traditional abstractions like desire and reason, love and duty. Part of our enjoyment lies in our watching him, through Sidney's fond but penetrating perspective, indulging himself in false logic (52), or in seeing his dutifully constructed arguments against love undermined by the simple appearance of his beloved, as in Sonnets 5, 10, or in the amusing self-contradictions of Sonnet 47:

> Vertue awake, Beautie but beautie is,
> I may, I must, I can, I will, I do
> Leave following that, which it is gaine to misse.
> Let her go. Soft, but here she comes. Go to,
> Unkind, I love you not: O me, that eye
> Doth make my heart give to my tongue the lie.

A major source of the confusion (and our enjoyment) is Sidney's placing Astrophil's internal struggles in the context of his public responsibility. The 'curious wits' (Sonnet 23) of the Court speculate on his 'dull pensiveness' or praise him for what he attributes to Stella's inspiration (Sonnet 41). Astrophil tries in vain to keep his two worlds and their discursive demands separate. He claims that love gives him a private place, a stable sense of self beside which the demands of courtly responsibility are shown to be trivial but, caught between conflicting worlds of self-indulgence and political responsibility, he ends by succeeding in neither. In some sonnets (or if we construct one of a number of narratives) we watch him corrupting his avowedly pure love into sensuality by the deviousness of political rhetoric. In Sonnet 23, he appears to reject the world; but in Sonnet 69, he expresses Stella's conditional encouragement of his advances in terms of the Court's own language. Since, he argues, she has 'of her high heart giv'n' him 'the monarchie', as king he too can take some advantage from that power:

> . . . though she give but thus conditionally
> This realme of blisse, while vertuous course I take,
> No kings be crown'd, but they some covenants make.

The traditional formula by which the man is subjected to his lady while at the same time the situation gives him the autonomy and power to try to seduce her is, not coincidentally, homologous with the relationship between the courtier and monarch. Both are built on a structure of absolute loyalty and subjection, frustration and rejection, and are interlaced with devious manipulations for the favours of the capricious, distant beloved. Thus while Astrophil speaks of the 'joy' inspired by Stella and of his own 'noble fire', he is attempting to manipulate Stella's vulnerability, seeking power over her in the way the devious courtier seeks hidden but real power over the monarch. In terms of the sexual politics of the Renaissance Court, Astrophil's world is one shared primarily by other male courtiers in relation to the monarch. Thus we watch Astrophil indulging himself in small but subtle ways. He continually twists Stella's words; he speaks openly of his love, but offhandedly and half-seriously, allowing (or being unable to prevent) the emergence of the underlying physicality of his desires in a series of fantasies of seduction. He professes great, unselfish devotion. He argues his love transcends any base motive; it is a private world of high ideals. But while Astrophil claims his love is independent of and superior to the public world, such an antithesis is self-deceiving. At the root of Astrophil's self-deception is the contradictions of Petrarchanism in the whole of the Court's life. As we have seen, it is at once a literary convention and a very serious courtly game, in which three powerful cultural discourses interact – love, religion, and politics.

Ann Jones and Peter Stallybrass have shown, indeed, that the compliments and manipulations Astrophil performs are curiously like those 'necessary to the new courtier in relation to his prince', and further down the social system, the poet in relation to patron. They demonstrate how these homologies between lover and beloved, suitor and patron, courtier and prince, shape both 'private' and 'public' texts alike. The courtier, like the lover, waits, hopelessly, using whatever devious means he can command to shape the responses of the capricious prince. The 'game' of Petrarchan love, the dangers of which we saw coming tentatively to the surface in Dunbar and Wyatt, was by the late sixteenth century, a powerful and acknowledged dimension of court life, as Ralegh's career, which we glanced at in Chapter 4, is a poignant reminder.[28]

If the structures of court politics dislocate the erotic titillation of *Astrophil and Stella*, so too do the demands of Sidney's deep commitment to Protestantism. As Sinfield puts it, 'the protestant humanist who felt the force of protestant doctrine as well as the imaginative excitement of literature was sited at the crisis point of a sharp and persistent cultural dislocation'.[29] Throughout *Astrophil and Stella*, Protestant theology constantly judges the ebullience and self-indulgence of Sidney's hero. Yet the results are never firmly settled. In Sonnet 5, three quatrains firmly put the Protestant rejection of self-obsessive erotic love, concluding that '[It is most] true, that on earth we are but pilgrims made.' And then, in a final (dismissive or plaintive?) line comes Astrophil's rejoinder: 'True; and yet true that I must Stella love.' As Sinfield comments: 'Either truculently or regretfully, Astrophil rejects all the assumptions'[30] of Protestantism. And yet while Sidney might invite criticism of Astrophil, he does not require it. Such poems – Sonnet 71, with its wonderfully poignant final line, '"But ah", Desire still cries, "give me some food"' is an especially interesting case – leave the reader balanced between the conflicting discourses of erotic love and Protestant theology.

It has recently become fashionable to see Sidney's poems as condemning Astrophil, even to see him by the end of the sequence learning from his moral errors. It is a reading that wishes, perhaps, to see 'Leave me ô love, which reachest but to dust', from *Certain Sonnets*, as a satisfactory conclusion to the collection. Hamilton's reading of the final *Astrophil and Stella* sonnets, 107 and 108, also insists on Sidney's desire to 'resolve the whole poem'.[31] But – apart from the oddity of seeing the sonnets as a 'whole poem' – we might consider: why is closure so necessary? The Petrarchan situation is built precisely on the power of a lack of closure, on the perpetual deference of desire's consummation. The Protestant insistence on moral criticism and therefore on narrative closure certainly feeds into the collection but it does not dominate it, nor does it reduce it to a kind of moral tract, as some modern readers seem to want. Sidney is almost in danger of being co-opted by the Moral Majority in some recent criticism (even though such a reading of Sidney does have a precedent in Fulke Greville's). But while Greville might well have liked to have seen his friend's poems in such a light, it is obvious from *Caelica* that it was because he saw *Astrophil and Stella* as potentially highly subversive of sound Protestant doctrine. Unless a modern reader shares such religious beliefs, it is the more open reading that most of us will prefer.

Astrophil and Stella, then, is a quintessential site of cultural conflict where a variety of discourses, including the reader's own, struggle for mastery. We should not see Sidney any more than any other poet, in 'control' of the discursive structures that speak through him. Astrophil may state that all his 'deed' is to 'copy' what in Stella 'Nature writes' (3), or assert that 'Stella' is, literally, the principle of love in the cosmos (28), or that the words he utters 'do well set forth my mind' (44), but Sidney knows, as we all do, that love and its significances and its relation to our words are far more complex matters. In love and poetry alike we are only partly in control of languages and logics we did not create and into which we find ourselves – sometimes painfully, sometimes hilariously – inserted.

Mary Sidney, Countess of Pembroke

In 1577 Mary Sidney married Henry, second Earl of Pembroke, and her home at Wilton became for some twenty years the centre of Sidney's attempt to give direction to Elizabethan high culture. Growing from informal gatherings of Sidney's friends and admirers at Wilton and elsewhere, after Sidney's death the Circle became centred on the Countess's attempt to continue her brother's ideals. Within the work of the Circle, its achievements and limitations alike, we can see a mixture of both residual and emergent cultural forms and practices, some of which look nostalgically back to medieval chivalric ideals and courtly practices, while others are struggling to articulate the emergent values· by which a new phase of English culture was taking shape.

One reason for the relative neglect, until recently, of the sixteenth century's most significant woman poet was simply that she was Sir Philip Sidney's sister. Mary Sidney, later Countess of Pembroke, was a distinguished patron of poetry, a fine poet herself, but above all, in her own eyes, she was a Sidney. She devoted most of her adult life to forwarding her brother's cultural ideals and, particularly, after his death, his hopes for the advancement of poetry. It was to his sister that Philip entrusted many of his manuscripts and it was she who oversaw the issuing, twelve years after his death, of an authorized edition of his works. During the last twenty years of the century, Wilton became a kind of salon to which many late Elizabethan intellectuals and poets came.

Nicholas Breton spoke of Wilton as 'a kinde of little Court' and compared it with Castiglione's Urbino, asking 'who hathe redde of the Duchesse of Urbina, may saie, the Italians wrote wel: but who knowes the Countesse of Pembroke, I think hath cause to write better'. He also calls attention – as did other commentators – to one feature of Wilton that differentiated it from Urbino: it was a place of piety and theological learning. In his devotional poems, *The Countesse of Pembrookes Love* and *The Passions of the Spirit*, Mary is depicted meditating at Wilton, 'a plot of earthly paradise' and visited by a procession of courtiers, divines, and poets. What Breton's slightly sentimentalized picture of Wilton suggests is borne out by other authorities. Wilton House became one of the Leicester–Sidney Circle's centres of power. On the other hand, Abraham Fraunce has left us a lighter, though still reverent, view of life at Wilton in *The Countesse of Pembrokes Ivychurch* where the 'peereless Pembrokiana', the damsels attending her, and the pastoral sports and hunting in Ivychurch, one of the family's properties near Wilton, are amusingly described.[32] Once again, we see the contradictions of the age brought together: courtliness and piety, Castiglione and Calvin. The 'little Court', set deep in the country, became in part a retreat from the corruption and insecurities of the Court of Elizabeth, and partly, deliberately, a powerhouse for the Sidneys' attempt to manipulate the direction of literary and wider cultural change. Most immediately it became the centre of the Countess's determination to find a wider audience for her brother's writings.

Over a period of a dozen years, the Countess undertook to edit and, with some reluctance, publish her brother's works. She argued with Greville over the nature and intentions of the *Arcadia*. She approved a corrected version of *Astrophil and Stella* after Thomas Newman had published, with a preface by Thomas Nashe, an extremely corrupt, pirated edition (1591). She added an approved edition of the *Defence* (first published separately in 1595) to the 1598 edition of Sidney's *Works*. It is this edition of 1598 which represents one part of the culmination of her supervision of her brother's writings.

Another is her own poetry. There is little evidence that Mary herself had written poetry of any substance or quantity before 1586 and she probably taught herself to write by closely following her brother's models and rules, then cautiously and with increasing confidence discovered her own literary talents. But in the next fifteen to twenty years she developed into a significant poet – in particular into the age's most important woman poet.

There are four categories of the Countess's writings: three original poems directly associated with her brother, an elegy and two poems dedicating the completed versification of the Psalms to the Queen and the memory of Philip; the *Psalms*; three translations from French and Italian, including the magnificent version of Petrarch's poem *Trionfo della Morte* in English *terza rima*; and a small handful of other poems.

We have no clear evidence of how soon after Philip's death the Countess contemplated writing her own direct tribute in verse to her brother. She seems to have immediately undertaken completing and improving upon his versification of the Psalms and, judging by the works for which we do have definite dates, she must have worked more or less simultaneously on a number of literary projects. Probably the earliest of the three poems she wrote to her brother's memory is the so-called 'Doleful Lay of Clorinda', published with Spenser's *Astrophel* in *The Ruines of Time*, but almost certainly written by the Countess.[33] The 'Lay', with its strange mixture of personal intensity, solid metrical competence, much flat padding, and tangled syntax, reads like the work of a competent amateur. Two other poems, written to Philip's memory, are a dedicatory poem addressed to the Queen, and another signed 'By the Sister of that incomparable Sidney', and entitled 'To the Angell Spirit of the most excellent Sir Philip Sidney'. The latter poem is especially interesting for the way the conventional *encomium* is interrupted by stanzas of private grief and dedication. Other poems written about the same time include a verse translation of Robert Garnier's *Antonie* and a pastoral dialogue 'between two shepherds, Thenot and Piers, in praise of Astrea', which was published in Francis Davison's court miscellany, *A Poetical Rhapsody*.

Of these poems, the *Triumph* deserves most attention here. Petrarch's *Trionfi* has been termed 'the most triumphant poem of the early Renaissance'.[34] For more than a century the reputation of the work outshone both that of the *Divine Comedy* and Petrarch's own lyrics, and in the mid sixteenth century, it was so popular Roger Ascham bewailed that Englishmen revered the *Trionfi* above *Genesis*. The separate poems that make up the work were written during Petrarch's period of exile in the 1340s and 1350, and were published first in 1470. Thenceforth it went into numerous editions, either singly or as part of collected editions of Petrarch's *Rime*.

Building upon the precedents of Dante's *Purgatorio, XXIX* (the meeting with Beatrice) and Boccaccio's *Amora Visione*, Petrarch's work is a series of dream visions portraying the successive triumphs of Love, Chastity, Death, Fame, Time, and Eternity. It is a solemn, learned, and at times moving, work especially in the *Trionfo della Morte* itself. In particular, there is a deeply poignant evocation of Laura who at last admits her long and faithful love for her poet. The combination of high romantic love and the *ubi sunt* theme seemingly appealed strongly to the Countess. It reflects, one might speculate, her own deeply idealized love for her brother, the impossibility of its consummation, and the realization that his poetic inspiration for her is the only real and lasting fruit of her love.

Earlier translations (by Thomas Morley and William Fowler) are clumsy and wordy; Mary Sidney's is undoubtedly the finest rendition into English of any part of the work before Ernest Hatch Wilkin's modern version, and the only one to reproduce Petrarch's *terza rima* in English. The most outstanding technical feature of the Countess's translation is her reproducing Petrarch's original stanzaic pattern: Petrarch's poem is written in *terza rima*, where the middle line of one stanza rhymes with the outer lines of the next tercet, – aba, bcb, cdc, etc. In the Countess's version, each of Petrarch's *terzine* is, almost without exception, rendered by an equivalent in English, yet as D. G. Rees remarks, 'in spite of this close adherence to her originals she succeeds in maintaining that fluency and naturalness which verse translations often lack'.[35] It is a remarkable performance. She shows constant ingenuity in changing the original eleven-syllable line into English iambic decasyllables and her determined practice to adhere closely to the original is remarkably successful, demonstrating that she had both an acute ear for the movement and tone of both the English poetical line and that of her original, and a consistent grasp of the high emotional level required. Her version is also remarkably succinct and there are few errors of translation. At the poem's great moments of idealized passion and elevated suffering, the Countess's version is especially impressive. The opening with its delicate vowels and stately movement is typical of her reading of the poem as a courtly pageant, and an allegorical revelation of the power of passion before the threat of death:

> That gallant Ladie, gloriouslie bright,
>   The statelie piller once of worthinesse,
>   And now a little dust, a naked spright:
> Turn'd from hir warres a joyefull Conqueresse.
>   Hir warres, where she had foyl'd the mightie foe,
>   whose wylie stratagems the world distresse,
>   And foyl'd him, not with sword, with speare or bowe,
>   But with chaste heart, faire visage, upright thought,
>   wise speache, which did with honor linked goe.[36]
>
>   (I, 1–9)

The grim description of Death, 'stealing on with unexpected wound', the praise of Laura, her voice 'repleate with Angell-lyke delight' (I, 44, 150), and the formal sombreness of the poem's conclusion all stand out as superbly evoked in image and tone, the more remarkable because of the tightness of form. Where the Countess does expand images or phrases, she consistently makes her original more concrete. 'In Petrarch's original', it has been suggested, in perhaps something of an overstatement, 'despite its eloquence and nobility, one feels at times that the language is a little vague, a little stylised. The poetic tool seems to have become a shade worn and blunted. Lady Pembroke seems to refurbish it and give it a new edge.'[37] She certainly uses vigorously active verbs and constantly ringing epithets. Some of Sidney's favourite devices occur: a liking for double epithets – 'never-numbred summe' (I, 74), 'devoutlie-fixed' (II, 40), 'sadlie-uttered' (II, 54), the frequent employment of simple and emotionally direct questions or statements. The emotions evoked in the *Triumph* are strong and passionate, and the poem's style is appropriately elevated and energetic. It is a triumph of tightly controlled, evocative verse, mixing passionate sorrow and celebratory affirmation, rising to the final culmination of Laura's farewell to the poet – and perhaps expressive of Mary's own farewell to her brother:

> Ladie (quoth I) your words most sweetlie kinde
> Have easie made, what ever erst I bare,
> But what is left of yow to live behinde.
> Therfore to know this, my onelie care,
> If sloe or swift shall com our meeting-daye.
> She parting saide, As my conjectures are,
> Thow without me long time on earth shalt staie.
>
>   (II, 184–90)

The most substantial expression of Mary Sidney's dedication to her brother is found in the *Psalms*, which were her works best known to contemporaries and which kept her reputation alive during the thirty or forty years after her brother's death. The 'Sidnean Psalmes', as John Donne called these poems,[38] were in fact mainly composed by the Countess. Sidney had translated Psalms 1–43; she revised his versions and then finished the remainder herself. She was, however, not merely content with a mere literal versification. From the manuscripts we can see the Countess feeling her way into the demands of both Psalm metaphrase and very basic matters of tone and texture. In taking the task of completing his versions upon herself the Countess also took up the problem of learning the sweat and grind of actual composition, the search for apt metaphor, flexible versification, and appropriate tone. She had her models – of positive and negative kinds – in other metrical versions. Her most important precedent was nevertheless the fertility of rhetorical and formal inventiveness and above all the grasp of appropriate tone shown in her brother's poetry. The metrical, stanzaic, and tonal variety of her Psalms is more a tribute to the inspiration of *Astrophil and Stella* than to earlier Psalters. By the late 1580s she had her own group of poetic protégés with whom she shared her problems: Daniel was with her between 1585 and 1587, actively encouraged by her; Fraunce was experimenting with some of the Psalms himself by 1588; and Breton's religious lyrics also date from the late 1580s and early 1590s.

But we should not overemphasize the group nature of her poetical experiments. Evidence for that is scanty and partly based on the remarks of writers anxious to be associated with her. So far as her poetry is concerned, the real work came in her own mulling over her brother's manuscript, altering his text not merely from perversity but from a constant desire to practise the rudiments of verse construction and, eventually, to bring what was obviously an unfinished manuscript entrusted to her to a stage of fuller completion. She was dissatisfied with Sidney's awkward phrasing at certain points; she removed irregular stanzas, smoothed rhymes and metres. She is usually especially adept at evoking a tone of joy or celebration (as in the opening of Psalm 81), and at changing moods of dramatically breaking up the syntax. She seems, in Rathmell's words, 'to have *meditated* on the text before her, and the force of her version derives from her sense of personal involvement . . . it is her capacity to appreciate the underlying meaning that vivifies her poems'.[39] Usually, if not exclusively, it is the 'underlying meaning' that she is concerned to evoke. She has an especial preference for the sharply ironical or paradoxical, and on occasions her verse can resemble that of Greville or Ralegh in its terseness of tone or sparseness of illusion. In other Psalms, her rhetoric can be elaborate and rich. To Psalm 148. 8–12, she adds a picture, typical of the most serene of Elizabethan cosmological thought, of the universe moving mysteriously at God's command in a complex, courtly dance:

O praise him Sunne, the sea of light,
O praise him Moone, the light of sea:
You preaty starrs in robe of night,
As spangles twinckling do as they.
Thou spheare within whose bosom play
The rest that earth emball:
You waters banck'd with starry bay,
O praise, O praise him all.

A particularly delightful 'courtly' addition to the religious original is Psalm 45, where a marriage ceremony is alive with the swirl of robes and dancing:

This Queene that can a king her father call,
Doth only shee in upper garment shine?
Naie under clothes, and what she weareth all,
Golde is the stuffe, the fasshion Arte divine;
Brought to the king in robe imbrodied fine. . . .

In these lines the religious allegory which Protestant commentators brought out in the Psalm is allied with a sensual description of courtly fashion – courtliness and Protestantism, Castiglione and Calvin, are brought together.

Although, as with most lengthy collections of poems, the quality of the *Psalms* varies greatly, at their best the Countess's Psalms, even more than Sidney's, display a remarkable intensity of poetic evocation, formal inventiveness, and intellectual subtlety. They constitute a landmark in the development of the English religious lyric. In Rathmell's words, 'when recognition is accorded to the Sidney psalter the history of the metaphysical revival of our time will have to be rewritten'.[40] They are as important a part of the late Elizabethan literary revolution as the *Shepheardes Calender* and *Astrophil and Stella*.

In looking at *Astrophil and Stella* we noted how its poems became the site of conflicting religious and political discourses. The Sidney *Psalms* are religious verse, but they are no less striated by contradictions. In general, the Countess's translations stay close to the Calvinist Geneva Bible, and there are even Psalms where her version intensifies the Protestant emphasis, sometimes taking up a suggestion from Calvin or Beza. But there are also examples where the intention of Protestant orthodoxy is undermined by a contrary position – where Castiglione, to return to my earlier distinction, contradicts Calvin. In many cases, these intellectual contraries reflect contrasting intellectual drives in the originals that more dogmatic translations smooth out; but as well, they often bring out the recurring intellectual dislocations of the Countess and the whole Sidney Circle. Most interesting are those Psalms where

Sidney imported not only the rhetorical vigour and flexibility of the court lyric, but also some of the sophisticated courtly philosophy that the secular lyric served to express. One example I have already noted is Sidney's version of Psalm 8, a paeon to the glorious creation of Man which worried the Geneva Bible translators so much that it notes that God had no need to come 'so low as to man, which is but dust'. It is especially uneasy on the Psalm's stress on the 'crowning' of man which is glossed as only 'touching his first creation'. Calvin is in even more difficulties. First of all, he disapproves of the Psalm's rhetorical extravagance – God, he comments on Psalm 8. 3, has no great need of great rhetoricians, but merely of distinct speech. He then argues that the Psalm stresses the miseries of man, 'this miserable and vyle creature', and comments 'it is a wonder that the creator of Heaven submitteth himselfe so lowe, as to vowtsafe too take uppon him the care of mankind'. Such a conjunction of divine grace and what Calvin sees as the depravity of man evidently worries him; he describes it tellingly, once again, as 'this matching of contraries'.

The Sidneys' version, certainly, has the appropriate Protestant wonder that man, a fallen creature, should be thus elevated by God, but at the same time there is a note of glorification that obviously reflects the sophisticated courtliness of the Elizabethan aristocrat:

> Then thinck I: Ah, what is this man
>> Whom that greate God remember can?
>> And what the race, of him descended,
>> It should be ought of God attended?
> For though in lesse than Angells state
>> Thou planted hast this earthly mate;
>> Yet hast thou made ev'n hym an owner
>> Of glorious crown, and crowning honor.

Courtly philosophy here is juxtaposed with Calvinist theology. With the celebration of man's creative autonomy the Calvinist view of man as a sinful and limited being is contradicted. As so often seems to be the case with all the Sidneys' poetry, the great intellectual contraries of the age interact and rewrite one another in the tissue of the Psalms.

Robert Sidney

The third of the Sidney poets is the younger brother, Robert. Unlike his more famous brother and sister, Robert was not a prolific writer. His career as a poet was probably confined to a few years, possibly as few as two. But the rediscovery of the manuscript of Robert Sidney's poems during the 1970s has added an important voice to the court poets of the late sixteenth century. In his manuscript's ninety pages of nervous, often corrected, handwriting are the works of a poet of outstanding interest for our understanding of the dynamics of the century's poetry.

The place of poetry in Robert's career is typical of most Elizabethan courtiers. Although references to the literary interests of all the Sidneys are found in many dedications, letters, and prefaces of the period, there are few if any references to him, specifically, as a poet. In 'To Penshurst' Jonson speaks of how Sidney's children

> . . . may, every day,
> Reade, in their vertuous parents noble parts,
> The mysteries of manners, armes, and arts

which, at the very least, is ambiguous. In 1609, Chapman wrote of him as 'the most Learned and Noble Concluder of the Warres Art, and the Muses'. There is a tradition that he wrote the lyrics for his godson Robert Dowland's *Musicall Banquet*, and he may have written verses in honour of his daughter's marriage. Certainly, like the rest of his family, Robert was widely praised as a generous patron of literature, and it is significant that the distinctive note of the other Sidneys' encouragement of poets was that they were poets themselves. 'Gentle *Sir Philip Sidney*', wrote Thomas Nashe, 'thou knewest what belonged to a schollar, thou knewest what paines, what toyle, what travel, conduct to perfection' – and clearly, now, the same can be said of Robert.[41] As with Mary, Robert's poetic career may have started seriously only after Philip's death.

During his life and after, Robert was overshadowed by the brilliance of his elder brother. In his early life, Robert had none of Philip's prestige or flamboyance. He dutifully went on a tour of Europe, pursued by letters of advice from his brother as to his reading, chivalric bearing, acquaintances, and finances. In 1585 he accompanied Philip, who had been appointed governor of Flushing, to the Low Countries, and was present at the Battle of Zutphen where Philip was mortally wounded. In short, Robert had undergone the usual initiation of the Elizabethan courtier – with the additional burden of being the younger brother of the mercurial Protestant knight so admired by European Protestants, statesmen, courtiers, and men of letters. In 1584, he married Barbara Gamage, a young Welsh heiress – after some rather sordid negotiations. Their letters later show them to have grown into a most loving couple. He constantly addresses her as 'sweet heart' or 'dear heart' and the letters are full of sadness of his absence from her. In 1594 he wrote 'there is no desyre in me so dear as the love I bear you and our children . . . you are married, my dear Barbara, to a husband that is now drawn so into the world and the actions of yt as there is no way to retire myself without trying fortune further'.[42]

The intense strain of being an honest courtier during the 1590s is evident throughout his letters. Indeed, we might say with a little (obvious) exaggeration that Philip had the good fortune to die in 1586; Robert had to live on. In 1587, he was his brother's chief mourner and like his sister Mary, may have turned to poetry as a similar, although less public, attempt to continue his brother's intentions for poetry. He may have decided that Mary, more permanently settled at Wilton in the 1580s with the increasing comings and goings of Greville, Spenser, Daniel, and other poets, was better placed to forward the Sidneian literary revolution. It is to her that he sent the one extant copy of his manuscript, possibly in one of his much anticipated but infrequent visits to England.

The obvious comparisons we should first make are, then, between Robert's poetry and that written by Philip and Mary. Like his brother's, Robert's poems take the form of a Petrarchan miscellany of sonnets and songs, although they show a greater variety of metrical and stanzaic patterns than the normal sonnet sequence of the 1580s and 1590s – and this is a characteristic he may have derived from Mary, whose *Psalms* involve the most impressive formal experimentation in English verse before Hopkins. Robert's are technically less ambitious, but they certainly reflect a similar interest in working with a variety of complex patterns of verse – as evidenced by the three unusual thirteen-line stanzas of 'Upon a Wretch That Wastes Away'. Here the complex rhyme scheme (aaab cccb ddeeb) and the varying line length (8886888633666 syllables) are reminiscent of the Countess's experiments, although none of Robert's patterns exactly matches any of hers, and his diction is naturally closer to the typical love poetry of the era (such as in *England's Helicon*) than to her *Psalms*. But they are born out of the same fascination with formal experimentation: just as in Mary's *Psalms* only once is the stanzaic pattern repeated, so in Robert's twenty-four songs he never repeats a pattern, and within particular poems, too, there is displayed a technical virtuosity comparable with his brother's and sister's: Song 1, 'O Eyes, O Lights Divine', for instance, skilfully mixes lines of varied length, with a predominantly iambic beat. Like both Philip and Mary, Robert uses feminine rhyme effectively in the songs (as in Song 10, 'You Who Favour Do Enjoy'), and his technical skill is seen in such sophisticated mixtures as the blending of rhyming anapaests with the regular iambics in Song 4 ('My soul in purest fire/Doth not aspire'). Like Mary, Robert shows an excellent control of movement and balance within single lines, as for instance in the final lines of Sonnet 21:

Or if on me from my fair heaven are seen
Some scattered beams – know such heat gives their light
As frosty morning's sun, as moonshine night.[43]

If Robert shares something of Mary's technical daring, nevertheless the most important influence is that of his brother. The sequence is clearly modelled on *Astrophil and Stella*: it mingles sonnets with longer, more emotionally diffuse songs, and like Philip's, Robert's sequence contains occasional transformations of biographical reference into devious fictions. The whole sequence is characterized by an opaque melancholy, a mood of disturbance and brooding which, while endemic to Petrarchan sonnets in general, nevertheless takes as its subject Robert's reading of his own political and personal career. But while the collection is a typical Petrarchan miscellany, it is united even less than *Astrophil and Stella* by narrative or characters; it is rather brought into play and held together, more explicitly than in any other collection of late Elizabethan lyrics, by the ideology of the Court.

When we set Robert's poems alongside *Astrophil and Stella* what can we discover? He does not possess Philip's dazzling control of changing dramatic mood within a poem: the emotions of his verse express themselves in broader sweeps, concentrating on generalized feelings about pain, disillusion, absence, and death. But his ear is highly sensitive, his poems reverberate with deep, sensuous moods. Perhaps the closest parallel is with a poet whose work we looked at in Chapter 4 – one who often (literally) just dropped his poems into ladies' pockets and who also never collected his verse, Sir Walter Ralegh. For both of them, poetry may have made up a small part of their lives, though their commitment to its craft and insight was intense. Like Ralegh's too, the strengths of Robert Sidney's poems lie in the ways their broodings over the great commonplaces of Elizabethan life and literature – time, absence, grief, deprivation – reveal much of the pressures upon poetry by its place in the ideology of the Court. The comparison is perhaps particularly apt because one of the most powerful poems of each poet was based upon the old Walsingham ballad (a version of which Ophelia sings in *Hamlet*) and while Ralegh's is tighter and more evocative in its rich, almost indefinable melancholy, Robert's is more personal, the emotions more diffuse yet no less keenly communicated. Both are poems by men who brooded with intensity over the experiences with which their poems attempted to deal; both, perhaps, turned to poetry occasionally as an escape from the world's pressures; and both found in it a commitment that went beyond mere emotional solace. Most interesting of all, both collections of poems reveal more than their authors recognized the ideological power of the Elizabethan Court upon those who struggled for articulation within its frantic centre or (in Robert's case) on its anxious margins.

Having looked at the affinities between Robert's poetry and that of his better-known brother and sister, let us look at it, then, in the context of the sixteenth century and, especially, the late Elizabethan Court. His poetry, like Ralegh's, is spoken *by* rather than just *for* or *in* the Court. Robert's poetry was probably written during his long, frustrating tour of duty in the Low Countries, perhaps started (like Mary's) in the late 1580s, but (at least in the one copy extant) copied probably at some time between 1596 and 1598. Perhaps turning to poetry was a reaction not only to his depressing exile from England, but to the melancholy duty of following in his brother's old post. It is possible that having used verse as an emotional relief, it lost its psychological and cultural functions for him once he had hopes of returning, and eventually did actually return, to England. Much of Robert's verse could therefore be read as a moving expression of a frustrated politician's escape-world, yearning for his wife and children and home at Penshurst, although in terms the significance of which he could only perhaps partly grasp.

But in tracing the 'poetical text' as a mediation of the 'social text', a merely biographical explanation of these poems would be to over-simplify them. Sidney's life is relevant as one typical of the late Elizabethan courtiers and courtly poets. With any newly discovered poet, it is perhaps inevitable that we will at first want to set the texts of life and poetry alongside each other. Criticism of his work to date (which after all dates only from the mid 1970s) has been predominantly of this kind. But as we have seen with other poets, Robert Sidney's verse is haunted by many pre-texts, subtexts (and post-texts) which call into question any naive biographical reading. Like Ralegh's or his brother's, Robert Sidney's poems are sites of struggle where the 'self' of the poems is a cultural creation not to be simply identified with the historical figure who held the pen and wrote them. They are the means by which Robert Sidney tried to write himself into the world. But there is, as we have seen before, a sense in which we should speak of 'Sidney' and 'his' poems alike as texts that need to be read against what they seem, or would like, to articulate, that speak as much in their silences as in their insistences.

So there are clearly poems where details from Sidney's life are certainly used, where 'the hardy captain, unused to retire', speaks directly of his turning from the Low Countries 'to the West' where 'love fast holds his heart' (Sonnet 7; Song 6). The sixth song of the collection is an especially revealing piece – as well as being perhaps the most impressive poetically. Like Ralegh's famous and haunting 'As You Came from the Holy Land', it is based upon the traditional lost ballad of a pilgrim travelling to Walsingham. Robert Sidney's version is an evocative 136-line dialogue between a pilgrim and a lady who pre-sumably represents Robert's wife, while 'the knight that loves me best', who 'griefs livery wears', and who 'to the West . . . turns his eyes' is Robert's wistful projection of his own exiled self, held by duty to the Low Countries away from 'the lady that doth rest near Medwayes sandy bed'. Penshurst Place, the Sidney home, stands on the Medway River just outside Tonbridge and almost due west of Flushing (Robert actually revised this particular line to read 'near ritch Tons sandy bed', which of course refers to Tonbridge).

The sixth song is the most clearly autobiographical poem in the sequence, projecting the partly calculated, partly wistful, view of a frustrated personal and political career. The bulk of the collection, in traditional Petrarchan fashion, is ostensibly concerned with love, and is similar to a host of sequences written in the 1590s such as Daniel's *Delia* or Drayton's *Idea*, although no poem mentions any identifiable or even coherently fictional mistress. The diction is typical of the English *petrarchisti*. The lover's 'soul' exists 'in purest fyre' (Song 4); he accepts both the joys and griefs of love, in his 'bonds of service without ende' (Sonnet 13). We encounter the familiar world of Petrarchan paradox: on the one hand, the high idealism of the lover who affirms the beauty of 'those fair eyes' which 'shine in their clear former light' (Song 12); on the other hand there are the 'pains which I uncessantly sustain' (Sonnet 2). The lady's beauties are 'born of the heavens, my sowles delight' (Sonnet 3), while the lover's passions are 'purest flames kindled by beauties rare' (Sonnet 4). As he contemplates in pleasurable agony how she takes 'pleasure' in his 'cruelty' (Sonnet 25), he asks her why she 'nourishes' poisonous weeds of cold despair in love's garden instead of the plants and trees of love's true faith and zeal (Song 22).

This basic Petrarchan situation of frustration, contradiction, and paradox is decked out in familiar Neoplatonic garb. The world is a dark cave where love's lights never shine except through the beloved's eyes, the 'purest stars, whose never dying fires' (Sonnet 1) constantly burn a path between the heavens and the lover's soul. Sexual desire is rarely explicitly mentioned: the dominant mood is that of melancholy, the recurring emphasis on the lover's self-torturing helplessness, and to an unusual degree, on torture, disease, and violence. The lover is a continually lashed slave, flung from rocks, a leper, racked by gangrene, or in violent wars.

Even with the marked emphasis on violence, we are in a world familiar to readers of Renaissance lyrics. Robert's work is less versatile, metrically and metaphorically, than Philip's, with no double sestinas, quantitative verse, and little of Philip's sly humour. What distinguishes Robert Sidney's poems from the mass of second-rate poems by Watson or Constable or from the anonymous verse of a miscellany like *England's Helicon* is the remarkable and usually consistent control of form, tone, and frequent use of a cryptic and direct address, not unlike the aphoristic tone of some of Greville's poems. Typical is the brief, pessimistic Song 17, which seems to reflect upon a deeply tragic event in the poet's experience. The first stanza sets the note of brooding melancholy:

> The sun is set, and maskèd night
> Veils heaven's fair eyes:
> Ah what trust is there to a light
> That so swift flies.

In the second stanza of this superb, cryptic little poem, the speaker (unusually, for Sidney) perhaps a woman, expresses a helpless, brooding bitterness:

> A new world doth his flames enjoy,
> New hearts rejoice:
> In other eyes is now his joy,
> In other choice.

Like Philip and Mary's, Robert's poetry shows a deep commitment to the craft of poetry as well as to its inspiring or calculated consolations of erotic or political favour. It is more than conventional Petrarchan regret when he asserts that even 'the most parfet stile kannot attaine' (Sonnet 11) to expressing the mistress's beauties or the pangs of love. The poems are the work of a poet with a highly sensitive ear, and a range of tone which while not broad, is deeply resonant, especially receptive to the way emotions may be attached to metaphors of absence and loss. It rarely, however, gets beyond the conventional Petrarchan motifs. In *Caelica* Fulke Greville often takes up the common Petrarchan assertion that, when apart, true lovers are paradoxically closer because of the spiritual nature of their love; but he demystifies the motif by placing it in a grimly realistic context acknowledging that 'absence is pain'. Robert Sidney's brooding over absence, delay, and loneliness have a conventional feel to them: the lover suffers incessantly from 'griefs sent from her whom in my soul I bless' (Song 23); constantly he feels that 'delays are death' (Song 18), as he waits 'on unknown shore, with weather hard distressed' (Sonnet 22). He presents himself as an exiled and neglected knight who has beseeched the pilgrim of the Walsingham poem to give his abandoned lady his undying devotion. Such common Petrarchan motifs are made peculiarly effective especially through the grave, deliberate, melancholic movement of the lines, which convey the passion, the hopelessness, and yet the continuing devotion of the lover. We are reading poetry of an exceptionally high level of craftsmanship, written by a poet skilled as well in the details of the poetic craft as in the range of poetic forms, which range from the courtly blazon or catalogue of the lady's beauties in Sonnet 32 to the more popular ballad form of the Walsingham poem.

Intellectually, Robert's verse is not as rich a revelation of the peculiar strains and repressions of the Elizabethan period as that of Philip or Mary. An aspiring and anxious courtier, directing his poems at particular (rarely, of course, stated) ends, the intellectual tensions of his poems remain the stock-in-trade of the Petrarchan poet; his sequence is poetically but not intellectually sophisticated. Nor, indeed, do the religious references in the poems suggest that he shared the intensity of theological interest of his brother, sister, or Fulke Greville. Where religious references do occur in the poems, they are used skilfully to darken the established mood of a poem or to glance at a necessarily understated political aim rather than to transform a conventional motif into a profound religious speculation.

The particular feature of Robert Sidney's poetry which makes his work of such interest to readers of the ideologically opaque power struggles of the Elizabethan aristocracy is the intense way it articulates the silent power of the Court. The exile of which Song 6 speaks, couched in speech seemingly depoliticized, is the political insecurity all Elizabethan courtiers felt within (or especially, as in Sidney's case, on the margins of) the Court. Most of the poems in the collection evoke not the frustrated sexual passion of a lover but use that basic Petrarchan situation as a metaphor for political powerlessness and aspiration. The 'lights divine' from which the lover is 'exiled', 'the only cause for which I care to see', 'these purest flames kindled by beauties rare', all may be read as conventional Neoplatonic compliments of a beloved only if the realities of Elizabethan politics and the Court's control of the discursive structures of both politics and poetry are ignored. The shepherd, with 'weights of change oppressed', and 'the hardy captain' who is 'scorned, repulsed, heartbroken', who is 'summoned by so great truth' yet in exile 'on unknown shore', and jealous of those 'who favour do enjoy/And spend and keep love's treasure', evoke not merely the bereft lover but the frustrated, anxious aspiring courtier, thwarted yet ambitious, powerless yet continually plotting for power – in Sidney's case, literally in exile, in the Low Countries and able to participate in the political manoeuvering of the Court only by proxy. No less than Ralegh's Scynthia poems or (if it is his) 'Praised Be Diana's Fair and Harmles Light', Robert Sidney's sonnets articulate the ideological dominance of the Elizabethan Court; unlike Ralegh's – except in their intense anxiousness and their over-insistent protest of absolute devotion – they do not articulate any opposition to that hegemonic discourse.

As *Astrophil and Stella* so triumphantly shows, one of the distinctive features of the Petrarchan sequence is its encouragement to readers to decode it in a variety of ways – as erotic self-evaluation, philosophical meditation, or moral debate. Robert's poems can be read as intense, extreme Neoplatonic poems of compliment and frustration, but they acquire an urgency and become rooted in the material life of late Elizabethan society when they are read as compensations for political powerlessness. Not all the poems can be read so directly in this way – there are a variety of translations, songs, and other miscellaneous pieces which may be seen as typical workshop exercises designed to show or practise his skills – but through the whole collection, we sense the enormous power of the Elizabethan Court, creating and controlling its subjects by the way it exerted power over their language, their metaphors of political as well as poetical expression. The political world in which Robert Sidney had, between 1586 and 1598, a marginal part, can be read from his poetical text: finally the poetical text (the poems we have in his slim notebook) and the social text (the events within which he wrote and tried to be a part of) are indistinguishable, each flowing into the other and together articulating the material and metaphorical dominance of the Elizabethan Court.

The Sidney Circle and beyond

Sir Philip Sidney's death, wrote his friend Fulke Greville, 'is a death that I think Death is sorry for'.[44] In choosing Sidney and his brother and sister as central figures in sixteenth-century poetry I am also pointing to their places, and the place of poetry, in Elizabethan culture generally. Philip Sidney's significance has clearly more than merely poetical dimensions; while the Countess of Pembroke's part in trying to continue the Sidneian ideals had wider significance. It was in part through her example and encouragement that late-sixteenth-century poetry was given particular energies and directions, and in carrying out their work, the other members of the Sidney Circle, especially Robert Sidney and Greville, Daniel, and (more independently but none the less paying due obeisance to the Wilton Circle) Spenser, were attempting to harness and guide more than the immediate needs of poetical reform.

They were, of course, already in the 1590s, being bypassed by a variety of cultural changes beyond their sympathy or understanding. The exception is perhaps Greville, whose increasing pessimism, as we have seen, is an articulation of his awareness of the changing nature of Jacobean society and his unease about the applicability of Sidney's idealism in such a corrupt world. Literary tastes changed; along with the radical new developments in public theatre, lyric and satiric poetry, picaresque prose, fiction, and the new sparseness in expository prose was growing a new social conjunction. Neo-classical drama, like the Countess's *Antonie*, polyphonic romance like Sidney's *Arcadia*, and the golden love lyric were not, as the next decade came through, the really significant developments in literature. The *Psalms* did help to initiate one of the new age's significant literary movements, but the tradition of religious lyric that links Mary Sidney, Greville, Herbert, Vaughan, and Traherne is significant as much for its representing a reaction against the dominant literary fashions and social patterns of the age as for its intrinsic merits as moving devotional verse. The kinds of poetry that dominated the sixteenth century were to become increasingly marginalized over the next sixty years or so.

To call the values and attitudes of the Sidney Circle reactionary would be correct but it would short-circuit an illuminating investigation of the forces that were in fact becoming dominant in late-sixteenth-century poetry and the wider culture. The transition in English culture marked by the Civil War, the Commonwealth, and the Restoration is part of a fundamental change in the cultural life of England, and it is not surprising that few writers in the 1590s and early 1600s were able to pick out and articulate the direction in which their world was moving. Shakespeare was certainly one whose works did; Donne, Webster, perhaps Jonson, were others. As well, a variety of lesser writers felt and fitfully expressed something of the transition and it is often the writers and artists who are not totally aware of what they are articulating who reveal most markedly the disruptive forces within a society making for important change. The period between the death of Sidney and the start of the Civil War appears to mark a fundamental change in English and European life. As Perez Zagorin puts it, it 'belongs to the handful of the "great revolutions" of Europe and the West – cataclysms which appear to mark the turning of times and to signify some fundamental change in the condition of humanity'.[45]

In a period when new experiences and values are disturbingly emergent, one understandable reaction is to take refuge in the past or in a belief in the degeneracy of the present. Sidney represented such a refuge for a significant number of courtiers, poets, and public figures in the Jacobean Court. In Sidney's poetry, in his life and ideals, increasingly in the myth that was built around him, many at Court in the reigns of James and Charles saw an ideal from which their times had degenerated. As certain aspects of the Stuart Court became increasingly unpalatable to those English courtiers who recalled, or thought they recalled, a more dignified age, the Spirit of Sidney as the epitome of that age was almost superstitiously invoked. His works went into numerous editions; poems or references to his memory abound, even as late as Ann Bradstreet's Elegy on him (1638). Ben Jonson often praised Sidney, his brother, and the whole family as embodying a virtue of which his contemporaries were losing sight. Fulke Greville spoke for the new age: 'it delights me', he wrote, 'to keepe companie with him even after esteeming his actions, words, and conversation the daintiest treasure my mynde could then lay up, or can at this daye impart with our posteritie'.[46]

If the perpetuation of the myth of Sidney as a reminder of the lost virtue and glory of the Elizabethan age is an example of the nostalgia and retrospective values of the Sidney Circle, can one find any points of cultural growth within the Sidneys' poetry? To answer that, we should perhaps return to Breton's description of Wilton as a 'little Court'. The myth of virtue and wholeness which Breton saw at Wilton was passing from the centralized Court of the high Renaissance to the great country houses like Wilton, Great Tew, or Penshurst. The culture of the early seventeenth century shows a widespread tendency towards de-centralization, paralleling such literary changes as the development of more introspective literary forms, such as the meditative devotional lyric, to replace the earlier lyrics of communal feeling. One central symbol of much seventeenth-century literature is the *hortus conclusus*, the enclosed garden of retirement of the mind: Herbert's rectory in Bemerton, Vaughan's retreat into the Welsh hills, Milton's retirement from the public world and his return to his epic ambitions. Another important symbolic focus is the virtue of the country gentry and the values of what Perez Zagorin and others have defined as the 'country party' of the early seventeenth century. Flattering courtiers or preachers like John Reynolds could continue to assert to the then Prince Charles that 'your Highnesse Court is a true and conspicuous Academie of Generositie and Honour', but men increasingly were experiencing the opposite. To quote Clarendon, 'by . . . the passion, insolence, and ambition of particular persons, the Court measured the temper and affection of the country, and by the same standard the people considered the honour, justice and piety of the Court'.[47]

Sidney's retirement to Wilton in the late 1570s, then, is not only a retreat from the Court, from the cultural centre of the high Elizabethan age. The establishment of the 'little Court' at Wilton in the late 1570s is a significant anticipation of an important cultural development in the next seventy years. The conflict between King and Parliament, 'Court' and 'Country', was not just fought out between members of the Commons and the King, but in the minds – in the conscious and dimly perceived structures of thought and feeling – of men and women. In the movement from the Court to the Country, from public responsibility to private virtue, concerns so typical of the poetry and other literature of the period, we can see a new consciousness struggling to emerge. The intellectual tensions, the conflicting languages of Philip's and Robert's love sonnets, the great house literature of the *Arcadia*, the combination of courtly sophistication and piety in the Sidney *Psalms*, and the moral strengths and sound learning of the neo-classical movement were, on the conscious level, the result of an attempt to hold back the forces of change, but paradoxically they contributed to the breakdown of the cultural hegemony of the Court and of aristocratic culture. The idealization of the feudal values of the Sidneys in Jonson's 'To Penshurst', for instance, shows us how a new ideology is slowly forming, as the pastoral moves from the Court to the country house. The Court is ceasing to be the dominant and respected centre of social existence and no longer monopolizes the allegiance of society at large. The result is a new society and with it, a new poetry. In the beliefs and the tensions of the Sidney Circle, we can see, better than they knew, the seeds of that new world and that new poetry.

Notes

1. Sir John Harington, quoted in A.C. Hamilton, *Sir Philip Sidney* (Cambridge, 1977), p.86; Sidney, *Astrophil and Stella*, 15; *A Defence of Poetry*, in *Miscellaneous Prose of Sir Philip Sidney*, edited by Katherine Duncan-Jones and Jan Van Dorsten (Oxford, 1973), pp. 116–17. Quotations from Sidney's poems are taken from *The Poems of Sir Philip Sidney*, edited by William A. Ringler, Jr (Oxford, 1962).

2. Hamilton, *Sidney*, pp. 34–35.

3. Terry Eagleton, *Criticism and Ideology* (London, 1976), p. 19.

4. Richard C. McCoy, *Sir Philip Sidney: Rebellion in Arcadia* (New Brunswick, 1978).

5. Hamilton, *Sidney*, p. 86.

6. Andrew D. Weiner, *Sir Philip Sidney and the Poetics of Protestantism* (Minneapolis, 1978), p. 70.

7. Sidney, *Defence*, p. 79.

8. Alan Sinfield, *Literature in Protestant England* (London, 1983), pp. 56, 57.

9. *The Correspondence of Sir Philip Sidney and Hubert Languet*, translated by Stewart A. Pears (London, 1845), p. 2.

10. Nicholas Breton, *Wits Trenchmour* (1593), p. 18; *The Pilgrimage to Paradise* (1592), sig. 12^r.

11. Hamilton, *Sidney*, p. 20.

12. Sidney, *Works*, III, 129.

13. *The Psalms of David with M. Calvins Commentaries*, translated by Arthur Golding (London, 1571), Psalm 8.

14. Stephen Greenblatt, *Renaissance Self-Fashioning* (New Haven, 1980), p. 8.

15. Sidney, *Defence*, p. 78.

16. Germaine Warkentin, 'Sidney's *Certain Sonnets*: Speculations on the Evolution of the Text', *The Library*, 6th series, 2 (1980), pp. 430–44 (p. 442); Ringler, p. lxiv.

17. Alan Sinfield, 'Sidney and Astrophil', *SEL*, 20 (1980), 25–41 (p. 35).

18. Neil E. Rudenstine, *Sir Philip Sidney's Poetic Development* (Cambridge, Mass., 1967), p. 50.

19. Sidney, *Miscellaneous Prose*, p. 50.

20. Roland Barthes, *S/Z*, translated by Richard Miller (New York, 1974), pp. 5–6; *Image, Music, Text*, translated by Stephen Heath (New York, 1977), p. 146.

21. J. P. Castley, S.J., '*Astrophil and Stella* – High "Sidneian Love" or Courtly Compliment?', *MCR*, 5 (1962), 54–65 (pp. 57–58).

22. Barthes, 'Theory of the Text', in *Untying the Text*, edited by Robert Young (London, 1981), pp. 31–47 (p. 42); Jacques Derrida, 'Signature Event Context', *Glyph*, 1 (1977), 172–97 (p. 174).

23. Michael Goldman, *Shakespeare and the Energy of Drama* (Cambridge, Mass., 1972), p. 4.

24. Barthes, *S/Z*, p. 15.

25. Lewis, p. 327; *Astrophil and Stella*, edited by Max Putzel (Garden City, 1967), p. xviii; Hamilton, *Sidney*, p. 86.

26. A. C. Hamilton, '"The Mine of Time": Time and Love in Sidney's *Astrophil and Stella'*, *Mosaic*, 13, no. 1 (1979), 81–91.

27. Ann Rosalind Jones, 'The Lyric Sequence: Poetic Performance as Plot' (unpublished doctoral dissertation, Cornell University, 1976), p. 144.

28. Ann Rosalind Jones and Peter Stallybrass, 'The Politics of *Astrophil and Stella*', *SEL*, 24 (1984), 53–69.

29. Sinfield, *Literature in Protestant England*, p. 23.

30. Sinfield, *Literature in Protestant England*, p. 57.

31. See Gary F. Waller, 'Sidney and the New New Criticism', *SNew*, 4, no. 2 (1984), 3–6.

32. Breton, *Wits Trenchmour*, p. 18; *Pilgrimage to Paradise*, Dedication, sig. 12^r; Abraham Fraunce, *The Third Part of the Countesse of Pembrokes Ivychurch* (London, 1592), sig. A2^r; *The Countess of Pembrokes Ivychurch* (London, 1591), sigs. B2^v, E1^v, E2^v.

33. For a discussion of the authorship question, see Gary F. Waller, *Mary Sidney, Countess of Pembroke: A Critical Study of her Writings and Literary Milieu* (Salzburg, 1979), pp. 90–5.

34. Robert Coogan, 'Petrarch's *Trionfi* and the Renaissance', *SRen*, 67 (1970), 306–27 (p. 311).

35. D. G. Rees, 'Petrarch's "Trionfo della Morte" in English', *Ital. Stud*, 7 (1952), 82–96 (p. 83).

36. Quotations from the poem are taken from *The Triumph of Death and other Unpublished and Uncollected Poems by Mary Sidney, Countess of Pembroke*, edited by G. F. Waller (Salzburg, 1977).

37. Rees, pp. 86–87.

38. John Donne, *The Divine Poems*, edited by Helen Gardner (Oxford, 1952), pp. 34, 35. For an account of the Psalms MSS, see Waller, *Triumph of Death*, pp. 18–28, 222–25.

39. *The Psalms of Sir Philip Sidney and the Countess of Pembroke*, edited by J. C. A. Rathmell (New York, 1963), p. xx.

40. Rathmell, *Psalms*, pp. xi, xv; J. C. A. Rathmell, 'Hopkins, Ruskin, and the Sidney Psalter', *Lon. Mag.*, 6, no. 9 (1959), 51–66 (p. 51).

41. Ben Jonson, 'To Penshurst', *Poems*, p. 79; Thomas Thorpe, *Catalogue of Manuscripts* (London, 1833), p. 96; Thomas Nashe, *Pierce Pennilesse*, in *Works*, edited by E. D. McKerrow, revised by F. P. Wilson and W. W. Gill (London, 1958), I, 159.

42. HMC, *De Lisle and Dudley*, II, p. 145; see also II, 160, 164.

43. Quotations from the poems are taken from *The Poems of Robert Sidney*, edited by P. J. Croft (Oxford, 1984).

44. HMC, *Salisbury*, III, 189.

45. Perez Zagorin, *The Court and the Country* (1970), p. 5.

46. Greville, *Life*, p. 105.

47. John Reynolds, *Treatise of the Court*, sig. A1^{r-v}; Clarendon, I, 5.

Chapter 6
Spenser and *The Faerie Queene*

Introduction

In 1590 were published the first three books of the one work of poetry
that, more than any other, epitomizes the glory and contradictions of
the Elizabethan Court and its poetry. In 1596 the poem was reissued,
with some revisions and with three further books. The reorganization,
revisions, and additions brought out what the early books, in retrospect,
can be seen to have largely, though not entirely, repressed – that *The
Faerie Queene*, the most ambitious poetic glorification of the Elizabethan
regime, could not celebrate the power which permitted it to exist
without revealing the strains and contradictions that were already
radically dislocating that power. Spenser's whole career, indeed,
epitomizes the way power was exerted over all literary and social
discourse by the Elizabethan Court. Perhaps the most faithful celebrant
of the regime which employed him, Spenser's epic manifests the
powerlessness of poetry but it also shows us its relative autonomy – how
it may offer, despite its intentions, a radical critique of the power that
brings it into being. We have seen how this dual process worked in
Ralegh's and Greville's poems; part of the distinctive interest of
Spenser's epic rests also on its capacity to bring such contradiction into
play – perhaps, except for Shakespeare's plays, more extensively than in
any writings of the period.

C. S. Lewis once remarked that everything that Spenser wrote outside
The Faerie Queene was 'something of a diversion'. However much of an
exaggeration that may be, none the less *The Faerie Queene* remains by far
his most important work. Students can be directed to the many detailed
studies of the minor poems that cannot be discussed, for reasons of
space, in this chapter. Spenser's early work, written in the late 1560s,
first flowered spectacularly in the *Shepheardes Calender* (1579) which was
praised by Sidney in the *Defence*, although Lewis notes that Spenser 'was
soon to write and perhaps had already written poetry which deprives the
Calender of all importance'.[1] He was certainly working on *The Faerie*

Queene during the 1580s and also produced a tribute to Sidney, *Astrophel* (1586), *Colin Clouts Come Home Again* (1589–90), and, about the same time, *Daphnaida, The Ruines of Time*, and *Muiopotmos*. Spenser's other minor poems include the four *Hymns* (the first two perhaps written as early as the late 1570s, the latter two maybe fifteen years later) and the *Amoretti*, a peculiarly (given the dominant English emphasis) Christianized Petrarchan sonnet sequence.

Much of Spenser's early work, including *Virgil's Gnat, Mother Hubbard's Tale*, and *The Teares of the Muses*, developed from the typical poetical preoccupations of the mid-century period – political allegory, heavy didacticism, experimentation with stanzaic and metrical patterns. These poems are still in the world of Googe, Turberville, and *A Gorgeous Gallery of Gallant Inventions*. Spenser was establishing himself as a serious Protestant poet. The publication of the *Calender* in 1579 is often seen as marking a turning-point in the age's poetry. But unlike *Astrophil and Stella*, the poem is not a courtly work – it continues rather in the tradition of the militant Protestant poets of mid century. The *Calender* is serious, moralistic, and satiric, all its elements incorporated into a firm Protestant didacticism. Spenser, in fact, seemed relatively indifferent to the Petrarchan fashions of his more courtly contemporaries. In part this was because he saw epic poetry as his vocation, and the lyric as a diversion from his aims. As Richard Helgerson points out, Spenser was unique in his generation for presenting himself not as a courtly amateur but 'as a Poet, as a man who considered writing a duty rather than a distraction'.[2] Above all, he is self-consciously the regime's servant in his poetry as he was as a minor civil servant and planter in occupied Ireland. As such he seemingly naturally turned to the most serious, most traditionally approved, poetic kinds in which to celebrate the regime.

The *Amoretti*, written in the early 1590s, is his only venture into the lyric, and it too is characteristically moralistic – in Sinfield's words, an 'unprecedented puritan humanist adaptation of the sonnet sequence to a relationship which ends in marriage'. The sequence is usually read as a fictionalization of Spenser's courtship of his second wife, Elizabeth Boyle. It sets out, occasionally amusingly but in clear moral terms, a pattern of desire that leads not to frustration and defeat but to marriage and mutual submission to God's will. Although the lover occasionally takes up the expected subservient role, the sequence is firmly articulated as a moral narrative: the mistress is even at times lovingly criticized. As Arthur Marotti notes, 'Spenser's speaker acts as his beloved's intellectual and ethical superior, a position from which he can comically, but affectionately, condescend to her at various points in the sequence.'[3] The Protestant, ever mindful of God's will and public duty, must subordinate sexual desire to higher goals. Although the early poems of the collection (those before Sonnet 67) are often light, even titillating, at the point at which the praise and gentle admonition of the beloved give way to a celebration of Christian marriage, the tone changes. Petrarchan praise is forced into the service of Christian duty: it is acknowledged that the beloved may often be a distraction from higher commitments, not only to God but also to the Queen and to Spenser's vocation to write the great poem in which he will 'enlarge' the Queen's 'living prayses', which is a 'sufficient worke for one mans simple head' (Sonnet 33). So in the latter part of the collection, notably in Sonnet 80 (where he defends the pleasure of the lyric) the primacy of the Queen, Christian commitments, and dedication to public duty are never wavered from. The primary role of his poems is that of the dutiful Protestant laureate.

Elizabethan poetry, I have argued, is characterized by fascinating fissures, contradictions, and repressions. Of all the age's poetry, *The Faerie Queene* is at once the most grandiose in its claims for ideological repleteness and the most dislocated and disrupted. It should now not be necessary to remind readers that to speak of 'fissures', 'flaws', 'contradictions', or 'dislocations', is not to play down a poem's importance or, to use the traditional term, its greatness. Spenser's epic is the most important single poem of the century precisely because it brings so compellingly to our attention the conflicting voices by and against which it was written; it allows us more richly than any other poem of the age to construct those voices which spoke so powerfully to create the hegemony of the Elizabethan regime. *The Faerie Queene* emerges in a cultural space radically crossed by impulses and structures which it vainly tries to discipline, and which over and over at key moments in its unfolding, articulate the ideological struggles of late Elizabethan society.

The last decade of Spenser's life, following Sidney's death, was when his epic reached its eventual, though probably not its intended final, shape. It coincides with an increasing restlessness in the Elizabethan Court, with many obvious and many underlying strains upon the economy and the broader social practices of the country – failing harvests, rural discontent, rising unemployment, increasing inflation, religious intolerance, and outbursts of unusually strong xenophobia directed against Spaniards, Catholics, and (as the plays of both Marlowe and Shakespeare witness) Jews. But the poem's history started much earlier. Spenser was working on what became *The Faerie Queene* at least as early as the time Sidney was experimenting with *Astrophil and Stella* and the *Defence*. By the mid 1580s, parts of the poem had been circulating in England; by 1589 Spenser had journeyed from his plantation in an increasingly rebellious and oppressed Ireland to be presented at Court by Sir Walter Ralegh. In 1590 the first three books were published, and the following year Spenser was rewarded for his devotion by the Queen by a lifetime pension of fifty pounds a year. Evidently disquieted by what he saw at Court, Spenser returned to Ireland. By 1592 Ralegh was in prison and something of his high risk (and in Spenser's highly partial view, misunderstood) career is reflected upon in Books IV and VI which, along with a fifth book closely based on Spenser's interpretation of the Irish occupation, were published in 1596. It was probably completed some years earlier – in *Amoretti*, Sonnet 80, he writes that his poem is 'halfe fordonne', with six books completed. In the last five years of his life he probably did not complete another. That, as well as the changes between the two parts, provides a profound revelation of the ways even such a loyal upholder of the regime was dislocated by the world he perceived – though as the ensuing discussion will show, his perceptions are revealing far beyond what he himself knew. He continued to serve in Ireland until 1598 when, driven from his house in Kilcolmen by an upsurge in the Irish resistance, he once again journeyed to England. He died early the next year, leaving behind a fragment of a further book.

In this survey of Spenser's career, it is important to stress the dislocations in the writing and revisions of *The Faerie Queene* because of the strange way it has been read by modern scholars if not as complete, at least as united, and in an almost mystical sense, whole. Only since the late 1970s, initially in the work of Jonathan Goldberg, Stephen Greenblatt, and Louis Montrose, have we seen the development of any symptomatic reading of the poem that did not try to explain away its dislocated nature. In part this is attributable to the success of an impressive Spenser industry fascinated with detailed annotations and even more with the assumption of the work's 'unity'. It is a fascinating instance of how an archaic political power maintains its hold over one of its cultural products even after 400 years. Most commentators, from the *Variorum Spenser* in the 1930s to the *Spenser Encyclopedia* of the 1980s, have largely taken for granted the ideological world foregrounded by the poem, and have depicted the poet as a master of intentional control and the poem as massively, complexly (even if often, it seems, inexplicably) unified. The authority of the Great Author and the unity of the Great Work have been unchallengeable – and the result has been that our own time's dominant reading is close to what would have been that of the regime itself. As a side-note, however, it is interesting to note one early reader of the poem whose perspective, eight years after his mother's execution and seven years before his own accession to the English throne she had (possibly) sought, was notably antagonistic and not at all in accord with the dominant reading. That reader was James VI of Scotland, whose remarks on Book V will be touched upon later.[4]

The Faerie Queene, then – and most especially its last books, particularly the sixth, in which Spenser deals directly with the Court and courtesy – is the most significant poetic document of its age. It is especially crucial to our understanding of the transition in English cultural life, and not only in poetry, between the death of Sidney in 1586 and the outbreak of the Civil War over fifty years later. Deliberately (and as it grew, increasingly) nostalgic, retrogressive, and disillusioned, *The Faerie Queene* opens for us, in the way the poetry of any transitional period does, the forces which were eventually to shatter the world it celebrates and from which it traced its origins and inspiration. Spenser criticism has rarely confronted this contradiction, preferring to explain away the frustrations, dislocations, and disruptions by searching – admittedly probably as desperately as Spenser himself might have – for principles of unity, harmony, and authority. Traditional readings have for the most part been what Goldberg, following Barthes, terms 'theological', assuming that the poem 'in some way . . . gains stability and order from replicating verbally the assumed harmony of the universe' it works to valorize.[5]

Even hostile critics have rarely challenged this view, preferring simply to find the poem archaic and dull. Derek Traversi, in the first edition of the *Pelican Guide*, wrote that the poem was the dead end of a medieval tradition and was an 'undeniable failure'. In the revised edition of the *Guide*, Spenser is elevated from the Age of Chaucer to the Age of Shakespeare, but W. W. Robson's assessment is no less astringent: 'modern readers, even those who still read poetry, simply find (Spenser) tedious'; his poems are 'the preserve of lovers of crossword puzzles and esoteric scholarship'.[6] But such a tradition of dismissive scepticism is still just as tied to notions of organic form, the authority of the great poet and craftsmanship, as the tradition it pillories – it is just that Spenser is seen to fail such tests. We do not read him (to return to F. R. Leavis's test for poetry) as we read the living. Where contradictions or a falling off in poetic power are acknowledged, traditional Spenser criticism has usually had recourse to the admission that every long poem has some weaknesses, or has put them down to Spenser's growing (but inevitably conscious) disillusion with the corruption of his age. The ending of Book II, especially the destruction of the Bower of Bliss, the (sometime) disturbing ferocity of Book V, the ambiguous allegiances to public duty of Book VI or the seeming renunciation of the world, even of his own poem, in the Mutability Cantos, have been diversely read, but rarely has Spenser's awareness of whatever he was doing been put into question. It is only recently that quite different readings have been occasionally risked or even seen as possible. This chapter attempts to continue the contemporary revision of our ways of looking at *The Faerie Queene*.

The Faerie Queene

First, what vision does Spenser himself want – at least when he first planned and wrote the poem and probably throughout its writing – a reader to gain? I use the archaic word 'vision' advisedly, since *The Faerie Queene* is designed to exemplify a poetic and a metaphysic of stasis; ultimately the poem reproduces the ideological universe of which it is a constituent part. *The Faerie Queene* is, primarily, a patriotic, Protestant epic. Throughout the poem, Spenser's militant Puritan humanism is insistently foregrounded. Book I, the Book of Holiness, embodies a theologically cautious but firm outline of the Reformed doctrine of justification by faith, the division of mankind into elect and reprobate, and the quest to find true salvation. While Spenser does not write as a systematic theologian, none the less the theological implications are solidly in accord with those of the moderate left wing of the Elizabethan Church on such doctrines as Providence, Predestination, the Fall, Grace, Free Will and Election. All history is set under the judgement of the Word of God, and the allegory directed to demonstrating God's purposes through his chosen people. Later books play down such explicit theologizing, but when Book I was written, Spenser's intentions seem clear enough.

Similarly clear is the intention, often announced quite explicitly, of building a magniloquent pageant-like celebration of the ordered universe's manifestation of harmony. The poem is built upon the traditional belief that reality is indivisible, that it embraces the whole of creation. Thus in Book VI, courtly behaviour – obligation, respect, obedience, magnanimity – is the social manipulation of an order expressed in the whole creation. The different facets of an indivisible reality, often presented as a dance, circle, or pageant, or in emblems of reciprocity, symmetry, and harmony, are expressed in the structure of the whole poem – in the parallel and symmetrical quests of the knights with their 'like' races 'to run', the graceful and continuous replenishment of the world from the Garden of Adonis and the pageant of Mutability, or the dance of the Graces on Mount Acidale. With such recurring metaphors, *The Faerie Queene* – like Sidney's *Arcadia*, the only work of the century to rival it in scope – attempts to stop the all too obvious flux and unpredictability of history by the assertion of timeless myths of origin, explanation, and cosmic destiny.

The poem uses the trappings of chivalry – knights, ladies, tournaments, dragons, talking trees – with which modern children are familiar in comic books or television programmes. In the Elizabethan Age, chivalry was obviously taken more seriously, but it may be that it constitutes a real barrier for the modern reader. Before dismissing it as arcane (and interestingly, there were a few Elizabethans who did just that), we should acknowledge that chivalry not only occupies in the poem an exactly analogous position to what it did in the Court at large, but that even at the time it was becoming increasingly old-fashioned. Both Sidney and Ralegh took part in a strange revival of chivalric tournaments, manners, and fashions, just as Wyatt must have been aware of Henry VIII's cultivation of the same outdated imperial trappings. Chivalry combined some very powerful contradictions – it had a reassuringly traditional emphasis on hierarchy along with the intense competitiveness of struggle; it insisted on a deference to the Queen's untouchable supremacy and yet encouraged her subject's individual prowess and ambitions. With its heraldic pageantry, it could define both the idealized history of the regime and its nervous competitiveness. Similarly, such rituals, progresses, and tournaments occupy a key role in both Spenser's poems and the Court. In the Court, they were cultural mechanisms designed at once to encourage and contain criticism and opposition – as we can see in Sidney's *Lady of May* or the pageant staged by Sidney, Greville, and other courtiers in 1581, *The Four Foster Children of Desire*, where antagonistic political positions were articulated and then reconciled. In *The Faerie Queene* chivalry likewise provides a mechanism for the establishment of asserting true allegiance and for the apparent reconciliation of contention. By presenting harmony as something achieved through the reconciliation of all disharmony, the poem affirms a belief that the values it celebrates are beyond challenge, even beyond history, and that its own order both reflects and is valorized by the whole cosmic order. To read *The Faerie Queene* in accord with such belief would be, in Spenser's view, to read it correctly. Hence, the poem thrusts at its readers a formidable repertoire of strategies designed to produce such a reading.

So far, I have tied discussion of *The Faerie Queene* closely to Spenser's career in, or in relation to, the Elizabethan Court. However, his life enters the poem in other ways, and much more than he knew. Raymond Williams notes on Sidney's *Arcadia* that the work 'which gives a continuing title to English neopastoral was written in a park which had been made by enclosing a whole village and evicting the tenants. The elegant game was then only at arm's length – a rough arm's length – from the visible reality of country life.'[7] *The Faerie Queene* was planned and partly written at a greater distance from the Elizabethan Court than the *Arcadia* and part of its intense idealization of the Court arises from Spenser's position as an outsider. His visit to the Court in 1589–90 must have forced him to see something analogous to the 'visible reality' of which Williams speaks. *Colin Clouts Come Home Again* is Spenser's pastoral re-creation of his visit, written as he contemplated both his reception at the Court of Gloriana and his continuing celebration of it.

One senses from the poem, in Josephine Bennett's words, that 'Ireland had never been "home" to him until he had been part of the court',[8] but Spenser still tries to insist on setting the all too evident corruption of the Court in the context of a redeeming ideal. As he contemplates the Court's sophisticated barbarism from what had seemed his exile among rude barbarians, he is still confident in his devotion to the Queen (who had, after all, rewarded him with fifty pounds a year):

> Her power, her mercy, and her wisdome, none
> Can deeme, but who the Godhead can define.
> Why then do I base shepheard bold and blind,
> Presume the things so sacred to prophane?
> More fit it is t'adore with humble mind,
> The image of the heavens in shape humane.[9]

The poem includes some devastating criticism of 'Courtiers as bladders blowen up with wynd' and of 'faire dissembling curtesie', but it is emphatic in its praise of the Queen and the 'ring' of those faithful courtiers who like the dead Sidney and his sister, truly reflect their Queen's glory.

This dual role of celebrating the ideal while warning against breaches of it is one that, as we have seen, characterizes court poetry throughout the century; it is also one that Spenser had adopted early in his career, when he similarly juxtaposed his criticism of corrupt courtiers with a radiant vision of Elizabeth in the April eclogue of *The Shepherdes Calendar*. It is the expected role of the court poet to conceal or reconcile ideological antagonisms and to replace the possibility of debating real alternatives by an assertion of their ultimate harmony. It is the role Spenser confidently continues in the first three books of *The Faerie Queene* and which also informs Book IV and most of Book V, one able to countenance and even give voice to attacks on the Elizabethan Court while celebrating un-ambiguously its glory and place in the cosmic order.

Thus Spenser combines the role of Protestant humanist moral critic with what he perceives as the Virgilian role of the poet's moral power in a society he at once loyally celebrates and judiciously criticizes. In the early books, Spenser's confidence in his role is seen as analogous to the plenitude with which the Queen herself embodies those same ideals. As he asserts at the start of Book II:

> And thou, O fairest Princesse under sky,
> In this faire mirrhour maist behold thy face,
> And thine owne realmes in lond of Faery,
> And in this antique Image thy great auncestry.
>
> (II. proem 4, 6–9)

In her allegorical role of Belphoebe, the Queen attacks and defeats challenges to her power with the same confidence that Spenser himself is attacking them in the poem as a whole. When in Book II Braggadocchio flatters Belphoebe (II. 3. 39) she sternly rejects Braggadocchio's view of the Court as a place of frivolity, just as Spenser himself did in *Mother Hubbard's Tale*, in *Colin Clouts Come Home Again*, and throughout the early books of *The Faerie Queene* itself. What is noticeable in such passages is not only the absolute distinctions made between the dedicated, active life and the frivolous life of pleasure, but the poem's confidence in moral absolutes, in the transcendent ideals that permit and even demand such absolutes, and in the power of the poet to articulate them. This is the confidence that gives *The Faerie Queene* its central place in the propaganda of the late Elizabethan regime and which attempts to sustain it (and, presumably, Spenser himself) through the acknowledged complexities, moral as well as poetical, of his treatment in Books IV to VI of chastity, friendship, and justice.

Such attitudes are central to the confidence of the early books of the poem. Spenser appropriates the Virgilian role of celebrating the nation: he is both the prophet justifying a providential reading of history, and the Protestant nationalist assuming the public good can be served in the order, harmony, and wonder of the most serious kind of poetry, the epic. Classical epic and Italian romance are combined to justify Christian heroism in an assimilation of the same elements of the past used throughout the century by educators, propagandists, and poets to create and uphold the Protestant Tudor regime. Thus in his letter to Ralegh, Spenser claims to be following Homer, Virgil, Ariosto, and Tasso; he echoes the *Aeneid* in the poem's opening, he alludes to Italian romance epic throughout; he speaks of 'magnificence' as the ethical basis of the poem, and he directs his reader continuously to Christian theology. Above all, he wants to root his syncretic ideals in the concrete particulars of the Elizabethan Court. As he put it to Ralegh, the poem was designed 'to fashion a gentleman or noble person in vertuous and gentle discipline'.

His letter to Ralegh is useful as a revelation of some of Spenser's intentions, at least at the time he wrote it. But the outline he gives there is just not reflected in the poem as we have it. He does not confine himself to 'Aristotles twelve morall virtues'; the relationships between individual knights and their particular virtues vary greatly; and Arthur never acquires the central place Spenser may have once intended. In short, the letter to Ralegh cannot, except in the most general terms, account for the poem's growth or suggest how it could be read satisfactorily. For today's readers, the letter is useful as a reminder that the poem calls into question any imposition of unity, even its author's. The poem is, in fact, a rambling, open-ended, disrupted work. It starts plot strands it cannot finish; its characters metamorphose continually; instead of the reassuring pleasures of a finished text which would reflect and teach about a stable world of universal values, *The Faerie Queene* is the quintessential example of *copia* in the period, a flow of textuality which undergoes what Goldberg terms 'continuous reconstitution'. Its continuities are those of repeated frustration and absence, a continual undermining of any 'possibility of fixed character and fixed meaning'.[10]

In the letter to Ralegh, Spenser also writes of his poem as a 'continued Allegory or darke conceit'. Once again, it is important not to treat allegory simply as a 'literary' device, but to root it in the material practices of the day, the 'social' text. Allegory was becoming increasingly archaic, however strong the interest in it at the Elizabethan Court was. A century later it was to be laughed at. 'It was the vice of those Times to affect superstitiously the Allegory', whereby 'nothing would then be current without a mystical meaning', wrote Rymer in 1674, in an age that was operating with quite different assumptions about the relation of signifier to meaning.[11] But for Spenser, allegory still seemed to grow naturally from an order of discourse whereby individual parts of the material world were given significance as parts of an interconnected universe of meanings. By Spenser's time, it looked back to increasingly archaic modes of thought – to *Piers Plowman*, to Lydgate, to *A Mirror for Magistrates* – and, interestingly enough, it was Spenser's fellow Protestants who were most scornful of it. They might well have considered the point that Puttenham makes when he wrote that both poet and courtier, he says, use allegory when 'we speake one thing and think another' and when 'our wordes and our meanings meete not'.[12]

Indeed, it is strange that given the Protestant suspicion of it, allegory did not strike the pious Protestant Spenser as a peculiar form for a self-consciously Reformed poet to use. Yet he showed himself more shrewd than his fellow Protestants, at least in his poetic practices if not in his own comments and glosses on his poem. The choice to write an allegory meant that the poem came to focus on the central poetic issue of the age, the relationship of meaning to language. Allegory is characterized by a deliberate and radical subordination of the signifier to the apparently signified; typically, it incorporates comments upon the process by which language works, by what is implied by the relation between icon and metaphor, and thus raises the fundamental question, in Isabel MacCaffery's phrase, of 'how far we may trust the basic medium, language'.[13] Jacqueline Miller has shown how such concerns grow out of the recurring Renaissance anxiety over an extra-discursive authority, whether conceived of as God or a political ideology, something beyond the poet's voice which would allow the reader's world to be reassuringly linked to another. Spenser's allegory continually tries to draw rich connections with such other worlds – with the Platonic forms in which he casts his quasi-Aristotelian virtues, with Christian theology, with the events of ancient and recent history or the constructs of myth. In all cases, the reality is asserted to reside with *res* and the final value of *verbes* is always outside the poem.[14]

Coupled with the need to establish an extraverbal authority is the need to repress aberrant readings of the text. Donald Cheney speaks of the 'strong universal compulsion of readers . . . to master books and every-day experience by imposing order and coherence where mere random circumstance is felt to be intolerable and threatening'.[15] How ironical it is, therefore, that the seeming endlessness of modern critical interpre-tations of Spenserian allegory does precisely the opposite of what Spenser consciously intended – multiplying in a promiscuity of signification the signs, whereas 'rightly' read, the poem should point to permanent, historical truths. But the point is a crucial one. Allegory represents an absolute desire to bring writing, and in one sense history, to an end. It tries rigorously to exclude anything that might disturb and challenge the monolithic readings the poet (as distinct, as we shall see, from the poem) intended. Allegory tries to create and position a reader who, educated correctly, will read not necessarily simple or single but certainly consistent and unified meanings, and repress undesirable ones: for instance that in Book I, Errour might stand for Protestant (rather than Catholic) heresy or that (in James VI's 'erroneous' reading) Mercilla in Book V, as a 'type' of Mary Queen of Scots, is mistreated, in both the text of the poem and the text of history. Spenser's formidable control of rhetoric, structure, and above all of the poem's atmosphere tries to pressure the reader to accept the poet's terms on such interpretations. As readers, we are continually called to insert ourselves into a discourse where instruction and enjoyment are real but none the less carefully controlled.

Yet any reading of *The Faerie Queene* is determined not by Spenser's intention but by its status as powerful language. And, paradoxically, the language-density of the poem itself continually expands and so subverts the author's attempt to control meaning. As Goldberg argues, the endless quality of the poem as text 'denies hermeneutic closure'. Con-tinually, the text invites us, lures us, to desire meaning, 'and then obliterates the possibility' of it.[16] *The Faerie Queene* encourages what it deliberately tries to avoid; despite its terms being selected with what Eagleton calls 'fetishistic' force, the promiscuity of its language spreads infinitely.[17]

One authorial guide by which Spenser tries to limit meaning is an insistence that allegory is a 'darke' conceit, that a correct reading is accessible only by arduous study, by the subordination of textuality to authorial intention, and by the insistence that the hidden 'true' meaning was available only to an élite. As Michael Murrin has argued, the Renaissance allegorist wanted his text at once to open the truth to the properly subordinate reader, but remain inaccessible to the undisciplined one.[18] Thus Spenser works hard to direct his reader by prefacing each canto with quaintly archaic quatrains, as if to underline the required meanings and thereby limit allegorical reading. As Maureen Quilligan notes, however, the quatrains only prove 'that Spenser, however great an allegorical poet, was not the best reader of his own poem when he had to resort to being an allegorical critic of it'.[19] But it is there, in the quatrains, where Spenser's affinities with the Protestant anxieties over the promiscuity of language become very clear. His is the dilemma not only of the allegorist, but specifically of the Protestant allegorist, anxious about how fallen man's words might embody God's truths.

If the quatrains fail to be of much use as signposts, the body of the poem is rich with more subtle structural and stylistic directions. To read the poem is to enter not a geographical landscape which provides a background to action, but a moral landscape – a world of moral choices. The poem speaks of Faeryland as a 'mirror', an 'antique image': it is designed to let us see and explore the significance of the material world in the way dreams momentarily explore the displaced or repressed significances of our waking world. Spenser wants to create the impression of an atemporal, mythic world where quests, conquests, fears and tensions are occurring all the time – and, where we are always (it is assumed) like Red Cross, engaged in a quest for perfection; like Guyon, in a quest for the appropriate and rational action; in our sexual relations, we are always faced with choices among different demands on our emotional and moral allegiances, like the lovers in Books III and IV. In short, the world of Faeryland is meant to be a world of complex psychological and cultural discoveries – and, most importantly, those discoveries are made by and about the reader. We can speak of the poem's psychological insights only in terms of our own experiences. We are not given insights into the 'characters' of Belphoebe or Britomart or Florimel; rather, they are parts of an attempt to create and educate the poem's readers as subjects within its seductive discourse.

The dominant narrative form of our culture since the early eighteenth century has been the novel, in which characters and their actions become part of an effaced illusion of realism, suppressing the contradictions of how those realistic effects are, in fact, constructed.[20] In particular, realism attempts to exclude any shifting in this involvement of reader, writer, and textual surface: we are asked to judge character and action by consistency and fidelity to a socially dominant norm. No such constraints are demanded by *The Faerie Queene*: what is foregrounded is rather a desire for rigorous ideological, not narrative or character, consistency. Character, landscape and setting, action and motive, are all manipulated without regard for verisimilitude or consistency. It makes no sense (except as revealing our own literary presuppositions) to ask: '"where" in the forest is Belphoebe's pavilion?' Or the House of Mammon? Or to ask whether Amoret 'really' loved Scudamour? Nor is narrative consistency as important. The poem simultaneously sets a goal before us and continually postpones achieving it by multiplying situations, characters, and complications into seemingly infinite variations. In short, instead of having the pleasures of classic realism and, especially, the consistency of the novel, we are thrust into a text populated with figures 'moving in flux, constantly resituated, momentarily lodged in relationships from which they are as quickly dislodged, inevitably undone', a world of textuality where the focus is always on the reader caught 'in the middest', manipulated, teased, and faced with what Lewis called 'states of the heart', with challenges to learn our own possibilities.[21] The ever-present threat is what Spenser would have seen as the fallen nature of the will, which he embodies in the dangerous, labyrinthine forest, and which is paradoxically embodied in the equally labyrinthine nature of the text. Goldberg suggests the poem is, in Barthes's terms, an exemplary writable text, one that by its very existence denies the closure which so many of its strategies desire. It is, one might add to Goldberg's claim, precisely this promiscuity of textuality that provides readers with the perpetual excitement of reading *The Faerie Queene*.[22]

In the space available, it would be foolish to provide a reading, even an outline, of the six books of *The Faerie Queene*. From the above argument, of course, one must conclude that any such reading would be, necessarily, culturally produced and therefore partial. For stimulating accounts, readers are directed to such critics as A. C. Hamilton on the first two books, Thomas P. Roche or A. Kent Hieatt on Book III, Jonathan Goldberg on Book IV, Donald Cheney or Michael O'Connor on Book V, and Humphrey Tonkin on Book VI. Spenserian scholarship of the last forty years is a monumental tribute to painstaking dedication and love for a great poem. It is perhaps best summed up in the *Spenser Encyclopedia*, which has attempted to bring together the best of modern and contemporary work on Spenser, its very multifariousness a tribute perhaps to a multifaceted post-modern Spenser just as the *Variorum* edition nearly fifty years earlier was to a Victorian and modernist Spenser. What follows here is necessarily the briefest of outlines of Books I to V, with some of the more interesting problems noted, followed by a detailed consideration of Book VI, where Spenser comes closest to and yet is most at odds with the ostensible centre of his poem of praise, the Queen and her Court. The Cantos of Mutability, the fragment of an unfinished Book VII, will then be considered in the final section where I attempt to provide a symptomatic overview of the place of *The Faerie Queene* in Elizabethan poetry and culture.

Book I, of Holiness, takes its reader into the adventures of a young, inexperienced quester, the Red Cross Knight, whose Christian significance is made clear from the start. In an opening symbolic montage, details are deliberately chosen to try to direct a reader's allegiances – the ideological exclusiveness of Red Cross's badge, the Protestant emphasis on struggle and alienation as value tests of faith, the vicious characterization of Catholicism as Error, and the threat and unpredictability of the forest. Yet the deeper we go into the moral landscape of Book I, the more problematic become the moral dilemmas. The narrative unravels as undecidable choices. The first and easiest battle, with Error, seems clearcut; thereafter, the issues are less easily decided. The high points in Spenser's overall plan are clear, however – Red Cross's temptations to suicide (Canto 9); and (an even more interesting temptation, especially given Spenser's later disillusion with the world of Elizabeth's Court) to abandon the quest and flee from Cleopolis, the Earthly City, the city of man, and immediately enter the Heavenly City; and finally, the magnificent emblematic stage-piece of Red Cross's battle with the dragon in the final two cantos.

Spenser's didactic Christian epic commences, then, with holiness, to emphasize man's dependence on God's grace. He combines his Christian allegory with the patriotic legend of St George, mixes history and theology with some vivid melodrama to persuade his readers to consider the issue of how to achieve a right relationship with God. Book II comes down to earth, and focuses on Sir Guyon, the Knight of Temperance, presented in Protestant humanist terms as the means by which human actions may be aligned to virtuous ends by self-control. One of the whole poem's most important episodes is the destruction of the Bower of Bliss (Canto 12). It marks the culmination of Guyon's task to overcome the witch Acrasia, depicted in forty-six extraordinarily evocative stanzas in which Guyon enters the Bower and lays violent waste to it and its inhabitants. The Bower has the alluring sensuality of a striptease, and Spenser's text is pulled in contradictory directions – by the stern moral demands of his didacticism and by the allurement of the unfolding seductiveness of the poetry. Here, explicitly for perhaps the first time in the poem, we can see some of the contradictions upon which it rests, as we observe the power of the poetry undo the didacticism of its plan. The very violence of Guyon's behaviour, hardly compatible with his role as the Knight of Temperance, points to a ruthlessness of authorial closure that increases throughout the poem. The Knight's goal is achieved; his power is upheld, but with a violence that points to more than the simple moral assertion of temperance. As Greenblatt argues, it is as if Spenser's text reveals what the poet could not face: the destruction of the Bower articulates his whole culture's 'violent resistance to a sensuous release for which it nevertheless' yearned with overwhelming intensity. Temperance itself is shown as inadequate to experience, and the poem is contradicting and (potentially at least) teaching the poet and (certainly) the reader.[23]

Book III is perhaps the most accessible to a modern reader despite its virtue – chastity. Spenser's poem gives a surprisingly Lawrentian reading of the quest for integrity in love. It is full of the violence and contradictions of love – obsession, domination, invasion, the violent imposition of the ways we express desire. The book's Knight is, significantly, a woman, Britomart, and we are taken through a complex process of misprision, naïvety, and over-reaction. But what marks a major difference is Spenser's technique which has become much more flexible in Book III than in the two earlier books. Where Books I and II tend to focus on the adventures of a single knight, Book III is much more polyphonic, a complex opening of mirrors-within-mirrors. Britomart disappears from the main action and is replaced by other heroines – Florimell, Amoret, Belphoebe – who take us into different, more complex, challenges to our experience of desire. Its major set piece, too, does not directly concern the Book's ostensible heroine: it is a richly evocative description of the Garden of Adonis, the birthplace of the twins Amoret and Belphoebe, and the seedplace of all the fecundity of the universe – including (an aspect to which we will return when we look at the remnant of Book VII) the great enemy, time. The book culminates in four of the most impressive cantos of the whole poem, and indeed one of the highest points of the whole age's poetry, the narrative of Amoret's capture by the magician Busirane, her subsequent rescue by Britomart, and (in the first (1590) version at least) her reconcilement with her lover Scudamour – who, significantly, as a male and thus the embodiment of so many of the myths by which Spenser's age apprehended love, has been unable to rescue her. In the 1590 edition, Canto 12, stanzas 43–47 brought the first published part of *The Faerie Queene* to its conclusion. In their celebration of unity through struggle and reconciliation they constitute an appropriate conclusion – confident, rapturous, serious – to what the poem's later edition would no longer be able to uphold. It is a replete and dignified ending in which Spenser turned to his lovers and his audience to exhort them: 'Now cease your worke, and at your pleasure play;/Now cease your worke, tomorrow is an holy day.'

Book IV, of Friendship, is at once the most disparate and, perhaps, in the poem's development, the most revealing. Spenser continues many of the polyphonic strands of Book III, and in some ways Book IV should be seen as a continued outfolding of the matter of Book III. It continues Book III's narrative technique, continually undermining, in

Goldberg's terms, 'the possibility of fixed character and fixed meaning'[24] in order to focus on the contradictory shapes of desire – Lust, Corflambo, Venus, the false Florimell, and (as the poem seems to move increasingly and uncomfortably closer to the world of Elizabethan politics) the love between Belphoebe and Timias, fictional projections of the Queen and Sir Walter Ralegh.

In Book V, the pressure of the Elizabethan regime upon the poem becomes most obvious, and most destructive of the poem's intentions. In Lewis's strong words, 'Spenser was the instrument of a detestable policy in Ireland, and in his fifth book the wickedness he had shared begins to corrupt his imagination.'[25] It deals fairly summarily with the execution of Mary Queen of Scots, the Armada, and then, in great detail, the English occupation of Ireland. During the late sixteenth century, Ireland was the battleground between Spain and England for continental hegemony and Spenser's attitudes were those of a planter, a landed gentleman, and a loyal Protestant Englishman with both an ideological and material stake in the colonization of Ireland. It is perhaps significant that in the 1970s some American critics have preferred to read Book V for an 'underlying' moral allegory rather than deal with the blatant political issues. Such readings are patently ideological, largely the product of the contemporary cold war, and interestingly attuned to attempts (like Spenser's, not totally deliberate) to cover and mystify awkward political realities. The fifth book undoubtedly expresses Spenser's unease before the strains of the last decades of the century just as these recent readings register a helplessness before the seeming inexorability of contemporary politics. We should remember too, that the first three books of the poem had been written before Spenser's visit to England where, for the first time in a decade, he saw something of the realities of court life. The 1580s had seen the death of Sidney and the rise of a new generation of such ambitious and ruthless courtiers as Ralegh and Essex. For Spenser himself, it had brought the responsibility of his duties in Ireland, first under Lord Grey whom he fictionalized in part as the Knight of Justice in Book V, and then under Grey's successors as Lord Deputy of Ireland.

When he came to England at the end of the decade, Spenser had certainly conceived and possibly finished Book IV. 'It belongs in spirit, design, and even execution, to the 1580s', Roger Sale notes, and parts of Book V also were written before Spenser's visit, at a time when he was anxious to defend the principles of Elizabethan power embodied in Grey's tough dealings with what the English, at least, saw as the Irish rebels.[26] From both Book V and his tract, *A Vue of the Present State of Ireland* (written 1596, although not published until 1633), we see how Spenser could be, as he was in his poem, critical of government policy. Yet he was fiercely, even brutally, loyal to its underlying principles, concluding in his treatise that Ireland should be immediately pacified by a massive application of English military force. As Helena Shire comments, while Spenser undoubtedly 'knew that the Irish were a language people of ancient culture who had inhabited the island for many centuries, that they were "lettered" earlier than the English, and that their way of life made sense to them', nevertheless, there is no acknowledgement 'whatsoever that the Irish had a right or an understandable determination to persist in their ancestral life-pattern, resisting the presence in the land of foreign overlords, who were intent on subduing them and colonizing the island completely'.[27] Spenser's criticisms of the details of Elizabeth's Irish policy, like his satire on court manners, were frequently harsh but certainly they never called the rights or ideals of the English into question.

Spenser's personal and literary careers, until sometime in the mid 1590s, therefore, both show similar patterns. But when we turn to Book VI of *The Faerie Queene*, something more disruptive can be observed. We start to see, more obviously than before, the ideological repressiveness from which the poem was born and to which, despite itself, it increasingly alludes. A note of disquiet starts to emerge that does more than simply call into question the cruder and more obviously reprehensible kinds of policies of the Elizabethan Court. In Book V, Spenser posed the problem of finding himself, as he must have done so often in Ireland, surrounded by acute contradictions between his ideals and what he saw as social realities. He looks back to the Golden Age and the note of criticism is an unusually sweeping one:

> For that which all men then did vertue call,
> Is now cald vice; and that which vice was hight,
> Is now hight vertue, and so us'd of all
>
> (V. Proem, 4)

Not surprisingly, therefore, his unease becomes more evident the closer the poem comes to the realities of the Elizabethan Court. The gloomy, unresolved ending of Book V testifies to Spenser's realization that the gap between the actual Court of Gloriana and his celebration of it was uncomfortably, perhaps unbridgeably, wide. In Book VI, he turns directly to the virtue that did, or should, uphold the life of the Court he served and by which, during both his visit to England and in his faithful service in Ireland, he felt so disturbed – courtesy.

The Book of Courtesy

The Book of Courtesy invites us to relax with a delightfully leisured, pastoral interlude, and enjoy exciting battles; it promises a civilized contrast with the gloomy brutality of Book V. Spenser presents courtesy as the manifestation in social relations of those higher virtues he has already treated. Among all the virtues, the poem serenely asserts in its opening, there

> . . . growes not a fayrer flowre,
> Then is the bloosme of comely courtesie,
> Which though it on a lowly stalke doe bowre,
> Yet brancheth forth in brave nobilitie,
> And spreds it selfe through all civilitie.
>
> (VI. Proem, 4)

But a poem by a poet whose disquiet at the Court had been expressed in *Colin Clouts Come Home Again* could not rest easy with that bland assertion, and throughout Book VI there emerges a deep anxiety about the reality of courtly life. While in the 'present age' the Proem continues, courtesy may seem to abound, 'yet being matcht with plaine Antiquitie ,/Ye will them all but fayned showes esteeme,/Which carry colours faire, that feeble eies misdeeme.' The mode of criticism in *Colin Clout* had been that of the servant of the Court appalled by the Court's irresponsibility and superficiality. Here the criticism goes much deeper:

> But in the triall of true curtesie,
>   Its now so farre from that, which then it was,
>   That it indeed is nought but forgerie,
>   Fashion'd to please the eies of them, that pas.
>
> (VI. Proem, 4, 5)

The central (if usually absent) figure of *The Faerie Queene* has been, to this point, the Queen: and, just as in *Colin Clout* the Lady Cynthia was excluded from the general criticism of the Court, so here too Spenser still highlights Elizabeth as the fairest pattern of courtesy, superior to all those of both Antiquity and the present. It is from her that the Court derives its being and also what reminders of grace and integrity it retains. Like the virtuous courtiers singled out in *Colin Clout*, the Queen is praised as the fountain, the ocean, the source, of all the 'goodly vertues' which 'well'

Into the rest, which round about you ring,
Faire Lords and Ladies, which about you dwell,
And doe adorne your Court, where courtesies excell.
                                                    (VI. Proem, 7)

But if, as the poem had sadly stated, *all* contemporary courtesy is 'but fayned showes', 'nought but forgerie', then the apparently excelling courtesy of the present age is mere surface. Similarly, while it is argued that 'vertues seat is deepe within the mynd,/And not in outward shows' and false courtesy is 'a glas so gay, that it can blynd/The wisest sight, to thinke gold that is bras', only eight lines later, the Queen herself, the source of the true courtesy, is also described as 'a mirrour sheene', her brightness also serving to 'inflame/The eyes of all, which thereon fixed beene' (VI. Proem, 5, 6). Spenser's choice of metaphor and the contradictions of his argument would seem to be produced by his repressed antagonism towards the political oppression of which he was part. Even though such confusions are marginalized, they point to fierce ideological tensions entering into the poem of which Spenser was perhaps not entirely conscious and yet which, by the end of the book, are radically undermining the ideals he is celebrating.

Social text and literary text, then, forcefully flow into each other. The England Spenser saw on his visit impinges more directly on the gentle, pastoral landscape of Book VI than might have first been imagined. But there is one characteristic of Book VI which opens up Spenser's disaffiliation with his world particularly revealingly. It is the near absence of the original inspiration for the poem: Book VI is the only one in which there is no allegorical representation of the Queen within the narrative. Everything that seems to be undermining the order Spenser had celebrated in earlier books is here embodied in the figure of the Blatant Beast – protean, indiscriminate, and, finally, impossible to enchain. Whether we see the Blatant Beast as detraction, slander, backbiting, or something more general, it stands for a distinctively courtly perversion and one that Spenser saw attacking the Court of Elizabeth so successfully that the chosen champion of courtesy, Sir Calidore, pursues but cannot finally defeat it. Presumably, it would have been possible for Spenser to have put an allegorical embodiment in the book finally to defeat or at least counterbalance the Beast. Such a confrontation would have been an assertion of belief in the continuing power of the Queen's inspiration. Instead he restricts her presence solely to the Proem and to brief references in later cantos. Even these references are uneasy or obligatory, and show Spenser coming closer than he knew to calling the ideals on which the Court was built radically into question.

There are other parts of Book VI where the realities of the 1590s provide a subtext which significantly swerves the poem from its intention. In the story of Timias, which started in Books III and IV, we can see Spenser dealing delicately with the controversial figure of Ralegh. It is, of course, too simple to say that Timias 'stands for' Ralegh: *The Faerie Queene* is too multiple in its focus to allow for such easy and unambiguous identification. But in Timias, Spenser seems to provide a very partial interpretation of his friend's relations with the Queen. Ralegh, after all, was perhaps the most blatantly manipulative of all Elizabeth's courtiers. Something of his flamboyant role-playing can be sensed in Timias's relationship with Belphoebe, where he takes the role Ralegh enacted to perfection in the English Court of the 1580s, that of the devoted yet unrewarded servant, 'captived in endlesse durance/Of sorrow and despaire without aleggeaunce' (III. 5. 42). But at some point in the second half of the poem, as (most probably) Spenser finished and revised his earlier draft of the Book of Friendship, contemporary events increasingly disturbed him into taking up the questions of courtly values in ways the first three books had not anticipated. There are signs that in considering Ralegh's fall from favour in 1592 Spenser found himself caught between conflicting allegiances to the Queen and to what he perceived as the injustice of his patron's treatment. In the earlier book, the delicate ambiguity of Spenser's treatment of Timias's guilt at being taken with Amoret, 'handling soft the hurts, which she did get' (IV. 7. 35), becomes a delightful comedy. Mistakes of misprision and overreaction occur on both sides and Spenser skilfully balances the seductive sensuality of Amoret with the fierce exclusiveness of Belphoebe who

> . . . in her wrath she thought them both have thrild,
> With that selfe arrow, which the Carle had kild.
> Yet held her wrathfull hand from vengeance sore,
> But drawing nigh, ere he her well beheld;
> Is this the faith, she said, and said no more,
> But turnd her face, and fled away for evermore.

(IV. 7. 36)

But when Timias reappears in Book VI, the ambiguity is no longer quite so comic or delicate. In Book VI. 3, Spenser attempts to deal, as Ralegh himself was attempting to do, with the Queen's anger at his marriage with Elizabeth Throckmorton. Spenser comes down firmly on his friend's side, and blames both the Blatant Beast, the slanderous enemy of courtesy, who 'in his wide great mouth' has seized Serena (VI. 3. 24), and the three Knights of Discourtesy, Despetto, Decetto, and Defetto, who have attacked and wounded the gallant squire. Like Ralegh himself, Spenser could not face the possibility that his commitment to the Court had proved so futile and unrewarding that the Court itself was corrupt and destructive; like Ralegh, he could only blame misunderstanding and malice which had, somehow, deceived even the Queen.

The world of the late Elizabethan Court, then, comes uneasily close to the surface of Book VI, despite the significant absence of the Queen herself within its narrative structure. Even more disturbing to the apparent serenity of this 'delightfull land of Faery', however, is a pessimism that contrasts radically with the tone of earlier Books. It is prefigured in the Proem to Book V, where Spenser broods over the 'state of present time' comparing it with 'the image of the antique world', and able to find evidence only for degeneration:

> Me seemes the world is runne quite out of square,
> From the first point of his appointed sourse,
> And being once amisse growes daily wourse and wourse.
>
> (V. Proem, 1)

All around is the dissolution of human history; only the chosen instruments of justice, like Artegall, stand between mankind and chaos. Implied here is a view of history startingly different from that of earlier books, where degeneration was seen as only a temporary phase in a pattern of natural replenishment and regeneration. An optimistic, cyclical view of history has been replaced by a view of history as entropic, a view that is stressed even more strongly at the start of Book VI. There too the Antique world's true virtue has been abandoned for 'fayned showes', 'forgerie', and deception, and Sir Calidore's quest, unlike that of any previous hero, has taken him further and further from fulfilment. At the end of the book, the Blatant Beast escapes and 'raungeth through the world againe' (VI. 12. 40). The poem's pessimism has become not merely that of a disillusioned, ageing courtier or public servant disturbed by the evident surface corruption of the late Elizabethan Court. The end of *The Faerie Queene* records a deeper disillusion, one that links the poem more closely than Spenser (or many of his modern admirers) would like to the generation of cynically quietistic, deeply disillusioned, radicals of the 1590s – with the tortured, dislocated writings of Donne, Marston, Greville and Webster, and with the deeply pessimistic Shakespeare of *Troilus and Cressida* and *Hamlet*. All of these younger men lived into the Jacobean period and each had his own, conscious or suppressed, ways of reacting to the pressure of that disillusion. Spenser was to die shortly before the peculiar Jacobean schizophrenia could claim him. What he must have started to grope towards is poignantly recorded in Book VI of *The Faerie Queene*.

At the start of the book, the poem turns to define courtesy and thus to set the expected quest in motion. We are told, in a conventional enough starting-point, that 'Courtesie' is derived from 'Court'. But the terms in which this commonplace is expressed are curiously contradictory:

Of Court it seemes, men Courtesie doe call,
For that it there most useth to abound.
                                        (VI. 1. 1)

'Seemes' and 'most useth' are more tentative than a wholehearted assertion of the virtue of courtesy might demand. 'Useth' suggests habitual or accustomed expectation as well as containing a hint of nostalgia; 'seemes' recalls the 'fayned showes' which the Proem has already mentioned. Furthermore, Spenser goes on: 'Right so in Faery court it did redound,/Where curteous Knights and Ladies most did won/Of all on earth, and made a matchlesse paragon' (VI. 1. 1). The switch to the past tense reinforces the tentativeness of Spenser's discussion of courtesy. Next we encounter a description of his Knight of Courtesy, and the same ambiguity continues. While Calidore is depicted as 'none more courteous', it is difficult to take the Greek origin of his name (Beautiful Gift) seriously without simultaneously admitting that either Spenser is verging on satire or is interestingly unaware of the contradictions. Calidore, we are told, has 'gentlenesse of spright', 'manners milde', 'gracious speech', 'faire usage and conditions sound', and is shown to be restrained, disciplined, and ceremonious. Yet the emphasis on such characteristics is qualified by Spenser's habitual use of 'seemes' (e.g. VI. 1. 2) and by the distinctive choice of terms to describe Calidore. To his natural graces, he 'add's 'comely guize'. While he is 'well approv'd in batteilous affray', yet his 'faire usage' 'purchast' him 'place' and reputation. It is difficult to argue that these terms do not undercut any affirmation of courtesy as the triumphant harmonization of opposites.

While Spenser sets up a strong contrast in the Proem between calculated externalized 'showes' of courtesy and the hidden virtues within, as he moves through Faeryland in Book VI, exploring, refining, and testing his initial definition of courtesy, a set of revealing contradictions emerges. At the start of the third Canto, the poem qualifies the earlier insistence upon true courtesy lying deep within the mind by asserting that outward manners can, in fact, be taken as a reliable guide to inward virtue. But now courtesy is said to be bound up with externals, behaving with decorum and bearing oneself 'aright/To all of each degree, as doth behove'. In the fifth canto, we are assured further that there is always a firm connection between gentle behaviour and noble birth, between external grace and internal virtue, even if it may not be easily discernible. Spenser asserts that Calidore 'loathd leasing, and base flattery,/And loved simple truth and stedfast honesty' (VI. 1. 3), but the difference between these admirable characteristics and the 'comely guize' and the 'greatest grace' that Calidore 'with the greatest purchast' is blithely not made clear. At one with his age's most conservative moralists, Spenser asserts that a noble, trotting stallion rarely begets an awkward, ambling colt. He seems to be deeply concerned to hold social change at bay and to preserve the traditional standards he clearly saw being eroded in the Court of the 1590s. Such contradictions show how the beginning of Book VI simply cannot maintain the moral distinctions on which his exploration of the nature of the Court and courtesy needed to be based. Even Spenser himself was perhaps increasingly unable to make such distinctions with his earlier certainty. The world he creates, instead of testing and so refining his chosen virtue, comes increasingly to call it radically into question.

In accordance with the expected pattern of the whole poem, then, Calidore goes off on his quest. It is striking that, embodying a virtue which 'useth' to be found at Court, Calidore will eventually find it best manifest in the country. It is also noteworthy that as a knight representing or searching for a distinctively social virtue, courtesy, he goes off alone. His world in fact becomes an increasingly lonely one, dominated by the unpredictability of fortune and the ambiguity of moral choice. 'All flesh is frayle, and full of ficklenesse', he learns, 'subject to fortunes chance, still chaunging new' (VI. 1. 41). The clear dichotomy between good and evil which is traditionally a central part of the chivalric quest is also missing here. Calidore's foe, the Blatant Beast – the savage vilifier of Timias, the adversary who has escaped Artegall's savage hand in Book V – emerges as a savage parody of courtesy, 'fostred long in Stygian fen,/Till he to perfect ripeness grew, and then,/Into this wicked world he forth was sent'. Such terms recall the nurturing of Amoret and Belphoebe, and the 'infinite shapes of creatures' bred in the Garden of Adonis (III. 6. 35). Indeed, part of the Beast's threat seems to lie in its being uncannily close to the virtue it seeks to undermine: the enemy of courtesy is not an alien force, but a variant of courtesy itself.

The impression that Calidore and his adversaries share a world of common values is brought out in Calidore's confrontation with Maleffort and Briana. Both sides in the battle use the language and the art of courtesy: she accuses Calidore of scorning and shaming the decorum of chivalry by murdering her servants and sends word to her champion Crudor to

> . . . desire that he would
> Vouchsafe to reskue her against a Knight,
> Who through strong powre had now her self in hould,
> Having late slaine her Seneschall in fight,
> And all her people murdred with outragious might.
>
> (VI. 1. 29)

In similar terms Crudor vows to 'succour her' and in appropriate chivalric manner sends 'to her his basenet, as a faithfull band' (31). In order to stress their shared values, Spenser does not, as he does so often in earlier books, give moral asides to direct his readers' responses. Instead, he stresses Calidore's precipitate entry into the battle. When he sees a knight approaching,

> Well weend he streight, that he should be the same,
>   Which tooke in hand her quarrell to maintaine;
> Ne stayd to aske if it were he by name,
>   But coucht his speare, and ran at him amaine.
>   (VI. 1. 33)

The two combatants are almost indistinguishable as they fight, and when Calidore is finally victorious, he comments upon the dubious outcome in a revealing line, confessing to his vanquished enemy that 'What haps to day to me, to morrow may to you' (41). It is as if they are struggling not in a world of moral absolutes, but for alternate versions of courtesy. Such relativism is a strange departure for *The Faerie Queene* and one that seems contradictory to Spenser's announced intentions.

The episode following, with the squire Tristram, also brings out the ways in which conservatism and moral relativism contradict each other. Calidore's initial hostility to Tristram's 'hand too bold . . . embrewed/In blood of knight' (VI. 2. 7) is tempered when he learns of the discourtesy of Tristram's victim, and instead of seeing Tristram's behaviour as discourteous, he accommodates the youngster's behaviour to necessity – 'what he did, he did him selfe to save'. He then enunciates a principle which would seem, logically, to justify the behaviour not merely of Tristram but of Crudor in the previous episode: that 'knights and all men this by nature have,/Towards all womenkind them kindly to behave' (VI. 2. 14). Spenser later tries to smooth out the moral contradictions: Tristram turns out to be of noble birth, the son of 'good king *Meliogras*' of Cornwall, and so his behaviour is legitimized.

These and the other early episodes in Book VI unravel, then, as nodes of contradiction. Spenser's difficulty in reconciling his conservative moral absolutism with an increasingly relativistic world comes out particularly in Calidore's need, most intriguing in a knight representing a supposedly inner virtue, to rely on the 'fayned showes' and the values of reputation and appearance which have been indignantly repudiated at the book's start. Calidore (and, in Canto 5, Arthur) are perfectly entitled, it seems, to use deceit, subterfuge, and cunning to achieve their ends. What seems to differentiate their true from others' false courtesy is simply success. Perhaps we are just meant to assume that Arthur is by definition right, but if so, an important moral ambiguity surfaces: his methods are difficult or impossible to distinguish from those of his or Calidore's enemies. We are meant to take his virtue for granted even though his actions seem indistinguishable from those of his enemies.

It may be that Spenser was partly aware of the contradictions he was building into his poem. But they undoubtedly articulate a more widespread unease and confusion than his 'intention' knew. We can recognize how such an earnest, committed servant of the Elizabethan Court would react to what he saw as the crumbling away of the ideals on which the Court was built. But what language did he have to articulate his distress? What he inevitably falls back on is the residual language of religious renunciation. Yet he did so only as the poem came to what was to be its premature end. In Book I the Red Cross Knight was given a vision of the Heavenly City, and, overwhelmed by its transcendence even of the Earthly City, Cleopolis, had prayed to be allowed to abandon his quest and enter into the world of eternity. He was sent firmly back into the world to complete his quest, just as Spenser applied himself faithfully to his duties in Ireland. But when, in the middle of Book VI, a similar situation arises in the Blatant Beast's attack on Timias and Serene the temptation of withdrawal from the world arises again. Timias and Serena take refuge with a Hermit, and for once, Spenser creates a character who, although unquestionably embodying what he wants us to see as a signpost towards truth, seems at odds with the ostensible virtue of the poem. He has, he tells them, renounced the Court:

> . . . he had bene a man of mickle name,
> Renowmed much in armes and derring doe:
> But being aged now and weary to
> Of warres delight, and worlds contentious toyle,
> The name of knighthood he did disavow,
> And hanging up his armes and warlike spoyle,
> From all this worlds incombraunce did himselfe assoyle.
>
> (VI. 5. 37)

The terms in which the Hermit is described suggest a restful reward for many years of devotion to the 'worlds contentious toyle', yet the cure he prescribes for Timias and Serena – who are still 'young' (VI. 5. 11) and 'faire' (VI. 5. 39) – is also renunciation of the toil of courtly strife. He entertains them

> Not with forged showes, as fitter beene
> For courting fooles, that curtesies would faine,
> But with entire affection and appearaunce plaine.
>
> (VI. 5. 38)

His counsel is to 'avoide the occasion' of their pain, to 'abstaine from pleasure', and 'subdue desire' (VI. 6. 14) – to give over, in other words, the delights of the courtly life. Obviously, the Hermit's advice is perfectly in accord with Spenser's earlier emphasis that true virtue lies deep within the mind, yet it does lie uncomfortably beside the active life of courtesy the book has so far celebrated.

The second half of Book VI brings these contradictions more into the open. What I have so far highlighted might be described as no more perhaps than a sense of unease on Spenser's part, most probably produced by his own experiences in the Court, his reaction to Ralegh's fall from favour, and, simply, his own increasing age and weariness. From Canto 7 onwards, this unease brings Spenser to focus on the one commitment to which, it seems, he held even more strongly than to his political duties – his poetry. As Book VI draws to its conclusion, the belief in national destiny that lay at the root of his original choice of the epic written to celebrate England and the Court of Elizabeth seems to falter, and we can see emerging an even greater contradiction. Unable to celebrate the Court and its virtues as unambiguously as he once did, his poem starts to evaluate even its author's role as the celebrant of the Queen and her Court. The Blatant Beast attacks not only virtuous and unwary courtiers, but the basis of the very art that has brought him into being:

> Ne spareth he most learned wits to rate,
> Ne spareth he the gentle Poets rime,
> But rends without regard of person or of time.

> Ne may this homely verse, of many meanest
> Hope to escape his venemous despite . . .
>
> (VI. 12. 40–41)

With this melancholy and somewhat waspish tone Spenser, in fact goes on to conclude Book VI: the forces which threaten society and civility are also attacking the poet and poetry itself, seemingly without restraint. Therefore how does the poet, whose life has been dedicated to celebrating the Court, deal with its rejection not only of the ideals of courtesy on which it is itself founded, but of the poet who would draw them back to those ideals? In the second half of the book, the power and value of poetry in the Court become a central subject, and what emerges is a deep unease about the reciprocity of Court and poet on which *The Faerie Queene* had been built. While the final six cantos of the book are ostensibly centred on Calidore, they have as an urgent underlying concern Spenser's commitment to the very poem to which he had devoted so much of his life. We can see perhaps Calidore and Colin Clout, who appears in Canto 9 as an embodiment of the figure of the troubled poet, as two aspects of Spenser himself, or more generally, of the court poet (a Sidney, a Wyatt, Ralegh, or Greville, all of whom, as we have seen, committed themselves so strongly to the importance of poetry in the Court). In the writing of *The Faerie Queene*, it may be that Spenser himself, however partially, became uneasily aware of an incompatibility between the courtier's life and the courtly poem. The poem itself starts to educate if not its writer at least its readers in ways its writer had not anticipated.

Let us trace something of this gradually opening fissure in the poem. The affinities between the Knight of Courtesy and his opponents become much more explicit when Calidore temporarily abandons his quest to live with the shepherds in the pastoral world. His quest has taken him throughout the world:

> Him first from court he to the citties coursed,
> And from the citties to the townes him prest,
> And from the townes into the countrie forsed,
> And from the country back to private farmes he scorsed.
>
> (VI. 9. 3)

When he finds a group of shepherds who have never seen such a creature as the Blatant Beast, he stays with them, and proceeds to woo a country girl, Pastorella. Calidore's addresses to her uncomfortably recall the 'outward showes' that were rejected at the book's start. He adopts shepherd's clothes and crook in the hope of making an appropriate impression. Once he sees that she had never 'such knightly service seene' and 'did little whit regard his courteous guize' he

> . . . thought it best
> To chaunge the manner of his loftie looke;
> And doffing his bright armes, himselfe addrest
> In shepheards weed, and in his hand he tooke,
> In stead of steelehead speare, a shepheards hooke.
>
> (VI. 9. 35, 36)

He defies Coridon, his rival, in terms strongly reminiscent of his earlier encounter with Briana and Maleffort, and then uses his superior courtly graces to win Pastorella from the angry shepherd. We are told by Spenser that all commended him 'for courtesie amongst the rudest breeds/Good will and favour' (VI. 9. 45), but the terms by which his victory is achieved are all too reminiscent of the patronizing, manipulative skills of the devious courtier. When he launches into a conventional praise of the pastoral life, and Pastorella's father replies, equally conventionally, that all men must accept their places in the universe since 'it is the mynd that maketh wretch or happie, rich or poore', Calidore does not see the irony of the comment, and moreover, immediately manipulates the discussion to further his desire for Pastorella.

When we are shown Calidore as the spectator of the stately vision on Mount Acidale, we are aware that as with other doctrinal nodes of the poem, Spenser is focusing with as much intensity as he can on the issues underlying his poem. In this superbly evocative episode, there is inserted a mysterious and striking figure. Besides the ring of dancers on the Mount is the figure of the poet named as Colin Clout. It is one of the most significant touches that Spenser should introduce what amounts to a charmingly deprecative self-portrait at a moment in the poem when the courtly vision seems closest to faltering. It is one of the high points of the whole poem – dignified, passionate, redolent with suggestiveness, and moreover, an episode into which Spenser put most explicitly his anxieties about his courtly vocation.

The episode starts by recalling the Book's opening, the terms of which have, as we have seen, become increasingly ambivalent as the adventures have proceeded. The pastoral world, we are told, far transcends the world of courtly vanity, 'Save onely *Glorianaes* heavenly hew/To which what can compare?' (VI. 10. 4). Perhaps Spenser's unease at where his poem is now turning makes him draw attention to this obligatory exception to courtly degeneration. Certainly, the vision Calidore is given on the Mount seems to call into question the value and power of the Court. In the centre of the Grace's dance is not the Queen, nor virtuous courtiers, nor an abstract, untested virtue, but Colin Clout's own shepherd lass who 'another grace . . . well deserves to be' (VI. 10. 27). There is a brief, though charming, apology for seeming to replace the Queen – and yet the transposition has been made. But of course, it is not Colin but Calidore who is the book's central figure and so it is he who breaks into the dance and makes the vision disappear. Interestingly, while Colin may instruct Calidore (and us) on its significance, there is no sense that (unlike the allegorical set pieces in earlier books) the Knight will benefit from the vision he has been given. Instead, he turns back to his devious pursuits and to his quest. Returning to Pastorella, he discovers the fact of her noble parentage and then that she has been captured by brigands.

How do we read this division in the book's culminating scene? It is as if we must choose between Calidore and Colin at this point. Book VI seems to have increasingly revealed contradictions in Spenser's celebration of the Court. We might argue that he seems aware of these contradictions to the extent that he can, with some unease, but without apology, project contradictory aspects of his vision into Calidore and Colin Clout. But it is the incompatibility which comes most strongly

through in the poem in ways the poet himself felt uneasy about. As at
the end of Book II, an act of authorial intervention had tried to direct,
very strongly, our response. The vision of the Graces does not merely
disappear; it disappears because of Calidore's intervention. Like the
Blatant Beast itself, he blunders in and destroys. At the book's end, we
are left with the situation with which it started. The Beast has infected
all estates of society, has been temporarily captured, and in the short-
lived triumph of its capture what the Knight and his enemy have in
common becomes quite explicit. All questions of moral superiority are
gone; instead, we have the spectacle of public adulation in which all
'much admyr'd the Beast, but more admyr'd the Knight' (VI. 12. 37).
The Beast then breaks his bonds and rages through the world again.

The Faerie Queene's place in Elizabethan culture

The Faerie Queene is the ultimate test case in Elizabethan poetry for the
ways in which power seeks to control language. It is a poem expressly
dedicated to the praise of the Queen, her Court, and the cultural
practices by which the Elizabethan regime established and maintained its
power. Spenser accepts his role as that of the Orphic bard, praising,
warning, and celebrating the society that not only rewarded but in a real
sense created him. Thus his poem's central figure is the Queen – as head
of the Church as well as the State, triumphing over heresy on the one
hand and political dissent on the other, and as the inspiration of the
poem itself. The Queen's response to the poem, at least to the first part
published, was to reward Spenser with a pension, and in 1598 she
requested his appointment as Sheriff of Cork. To have even a self-styled
laureate praising her regime so fulsomely was to acknowledge poetry's
usefulness as part of its ideological underpinning. More consciously than
any other poem in the last two decades of the century, *The Faerie Queene*
is 'Art become a work of State', asserting that beneath the contingent
world the values of the regime are without contradiction and that when
its norms are transgressed, chaos will result. The poem is offered as a
microcosm of this truth.

To speak of *The Faerie Queene* as the most magnificent articulation of
the Elizabethan Court's dominant ideology is, however, a claim that is
contradicted by the poem itself. The poem raises the question of how a
deeply conservative poet can be surpassed by his own poem so that his
readers see the ideological contradictions, not just the ideological
mystifications, of his society. If we submit *The Faerie Queene* to a

symptomatic reading, and are alert to its contradictions, to what is absent or silent, then we can see how to construct the latent text which is struggling to emerge.[28]

The very length of time Spenser spent on his poem, perhaps twenty years, helps us open up the poem to such a symptomatic reading. The poem may have started as a celebration, and even with some plan like that which Spenser outlined in a letter to Ralegh, where he spoke of twelve books, each with its own virtue and a culminating feast in the Court of Gloriana. But by 1596, the original design had been abandoned. Lewis suggests we speak not of a 'whole' poem, but rather of fragments A (1590, Books I–III), B (1596 IV–VI), and C (Mutability).[29] Certainly, between the image of mutuality and confidence in the reconciliation of Amoret and Scudamour in the cancelled final stanzas of the 1590 edition and the darker late books there are too many contradictions to ignore. The poem encodes many of the real historical conflicts and tensions of its time, dealing with them not (as Shakespeare was already starting to do in the mid 1590s) by juxtaposing and so exploring their rival claims to truth and allegiance, but by trying arbitrarily to displace and condense them to maintain the power of the dominant ideology. The poet's desire is clear: to justify the cultural and ideological practices of the Elizabethan Court. And yet his poem is fragmented by potent ideological breaks and contradictions. Book V is particularly revealing: in the opening canto, for instance, Artegall dismisses chivalric reconciliation as ineffective in deciding the conflict between Sanglier and his opponent, asserting that 'doubtfull causes' can be decided only by force. Conflict is settled not by the knights acknowledging their places in a hierarchy but by brutal militarism. Ultimately, ideological domination is dependent on force.

What the poem attempts – in the early books buoyantly, in the later ones desperately – is a denial of historical change. *The Faerie Queene* yearns for stasis, to project truth as unalterable in the face of unpredictability and, in its manifestation in Elizabeth and her Court, as natural, given, and unassailable. It is built therefore on a poetic that tries to avoid debate, to efface all contradiction, and to reconcile all partial truths into a higher harmony or ruthlessly to exclude them as heretical or unnatural. It tries likewise to create a reader who is active but subservient – a loyal participant in the decipherment of emblem, hieroglyph, and allegory. He or she is interpellated as part of a great celebration of ideological plenitude, just as the Elizabethan courtier was enculturated and socialized by accepting his or her proper place in the Court. But just as there was in the Court, so in Spenser's poem there is an anxiety that emerges as continual contradiction. As we have seen, Sidney's independence of mind, Ralegh's devious rebellion (and earlier, Wyatt's bursts of moral scepticism) could be dealt with by various state apparatuses – by exclusion, imprisonment, silence, or threat. But in Spenser's poem the pressures and contradictions of the history which it tries to exclude – the real as opposed to the ideological – continually seep back into it. Despite its epic claim to speak for the Elizabethan regime, thoughts and actions that were not permitted beyond preserved limits none the less enter the poem. Oppositional cultural practices barely allowed voice elsewhere in Elizabethan poetry fracture and disrupt *The Faerie Queene*. However marginalized, ridiculed, or (by the mechanics of the allegory) repressed, none the less they come through to mark the seeming serenity of the ideology which produces the poem. Like any text – and the greater the text's desire for 'universal' meaning, the more this occurs – *The Faerie Queene* emerges in a cultural space where cultural contradictions surface and there are inevitably indeterminacies and gaps in the poem where it cannot say what its own logic demands.

Even sympathetic readers note this unease in the poem, although they might put it down to failures of poetic style instead of symptomatic, culturally produced, characteristics. It is the role of the reader *not* to accept the poet's demands (which were, after all, the Elizabethan regime's demands) but rather to reconstruct the ways by which the text was produced by the operation of its power, just as, to return to Alan Sinfield's comparison, we might argue it is the role of the reader of contemporary Soviet writing to probe beneath the bland superficialities of official pronouncements on the writers duty to produce patriotic 'realism'. This is why it is important to look for the signs of contradiction, uneasiness, and incompletion in *The Faerie Queene* – because of the very power of the dominant reading. Again, such revealing moments should be viewed not as 'faults' in any 'aesthetic' sense, but rather perhaps in something like the geological sense – as signs of the eruption of history into the production of the text. The text is, as we have seen with all the sixteenth-century poets, a site of struggle: it is fought over by the ideological strains within the society at large, and centred on an attempt to efface all traces of those struggles by which it is, in fact, produced.[30]

Two further, brief, examples may be given from the later books. As was noted earlier, Spenser's unease before the Queen's treatment of Ralegh is one that surfaces in Books IV and VI. It is an episode the poet himself foregrounds, no doubt because Ralegh was one of his sponsors; but Spenser is none the less controlled and limited by Elizabeth's own reading of the situation. In Book IV, Belphoebe's absence limits the claims of mistreatment Timias can make; in Book VI, the poem is further paralysed by Ralegh's fate. We note the powerlessness of the court poet: all his poem can seemingly do is acknowledge the power that was, outside the poem, imprisoning and condemning his patron. We can even construct Ralegh's own reading of the Timias episode, perhaps, in his own poetry, especially in 'Ocean to Scinthia' where he grimly complains of his twelve years in the Queen's service.

A second example comes from Book V. Goldberg has pointed out how one particular reader of the poem whose misreading, however creative or 'powerful' in the sense I suggest modern readings should be, is deliberately rejected by Spenser's allegory and would be not only considered 'wrong' but heretical by Spenser. James VI of Scotland read Book V as an insult to his mother, Mary Queen of Scots, executed in 1588, and demanded (in vain) that the poet be punished. In the poem, in fact, the very same demand that Duessa (Mary's allegorical surrogate) receive fair treatment is rigorously 'raced out' (V. 9. 26), and her poet Bonfont is renamed Malfont and has his tongue nailed to a post. As Goldberg notes, 'public dismemberment – including the beheading of Mary Queen of Scots – is congruent with numerous actions' that occur in Book V: it 'was one way in which the power of the monarch displayed itself, inscribing itself on the body of the condemned'.[31] What James's objection assumed was that the power of the Elizabethan regime stood behind Spenser's poem – after all, it is Spenser himself who insists that *The Faerie Queene* is indeed Elizabeth's, that Artegall is her, not his, knight (V. Proem) and that he is merely the articulator not the originator of the unchanging principles, beyond argument or opposition, of law and justice. Artegall's imposition of justice is a confirmation not of eternal principles but of force. Book V enacts the ways the Queen's power operates over poetry; it displays *The Faerie Queene*'s origins in Elizabethan ideology – and we can see James's reading of the poem as perhaps the earliest unveiling of those origins. James, who loved flattery, might not have been quite so pleased with being described as an early demystifier of ideological repression, but his reading is a model for the kind I am suggesting modern readers produce – where a body of powerful questions are asked of the poem, especially ones the poem does not want to answer.

Further, observing such explicit ways ideology marks the seemingly innocent literary text – done not by going outside the text as by probing a site of struggle within it – allows us to look at other places in the poem where similar struggles occur and where they have been, perhaps, more successfully effaced. Judith Anderson has observed how even in Book III, the portrait of Belphoebe distances her 'as a mythic ideal' from 'any living referent' – precisely the process which we can observe in the way the Queen operated within the social text of Elizabethan culture. In Book IV, the same process is at work in the reconciliation of Belphoebe and Timias, which can be read as a desirable fantasy, but what in the dangerous world of late Elizabethan politics was becoming increasingly impossible, and before which poetry was increasingly helpless.[32]

The closer we probe the textual practices of *The Faerie Queene*, the more we must ask whether it makes sense to speak of the 'unity' of *The Faerie Queene* at all. It is a different question from: to what extent would Spenser have wanted to have his readers find unity in it? The dislocations are obvious in later books but even in the early books, ideology and textuality seem to pull in different directions. Carol Kaske has pointed to the unsettling relativistic universe the poem creates – as distinct from the assertions of absolute principles with which it asserts – by its unfinished quests, the increasing heterogeneity of its virtues, the uneasy slippage between Christian and classical principles. Even back in the opening canto, there is a real sense in which the poem's first adversary, the Monster Error, embodies a fundamental principle of its writerly quality. As Patricia Parker notes, 'Spenser's own book is like the monster "Error" in that it, too, has swallowed a multitude of books and recognizing them is part of the devious process of "reading".'[33]

As we have seen, of the books that Spenser completed, it is in Book VI that the contradictions and silences are most clearly evident. Spenser's loss of epic vision is taken a further step in Lewis's fragment C, the Cantos of Mutability, where one of the recurring enemies of the poem's vision is at last faced. The Garden of Adonis (II. 6) had been an earlier attempt to turn history to myth by showing how the universal changes of nature had an underlying principle of stability. The Garden is the source 'of all things, that are borne to live and die'. And yet it is dominated by the figure that recurs so powerfully in Elizabethan mythology – Time. Time is the arbiter of human life, the destroyer of youth, beauty, and the rude challenger to the order of human society. Time, we are told

. . . with his scyth addrest,
Does mow the flowring herbes and goodly things,
And all their glory to the ground downe flings . . .
All things decay in time, and to their end do draw.

(III. 6. 39–40)

But, in the vision of plenitude Spenser asserts, Time's power over each creature can be only a partial representation of truth. Without change and death, Nature could not fulfil its regenerative purposes. What matters is not that individual creatures are inevitably subject to transience, but that through all change, the universal and God-given natural principles of procreation and fertility continue. The principles of the universe are 'eterne in mutabilitie'.

In the Cantos of Mutability Time reappears in the form of the demi-goddess, Mutability, who challenges the power of the gods and claims to be the single universal principle. Occasionally, modern scholars have pointed out Spenser's affinities with avant-garde

philosophers, such as Giordano Bruno, in this Book. But if any ideas
from Bruno are referred to here, they are invoked only to be rejected.
The Lucretian law that all things are powerless to resist time is firmly set
in the contexts of the natural creative order and the explicitly Christian
perspective of God's eternity. In one of Bruno's dialogues, *The Expulsion of the Triumphant Beast*, Fortune (like Spenser's Mutability)
argues for the god's recognition of change as an autonomous principle of
the universe. For Bruno, mutability is a discovery of liberation and
creativity. For Spenser, however seductive Mutability appears, she is the
enemy and must be rejected. Mutability's claim is that both heaven and
earth are subject to change:

> For, who sees not, that *Time* on all doth pray?
> But *Times* do change and move continually.
> So nothing here long standeth in one stay:
> Wherefore, this lower world who can deny
>   But to be subject still to *Mutabilitie*?
> (VII. 7. 47)

Once again, Time and its power are placed in the context of a larger
purpose: the more Mutability demonstrates the facts of change, the
more it is obvious that Nature includes Mutability in itself, that change
and death are part of a universal order – just as the Elizabethan regime
itself must be seen as unchanging and constant, centred, in Ralegh's
words, on the 'Lady whom Time hath forgot'. Ideology smooths over
any opposition.

In the final stanzas of this fragment of two cantos and two disconnected stanzas, Spenser explicitly invokes the orthodox Christian
framework, in which time is transcended by an eternal realm which

> . . . is contrayr to *Mutabilitie*:
> For, all that moveth, doth in *Change* delight:
> But thence-forth all shall rest eternally
> With Him that is the God of Sabbaoth hight:
> O that great Sabbaoth God, graunt me that Sabaoths sight.
> (VII. 8. 2)

So, at least, is the argument of the Mutability Cantos. Its fragmentary
nature makes it difficult to see it unambiguously as a coherent whole or
as a continuation of the rest of the poem. Many aspects of the cantos
continue the concerns of earlier books but there are many which do not
fit. As Marion Campbell notes, 'for all their affinities with the rest of the
poem, what the Mutability Cantos offers us is not so much a re-
capitulation as a reversal, or at least a dislocation of our experience of the

world of *The Faerie Queene*'. The stance of the narrator is one such dislocation: perhaps for the first time, he is 'clearly shaken by the tale he tells and he finds himself unable to proceed with his customary confidence and objectivity'.[34] Even more telling is the apocalyptic note in the final cantos in which the poet turns back to his poem and, in effect, rejects the poem itself.

There is an irony in the poem's final fragments that may turn a reader back to that point in Book I where the Red Cross Knight was enjoined not to turn his back on the world but to pursue his quest to the end. There, he did so in part to enforce the reader also to pursue a quest for the principles of holiness, temperance, love, friendship, justice, and courtesy upon which the poem's vision would be built. Yet, as the poem proceeded and we read on, those virtues became increasingly blurred. The Mutability Cantos likewise show an uneasiness before the terms they propose. The two great adversaries, Cynthia (representing the status quo) and Mutability, both appeal to the same 'sterne' principles (V 6. 12, 13) and even when they turn to Jove for judgement, he has no firm means of distinguishing between them. As Jove and Mutability face each other, it is also difficult to distinguish their speeches as if, in Jacqueline Miller's words, by the end of these two encounters there is no hierarchy remaining except by the force of assertion.[35] As we saw in Book VI, the poet has to step in himself to show the truth. But here he does so in such terms that the poem itself is rejected. Throughout, part of *The Faerie Queene*'s energy has been built upon its author's firm intentions, and the clash between those intentions and the multiplicity and deferrals of the poem itself. As Richard Neuse puts it, '*The Faerie Queene* opens up what Elizabeth and her regime tried to prevent, a public space for debate.'[36] Now, in the Cantos of Mutability, the despair of the poem to affirm a final truth finally surfaces explicitly. Just as Sidney here, at his death, was to ask for his 'toys' and 'vanities' to be destroyed, so Spenser is, in effect, rejecting his whole poem. The final stanzas concede the failure of his undertaking: they look back and see that as the poem has developed, there are secretly proliferated contradictions which break the poem apart. Spenser might have attributed it to mutability or the fall, but in the final stanzas of the poem as we have it, Nature vanishes, the world is dismissed, and so too is poetry. What remains is an absence that undermines what Spenser has devoted his whole life to make present in his poem.

Set in the context of sixteenth-century poetry (and even if we look ahead and acknowledge the presence of Renaissance England's other great epic, *Paradise Lost*), *The Faerie Queene* can be seen as the last attempt to decipher the world by affirming as natural, given, and eternal the secret resemblances and hierarchy behind its plethora of signs. It attempts to create a reading of nature, society, man, and poetry as an interconnected network of harmony and hierarchy, the whole recognized and valorized by each individual part – only to find that each part breaks into its separate world. At the poem's end, left with only his words, he discovers that they too have lost their divine resemblance. It is as if Spenser sensed how language could no longer function as marks of a divine order, but was revealed as signs of power. Earlier in the poem it was for Spenser a seemingly natural impulse to refuse history, to erect myths by which the promiscuous overflow of words could be refused reality. And as we read *The Faerie Queene*, from the confident opening stanzas to the Cantos of Mutability, we can see how Spenser could not foresee that the productivity of his text and of the world it purported to represent would again and again contradict his determinations.

If we say then, as this chapter asserted at its start, that *The Faerie Queene* is unquestionably the 'greatest' poem of the century, what do we mean? Clearly not that it is united, finished, replete; or that its vision is noble, coherent, let alone 'true'. Spenser's poem is one of the most fascinating in all our poetry, at once one of the richest and the emptiest poems, one to which readers can return endlessly because it is an encyclopaedia of the ways ideology and textuality interact, and of the processes by which languages intersect and rewrite one another. There is a deep longing for meaning and stasis in *The Faerie Queene* which is contradicted at the deepest level by its own being. It attempts to transform history into culture, culture into nature, and to fix that which inevitably changes in stasis. As such it epitomizes all that the Elizabethan Court itself likewise tried and failed to do. Spenser's poem may be described as 'great' on two main counts. First, like the society which produced it, it could not remain faithful to the desires which motivated it, and the more those were asserted to be natural and true, the more their falsity and the naked power on which they rested, is revealed. *The Faerie Queene* is thus a rich and fascinating articulation of a complex and fascinating cultural formation. Second, as text (as, to be precise, textuality, as the stimulus to seductive and multiple readings), it remains intriguing, perplexing, rich, unmistakably a great work of poetry.

Notes

1. C. S. Lewis, *English Literature in the Sixteenth Century Excluding Drama* (Oxford, 1954), pp. 358–64.

2. Richard Helgerson, 'The New Poet Presents Himself: Spenser and the Idea of a Literary Career', *PMLA*, 93 (1978), 893–911 (p. 893).

3. Alan Sinfield, *Literature in Protestant England* (London, 1983), p. 66; Arthur F. Marotti, '"Love is not Love": Elizabethan Sonnet Sequences and the Social Order', *ELH*, 49 (1982), 396–428 (p. 417).

4. Jonathan Goldberg, 'The Poet's Authority: Spenser, Jonson and James VI and I', *Genre*, 15 (1982), 81–121.

5. Jonathan Goldberg, *Endlesse Worke* (Baltimore, 1981), p. 27.

6. Derek Traversi, 'Spenser's Faerie Queene', in *The Age of Chaucer*, edited by Boris Ford (Harmondsworth, 1959), pp. 211–26 (p. 217); W. W. Robson, 'Spenser and *The Faerie Queene*', in *The Age of Shakespeare*, edited by Boris Ford, revised edition (Harmondsworth, 1982), pp. 119–36 (p. 120).

7. Raymond Williams, *The Country and the City* (London, 1973), p. 33.

8. Josephine Bennett, *The Evolution of 'The Faerie Queene'* (Chicago, 1942), p. 157.

9. Quotations from *The Faerie Queene* and the Letter to Ralegh are taken from *The Faerie Queene*, edited by A. C. Hamilton (London 1977); from Spenser's other poems, from *Spenser's Minor Poems*, edited by Ernest de Selincourt (Oxford, 1910).

10. Goldberg, *Endlesse Worke*, pp. 9, 21, 77.

11. Quoted by Rosemary Freeman, *Elizabethan Emblem Books* (London, 1948), p. 2.

12. George Puttenham, *The Arte of English Poesie*, edited by Gladys Doidge Willcock and Alice Walker (Cambridge, 1936), pp. 186–88.

13. Isabel MacCaffery, *Spenser's Allegory: The Anatomy of Imagination* (Princeton, 1976), p. 9.

14. Jacqueline T. Miller, 'Authority and Authorship: Some Medieval and Renaissance Contexts' (unpublished dissertation, Johns Hopkins University, 1980), p. 104.

15. Donald Cheney, review of Jonathan Goldberg, *Endlesse Worke*, in *SpN*, 13, no. 2 (1982), 34–37 (p. 35).

16. Goldberg, *Endlesse Worke*, p. 76, no. 1.

17. Maureen Quilligan, *The Language of Allegory: Defining the Genre* (Ithaca, 1979), p. 35; Terry Eagleton, *Walter Benjamin or Towards a Revolutionary Criticism* (London, 1981), pp. 10, 22.

18. Michael Murrin, *The Veil of Allegory* (Chicago, 1969), p. 168.

19. Quilligan, pp. 29, 31.

20. Catherine Belsey, *Critical Practice* (London, 1980), pp. 74, 82.

21. Lewis, p. 380.

22. Goldberg, *Endlesse Worke*, pp. 9, 76, no. 1.

23. Stephen Greenblatt, *Renaissance Self-Fashioning* (New Haven, 1980), pp. 157–92.

24. Goldberg, *Endlesse Worke*, p. 77.

25. Lewis, p. 349.

26. Roger Sale, *Reading Spenser: An Introduction to The Faerie Queene* (New York, 1968), p. 162.

27. Helena Shire, *A Preface to Spenser* (London, 1978), p. 51.

28. Eagleton, *Benjamin*, p. 8.

29. Lewis, pp. 378–79.

30. Fredric Jameson, *The Political Unconscious* (Princeton, 1980), pp. 8, 3; Pierre Macherey, *A Theory of Literary Production*, translated by Geoffrey Wall (London, 1978), p. 131.

31. Jonathan Goldberg, *James I and the Politics of Literature* (Baltimore, 1983), p. 5.

32. Judith H. Anderson, '"In Living Colours and Right Hew": The Queen of Spenser's Central Books', in *Poetic Traditions of the English Renaissance*, edited by Maynard Mack and George de Forest Lord (New Haven, 1982), pp. 47–66 (pp. 49–50).

33. Goldberg, *Endlesse Worke*, p. 88; Carol V. Kaske, 'Spenser's Pluralistic Universe: The View from the Mount of Contemplation (FQ.1.x)', in *Contemporary Thought on Edmund Spenser*, edited by Richard C. Frushell and Bernard J. Vondersmith (London, 1975), pp. 121–49; Patricia A. Parker, *Inescapable Romance* (Princeton, 1980), p. 14.

34. Marion Campbell, 'Spenser's *Mutabilitie Cantos* and the end of *The Faerie Queene*', *Southern Review* (Adelaide), 15 (1982), 46–59 (p. 53).

35. Miller, 'Authority', p. 111.

36. Richard Neuse, in *SpN*, 14, no. 2 (1983), 49.

Chapter 7

The Poetry of Shakespeare and the Early Donne

Shakespeare

By the 1590s, the public theatre was already promising to become one of the age's most powerful counter-dominant cultural forces. What Alvin Kernan has called the 'new theatre of the late sixteenth century' was revolutionary in many ways that were not obvious at the time.[1] More easily than any other literary form, in part because it grew up outside (though still subject to the control of) the Court, the public drama acquired a relative autonomy to articulate the conflicts and growing points of the new age. Its growth illustrates how the lived experiences of any society can never be equated with its explicit, dominant ideology. The Jacobean Court's preferred literary form, the masque, was devised to inculcate order, hierarchy, and royal supremacy, while the plays of the public theatre were learning to deal with the issues that were gradually challenging the Court's hegemony, such as the centralizing of state power, political corruption, the restriction of ancient liberties, and the subordination of personal values to the State.[2]

Among the plays of the public theatre, Shakespeare's stand supreme; he worked superbly in the literary form that, although explicitly under the watchful eye of court officials, none the less uncannily came most clearly to articulate those forces which would dislocate and, by the 1640s, finally overthrow it. Among Shakespeare's audience in the 1590s was a law student, an ex-Catholic, an aspiring courtier, and an increasingly fashionable poet (at least among his friends). His name was John Donne – and it is Donne's poetry which, along with Shakespeare's, marks the culmination of sixteenth-century poetry and points beyond it. Their poetry will be the subject of this chapter.

In writing of Shakespeare at all, of course, we are face to face with the epitome of the idealization of the Elizabethan age I discussed in Chapter 1. We are dealing less with a body of poetry than with an institution – or rather a concept mediated through a series of institutions, educational, cultural, political. 'Shakespeare' seems, even in the dominant ideology of our time, safe from both his own history and ours, a transcendent figure, somehow a guarantor of the national culture. But like every collection of texts, Shakespeare's poems (and plays) have a history, even if in this case, that history is largely one of successive mystifications into a symbol of high culture, civilization, and educational standards. Nor is Shakespeare simply a British phenomenon: the success of transatlantic Shakespeare festivals, Shakespeare societies, lecture series, celebrations, not to mention university courses, textbooks, and libraries, have turned 'him' into an international guarantor of Western civilization.

The approach here to Shakespeare's poems – themselves a marginal part of his activities and therefore in some ways easier to read and write about with some fresh perspective – will be in accord with the rest of the study. I will attempt to place the life of Shakespeare's texts (in this case the non-dramatic poems) in their history *and* ours, to ask some of *our* questions of them as well as consider the questions their original readers might have posed. And I will start by locating the poems in relation to the sixteenth century's dominant institution, the Court.

Although we consider him the greatest dramatist of our language, we should not forget that Shakespeare also served an apprenticeship in the other literary forms more directly controlled by the Court's values and practices. As a dramatist working in the public theatre, he was afforded a degree of independence from the Court's power. The very nature of script and performance provided, in practice if not in law, a relative autonomy alongside the more obviously court-controlled arts of music, lyric poetry, romantic fiction, and propagandist masque. But early in his career, Shakespeare did turn briefly to the fashionable courtly form of verse romance, and to the courtly fashion for sonnets; in doing so, he was moving closer to the cultural and literary dominance of the fashionable court modes dominated by Ovid, Petrarchanism, and Neoplatonism. His short erotic verse narratives, *Venus and Adonis (c.* 1592) and *The Rape of Lucrece* (1594), are typical examples of a fashionable literary genre, and show his versatility in a poetic mode which, while clearly a sideline for him, none the less demonstrated his considerable skill. Other incidental verse he wrote in the 1590s included contributions to the miscellany, *The Passionate Pilgrim* (1599), and *The Phoenix and the Turtle*, a cryptic allegorical poem written for a collection of poems appended to *Love's Martyr* (1601), an allegorical prose treatment of love by Robert Chester. All of these incidental poems, however, pale alongside the achievement of the *Sonnets*. In an age of outstanding love lyrics, the *Sonnets* attain a depth, suggestiveness, and power rarely matched in men's and women's struggles to match desire to language.

The minor poems can therefore be dealt with only briefly here. First, to *Venus and Adonis*. In his initial venture into public poetry,

Shakespeare chose to work within the generic constraints of the fashionable Ovidian verse romance. The presence of Ovid in Elizabethan verse is a particularly pervasive one. The *Metamorphoses* in particular not only provided intriguing and spicy narrative, but also philosophical and moral insights and a lush melancholy that appealed increasingly to readers of poetry late in the century. It also appealed to the fascination for *copia* Elizabethans liked to indulge in. Ovid is intriguing because rather than asserting an unchanging reality 'behind' the world which words exist to 'express', his writing suggests that change and copiousness are the primary realities of experience, and that poetry should likewise express that. Where the Middle Ages (and, indeed, some Elizabethans, like Sidney's friend William Golding) moralized Ovid, finding sound philosophical truths in the *Metamorphoses*, increasingly he was admired and imitated for less rigid qualities.

In the 1590s fashion for Ovidian romance, Marlowe's *Hero and Leander* and Shakespeare's *Venus and Adonis* stand out as most readable today. *Venus and Adonis* especially appealed to the taste of young aristocrats like the Earl of Southampton, to whom it was dedicated. It is a narrative poem in six-line stanzas, mixing classical mythology and surprisingly (and incongruously) detailed descriptions of country life designed to illustrate the story of the seduction of the beautiful youth Adonis by the comically desperate ageing goddess, Venus. Alongside Marlowe's masterpiece, Shakespeare's is regretfully static, with just too much argument and insufficient flowing sensuality to make it pleasurable reading. Its treatment of love relies too heavily upon Neoplatonic and Ovidian commonplaces, and (unlike *Hero and Leander*) upon heavy moralizing allegory, with Venus representing the flesh and Adonis something like spiritual longing. Its articulation of the nature of the love that separates them is abstract and often unintentionally comic – although Shakespeare's characterization of Venus as a garrulous plump matron does bring something of his theatrical power into the poem. *Venus and Adonis* was certainly popular, going through ten editions in as many years, possibly because its early readers thought it fashionably sensual.

The Rape of Lucrece is the 'graver labor' which Shakespeare promised to Southampton in the preface to *Venus and Adonis*. Again, he combines a current poetical fashion – the melancholy verse complaint – with a number of moral commonplaces, and in effect writes a novelette in verse: a melodrama celebrating the prototypal example of matronly chastity, the Roman lady Lucrece's suicide after she was raped. The central moral issue – that of honour – at times almost becomes a serious treatment of the psychology of self-revulsion, but the decorative and moralistic conventions of the complaint form certainly do not afford

Shakespeare the scope of a stage play. There are some fine local atmospheric effects, which in their declamatory power occasionally bring the directness and power of the stage into the verse. But overall it is less impressive than might be expected from Shakespeare.

Likewise, *The Phoenix and the Turtle*, an allegorical, highly technical celebration of an ideal love union, is a rather static piece. It consists of a description of a funeral procession of mourners, a funeral anthem, and a final lament for the dead. It is dignified, abstract, and solemn but never achieves much sense of life. Readers have fretted, without success, over the exact identifications of its characters. What power it has lies in the mysterious, eerie evocation of the mystery of unity in love.

As this brief survey shows, Shakespeare's incidental poems clearly grew out of fashions of the 1590s. Like other ambitious writers and intellectuals on the fringe of the Court, Shakespeare was locating his poems in relation to fashionable kinds, and they are interesting primarily because it was Shakespeare who wrote them. His sonnets, on the other hand, to which detailed attention must be given, constitute perhaps the language's greatest collection of lyrics. They are love lyrics, and clearly grow from the social, erotic, and literary contexts of his age – but part of their greatness lies in their power to be read again and again in later ages, and to raise compellingly, even unanswerably, more than merely literary questions.

Probably more critical ingenuity has been wasted on Shakespeare's sonnets than on any other work of our literature, even perhaps including *Hamlet*. In the five and a half pages of the refreshingly sensible Appendix I to his outstanding edition of the *Sonnets* (1978), Stephen Booth briefly summarizes facts that, however few, have led (or led away) to a plethora of speculation on such matters as text, authenticity, date, arrangement, and, especially, the *Sonnets'* biographical implications. The *Sonnets* were published first in 1609, although Sonnets 138 and 144 had appeared in *The Passionate Pilgrim* a decade before. There is no reason to doubt they are Shakespeare's. Some were composed before 1598 and they are usually dated in the late 1590's.

It is conventional to divide the *Sonnets* into two groups – 1–126, purportedly addressed to or related to a young man, the so-called 'Fair Youth'; and 127–152, addressed to the so-called 'Dark Lady'. Such a division is arbitrary at best: within each major group there are detachable sub-groups, and without the weight of the conventional arrangement, many sonnets would not seem to have a natural place in either. Sonnets 1–17 (or perhaps 18) are, ostensibly, concerned with a plea for a young man to marry, but even in this, what many readers have seen as the most conventional and unified group there are disruptive suggestions that break out of such a conventional arrangement. The order in which they appear in 1609, in Booth's words, feels throughout 'both urgent and wanting', purposeful and yet 'to have just barely failed of its purpose'.[3] Their order has provoked many attempts at reordering, usually according to some narrative principle, to create a story of dedication, rivalry, and betrayal among the 'Poet', the 'Rival Poet', the 'Dark Lady', and other 'characters'. Many of the suggested rearrangements construct ingenious narratives and Booth's cool remark is that the *Sonnets* are an 'aleatory composition', allowing their performers the latitude to arrange and select so that, he concludes, 'all the rearrangers are right'.[4] In short, none of the subsequent attempts to 'reorder' the *Sonnets*, however varied and creative, represents the 'correct' order. Perhaps (as we saw with attempts to construct a narrative from *Astrophil and Stella*), they largely fulfil an understandable anxiety on the part of some readers to see narrative continuity rather than variations and repetition in the *Sonnets*. The so-called story behind the *Sonnets* has also, as Booth puts it, 'evoked some notoriously creative scholarship': speculation on the identity of the young man mentioned in many of the first 126 sonnets, of Mr W. H., to whom the sequence is dedicated by the printer (and who may be the same young man), of the so-called 'Dark Lady' of some of Sonnets 127–152, and of the rival poet or poets mentioned in some. All these matters have filled many library shelves, as has the question whether Shakespeare had any deviant sexual preferences. On this latter subject, Booth's remark may sum up all such speculation: 'William Shakespeare', he majestically concludes, 'was almost certainly homosexual, bisexual, or heterosexual. The sonnets provide no evidence on the matter.'[5]

Such speculations – which reached their peak in critics and readers wedded to the sentimental Romantic insistence on an intimate tie between literary and historical events – are in one sense a tribute to the power of the *Sonnets*. They are arguably the greatest collection of love poems in the language, and they provide a crucial test for the adequacy of both our love of poetry and our sense of the fascinating confusion which makes up human love. It is often extraordinarily difficult to expose oneself to the raw power of many of the *Sonnets*, which at their best seem to demand that they judge us, not the reverse. The insistence on an audience's participation in the production of meaning which, as we have seen, is so central to sixteenth-century lyrics, here becomes most challenging and intense.

What the *Sonnets* thrust at their readers is an intricate nexus of sex, power, and knowledge. Not only 'love' poems, they are also an intense interrogation of the received languages of love. We are given a collective portrait of the internal dialogue of eroticism far beyond any other collection of lyrics, excepting perhaps Donne's. But they are not an idealistic celebration. Love, more explicitly and vulnerably than in any earlier Petrarchan collection, is shown to set in operation an intense fragmentation of the self. It operates especially by means of the discrete and unsystematizable occasions which falling in love imposes upon its subjects and, not least through the language within which lovers struggle to articulate themselves. Dislocation and fragmentation, experiences that are so endemic to the Petrarchan sonnet collection, never tend anywhere or finally come to a conclusion. Shakespeare's sonnets exemplify Barthes's words, that 'to speak amorously is to expend without an end in sight, without a crisis'.[6]

With these sonnets, as with few other literary works, we can be overwhelmed by them or (on the other hand) fly their seductive power and take refuge in the all-too-easy search for contextual or biographical knowledge as an escape from the living responsiveness they demand. Above all, they stand, as it were, like crystals refracting light according to the angle on which we hold them – they illuminate not Shakespeare's life, let alone the imagined lives of his 'characters', but the lives of his readers. In a sense, they are as dramatic as any of his plays. Better than any other lyrics of the age, they illustrate how meanings can be concretized only in the different lives of readers: as we read Shakespeare's sonnets, we may easily find ourselves as we all struggle for self-understanding.

Each sonnet is like a little script. Each certainly contains (often powerful) directions on reading and enactment, but finally each is built as an awareness that textual meanings are not given but made anew in every performance, by every new reader within his or her own individual and social life. What Sonnet 87 terms 'misprision' stands for the necessary process by which the sonnet is produced within each reading through its history.

Such an approach to Shakespeare's poems should be, by now, familiar to readers of this study. The *Sonnets* are not *sui generis*, but grow out of the shared socio-cultural expectations of English Petrarchist poetry. How, then, should we relate the *Sonnets* to their ancestors, not least those powerful sequences of the early 1590s, those by Spenser and Sidney and, behind them, to Petrarch? On the simple level of verbal echoes and borrowing, inevitably the *Sonnets* are criss-crossed by the ubiquitous language of Petrarchan and Neoplatonic praise, the conventional motifs of praise, fear, betrayal, temporality, dedication, sacrifice, and disillusion. A. Kent Hieatt has made an unusually striking case for Shakespeare's knowing and brooding over with special concentration Spenser's *Ruines of Rome* (printed with the *Complaints* in 1591), a meditation on the mutability of civilizations. Hieatt argues that Spenser is 'nearly as important as Marlowe in the development of Shakespeare's early style' and produces many verbal parallels such as Sonnet 16's 'Make war upon this bloody tyrant time' and 'Make war/ Gainst time' in *Ruines of Rome*, Sonnet 27.[7] But beyond such verbal parallels and echoes – always the means by which the intertextual network of Petrarchanism spread its linguistic power – Shakespeare's sonnets are also inevitably drawn into a wider socio-cultural nexus. The *Sonnets* are not merely literary texts; like Sidney's, Ralegh's, Greville's, or Spenser's, Shakespeare's sonnets are part of the distinctive social text of the 1580s and 1590s. As Giorgio Melchiori notes, 'the English sonnet is the typical expression of the poet who is either already at the top of fortune's hill or who hopes to reach it';[8] even when its subject-matter seems to be the ubiquitousness of unsatisfied personal desire, sonnet writers are none the less putting their claim for a right to enter the magic circle of the aristocracy or the Court.

Our residual way of reading the *Sonnets* as great *love* poems should not hide this dimension. Thus they adopt the tone of the gracefully adroit petitioner, praising the virtues and values of the embodiment of society's dominant class which are seen pre-eminently embodied in the 'Fair Youth'. Yet the relationship between the poet's voice and the object of his devotion is a distinctive one in curious ways, very unlike that of the typical Petrarchan lover like Astrophil. Shakespeare's sonnets in fact articulate, as Kernan has argued, the failure of the patronage relationship. The poet–patron dynamic simply forms a 'framework or social setting' within which more important psychological, moral, and linguistic issues are wrestled with. In most of the *Sonnets*, the patronage relationship becomes irrelevant and we watch 'the birth of the professional poet out of the sea of anonymity'.[9] Werner L. Gundersheimer suggests that Shakespeare preferred the 'support of his London crowds to that of a single *patronus*' and thus the *Sonnets* can be read as his whole career in miniature, 'less as a product of, than a departure from and perhaps a challenge to, the traditional relations that define patronage in the Renaissance'.[12] In this, they look forward to an era when the lyric poet would be cut off from the central power of his culture – to the poets of forced or deliberate retirement like Vaughan or Traherne some fifty or more years later. In short, Shakespeare's sonnets raise the question we have seen to be implicit in Petrarchanism, that of the nature of the self, in ways that uncannily anticipate the Cartesian anxiety about selfhood and permanence. As we shall see, the poems in Donne's *Songs and Sonets* also, in their own way, grapple with the same issue.

Like every Petrarchan collection, Shakespeare's sonnets see the nature of the self as intimately bound up with sexuality. But nowhere among earlier collections are the extremes of erotic revelation offered in such rawness and complexity or with such obsessive anguish over the glorious failure of language to constitute or reassure the vulnerable self. They are a unique imaginative proving-ground where the feelings about love and the language traditionally used to capture them intermingle with and contradict each other. It is easy to see the repeated moves of Petrarchanism in the *Sonnets*. Most of the conventional topoi of traditional poetry are there – the unity of lovers (Sonnets 36–40), the power of poetry to immortalize the beloved

(Sonnets 18, 19, 55), contests between eye and heart, beauty and virtue (Sonnets 46, 141), the contrast of shadow and substance (Sonnets 53, 98, 101). As with Petrarch's *Rime* or Sidney's *Astrophil and Stella*, it would be easy to create a schematic account of commonplace Renaissance thinking about love from the *Sonnets*. But to do so would be to nullify their extraordinary power of creation – the way they force ejaculations of recognition, horror, or joy from their readers.

What often strikes contemporary readers, and not merely after an initial acquaintance with the *Sonnets*, is the apparently unjustified level of idealization in many of them – the tone of adulation, an idealization of noble love that to a post-Freudian world might seem comforting but rather archaic. The *Sonnets* which express seemingly serene affirmation seem so idealistic, so absolute. They lack our insights into the complexity and contradictions that we take as central to our experience of love – of which, indeed, the Renaissance was certainly not unaware. The early sonnets are saturated in the clichés of Petrarchan and Neoplatonic praise, as are later groups like 105–108 where the language verges on the sacramental. While the lover protests that his love cannot be called idolatrous, none the less the beloved is the culmination of centuries of 'antique' praise (Sonnet 106), such that the rest of history is seen as waste. A true love is one that inspires a language that can never lose its richness, words that aim for and achieve the fullness of presence that only the beloved inspires:

> So that eternal love in love's fresh case
> Weighs not the dust and injury of age,
> Nor gives to necessary wrinkles place,
> But makes antiquity for aye his page,
> Finding the first conceit of love there bred,
> Where time and outward form would show it dead.
>
> (Sonnet 108)

The continual self-effacement of the anguished lover, the worship of the 'god in love, to whom I am confined' (110), the poet's claim to be immortalizing 'his beautie . . . in these black lines' (63), helpless idealizations of absolute commitment – are all born, it seems, out of a world of beliefs we have largely lost. Today we come across such sentiments in the lyrics of second-rate pop songs. Indeed, an interesting exercise is to compile a list of the metaphors of idealization in today's popular songs – not to show how degenerate they are (or the whole modern world has become), but to point up the difficulty of seeing the idealization of the beloved in Shakespeare's lyrics as fresh and untouched by history. Of course, students of sixteenth-century poetry (including readers of this book) will then further point out just how conventional they were even then – we are, they might say, always already in such conventionality.

But today we habitually respond more easily to the darkness of what R. P. Blackmur called a 'poetics for infatuation', with its attendant acknowledgement of frustration and anguish. But even when we acknowledge that too is conventional we do not respond, perhaps, so easily to a poetics of deification like Shakespeare's. The most celebrated sonnets of idealism, like 'Shall I Compare Thee to a Summer's Day?' (18) or 'Let Me Not the Marriage of True Minds' (116) may even seem cloyingly sweet, their texts seemingly rejecting (or is it repressing?) any subtextual challenges to their idealism. Sonnet 18 is indeed the classic case. It seemingly requires to be read in a solemn murmur, almost as if one were in church. It is serene, replete, seemingly taking into consideration all possibilities to settle on the uniqueness and irreplaceability of the beloved. It is certainly a wonderful performance in its assertion that it is such unique fragile beauty that allows the poet his affirmation and his defiance of time:

> But thy eternal summer shall not fade,
> Nor lose possession of that fair thou ow'st,
> Nor shall death brag thou wand'rest in his shade,
> When in eternal lines to time thou grow'st.

So powerful a part of our literary and erotic heritage are such sentiments that we may feel guilty if we choose to query such confidence and read such sonnets against the grain, so to speak, against their seeming intentions, trying to make them give us insights into love as we know it today.

Yet part of the greatness of the *Sonnets* is, perhaps, the way they invite such scepticism and thus try to make us reverse their idealism. As the sonnet had developed in the 200 years since Petrarch, it had become, as we have seen, a potent rhetorical instrument for evoking a reader's or a listener's participation in the making or the concrete particularization of its meanings. Shakespeare uses an extraordinary number of deliberately generalized epithets, indeterminate signifiers, and floating referents which provoke meaning from their readers rather than provide it. Each line contains echoes, suggestions, and contradictions which require an extraordinary degree of emotional activity by the reader. The so-called Shakespearian sonnet, with its three quatrains and concluding couplet, allows especially for the concentration of a single, usually meditative, mood. It is held together less by the apparent logic (for instance, the recurring 'when . . . then' pattern) than by its atmosphere of invitation to the reader to enter into and become part of the dramatization of a brooding, devoted, self-obsessed mind. The focus is on emotional richness rather than logical coherence; on evoking the immediacy of felt rather than rationalized experience. The concluding couplets also frequently offer a reader powerfully indeterminate statements. Even in reading they seem to break down any attempt at limiting meaning, as in the conclusion to Sonnet 33: 'Yet him for this my love no whit disdaineth ;/Suns of the world may stain when heav'n's sun staineth.' The weighty generality of 'him', 'this', 'love', and, especially the unstateable weight of 'stain' and 'staineth' attempts to set up an indeterminacy, an undecidability of meaning, that can only be resolved by particular and changing applications in Shakespeare's readers' own lives.

In particular lines, too, these poems achieve amazing power by their lack of logical specificity and their emotional openness. As Booth points out, many lines show 'a constructive vagueness' by which a word or phrase is made to do multiple duty – by placing it 'in a context to which it pertains but which it does not quite fit idiomatically' or by using phrases which are simultaneously illogical and amazingly charged with meaning. He instances 'separable spite' in Sonnet 36 as a phrase rich with suggestion which can be vitiated by scholarly teasing out of a limited if coherent sense[11]:

> In our two loves there is but one respect,
> Though in our lives a separable spite,
> Which though it alter not love's sole effect,
> Yet doth it steal sweet hours from love's delight.

Another example would be the way in which the bewilderingly ordinary yet suggestive epithets sit uneasily in the opening lines of Sonnet 64:

> When I have seen by time's hand defaced
> The rich proud cost of outborn buried age,
> When sometime lofty towers I see down razed,
> And brass eternal slave to mortal rage . . .

The greatest of the *Sonnets* – 60, 64, 129, and many others – have this extraordinary combination of general, even abstract, words and unspecified emotional power that we may take it as a major rhetorical characteristic of the collection. An intense and concentrated reading can be caught up in a seemingly endless and indeterminate flow as the words bump against one another, setting up multiple and never fully identifiable suggestions of power, determinism, and helplessness by the undecidability of their con- nections. It is extraordinarily difficult, probably impossible, to paraphrase such lines without nullifying their power. Often this process occurs by a syntactical movement which is modified or contradicted by associations set up by words and phrases. Booth argues that such constructions are usually made meaningful 'because of clear intent implied by context, or because of a syntactical momentum that carries a reader into clarity and thereby dispels puzzlement'. Yet when he wants to see the 'capacity to communicate' as the 'most important' effect of a Shakespeare sonnet, he misses the point. The reader is simply forced on, into the void of the insecure and journeying self the poem brings into existence. There is, indeed, usually a syntactical or logical framework in the sonnet but if we read slowly and carefully, so powerful can be the contradictory, random, and disruptive effects occurring incidentally as the syntax unfolds that to reduce any sonnet to its seemingly logical framework is to miss the most amazing potential effects of these extraordinary poems.[12]

To discuss these poems adequately, we need an adequate vocabulary. Perhaps that is why, after half a century of even a hazy knowledge of Existentialism, readers in the late twentieth century are unusually well equipped to understand what L. C. Knights pointed out many years ago – that one of the most urgent subjects of the *Sonnets* we usually notice today is not the commonplaces of Renaissance thinking about love, not the powerful concern with the power of art, but rather what Sonnet 16 calls our 'war upon this bloody tyrant Time'.[13] It is no accident that the 'discovery' of the *Sonnets'* concern with time and mutability dates from the 1940s when the impact of Kierkegaard, Nietzsche, Heidegger, and Existentialism was starting to be widely felt in Britain and America. It is from such sources that we have gained what now seems to be a 'natural' vocabulary in which to discuss the *Sonnets*. They invite us to see our temporality not merely as an abstract problem but as part of our ever-changing nature, and what Heidegger terms our 'thrownness', our sense of being thrown into the world, seems central to our perception of the *Sonnets'* power. Such perceptions, it now seems commonplace to say, are 'in' the *Sonnets*. In fact, it has needed the epistemological breakthrough of post-Nietzschean philosophy to provide us with vocabulary adequate to express them. It is perhaps the best example in the period of what in Chapter 1 I termed a powerful reading meeting a powerful text. Even so, even with what seems an adequate vocabulary, we are still in the paradoxical situation of finding a language adequate only to point up language's inadequacy. Frustration, incoherence, unpredictability, and change are at the heart of the *Sonnets*. But it is a continually shifting heart, one that conceives of human love as definable only in terms of such change, finitude, and final silence.

To speak, then, of the theme or motif of time and mutability in the *Sonnets* has become a critical commonplace. It seems to point to something seemingly given, apparently ineradicably there. Yet even on such a reductive level, the *Sonnets'* anxiety about time shifts under our gaze. It does not provide a stable centre. The cry of protest the *Sonnets* direct us towards deliberately avoids (except in the strangely detached Sonnet 146 with its apparent medieval Christian emphasis) the transcendentalism of Chaucer's beseeching his young lovers to turn from the world, or Spenser's rejection of change for the reassurance of God's eternity and His providential guidance of time to a foreknown, if mysterious, end. Like the speculations of Heidegger or Nietzsche, Shakespeare's sonnets instead overwhelm us with questions and contradictions, with the sheer perplexity of our own contingency. They involve us less in abstract solutions to the problem of time than in the experience of it upon our pulses:

> Like as the waves make towards the pebbled shore,
> So do our minutes hasten to their end,
> Each changing place with that which goes before,
> In sequent toil all forwards do contend.
>
> (60)

In such lines, it is not an abstraction like 'time' but we ourselves who are the problem – decentred, swept along in the very movement of the lines, defined by the change the poem purports to deal with. Time is not thrust at us as an impartial or abstract background. Even where it is glanced at as a pattern observable in nature or man, it is evoked as a disruptive, disturbing experience which cannot be dealt with as a philosophical problem or by the assertion that our experiences are held together by a vulnerable yet none the less central self. Some sonnets face us with time as a sinister impersonal determinism; others thrust time at us instead as unforeseeable chances and changes, what Sonnet 115 calls our 'millioned accidents'. We are taken straight into a moment of insight that immediately, and as we read, dislocates us – 'When I consider everything that grows/Holds in perfection but a little moment . . .' (Sonnet 15) – until we are faced with what we fear most, that our most cherished ideals, our most defended integrity, our sense of the presence and irreducibility of our inner selves, are always already disintegrated: 'Ruin hath taught me thus to ruminate,/That time will come and take my love away' (64).

With such awareness, what affirmations are possible? Whether time is felt as determinism or chance, each reader of the *Sonnets* may find that the very formal characteristics of the sonnet sits uneasily with such insights. How could, we might say, Shakespeare write in this artificial form when he saw, with such clarity, the darkness within? To read Sonnet 15, for instance, tempts us to articulate an understandable protest against time's inevitably destroying its own creations (a commonplace enough Renaissance sentiment), and accede, in abstract, to a sense of helplessness before a malignant force greater than the individual. But as the sonnet tries, by virtue of its carefully structured argument, to create in us a conciousness that seeks to understand and so control this awareness, it thrusts at us lines, or words, that uncannily undermine that temporary satisfaction of the sonnet form. Such, for instance, is the force of Sonnet 15's 'everything that grows/Holds in perfection but a little moment'. If we pause over the words, what is the application of 'everything'? Or the emotional effect of the way the line builds to a seemingly replete climax in 'perfection' and then tumbles into oblivion in 'but a little moment'? The sonnet does not and need not answer such questions – and, in a real sense, cannot answer them, for we all, in so far as we are attentive to what the poem opens up in us, can only acknowledge its power in our own contingent lives. It is we who must answer, or run from, them. Similarly, what is shocking is not merely the commonplace that 'never-resting time leads summer on/To hideous winter and confounds him there' (Sonnet 5), but that each reader fights against and so disrupts the logical and aesthetic coherence offered by the sonnet and with it his or her own personal sense of change and betrayal.

There is, in short, in the *Sonnets* not merely a thematic concern with time, but the appallingly relentless process of reading ourselves into an awareness of our own fragility. As we read, each of us (like the young man of Sonnet 16) is being exhorted to realize the difficult truth that 'to give away yourself' paradoxically 'keeps your self still'. What can that mean? Perhaps we apprehend it as a challenge to open ourselves at our points of greatest vulnerability. Yet, again, we may pause over the unpredictability of that 'still'. Do we gloss it as 'nevertheless', 'continually', 'forever'?

To attempt to place the *Sonnets* within our personal histories is, therefore, to an unusual degree to be challenged to expose ourselves to a kind of creative therapy. In this way, the *Sonnets* are the culmination of sixteenth-century poetry's attempt to involve its audience in the making and remaking of the poem. They try to manipulate their readers into areas of vulnerability, and the result is a creation of a shifting, vulnerable self which reads, ponders, and returns to the suggestive futility of the words. Like every 'I' in a Petrarchan sequence, the 'I' of Shakespeare's sonnets is never stable. It is not the Wordsworthian egotistical sublime or the collective 'I' of a medieval hymn or Anglo-Saxon elegy. It is a shattered, decentred voice that searches in vain for stability, as in Sonnet 75:

> Now proud as an enjoyer, and anon
> Doubting the filching age will steal his treasure;
> Now counting best to be with you alone,
> Then bettered that the world may see my pleasure;
> Sometime all full with feasting on your sight,
> And by and by clean starvèd for a look;
> Possessing or pursuing no delight
> Save what is had or must from you be took.
> Thus do I pine and surfeit day by day,
> Or gluttoning on all, or all away.

In such sonnets, the radical break with the collective 'I' of the medieval and Petrarchan lyric has been finally made. Instead, we have a montage of the subject, caught up into language, undertaking to speak its desire, reaching to relate to another 'I' and finding there is no such thing and that fragmentation is the only universal characteristic of the human condition. The 'I' of the

Sonnets is constituted as a subject only because it continually experiences itself as changing. The 'I' is aware only of a lack, which has set desire in motion; it articulates this lack by inserting itself in language, which serves only as a further decentring, as it moves along an endless chain of signification, unable to capture the derived plenitude of significance it attributes to the object of desire. As Terry Eagleton comments, 'to speak is to lack: and it's in this lack that the movement of desire is set up, the movement whereby I move restlessly from sign to sign without ever being able to close my fist over some primordial plenitude of sense, a movement which will be satisfied only in death'.[14] The Cartesian ego, fifty years later, would try desperately to pin down some unassailable centre to the experience of 'I'. Shakespeare's sonnets, like Donne's, show the futility of the attempt. The 'I' strives to constitute itself a basis for identify, coherent, and primordial, as a source of order and control, and finds itself always already a function of an endlessly frustrating plethora of differences while producing the illusion of autonomy and control.

A further example of the way in which vulnerability is both a key thematic obsession and a stratagem of the readers' involvement in the *Sonnets* is the recurring dwelling upon the lover's age. Indeed, perhaps the most pressing concern with the Fair Youth's vulnerability to time and the shifting self is found in the recurring motif of growing old. It starts, usually, as protest or defiance and ends in fear:

> My glass shall not persuade me I am old
> So long as youth and thou are of one date,
> But when in thee time's furrows I behold,
> Then look I death my days should expiate.
>
> (Sonnet 22)

More brutally, the relationship with the Dark Lady is also one where the lover is '. . . vainly thinking that she thinks me young,/Although she knows my days are past the best' (Sonnet 138). So, in the same poem's question, 'wherefore say not I that I am old?' Why this insistence on old age?

The simplistic answer is that the speaker *is* older. But even if we concede there are biographical origins for the *Sonnets*, there is no evidence that Shakespeare *was* in fact old: if we can make the too-easy equation between poet and speaker, he was probably thirty to thirty- five when he wrote the *Sonnets*. Of course he may have *felt* old. But put it in the context of a possible biographical situation for a moment: when one falls in love with a much younger woman or man, does one not inevitably feel the insecurity of a generation gap? Grey hair, middle-age spread on the one side; inexperience on the other. Clearly that is something of what is alluded to. But what is insisted upon by the *Sonnets* more strongly is that age or youthfulness are not important in themselves: it is rather that the insistence itself is important, not the mere fact of age – just as it is the anxiety with which a man or woman watches the wrinkles beneath the eyes that is important, not the wrinkles themselves. The note of insistence, in other words, is not attached merely to the speaker's age: it stands for some wider psychological revelation, a desire to face (or not face) the vulnerability which we all encounter opening up in ourselves in any relationship that is real and growing, and therefore necessarily unpredictable and risky. Such a revelation usually starts with a confident boast:

> To me, fair friend, you never can be old,
> For as you were when first your eye I eyed,
> Such seems your beauty still.
>
> (Sonnet 104)

Here the pun on 'I' – a play that occurs throughout – concentrates, as Booth notes, in a 'showy combination of pun (eye, I), polyptoton (eye, eyed) and epizeuxis',[15] focusing our attention on the interrelation of the self and ageing. But then, characteristically, boasting inevitably succumbs to shock:

> Ah yet doth beauty, like a dial hand,
> Steal from his figure, and no pace perceived;
> So your sweet hue, which methinks still doth stand,
> Hath motion, and mine eye may be deceived.

The delusion that the 'I' stands still is harshly undermined.

And yet without vulnerability and contingency, without the sense of being thrown into the world, and so of ageing – without, in short, the decentredness of the 'I' – there can be no growth. Hence the poet invites us ruefully to accept what the fact of his greater age evokes – an openness to ridicule or rejection. Today perhaps we have something of the same fixation on the insecurity of age, although our more natural equivalent might equally be the insecurity of overweight (for Shakespeare, or Ben Jonson for that matter, fat, as Falstaff might have put it, is beautiful).

The *Sonnets'* insistence on being open to the insecurity represented by age points not merely to a contrast between the speaker and his two lovers but rather to a radical self-division. This is so especially in the so-called 'Dark Lady' sonnets, where we are invited to witness and participate in some of the most savage self-laceration ever evoked in language, particularly in the fearful exhaustion of Sonnet 129, where vulnerability is evoked not as potential or growth, but as paralysis. At once logically relentless and emotionally centrifugal, as we read it, Sonnet 129 has the power to draw in our own memories, fears, or vulnerability to its compulsive ejaculations of self-disgust. Nothing is specified: the strategies of the poem work to make a reader reveal or recognize his or her own compulsions and revulsions:

> Th'expense of spirit in a waste of shame
> Is lust in action, and till action lust
> Is perjured, murd'rous, bloody, full of blame,
> Savage, extreme, rude, cruel, not to trust . . .

The physical, psychological, and cultural basis of such lines are all too easily recognizable to 'all men'; we are invited to face our most vulnerable experiences which are never quite specified by the poem's words but, as we read, are difficult not to acknowledge. Shakespeare's sonnet does not give us words for the experiences, or incidents, that come to mind as we read them – in fact it may make us aware of our awful drive to repress them because they are potentially so embarrassing or so destructive.

This strain of insecurity and uncertainty, to which we are asked to repeatedly contribute, is not only found within the explicit lacerations of the Dark Lady sonnets. Even those sonnets celebrating the Fair Youth are frequently undermined by contradictions, weak logic, and helpless self-torturing before the unacceptable. 'That thou are blamed shall not be thy defect' (Sonnet 70), or 'I in your sweet thoughts would be forgot,/If thinking on me then should make you woe' (Sonnet 71), are typical protests of willing self-immolation that echo throughout the *Sonnets*. The absolute self-denial of love is of course an emphasis familiar in both Christian and courtly Petrarchan codes: 'You are my all the world, and I must strive/To know my shames and praises from your tongue' (Sonnet 112) is recognizably self-denying and not perhaps threatening to us. We may indeed admire such devotion. But do we respond with more uneasiness, perhaps, to the masochism of 'That god forbid, that made me first your slave,/I should in thought control your times of pleasure' (Sonnet 58) or of 'the injuries that to myself I do ,/ Doing thee vantage, double vantage me' (Sonnet 88), coupled with the obsession of Sonnet 113 where whatever is seen, 'sweet favor or deformèd'st creature', is shaped to the beloved's taste and feature? Do we find the invitation to participate in such painful self-immolation as an experience of growth or maturity? At what point does devotion become self-destructive?

We habitually use words like 'maturity' or 'fulfilment' about love experiences which are mutual, awakening in the partners some authentic and creative springs. Yet even in the seemingly most serene sonnets in the collection that affirm such experiences, there are inevitably dark shadows of insecurity and anxiety. Absence and loss were always the primary subjects of the Petrarchan sonnet, as the lover seeks to recover what he imagines into being precisely *as* loss and, on the level of the signifier, the poem strives to materialize an object which always escapes.

Sonnet 116 is perhaps the best-known and loved example of a poem seemingly triumphant over such anxieties. As Booth notes, it is 'the most universally admired of Shakespeare's sonnets'. It is, he asserts, a 'grand, noble, absolute, convincing and moving gesture', a 'single-minded presentation of constancy as the only matter worth considering'. Its argument – at least as our dominant critical tradition has valorized it – is that a love which alters with time and circumstances is not a true, but a self-regarding, love, and the heterogeneous effects of the world's impermanence do nothing to diminish or intrude upon such single-mindedness:

> Let me not to the marriage of true minds
> Admit impediments. Love is not love
> Which alters when it alteration finds . . .

Booth's argument is the one to which many, perhaps most, readers of the *Sonnets* would accede: the sonnet is so strongly yet serenely assertive that, he asserts, no challenges to its power enter a reader's mind – 'the poem's assertions sound as if they took cognizance of all viewpoints on all things related to love and were derived from and informative about every aspect of love'.[16]

Yet what if a reader were to resist the pressure of the poem's syntactical sweep? In what interesting ways might a contemporary reader read it against the grain, against its own seeming intentions, and thus make it answer our questions, not only its own? Once again consider the way the courtly lyric characteristically invites its reader's participation. Where Sidney's poems encourage us, tantalize us, even with the pleasure of participation, exhibiting and delighting in the poem's disintegrative self, Shakespeare's exposure of the decentring of the self in language is much less comforting. Sonnet 116 looks as if it is a triumphant rejection of such painful insecurity. Its pressure is enormous, its confidence seemingly replete. Yet, as with a dream, even if the struggles beneath are not revealed, the marks of the erasure of those struggles can be seen. What has been repressed, crowded out of the passageway to consciousness, in the making of Sonnet 116? What, to use Derrida's metaphor, is there that 'remains in the drawing, covered over in the palimpsest'?[17] Our generally received reading of the sonnet has eliminated all the struggle of its production. The sonnet purports to define true love by negatives. If we deliberately negate these negatives, what emerges may be seen as the dark, repressed underside of the poem's apparently unassailable affirmation of a mature, self-giving, other-directed love. If we *do* admit impediments, if we assert, against what (apparently) the poem wants, and play with the idea that love is indeed love which 'alters when it alteration finds', that is a *never* 'fixed' mark and, most especially, that love *is* indeed 'time's fool', we can connect the poem to the powerful strain of insecurity about the nature of change in human love that echoes throughout the whole collection and that strikes a curiously modern note. Such apparent affirmations as Sonnet 116 provides, that is, may be read as acts of repression, attempts to regiment the unexpectedness and challenge of love and the disintegration of the self into language.

There are poems in the collection which, although less assertive, do show a willingness to be vulnerable, to re-evaluate constantly, to swear permanence within, not despite, transience – to be, in the words of St Paul, deceivers yet true. In short, what Sonnet 116 can be seen to repress is the acknowledgement that the only fulfilment worth having is one that is struggled for and which is achieved through, not affirmed against, disintegration. The kind of creative fragility Sonnet 116 tries to ignore is that evoked in the conclusion to Sonnet 49 when the poet admits his vulnerability: 'To leave poor me thou hast the strength of laws,/Since why to love I can allege no cause.' This is an affirmation of a different order – or rather an acknowledgement that love must not be defined by confidence as by vulnerability. We can affirm the authenticity of the erotic only if the possibility that it is not absolute is also admitted. Love, that is, has no absolute legal, moral, or casual claims to make upon us; nor in the final analysis, can love acknowledge the bonds of law or family or State – or if, finally, they are acknowledged, it is because they grow from love itself. Love moves by its own internal dynamic; it is not motivated by a series of external compulsions. Ultimately it asks from the lover the *nolo contendere* of commitment: do with me what you will. A real, that is to say, an altering, bending, *never* fixed and unpredictable love is always surrounded by, and at times seems to live by, battle, plots, subterfuges, quarrels, and irony. And at the root of such experiences is the acknowledgement that any affirmation is made because of, not despite, time and human mortality. As Sonnet 12 puts it, having surveyed the fearful unpredictability of all life, finally we must realize that it is even 'thy beauty', the beauty of the beloved, that the lover must question. This thought may be 'as a death' (Sonnet 64), a 'fearful meditation' (Sonnet 65). Even the most precious of all human creations will age, wrinkle, fade – and we should extend the list since, subtle Petrarchan that he is, Shakespeare makes us feed in our own fearful meditations – get fat, bald, impotent, and die. Just how can one affirm in the face of that degree of reality?

Under the pressure of such questioning, to accept the affirmation of Sonnet 116 might, therefore, in the argument – the strong reading – I am pursuing, be seen as a kind of bad faith, a false dread – false, because it freezes us in inactivity when we should, on the contrary, accept our finitude as possibility. Frozen in the fear of contingency, which Sonnet 116 so ruthlessly represses in its insistent negatives, we may miss an essential insight that it is in fact the very fragility of beauty, love, poetry, Fair Youth and Dark Lady alike, that enhances their desirability. Paradoxically, it is just because they are indeed among the wastes of time that they are beautiful; they are desirable not because they are immortal but precisely because they are irrevocably time-bound. One of the most profound truths that perhaps we know is expressed in arguably the greatest (certainly among the simplest) lines in the *Sonnets*:

> Ruin hath taught me thus to ruminate,
> That time will come and take my love away.
> This thought is as a death, which cannot choose
> But weep to have that which it fears to lose.
>
> (Sonnet 64)

The power of such lines goes far beyond the serene platitudes of Sonnet 116. At our most courageous, we do not merely affirm our love as some of the *Sonnets* try to insist, *despite* the forces of change and unpredictability which provide the ever-shifting centres of our lives. On the contrary, we discover our greatest strengths not despite, but *because* of, and within, our own contingency.

It is worthwhile perhaps stressing the importance of the difference. Shakespeare does often dramatize the familiar, and comforting, posture of hyperbolic defiance, as in the conclusion to Sonnet 19: 'Yet do thy worst, old Time: despite thy woes,/My love shall in my verse ever live young'. There is the 'despite'. But elsewhere, we realize that it is rather because there is no fixed centre in love, that it is precisely because of, not despite, time – because 'your' beauty, wit, virtue, or youth are subject to time – that they are so valuable. To accept rather than deny time is to prove that our deepest life ultimately does not recognize stasis but always craves growth, and that fulfilment is built not upon the need for finality, for being 'ever fixed', but on the need to violate our apparent limits, to push forward or die.

So, unlike Sonnet 116, many of the *Sonnets* depict love not as a serene affirmation of an irreducible core of commitment. Rather they challenge us radically to reorient our understanding of ourselves even while time passes and continues to change us. We are asked not to dismiss our fears of limitation, but to affirm that while, as Sonnet 29 puts it, 'I all alone beweep my outcast state', I may discover that:

> . . . in these thoughts myself almost despising,
> Haply I think on thee, and then my state,
> Like to the lark at break of day arising
> From sullen earth, sings hymns at heaven's gate.

So it is in the midst of contingency, when our meditations are overwhelmed by the betrayals of the past, while 'I sigh the lack of many a thing I sought,/And with old woes new wail my dear time's waste'

(Sonnet 30), that love may open up the future as possibility, not as completion – so long as we accept that it is time itself that offers us such possibility, not any attempt to escape from time.

At this point in my construction of what may seem to be an exclusively 'contemporary' reading of the *Sonnets* a historical comparison is useful to get some additional perspective. The typical Renaissance attitude to time and mutability is one of fear or resignation unless, as in Spenser, the traditional Christian context can be evoked as compensation. There seemed to be no other language with which to deal with it. But for Shakespeare – Giordano Bruno is again the only contemporary who comes close to him here – the enormous energies released by the Renaissance are wasted in trying to escape the burden of temporality. The drive to find some stasis is a desire to escape the burden of realizing that there are some transformations which love cannot effect. Ultimately we cannot get inside our lover's soul, even under his or her skin, however much we tear and seize and penetrate. The drive to possess and so to annihilate is a desire derived from the old Platonic ideal of original oneness, which only Shakespeare and Donne among the sixteenth century poets seem to have seen as a clear and fearful perversion. It certainly haunts the lover of the Dark Lady sonnets and we are invited to stand and shudder at the poet-lover's neo-Augustinian self-lacerations. In Sonnet 144 the two loves he has 'of comfort and despair/which like two spirits do suggest me still', are not just a 'man right fair' and a 'woman colour'd ill': they are also the contradictory aspects of the lover's self, and the two loves that a dualistic mind cannot affirm and by which we may be paralysed unless we realize that the self is not whole, but multiple and changing.

Throughout this discussion of the *Sonnets* what has been stressed is that their power rests on the seemingly fragile basis not of Shakespeare's but their readers' shifting and unpredictable experiences. In this they stand not as certain affirmations but, as Sonnet 60 puts it, 'to times in hope'. They insist that, at their most authentic, our affirmations are made, often, through pain – pain faced and not vanquished but accepted as the dark visceral element in which we all must live and struggle. Many of the Dark Lady sonnets are grim precisely because the lover can see no way to break through such pain. What they lack, fundamentally, is that open-endedness of hope. Sonnet 124 is particularly suggestive here – perhaps it is one of the key sonnets of the collection precisely because it is so radically undecidable at crucial points. The sonnet categorizes love as 'dear', costly, not only because it is 'fond', beloved, but because it is affirmed in the knowledge of the world. Moreover, while it 'fears not policy' it is none the less 'hugely politic'. How do we explain the strange equivocation here? It is as if love must be adaptable, cunning, even deceptive, aware of the untrustworthiness of the world from which it can never be abstracted: 'it nor grows with heat, nor drowns with showers'. Finally the poet affirms with a strong and yet (when we recall Sonnet 116) ironic twist: 'To this I witness call the fools of Time,/Which die for goodness, we have lived for crime.' As Booth notes, Sonnet 124 'is the most extreme example of Shakespeare's constructive vagueness'; its key word is 'it' which, 'like all pronouns, is specific, hard, concrete, and yet imprecise and general – able to include anything or nothing'. 'It' occurs five times. Each time it becomes more indeterminate, surrounded by negatives and vaguenesses, 'precisely evocative words in apparently communicative syntaxes which come to nothing'. By contrast, 'the word *it* stands sure, constant, forthright, simple and blank'.[18]

The blankness to which Booth points has been filled very specifically by many puzzled readers to yield up a reading consistent with the dominant reading of Sonnet 116. For instance, the key phrase, 'the fools of time', is usually glossed as examples of political or religious time-servers. But less anxiously pursued for exact meaning, the phrase suggests rather that we are *all* fools of time, without more specific reference. When Sonnet 116 affirms that 'Love's not time's fool' it betrays, it might be argued, a deliberate and fearful repression, an unwillingness to acknowledge that Love is not able to overcome Time as something that can be fulfilled only as it presents opportunity and possibility to us. In Sonnet 124, we are challenged to become fools – jesters, dancers in attendance to Time, holy fools before the creative challenge of our finitude – and we 'die', are fulfilled sexually, existentially, only if we submit ourselves, 'hugely politic', to the inevitable compromises, violence, and disruption which is life. We 'die for goodness' because in a sense we have all 'lived for crime'. We are deceivers yet true; or, to quote Shakespeare himself, the truest acts, like the truest poetry, are the most feigning.

The sonnet conventionally regarded as the culmination of the first part of the sequence, the twelve-line Sonnet 126, provides an interesting gloss on this particular reading I am constructing. It is also a serene poem, yet its serenity is very unlike that of Sonnet 116. It acknowledges that, even if the Fair Youth is indeed Nature's 'minion', even he eventually must be 'rendered'. And this realism does not detract from the Youth's beauty or desirability – in fact, it constitutes its power. Because we must 'render' (give back as well as destroy) our deepest experiences and richest language, they are the more valuable to us.

I have so far looked at Shakespeare's sonnets as part of the – perhaps, indeeed, *the* – culmination of the Petrarchan obsession with the vulnerability of the 'I' in the discourse of love. And undoubtedly, through their history, the *Sonnets* have been primarily read as documents of erotic desire, and unfortunately, too often as documentation of the author's lovelife. But there is always a wider socio-cultural dimension to consider. The *Sonnets'* concern with sexual desire and its language coexists with a concern with other, especially political, desires and contradictions. Shakespeare's presentation of the self of the poems as the socially insecure petitioner searching for an influential patron is obvious enough, but less obvious are the ways in which the public roles of the actors in the drama force greater insecurity upon the I of the poems. As Arthur Marotti has argued, even the serene affirmation of Sonnet 29, with its assertion of the saving compensation of love's 'power to compensate wonderfully for social losses and defeats' none the less has a manic quality which 'suggests the degree to which the self-consolation is forced and inadequate'. 'When, in disgrace with fortune and men's eyes/I all alone beweep my outcast state' is succeeded by, as compensation, 'Yet in these thoughts myself almost despising/Haply I think on thee. . . .' However desirable it would be, the private world cannot be isolated from the public; both are traversed and constituted by the same languages.[19]

Within our writing of the history of the poetry of the sixteenth century, Shakespeare's sonnets occupy a pivotal place. They are both the culmination and the destruction of a long and richly contradictory tradition; they anticipate the intensification and the demise of the lyric in its characteristic Renaissance form. They partake of the collective scriptoral tradition of the Petrarchan lyric and yet anxiously anticipate the fragile ego of Cartesianism that was to dominate Europe for the next 300 years. They are also an enigma within our cultural history. Whether we try to identify the Fair Youth or the Dark Lady sonnets, whether we attempt to see a 'hidden' order to the *Sonnets,* or even if we wish to see a story of even some kind of biographical origin 'within' them, perhaps their greatness rests on their refusal to offer even the possibility of solutions to the problems they make us raise. They disturb, provoke, and raise more than merely 'aesthetic' values or questions; read singly or together, they make us face (or hide from) and raise questions about the most fundamental ways we live. Poetry, love, time, death, values, all are put into question. It almost seems superfluous to speak of the *Sonnets* in traditional academic ways – more than most literary works, they offer insights into and raise questions about our whole, not merely our scholarly or literary, lives.

The early Donne

After reading the Elizabethans, when we encounter Donne, wrote F. R. Leavis, at last we read 'as we read the living'.[20] From Grierson's

1912 edition and T. S. Eliot's influential essays in the 1920s, our century has valued Donne over any other sixteenth-century poet except Shakespeare. Why should this be? One answer is that we discovered, at last, that he was a 'better', more lifelike, poet than the others. Literary gossip undoubtedly helped. Donne's reputation as a reformed rake, a handsome roué, who married unwisely but passionately, and ended as Dean of St Paul's, all added to his appeal. His poems also lent themselves to those crucial confining strategies of close formalist reading, the explicationary class or seminar. In Jonathan Z. Kamholtz's words, his poetry could be exhibited as a 'conjunction of static visual symbols, expressing the invisible by means of the visible paradox'.[21] Donne's poetry was thus at once difficult poetry for a difficult age and yet conquerable within a fifty-minute class period.

As is always the case, there were deep-seated ideological reasons for this modern – perhaps more accurately, modernistic – revaluation of Donne's poetry. For many twentieth-century liberals his poetry perhaps articulated some of their own aspirations: Donne was born into a persecuted minority, was a bold experimenter, a man who dared to face the emotional consequences of the 'new philosophy', and who explored in his poetry a refreshingly direct sexuality and then gradually found a way of integrating his youthful radicalism into a mature and ordered framework which he accepted with no less energy but a more ordered perspective. A few revisionists criticized this narrative. William Empson termed it a 'slow capitulation to orthodoxy'.[22] Some recent commentators have written more of Donne's vacillations and contradictions, but the consensus has been that we can observe the emergence of a wiser, chastened Donne, whose writing is no less rich in his sermon than in his lyrics, a man who continued to speak with the voice of the living not only of the disturbing new discoveries of his time but also of the reassuring wisdom of European scholasticism and humanism. Would it were true, so this narrative suggests, of our own time.

To read Donne anew now, at the end of the twentieth century and set him again in the history of sixteenth-century poetry from his own time to ours is therefore to have to take notice of what our recent history made of him. It is also to have to examine the other conventional context into which his work is put – that of a 'transitional' poet between the late Elizabethan Petrarchans and the Metaphysical Poets. The poems with which this chapter is concerned are necessarily those written before or around the end of the century – mainly the *Satires*, and most of the *Songs and Sonets*. Thus they are more or less contemporary with Spenser's late work, Shakespeare's sonnets and the satiric and erotic poetry of Donne's ambitious fellow students in the Inns of Court. Nor should it be forgotten that they are written in the same decade as

Shakespeare's and Jonson's early plays. Donne has often been seen not as a sixteenth-century poet at all, but as initiating a new school, sometimes termed the 'Metaphysicals' or 'the School of Donne' and vaguely located in the early seventeenth century. 'From Donne to Marvell' is both the title of an influential study of the period and a typical title of a university course. More recently, however, Donne has been seen as looking back – to medieval philosophy and theology and to the Petrarchan tradition. His poetry has also been used by Yvor Winters and his followers as the culmination of a robust 'native' school of versification.

The 1590s are widely seen as a more than unusually transitional decade. The dominant cultural trends of the 1580s and the 1590s – those centred in particular on the Sidneian ideals of the Wilton Circle and on the Court of Elizabeth – were being transformed by a variety of deep-seated cultural changes. It is not surprising that few writers at the end of the century were able to articulate explicitly the direction in which their world was moving. We have often valorized Shakespeare as one who, to an unusual extent, could do so; Donne is often looked to as another. Of all the new poets of the 1590s, Donne presents us with an especially interesting case – not only because his poetry has been used to define the transition to the next century, but because his career articulates so compellingly the peculiar pressures under which poetry came late in our period.

Since the presence of Petrarch is so ubiquitous in sixteenth-century poetry, let us glance briefly at Donne's relations with Petrarchanism. Like any poet, Donne had to work against the pressures of his predecessors, and among the voices which speak through his lines one of the most insistent is probably, naturally enough, Petrarch's. Donne wrestles to rewrite Petrarchan motifs and tropes as emphatically as he can. 'The Blossom', for instance, uses the broken, unwanted heart motif, and throughout the poems the tyrannical, sudden nature of love, its violence and surprise, are 'givens' with which the poems struggle. Like the poems of the other English *petrarchisti*, too, Donne's are obsessed with their own failure as language. In the face of the beloved's absence, the Petrarchan poem broods over its own status as discourse, asking questions about the adequacy, even the impossibility, of constructing words for desire. Donne's approach is typically one of bravado: 'I am two fooles, I know,/For loving, and for saying so/In whining Poëtry' ('The triple Foole'). The helpless inevitability of bringing 'grief' to 'numbers' is matched only by its impossibility.[23]

The Petrarchan frustration at the impossibility of conjuring the beloved's presence into words is rendered especially intensely by Donne. Overall, and frequently within a single poem or line, his poetry presents such a variety of tones and moods that it is often difficult to pin down any centre of serious commitment that purports to lie behind it. It is unnecessary (though for some people clearly tempting and reassuring) to construct a systematic metaphysic of love out of the totality of Donne's poems. Each poem grows out of or evokes a different, often isolated, mood in the vast and contradictory range of human experience. What is impressive about the variety of moods of the poems is Donne's attempt to be faithful to individual moments of experience and to the importance of crucial points of time, each of which overwhelms us with the sudden awareness of limitless significance. This is not merely a repeated and effective trope. One of the reasons Donne's poetry is so valuable to us is that it not only brings into play many conflicting voices, but because they are voices that are demonstrably culturally produced. Probably more than any poetry of the 1590s, he dramatizes (his well-attested liking for the theatre is relevant here) these voices. Like the plays he supposedly liked to frequent, his lyrics let us witness intimate scenes of conflict and contradiction. Furthermore, unlike Sidney's or Spenser's, Donne's lyrics are notoriously indifferent to consistency and closure. Vibrant in all the lyrics – expressed in the diverse poses of advocacy, negative argument, positions momentarily held, rhetorical extravagance, or dramatic peripeteia – is a continually decentred subject that tests and is tested by the conflicting discourses that bring it into awareness.

Donne's poetry makes us pay meticulous attention not merely to a marvellous and subtle sensitivity to tone and feeling, but to the infinite (and often fearful) multiplicity of human experience to which his words try to cling. The opening of 'The Canonization', 'For Godsake hold your tongue and let me love', opens up innumerable contexts in readers' minds – personal and dramatic, erotic, social, and intellectual. Not only is there anger, anxiety, over-reaction, as we read that line; there are, as well, the pressures, social as well as personal, that produce their sharp urgency. Their impact is derived from a fascination with the complexity and unpredictability of experience however complex or contradictory it might sometimes be. It is a characteristic summed up by a line in one of Donne's verse letters where he asserts that things 'as they are circumstanced, they be'. Experiences struggle with words not to produce an ideal unity of signifier and signified but only as things are 'circumstanced'. The voices of the poems continually shift, cancelling the seemingly confident conclusions elsewhere in the same poem. If we look at the *Songs and Sonets* as a whole, there is no pretence at narrative order or consistency. As Tilottama Rajan puts it, the poems 'mutually qualify each other within a larger structure which cannot be grasped by any one poem', and any meanings which we may confidently take from a particular reading disintegrate as we leap from one poem to the next. It may even be, as Rajan speculates, that Donne 'deliberately randomised the arrangement of his poems in order to challenge the conventional assumption of the reading-process as a linear movement in which a "truth" is progressively explored and consolidated as the reader moves forward'. The unity or fulfilment, even the presence, of love is never possessed and never final. In Donne's own words, mankind 'hath raised up nothing . . . if these things could fill us, yet they could not satisfie us, because they cannot stay with us, or we with them'.[24]

How do we account for this peculiarly dislocative poetic mode? It is like something that Wyatt's or Sidney's poetry acknowledges as disturbance but that must (if possible) be dealt with; it is akin to what Spenser views with anxiety and, finally, renunciation; it is what Shakespeare's sonnets articulate as part of the melancholy and ambiguity of love, what we all must fight through. Donne characteristically refuses to look for a philosophical absolute beyond the way the self is 'circumstanced'. What we get is his fascination with the problematic nature of the self. Moreover he 'circumstances' that self in a recognizable and appropriate setting for such dislocation. Donne is our earliest, and still one of the best, articulators of the characteristically anxious, over-stimulated, dislocated urban sensibility. Barbara Everett has depicted him as the typical East Ender, looking anxiously westward to Westminster – the son of a city merchant who aspired to and eventually reached the Court, on the fringes of which he spent most of his youthful adult life.[25] His satires in particular take us directly into the restless confusion of the aspiring intellectuals living in London, and in particular into the peculiarly brittle and artificial self which, in a mixture of longing and antagonism, wishes to locate itself in that world. Donne's satires operate by creating an impression of tactile, optic shock, conveying the countless and restless movements that walking through a city involves the individual in – the shocks, collisions, impulses, contradictions.

But Donne brought to his early poetry more than just the culturally created sensibility of the urbanite aspiring to enter the seemingly more secure world of the Court. His early ambitions for a public career must have been tempered by his awareness that with a recusant background, he had a special need for tact, caution, and loyalty not only to the Elizabethan regime but to a particular life-style. John Carey has recently presented a view of Donne as a man writing under intense, even paranoid, alienation in the growing religious intolerance of late Elizabethan England. In this view, Donne grows up in apostasy – he feels himself superior to the ordinary Englishman because of his religion, his European education, and his temperament, and his love poems raise questions 'affected by his betrayal of Catholicism and the anxieties it bred'. What Donne does, argues Carey, is to use his love poems as 'a veil for religious perturbation', as a 'private theatre in which unresolvable oppositions could be entertained as they could not in the decisive business of life'. Treachery and betrayal, experiences which must have loomed so large to the young recusant Donne, could be removed from the dangerous sphere of religion 'where in real life it belonged', and transferred 'to the relatively innocuous department of sexual ethics'.[26]

But Donne's situation as an alienated intellectual is not to be discussed totally in terms of his religion. His situation was not unique: the families of most Englishmen in the sixteenth century were, at some time, at least nominally Catholic. During the last twenty years of the century there was a growing number of intellectuals without secure or continuous attachment to the centres of the country's political power. They constituted insoluble groups of either Catholic or (increasingly) Puritan intellectuals who became alienated in a period of growing restlessness and could find employment spasmodically or only on the fringes of the Court.[27] Donne is typical of this class of dislocated intellectuals and his career may be read as an attempt to integrate himself into the establishment. His satires all display the witty irreverence and gusto of a typical 1590s Inns of Court man, but they are careful to articulate very clearly a sense of moral dedication to the appropriate public concerns of the ambitious public servant. They take us into the cynicism of that group, especially into its desire to occupy a place within power. Their rhetorical pose is that of surveying the more bizarre or corrupt aspects of society in the light of the traditional sources of humanist wisdom; they stress the evils of ambition, affirm the contemplative life over (without scorning) the active, and above all express allegiance to the traditional ideals of justice, harmony, piety, and truth which have seemingly been lost by the 'age of rusty iron' (Satire 5) – except, needless to say, by those like Donne who serve the 'greatest and fairest Empresse', and his employer Egerton.

Donne's satires, then, like Marston's or Hall's, are radical only in their self-conscious choice of a modish rhetoric. Accents are deliberately harsh, lines dislocated, the structure of argument developed by rapid shifts rather than smoothness, details are piled up seemingly at random, and the whole held together, seemingly, only by the indignant voice of the speaker. But the rhetorical fireworks are belied by the cannily, even cynically, conservative values. Only Satire 3 stands slightly aside; it is valuable because it seems to use satiric means to non-satiric ends, and provides a valuable commentary on both the fashion for verse satire and on some of the contradictions of the age upon which Donne was brooding, yet trying to accommodate. The satires are playing a habitual game: they are competitive, aggressive, and rhetorically self-conscious because of fashion; they are episodic in the way that Marston's *Scourge of Villanie* and Guilpin's *Skialetheia* are, crowding together seemingly randomly and scattered experiences of the city and Court and yet asserting that the satirist knows how he can surmount and control them.

Richard Helgerson has described the typical Elizabethan amateur poet of this period as one who sets himself in opposition to literary fashions in order precisely to demonstrate his 'fitness for the sort of service against which he was rebelling', in particular rejecting the 'self-as-poet in order to reveal the dutiful and employable self-as-civil-servant'.[28]

Here, then, in the satires Donne's poetry brings into play some of the age's most crucial cultural contradictions. They are not merely the product of a personal crisis, even though they are insistently articulated as confusing and wounding the self. The satires record a fascination with being thrown into experience and finding no way of examining its meaning except from within: even when the observer feels cut off from the world of politics, none the less he wants desperately to be a participant. In Satire 1, we meet two characters, a long-winded philosopher who is 'consorted' with his books and a giddy, unpredictable, and ambitious courtier who is at once fascinated and repulsed by the world. The poem gives us the conventional rejection of the Court as corrupt and trivial; but there is as well a clear fascination with it as a place where the self can acquire experience and employment. The discourse precedes the speaker of it: the Court is the emblem of the world-at-large; although the traditional humanist commonplaces, by which the self's seeming stability is valorized, reject the Court as corrupt and immoral, none the less the self is in fact defined by it. We have been taken into a world of intrigue and gossip, a world of men who, we are told by the 'brisk perfumed pert courtier'

> . . . all repute
> For his device, in hansoming a sute,
> To judge of lace, pinke, panes, print, cut, and plight,
> Of all the Court, to have the best conceit.

If we see the satires in their literary context, they show a particularly brilliant manipulation of a Horatian persona in a Juvenalian context, the careful observer among the frantic and bewildering randomness of experience. They produce a self simultaneously gripped by, and yet determined to discriminate among, the flurry of experiences passing by. Cloyed with quickly passing detail, we are never certain whether boredom may suddenly become grippingly significant, or when trivial remarks may suddenly alter our hold on power. The Court may be a 'bladder' where the 'puffed nobility' are all 'players' of various seemingly pointless games (Satire 4), but we also realize that tedium, impatience, role-playing (including playing that of the apparently uninvolved spectator) are unavoidable if one is to prosper. Satires 4 and 5 grapple with this overwhelming realization. In one manuscript, Satire 4 is subtitled 'A Satire against the Court'. The poem opens with an

ejaculation of relief for surviving an unwanted visit to the Court and is
followed by a re-creation, with grim hilarity, of the pressures upon an
especially sensitive observer of the fashions, viciousness, and unpredictability of the Court, of which 'there be few/Better pictures of vice'.
We perceive the Court not merely through commonplace description
but through the reactions of the speaker. In the Horatian tradition he
tries to set himself apart as a discriminating observer who prefers to be
'at home in wholesome solitariness' rather than among the 'gay painted
things' of the Court. And yet, despite the disclaimers, there is a relishing
at the sheer detail and outrageousness of the Court's habits. We may
sense the gusto with which the observations are rendered as he notes
'who wasts in meat, in clothes, in horse . . . who loves whores, who
boyes, and who goats'. The outrageousness undermines the con-
demnations – after all Donne's primary audience shared his amused
tolerance of the Court as a given, even while they sensed its moral
offensiveness. So they would not simply condemn it for its apparent
indifference to traditional values. While they would be aware of the
Court as immoral – why, we are asked in Satire 4, with mock-naîvety, is
the 'great chamber' hung 'with the seaven deadly sinnes?' – they recognize that in its variety, colour, and stimulation, it is both autonomous
and inescapable, indifferent to any effective moral categories they might
attempt to impose upon it yet (no little matter) alluringly attractive. So
it is with the narrator. Whatever peace is restored by his leaving it,
something fascinating has gone out of his life. He can moralize over
what he sees, but morality seems irrelevant to the way the world is
'circumstanc'd'. The Court is a play, the would-be courtier an actor.
The picture of the Court at the poem's end is not morally indignant, but
conveys the superiority of the witty and sophisticated courtier enjoying
himself and looking to an audience with similar responses.

My reading of Satire 4 is meant to point less to the sources of Donne's
moral criticisms of the Court – which, patently, his audience would
have seen echoing Horace and the humanists – as to the tone which
disrupts the humanist commonplaces. The rhetorical stratagems assume
the existence of an audience which knows moral diatribes on court
corruption would be just but beside the point. The Court is *there*; it is
inescapable, fascinating, and above all, powerful. So the moral con-
demnations that have paradoxically educated Donne and his fellows to
seek court service are made irrelevant.

Satire 5 starts with a similarly dislocative *jeu d'esprit* – it may be
possible to have rules to 'make good Courtiers, but who Courtiers
good?' The satire seems to be addressed indirectly to the Queen,
'greatest and fairest Empresse', and to Donne's employer, Sir Thomas
Egerton – 'You Sir, whose righteousness she loves, whom I/By having
leave to serve, am most richly/For service paid . . .' The basis of its

observations is, however, the contingent practicality of administration rather than humanist moral principles. Here is a further decentring. Donne's employer, Egerton, was a member of Elizabeth's civil service. He was an illegitimate child who, after Oxford and Lincoln's Inn, had by hard work and graft become Lord Keeper of the Great Seal in 1596, and, later, Lord Chamberlain under James. Donne was also a Lincoln's Inn man and when in 1597 he became Egerton's secretary, his security seemed assured. In 1599, he was a sword bearer at the funeral of one of Egerton's sons, and by 1601, under Egerton's patronage had become MP for Brackley. The tone of Satire 5 is therefore not that of the angry outsider but rather of a confident, talented junior associate of one of the highest cabinet officials of the time, a man who had access to the details of Elizabethan policy and who thought with seriousness and practicality about its principles and application.

Donne's letters written about this time (c. 1599–1600) show him, in fact, to be on the edge of the Essex Circle: he had participated in Essex's attack on Cadiz in 1596 and may well have admired the flamboyance of the Earl, another brilliant young man challenging the dominance of a staid establishment. After the fall of Essex in 1601, Donne wrote the bitter and cryptic poetic fragment, 'The Progress of the Soule', which seems to reflect on the fall of the Earl and his own change in fortune. But in 1599–1600, the probable date of Satire 5, Donne's disappointments lay in the future. The poem is, therefore, written with the restrained vehemence of a concerned insider, and both its rhetorical fireworks and its moral platitudes are subordinate to practical policy. Bald comments that Donne's writings at this time are 'so full of contempt for the ways of the court and of a sense of the depravity of the age that one is inclined to wonder how Donne could have been satisfied with the way of life he had chosen'.[29] But the moral stance of the satire is very much attuned to the Court's dominance. Donne's closest friends of the time were men of similar ambitions and provided him with the primary audience for his satires and verse letters: Christopher Brooke, Rowland Woodward, Henry Wotton, and Thomas Goodyere were all lawyers, courtiers, diplomats, or clergymen, perhaps without Donne's flamboyance or poetical talents, but certainly sharing similar ambitions. They had read their Castiglione and their Machiavelli as well as their Livy and Cicero. They were members of the ambitious, cynical, post-Sidneian generation, determined to make their way in a competitive and at times ugly world. Their favourite art forms were the public theatres, Ovidian verse, and this new satiric poetry. They were politically or socially radical only to the extent of, perhaps, looking to a charismatic figure like Essex to provide a sense of newness or excitement in a time that seemed to be, at its gloomiest, what Donne called an 'age of rusty iron', but one in which they were determined to be successful.

How typical, then, are Donne's satires? There is, argues Puttenham, 'another kind of Poet, who intended to taxe the common abuses and vice of the people in rough and bitter speaches, and their invectives were called *Satyres*, and them selves *Satyricques*. Such were *Lucilius, Juvenall* and *Persius* among the Latines, and with us he that wrote the booke called Piers plowman.' Associating 'satire' with base, rough reprovers, the 'gods of the woods, whom they called *Satyres*', accounts for the peculiar etymology of the term and leads the English satirists of the 1590s to adopt a rough and aggressive manner. Sidney suggests a milder alternative, that the satirist's attacks 'sportingly' are directed 'at folly, and . . . to laugh at himselfe'.[30] But the fashion for epigram and satire in the last decade of the century is peculiar for its virulence, its focus on social scandal and moral corruption: Davies, Guilpin, Hall, Marston, Wither, Rowlands all work variations on the equivalence of 'satire' and 'satyre'. Of the three major satirists, Hall's are more literary exercises – six books, divided into 'Toothlesse Satyrs' and 'byting Satyres', including many literary references, pastiche, some vicious pen-portraits. Marston's are more obscure, violent, sexually obsessed and pessimistic. Donne's stand aside but for their intensity of dramatization and the underlying fragility and waywardness of the self in a powerful public world.

Satire 3 is, perhaps, the exception. John Carey terms it 'the great, crucial poem of Donne's early manhood',[31] and sees its contradictions and insecurities pointing back to his religious anxieties as he moved out of his family Catholicism. Certainly, like the most powerful of the *Songs and Sonets*, it seems to articulate a distinctive anguish. In Satire 3 what Carey sees as the anxiety of Donne's apostasy is clearly visible, with its noble exposition of the need to seek 'true religion'; but so too is Donne's helplessness before the discourse of ambition and worldly success. 'Wee are not sent into this world to Suffer but to Doe', he writes, and the first decade of his life in London exemplifies a brilliant attempt to insert himself, flamboyantly but safely, into the given structures of Elizabethan public life. As with Shakespeare's sonnets, the 'self' of Donne's satire is, then, a peculiarly brittle one. Personal value is a consequence of social value, 'an aspect', as David Aers and Gunther Kress put it, 'of market transactions',[32] and including an awareness that to be outside the public world is not to be at all.

By the turn of the century, then, Donne was an MP, private secretary to Egerton, a rising young man confidently waiting on the fringes of the Court, his satirical poetry and verse letters those of a fashionably cynical young man on the make. By 1602, he was in prison, married but out of a job, his career at Court in ruins. Much has been written of the social disaster and private fulfilment of his marriage. Reading Donne's first letters to his new, somewhat reluctant father-in-law, we might be struck not only by the appropriately desperate sincerity of his professions of love, but by his superficially confident insistence that his private affairs should not affect his public career. He insists on the reciprocity of love – 'we adventured equally' – and on the public priority and social decorum of his actions, assuring Sir George More that he deliberately avoided involving 'any such person who . . . might violate any trust or duty' towards him. But that was not the way More saw the matter; nor did Egerton who, under some pressure, dismissed Donne. From prison and after, Donne wrote to Egerton in more anxious terms, petitioning for reinstatement, but neither his requests nor those of his friends could restore his position. Egerton remained firm: it was 'inconsistent with his place and credit to discharge and re-admit servants at the request of passionate petitioners'.[33] A young man, however promising, was obviously expendable. As the century and Elizabeth's reign ended, so another brilliant young aspirant had found himself excluded by the Court's power.

So far I have hardly mentioned Donne's most celebrated poetry. How can we set the *Songs and Sonets* in this all too typical account of the ruthlessness of power? Modern commentators on the poems collected as Donne's *Songs and Sonets* have tended to concentrate on seemingly purely literary considerations: their relation to Elizabethan rhetoric, Petrarchanism, their striking conceits and dramatic voice, or Donne's biography. Yet even on a cursory reading they are not simply love poems. His women are even more shadowy figures than those of most Petrarchan poets; even more than *Astrophil and Stella* they tease by demanding to be read straightforwardly as personal lyrics and yet by giving us a radically hollow 'I' to fill. Their status as *rime sparse* is extreme. They are repeated gestures at bringing dislocation into discourse; erotic desire is spoken of as the slippery place where other pressures – linguistic, political, religious – continuously try to locate themselves. We can, of course, radically simplify the poems into an almost infinitely adaptable handbook of seduction, compliment, frustration, and anger, but the interest of these poems is not their focus on the psychology or physiology of love.

Most of Donne's lyrics simulate the dramatic voice. Given the increasing cultural dominance of the public playhouse, they ask to be read with the immediacy of a stage performance, with the urgency and authority of the speaking voice and a sense of a multiplicity of an audience which is required to validate and assess their demands. Readers are invariably asked to imagine a pre-existent situation that the speaking voice is attempting to control. The poems are willing to abuse logic, shift ground, make magniloquent or devious gestures, reply to unspoken objections, and even end by denying the premises of the original situation. The reader's stated role is usually that of witness and admirer, but inevitably the poem's rhetoric, its sense of theatre, allow for our active involvement.

The I of the *Songs and Sonets*, then, seems even more wildly dislocated than most Petrarchan poetry. There is no pretence even at continuity or sequence. The site of meaning is wherever the 'I' is thrown; the drama of the poem is the gestures and struggles whereby the 'I' tries to carve out an area of significance in situations that insist on continuous decentring. One way to describe the effects of the poems' dramatic form would be to say there is no systematic philosophy of love that can or cannot be extracted from Donne's poems; they are 'about' the unsystematizable nature of love. Perhaps more fruitful is to point out that in an age where, as we have seen, the self is simultaneously reified and dispersed, Donne's poems, probably better than any others in the century, exemplify the decentring process. Thirty years later Descartes would attempt to hypostasize the stable ego, and for two centuries the individual or 'mankind' would be the stable object upon which the human sciences would be built up. Donne's poems register the enormous insecurity that underlies that reification.

Just like Spenser's or Shakespeare's poetry, Donne's *Songs and Sonets* voices this complex anxiety in the most common language afforded by his age – that of time, mutability, and change. Most of the poems are obsessed with the same commonplaces as the Cantos of Mutability or Shakespeare's sonnets. But there is a major difference. Donne consistently accepts the momentary as the given characteristic by which all human relationships are experienced. As 'Woman's Constancy' puts it, 'we are not . . . those persons, which we were'.

In particular, there are two contradictory obsessions with temporality that haunt those poems. One is a preoccupation with the residual philosophical concern with stasis, moments of permanent significance, within time. D. W. Harding has argued that Donne indulges in 'fantasies of permanence', attempts to escape the pressures of mutability on human life by anticipation or artificial prolongation of an event.[34] We might question whether 'fantasy' is too dismissive for the kind of imaginative elaboration of the experienced moment Donne seeks to evoke in a poem like 'The good-morrow'. Unlike the wish-fulfilment poems of the Caroline Cavaliers, there is little *carpe diem* melancholy in Donne: the awareness of time and death may be all-important in, say, 'The Anniversarie', but there is no hint of a melancholy seizing of fleeting joys, only the joyous affirmation of the moment that fulfils time while time's passing is admitted and faced. For a man so imbued with religious and philosophical traditions which affirmed man as an irreducible self created by an eternal God, it is fascinating to note how many of the *Songs and Sonets* acknowledge that time and mutability are categories bound up with man's deepest nature. The lover of 'A Feaver' asserts that he 'had rather owner bee/Of thee one houre, then all else ever'. It is noticeable that the strength of such a claim is found not in the irreducible selves of the individual lovers themselves, but in their explored and growing relationships. 'Aire and Angels' is particularly powerful for the way it rejects the error of anchoring the reality of love in anything but the indefinable, changing, love of a relationship. 'The Anniversarie' similarly depicts a mutual love that is at once limited and yet fulfilled by time's power. Indeed, it is precisely because of time's passing that love exists and grows. The real fears that transitoriness, loss, and death can bring are faced clearly and then calmly set aside. There is no sense of escapism in the poem's conclusion:

> Let us love nobly, and live, and adde againe
> Yeares and yeares unto yeares, till we attaine
> To write threescore: this is the second of our raigne.

Two great philosophical languages conflict in such poems: the contemplative-mystical tradition inherited from medieval Christianity and reinforced by Neoplatonism, and a strain of secular activism represented by, say, Montaigne or Bacon. The result is the intertwining of contradictory attitudes of time – on the one hand, time is to be redeemed from outside by values that lie beyond its grasp; on the other, time is something that can only be exploited from within its flow. In the words of Giordano Bruno, whose views seem strikingly akin to Donne's on this point, we seize our opportunities only 'amid the changes and chances of life', for if 'there were not mutation, variety, and vicissitude, there would be nothing agreeable, nothing good, nothing pleasurable'.[35]

Donne's poems, therefore, articulate not only something of the same frustrations and affirmations as Shakespeare's sonnets but something of the same unease before the residual ways of dealing with time and mutability. Where the traditional languages saw time predominantly as an unreal realm beneath eternity, what comes through Donne's poems is the struggle to put into language a felt, perhaps growing sense, that fulfilment can come only through the acceptance that 'change is the nursery/Of musicke, joy, life, and eternity' (Elegy 3). Such poems admit the self is above all else subject to time: the lovers *cannot* be isolated from time in their own élitist world.

As with Shakespeare's sonnets, too, in some of the most interesting poems it seems that it is only *because* of time's passing that love can exist and grow. The real fears that transitoriness, loss, and death can bring are faced clearly, and an affirmation is made only *because* time had been faced and lived through. The lovers' seemingly self-sufficient world can be complete only by accepting the need to move beyond it. Just as 'Love must not be, but take a body too', ('Aire and Angels') so love's growth can occur only through time. 'Love's growth' suggests that the fullest experience of life involves the acceptance of change: 'Me thinkes I lyed all winter, when I swore,/My love was infinite, if spring make'it more'. Love is 'elemented' and must 'endure/Vicissitude, and season, as the grasse'. 'A Valediction: Forbidding Mourning', rejects the conventional Platonic analogies to describe the lovers' disdain for temporal and spiritual separation, and similarly ends on a note which affirms the necessity of both eternal fixity and temporal movement. Indeed, the very movement of the free compass arm through time and space describes a circle, the symbol of eternity, making time and eternity one.

How have modern readers, inheriting 300 years of the reified self of Cartesianism, dealt with these contradictions in Donne? The modern admiration for Donne has been built, since Eliot and Leavis, on the captivating and controlling unified voice of the poems. Peter Dane sums up this view: 'What captures us is Donne's "voice". . . . Donne's voice is vibrantly present in all he wrote.' For Wilbur Sanders, Donne's poetic utterance is 'a way of discovering, creating, realising his feelings'. For other readers, it is a way of *dramatizing* such a process. Thus 'Woman's Constancy', with its self-contradictory cynicism, dramatizes the struggles of a Petrarchan lover with sexual desire; 'Aire and Angels' is a 'dramatic peripeteia'; 'Communitie' is voiced by an unreliable narrator whose logical inconsistencies are revealed as the poem proceeds.[36]

But where, if at all, is the still centre of such poetry? Is there a single 'voice' that we listen to? Each poem articulates not only different but incomplete stances. Read either collectively or at random, Donne's *Songs and Sonets* make up the most powerful articulation of dislocation and self-contradiction in the period. The *variatio* of the Petrarchan *rime sparse* gives voice to the decentred self that the Cartesian assertion would attempt to deproblematize. In Rajan's words, the poems 'mutually qualify each other within a larger structure which cannot be grasped in its entirety from the standpoint from any one poem'.[37] Any meanings emerging do so as dislocation, as continual deferment. 'The Triple Foole' voices what looks like the obligatory Petrarchan despair or irritation at the ineffectiveness of language in capturing the beloved: 'I am too fooles, I know,/For loving, and for saying so/In whining Poetry.' The poet-lover is the third fool because he is further betrayed by language, by the dissemination, being set to music, of the words by which he had attempted to 'fetter' love. Hence '. . . I, which was two fooles, do so grow three'. There is no language that does not spread and distort; there is no *écriture degree zero*, no articulation that does not betray itself.

Yet language is clearly all that we have; Donne's poems, like those of all good Petrarchans, rage, despair, and amuse in their failure to make language embody truth. The Petrarchan poet tries and fails to create the presence of the beloved in language; Donne tries, and fails, to find a space for truth in language. Already by the late 1590s, some poets were starting to tire of that rage, and taking on a more instrumental view of language – the Ramists in rhetoric, Jonson in his drama and poetry, the writers of picaresque prose tales, even someone like Greville in poetry, were all moving towards a view of language as instrumental, the so-called 'plain style'. Donne's poetry is less simplistic, as if aware that language can never escape metaphor. To write is to trope. Each poem settles for a sophism, using the wiles of rhetoric to create the illusion of truth, which will inevitably be countermanded by its very reading. In Rajan's words, Donne 'cannot envision, for more than a moment, a language free of shadow: free of unsaid implications that contradict and deconstruct what is being said'.[38]

But Donne's poems do not stand simply as triumphant confirmations of the self-deconstruction of textuality. Speaking through the contradictions of his poems is the force of ideological contradiction. 'The Canonization' has become a crux in this regard. For Wilbur Sanders, the poem is a failure of nerve, an irresponsible slip into triviality. He points to what most readers observe, the poem's continual shifts of voice, and the contradictions of logic by rhetoric. But these contradictions and shifts are not simply signs of an especially brilliant *glissage* of language: they are related to a silent pressure which is inseparable yet deliberately excluded from the literary text. 'The Canonization' probably belongs to the years 1601–5, following Donne's disgrace, and (if we take the reference to the King literally) to after 1603, but it epitomizes, perhaps because of its hindsight, so much that was swirling round during the last years of the century. What it sets before us is what we have observed throughout the age – the power of the Court.

Helen Gardner has argued persuasively that we can identify a group of the lyrics written around the turn of the century, including 'The Canonization', all of which are centred on an opposition between the values of love and the values of the Court.[39] These are, therefore, crucial poems for our understanding of Donne, especially for the way they articulate a conflict that was neither a purely personal one, but one rooted in his whole age. The Court was for Donne both a place of fascination and a set of demands upon him which both excited and drew him into activity. In 'The Canonization', however it is reviled, the power of the Court is never questioned. What is at issue is how, while acknowledging its overwhelming pressure, the individual can affirm a commitment to experiences and values which the Court denies. What place does love occupy in its economy? What place does language? Gardner describes 'The Canonization' as *contemptus mundi* poetry,[40] but this is too crude; the opposition between the Court and love seem on the surface total, but neither is unambiguously affirmed or abandoned. With a marvellous combination of anger, petulance, flippancy, and solemnity, the poem dramatizes an attempt to assert private commitments which are contradicted by public demands that seem sensible and, above all, unavoidable. The initial outburst of anger sets up an absolute opposition between the ambitious, responsible courtier and the indignant lover, but the anger is all the stronger because of the overwhelming logic of the unspoken argument. We might want to read the outspoken lover and the sensible courtier alike as two manifestations of the same dislocated self angrily torn by the contradictory claims of incompatible sets of values. The power of the poem's defiance, its urgent search for justification, and its triumphant or irresponsible abandonment of the glories of the public world – war, glory, fame, chronicle – for the more fragile fulfilment of love, are dependent upon the acknowledgement that the argument can be defeated only by being ignored. Even where the Court is most vehemently rejected and triumphantly transcended, its power and demands are irresistible.

In other poems of the same group (if we accept Gardner's linking of them) it is noticeable that even when the logic of the poem demands otherwise, the integrity and importance of love are acknowledged to be always under pressure from the Court and its values. Even when the autonomy of the lovers' world is asserted, in 'The good-morrow', for instance, their love's maturity is likened not to pastoral innocence but to the sophistication of the Court or city: 'I wonder by my troth, what thou, and I/Did, till we lov'd? were we not wean'd till then?/But suck'd on countrey pleasures, childishly?' Like the Court itself, love is distinguished by refinement and complexity, not by innocence. In 'Love's exchange' love is mockingly called a 'devil' and thus compared to other sophisticated, devilishly attractive, courtly activities:

> *Love*, any devill else but you,
> Would for a given Soule give something too,
> At Court your fellowes every day,
> Give th' art of Riming, Huntmanship, or Play. . . .

Here, love is distinguished from its fellow devils of the Court, but the contrast demands an acceptance of the likeness, not an absolute opposition. Even a poem like 'The Sun Rising', which asserts so confidently the autonomy and serenity of love's fulfilment, does so only by acknowledging and trying to match the power of the Court from which it asserts its independence. It expresses a view of the lovers as distinctive from the claims of the public world, 'the rage of time', and yet describable only in the terms of the world they reject.

Just as love is inseparable from the slippage of language, so the self which yearns to find itself in that love is inseparable from history and the world. Sidney's Astrophil had acknowledged, sometimes with resignation, at other times willingly, that the world of the Court could not be exorcized. Donne's poems may attempt to reject the world, to assert as in 'The good-morrow', that 'each hath one, and is one', but the self that the poems try to create is called into being by that alien world. 'The Sunne Rising' tries to situate its lovers in an intense, fixed moment, but its very power is based on its context. By denial we are made aware of what it tries to exclude. 'I wonder by my troth, what thou, and I/Did, till we lov'd . . .' has its corollary: and what will we do after? What do we do this afternoon? Tomorrow? The very intensity of the physical setting – bedroom, bed, room – creates a performative site which draws in as an unwanted but inevitable pressure the world outside, and with it the darkness that frantic activity has (momentarily) kept out.

The strategy of such poems is usually, then, to acknowledge by denial or exclusion the pressure of the world, and then by rhetorical mastery, to try to control the reader's acknowledgement of it. In 'The Sunne Rising' Donne uses an extended personification of the sun to order it around, and by the vigour of his rhetorical sophism to make us, as representative of that outside world where language and history will master him, a part of his world. Hence the sense, often, that Donne's readers have of being overwhelmed, possessed, rendered powerless.[41]

Donne's poems are so rich, it seems (as with Shakespeare's sonnets) almost blasphemy to tease out the warring strains within them and speak of them as sites of contradiction rather than as masterpieces of achieved unity, reconciliation of opposites, or expressions of his own united sensibility. But such descriptions would be to take Donne out of history – his and ours. So far as his love poems are concerned, what we might call their glorious failure to hold together warring elements is what makes them so suggestive and so fitting a climax to an exploration of sixteenth-century poetry.

Indeed, if we turn outside the Songs and Sonets to Donne's other writings at the time, this case is made even stronger. If we look at his letters, in both prose and verse, we can see something of the same fascination and, in more private moments, of a bitter frustration at his lack of activity in the wider world from which he had been excluded. Many of his letters express what was clearly anguished frustration at his inactivity in the decade following his marriage. He was forced to exist, in relative penury, on the edge of the Court, in what, like Ralegh and Greville, he experienced as exile. He confessed to Goodyere that he still retained 'the same desires' as 'when I went with the tyde, and enjoyed fairer hopes than now', and in a verse letter to Wotton, he similarly bewailed 'the tediousness of my life'. Continually, his correspondence begs for news of the Court. In 1608, he complains to John Harington of being 'far removed from Court and knowledge of foreign passages' and of his 'emptiness'. While his letters show that he can wittily caricature the Court, nevertheless he yearns relentlessly to be in it.[42]

It is interesting to contrast two of his verse letters to Wotton, one written before his marriage (probably about 1598), the other after (in 1604). The first is witty, familiar, rejecting the temptations of 'Countries, Courts, Towns' with the assurance of one totally at ease in all three. Donne can afford to depict himself as 'Parch'd in the Court' and of the Court as a 'Theatre' just because of his own total security within its roles and acts. The tone is of a young man generalizing suavely about the world with the easy dismissiveness of one for whom everything, seemingly, lies open. The description of his fellows as 'Utopian youth, growne old Italian' is disarmingly amusing, but has no sense of giving up the charms of such a tempting world. The later letter has an entirely different tone. It is entitled 'To Sir H[enry] W[oton], at his going Ambassador to *Venice*', and contains lines which are immensely revealing of Donne's exile from court life:

> 'Tis therefore well your spirits now are plac'd
>   In their last Furnace, in activity;
> Which fits them (Schooles and Courts and Warres o'rpast)
>   To touch and test in any best degree.

'Activity' is the crucial term here: the self must be tested, not merely find its own self-satisfaction. Love, of course, may be an activity – it may 'sometime contemplate, sometime do' – but exiled from the dangerous, artificial, but always alluring Court, Donne seems to have lost his most exciting challenge to discover meaning in life's (and love's) variety. The result is a restlessness which is expressed as a calling into question of his whole self:

> For mee, (if there be such a thing as I)
>   Fortune (if there be such a thing as shee)
> Spies that I beare so well her tyranny,
>   That she thinks nothing else so fit for mee.

'Fortune' here is not a general malevolent force; it is the symbol of the 'chances and changes' of life that still made the Court so alluring for Donne. It has been replaced by a paralysing inactivity which he interprets as 'tyranny'. It is interesting that Donne was so clearly incapable of taking his own advice to Wotton, to 'be then thine own home, and in thyself dwell'. Such noble neo-Stoicism was all very well when one is actually in the world; in exile, what struck home was his restlessness and insecurity.

Another later letter, to Goodyere, reinforces this point. In 1608, he wrote:

> Every Tuesday I make account that I turn a great hour-glass, and
> consider that a week's life is run out since I writ. But if I ask
> myself what I have done in the last watch, or would do in the
> next, I can say nothing; if I say that I have passed it without
> hurting any, so may the spider in my window . . . I would fain do
> something, but that I cannot tell what is no wonder . . . to be no
> part of anybody is to be nothing. . . . At most, the greatest
> persons are but great warts and excrescences; men of wit and
> delight conversation but as moles for ornament, except they be so
> incorporated into the body of the world that they contribute
> something to the sustenation of the whole.[43]

The world of activity, of great persons, wit, and public service – the world in which Donne could see Wotton acting – is for him the ultimate 'furnace', when alone he could be fired and purified. That is how life is 'circumstanced'.

To continue this account would be to take us beyond the confines of the sixteenth century. There seems little to challenge Empson's judgement that the first decade of the new age shows, for Donne, a 'slow capitulation to orthodoxy' – except to say that 'orthodoxy' had always been the centre of Donne's world. In 1614 he took orders in the Church of England, and his ordination gave him, however unexpectedly, what his struggle in the 1590s had aimed at: a place in the Court which he had first, confidently then despairingly and at times even tastelessly sought. He willingly became one of the clergy who were increasingly crucial to the Stuart regime as the Civil War came closer, and who were responsible for articulating government policy to the faithful, just as the homilies had been promulgated by the clergy of Elizabeth's reign. Despite our century's romanticizing of him Donne was a court poet, whose self and texts alike speak of the vast power of the institutions he inhabited and which (in a real sense) inhabited him.

Notes

1. Alvin Kernan, 'The Plays and the Playwrights', in *The Revels History of Drama in English*, edited by J. Leeds Barroll *et al.* (London, 1975), pp. 251–94 (p. 251).

2. Robert P. Adams, 'Transformation in the Late Elizabethan Tragic Sense of Life: New Critical Approaches', *MLQ*, 35 (1974), 352–63 (p. 356).

3. *Shakespeare's Sonnets*, edited by Stephen Booth (New Haven, 1978), p. 545. All quotations from the *Sonnets* are taken from this edition.

4. Stephen Booth, *An Essay on Shakespeare's Sonnets* (New Haven, 1969), p. 116.

5. Booth (ed.), pp. 546–48.

6. Roland Barthes, *A Lover's Discourse*, translated by Richard Howard (New York, 1978), p. 160.

7. A. Kent Hieatt, 'The Genesis of Shakespeare's Sonnets: Spenser's Ruines of Rome: by Bellay', *PMLA*, 98 (1983), 800–14.

8. Giorgio Melchiori, *Shakespeare's Dramatic Meditations* (Oxford: Clarendon Press, 1976), pp. 12–13.

9. Alvin B. Kernan, *The Playwright as Magician* (New Haven, 1979), pp. 27–38.

10. Werner L. Gundersheimer, 'Patronage in the Renaissance: an Exploratory Approach', in *Patronage in the Renaissance*, edited by Guy Fitch Lytle and Stephen Orgel (Princeton, 1981) p. 23.

11. Booth (ed.), p. 366.

12. Booth (ed.), p. 367.

13. L. C. Knights, *Explorations* (Harmondsworth, 1946).

14. Terry Eagleton, 'Marx, Freud and Morality', *New Blackfriars*, 58 (January 1977), 22–29 (p. 27).

15. Booth (ed.), p. 333.

16. Booth (ed.), pp. 387–89.

17. Jacques Derrida, 'White Mythology: Metaphor in the Text of Philosophy', *NLH*, 6 (1976), 5–74 p. 11.

18. Booth (ed.), p. 419.

19. Arthur F. Marotti, '"Love is not Love": Elizabethan Sonnet Sequences and the Social Order', *ELH*, 49 (1982), 396–428 p. 411

20. F. R. Leavis, *Revaluation*, (London, 1936), p. 11.

21. Jonathan Z. Kamholtz, 'Immanence and Eminence in Donne', *JEGP*, 81 (1982), 480–91 (p. 483).

22. William Empson, 'Donne in the New Edition', *CQ*, 8 (1966), 255–80 (p. 274).

23. Quotations from Donne's poems are taken from *The Poems of John Donne* edited by H. J. C. Grierson 2 vols. (London, 1912).

24. Tilottama Rajan, '"Nothing Sooner Broke": Donne's *Songs and Sonnets* as Self-Consuming Artifact', *ELH*, 49 (1982), 805–28 (pp. 822, 823).

25. Barbara Everett, *Donne: A London Poet* (London 1972), p. 13.

26. John Carey, *John Donne: Life, Mind and Art* (London, 1981), pp. 37, 38, 46.

27. David Aers and Gunther Kress, '"Darke Texts Need Notes": Versions of Self in Donne's Verse Epistles', *Literature and History*, no. 8 (Autumn 1978), 138–58 (p. 147); Michael Walzer, *The Revolution of the Saints* (New York, 1965).

28. Richard Helgerson, 'The Elizabethan Laureate: Self-Preservation and the Literary System', *ELH*, 46 (1979), 193–200 (p. 200).

29. R. C. Bald, *John Donne: A Life* (London, 1970), p. 122.

30. George Puttenham, *The Arte of English Poesie*, edited by Gladys Doidge Willcock and Alice Walker (Cambridge, 1936), p. 26; Sir Philip Sidney, *A Defence of Poetry*, in *Miscellaneous Prose of Sir Philip Sidney*, edited by Katherine Duncan-Jones and Jan van Dorsten (Oxford, 1973), p. 95.

31. Carey, p. 26.

32. Aers and Kress, p. 138.

33. *Life and Letters of John Donne*, edited by Edmund Gosse (Gloucester, Mass., 1959), II, 113.

34. D. W. Harding, *Experience into Words* (London, 1963), pp. 11–13.

35. Giordana Bruno, *De Immenso*, quoted by I. Frith, *Life of Giordano Bruno* (London, 1887), p. 213; *The Expulsion of the Triumphant Beast*, translated by Arthur D. Imesti (New Brunswick, 1964), p. 89.

36. Wilbur Sanders, *John Donne's Poetry* (Cambridge, 1971), p. 13; Peter Dane, review of Sanders, in *AUMLA*, 37 (1972), 83–84 (p. 83).

37. Rajan, p. 822.

38. Rajan, p. 818.

39. *The Elegies and the Songs and Sonnets*, edited by Helen Gardner (Oxford, 1965), pp. lviii–lx.

40. Gardner, *Elegies and Songs and Sonnets*, p. lx.

41. Dane, p. 83.

42. Donne, *Letters*, I, 168.

43. Donne, *Letters*, I, 190.

Chapter 8
Conclusion – Reopening the Canon?

Beyond the sixteenth century

As I noted in Chapter 1, we have long looked back to the sixteenth century as one of the glorious periods of English culture. It is an evaluation that would have pleased most of its original readers. While the drama of the public theatre, especially that of Shakespeare, has rightly been accorded great reverence, none the less the poetry of Wyatt, Sidney, Spenser, Donne, and Shakespeare has been revered in ways their writers and first audiences would have wished, as glorious manifestations of a noble, idealistic, and ordered culture. Moreover, if today we read or listen to the poetry studied in this volume outside the school or university classroom, we quite often do so in a context uncannily like that of its origins – as background music to dinner parties, or cocktail parties in middle- or upper-middle-class homes – or, in America at least, with that delectable and ubiquitous institution, Sunday brunch. The dominant cultural groups of our time have appropriated the songs of the early Tudor Court, and along with Vivaldi, Bach, or more modern manifestations like Mike Oldfield or Sky, they reside in the genteel background music section of the record collection. Groups like the Deller Consort have helped to popularize Elizabethan poetry and music for audiences far larger than the original writers could ever have hoped for in their lifetimes. Of all the great Elizabethan poetry, only Spenser's *Faerie Queene* remains an arcane and almost totally academic pursuit.

Of course this study has been written in part to *rewrite* this account of sixteenth-century poetry. I have just written of the uncannily similar social functions of the Renaissance lyric as if 400 or 500 years of history can be ignored. We live in a quite different world and the uses to which we put sixteenth-century poetry are acts of cultural selectivity and appropriation no less partial than Palgrave's or Eliot's or the New Critics'. No history is innocent; no use of any cultural product is ever pure – and that includes, needless to say, the original uses. To study our history is to study, from within, a discontinuous struggle to appropriate and control the production of the history and the languages that have written us and in which we struggle to speak. We write and rewrite our history – and that includes the history of our literature – not to re-create a 'true' picture, or (let us hope) to construct an antiquarian's dream of a lost glorious past, but to realize what struggles, what achievements, and exclusions alike, have made us what we are in the present. Major revaluations of history occur when an especially strong rewriting of the past is acknowledged and, in its turn, appropriated. In all cases, we battle with the dominant, residual readings of that past to make our own readings plausible and, indeed, perhaps to let them be heard at all.

In the present account of the poetry written between, approximately, the late fifteenth century and the final years of Elizabeth I's reign, necessarily, many familiar aspects of our residual history have been ignored or downplayed. In part these shifts in perspective have been matters of space – and it is hoped that material in the appendices will direct readers to further considerations or at least serve as acknowledgements that some other writer or topic has not been adequately considered. But in part they have occurred because I have attempted to reread the poetry of the period through late-twentieth-century eyes. This study has been, unashamedly, an essay, *un essai* in Montaigne's sense, an attempt to pose and suggest possible answers to the question Marx asked about ancient Greek tragedy over a century ago: how is it we can still admire works when their original occasion, social structure, cultural assumptions, and socio-economic system have all long disappeared? That is a question that during the middle of our century was asked, by E. M. W. Tillyard and others, as a way of relating the anxieties and problems of that time and its interests to their understanding of the sixteenth century. It saw Elizabethan literature not as produced by a distinctive, complex, but changing social system, but as the product of a universal order and growing from a national unity that seemed an enviable contrast with a disordered twentieth century. Such a view of both periods was, of course, highly partial, but even while (let us hope) we can reject it as different from our concerns, we can acknowledge that a later reading of the period is also, necessarily, one that arises out of a particular horizon of expectation and needs. History needs constant rewriting not because its object of study changes so much as historians (readers, critics, teachers, students) change. The view of the sixteenth century I am advocating here, therefore, is necessarily different. We ask our questions of our past: we find our own ways to make the languages of the past which speak through us (often largely unknown to us) more clearly articulated. Thereby we open in the present the cultural choices we have had made for us in the past – and so open up the nature of cultural choice itself.

But why choose literature, and in particular poetry in this way? Is poetry somehow not separate from the changing social or political pressures that are felt by its readers? As Roland Barthes once noted, in a remark which should give reassurance to the beleaguered humanist and avid deconstructionist alike, if we were unfortunate enough to lose all the human sciences, the one we must keep above all else is the study of literature and the ways its languages have formed and speak through us. This is why, finally, we privilege literature, including poetry – not to 'preserve' it (with all the revealing smell of formaldehyde or pickle jars in that metaphor) but to use it for a perspective on the present and the languages which speak through us. It is in the potential, or unrealized, power of the texts we read that we find the ways to get a perspective on our own place in history, to extend our possession of the pasts which have made us and therefore which are making our possible futures. We are, as Foucault would argue, never outside coercion, and discovering the ways our past has been coerced into particular shapes is one of the ways of understanding and inserting ourselves meaningfully into the present.

In this concluding chapter, I wish to look briefly beyond the period, and then at two kinds of poetry which, if considered in more detail than this study affords, could reopen the questions of both the received canon of sixteenth-century poetry and, even more important, raise the matter of how it is that canons are in fact created.

First, then, to glance ahead, beyond sixteenth-century poetry to what eventually came through into the next century – and to raise the question of what did *not* come through. We should have a quick look ahead at the increasing power of what was to become the dominant mode of literary discourse less than a century later – at the rise of neo-classicism, where, in Francis Barker's words, it seems 'we emerge at last into a clear, known world of facts'.[1] For more than a century, classicism was to become the hegemonic period style. It is more than a literary phenomenon since its hegemony was incorporated into a peculiarly repressive cultural apparatus, the effects of which were felt in every field of human production from economic organization to educational practices.

There was, of course, a developing classical movement long before Jonson's poems, plays, and prefaces started to appear in the 1590s. One of the residual clichés about the Renaissance is that it involved a rediscovery and appropriation of ancient literature. That view, promulgated especially by Burckhardt in the nineteenth century, is today heavily qualified, but it was certainly a view advocated by humanist propagandists like Erasmus, More, or Ascham, and appropriated by the Tudor propaganda machine. A radically rewritten and idealized classical past was ruthlessly made to stand as a reminder of a stability and clarity which the barbarous, dark, papist Middle Ages had lost. On the level of language, what evolved into a systematic set of principles concentrated not merely on revising, Christianizing, and then propagating Greek and Roman authors, but on the control of the signifier, on simplifying the message-transferring function of language. The instrumentalizing of language is given its first full literary articulation in Jonson's theory and poetical practices. Poetry was to serve as the vehicle of permanent truth, of 'matter'; and to achieve an unhindered transference between auth-or(ity) and reader. Metaphor is suspect; substance is stressed over the deceptive promiscuity of rhetoric; Sidney's 'moving' is made strictly subordinate to 'teaching'. When we think of revolutionary movements in the 1590s, we usually think of Donne or the theatre. But it is Ben Jonson who is the real radical. If we look ahead, to the time of Milton – the founding of the Royal Society in the 1660s is often pointed to as a landmark – a new view of language, and with it, a whole new order of things, to use Foucault's phrase again, has emerged. We can find traces of opposition – in Milton, the sectarian writers, and in the last trickle of the lyric before it goes underground into the Methodist hymns or folk-song – but the dominant voices of the eighteenth century (or that view of it that has come down to us) is one in which Jonson's principles have triumphed.

Jonson's literary career starts to take shape in the 1590s and it is in that turbulent decade (perhaps it should be extended to the whole period 1586–1603, between the symbolic deaths of Sir Philip Sidney and that of the Queen, the lady of whom Ralegh, characteristically pious in his hypocrisy, once remarked that time had forgot) that we may perceive many changes and disruptions symptomatic of wider cultural change. Conventional literary histories have rightly pointed to the upsurge and popularity of many new or revived literary genres, most especially in the drama. But in the poetry of the time, too, some significant dis-locations and new directions can be sensed – and not only the new poetical kinds which were becoming fashionable, but in a distinctive confusion of kinds. Polonius's disdainful recitation of the mixture offered by the players visiting Elsinore – 'pastoral-comical, historical-pastoral, tragical-historical, tragical-comical-historical-pastoral' (*Hamlet* II. 2. 397) points to a wider cultural dislocation. In poetry something similar can be sensed – for instance in the epyllion, the short, versified Ovidian narrative (variously serious, comic, erotic, serious- or comic erotic like *Venus and Adonis* or the richly sensual *Hero and Leander*, by Marlowe and (completed and thereby dislocated in a more serious vein) Chapman. It is in the erotic–comic mixture that the generic unease can be seen most easily to connect with wider social dislocation. The writers of such poems were working within the tradition of *Ovid moralisé* and inevitably undermine it – by irony, by lengthy passages of sensuality, and especially by bringing in their hostility to the dominant courtly modes of idealized lyricism and traditional civic and Christian moralization. The romanticized comments of virtuous lovers are invariably undermined by ironic narrators and by cleverly involving their readers in acknowledging their own sensuality – a wonderfully subversive parody of Sidneian 'delight' and 'moving'. It is the poetry of a generation increasingly unsure of its cultural allegiances. The dialogic nature of textuality is foregrounded, the conflicting discourses clash and rub against one another. It is typical of all avant-garde literature: the languages that can be teased out of these texts are tentative and self-dislocating. The poets were facing, as it were, several ways at once, maintaining an ironic distance from a culture from which they were breaking and yet to which still were irresistibly tied.

In the same way the much commented upon fashion for verse satire in the 1590s shows its ambivalent, uneasily transitional, nature. Typical of the decade, it is vigorous and iconoclastic. Hall, for instance, in his *Virgidemiae*, attacks courtly romance as extravagant and incredulous. He rejects romantic Petrarchan sonnets as conventional, idolatrous, and insincere:

> The love-sicke Poet, whose importune prayer
> Repulsed is with resolute dispayre
> Hopeth to conquer his disdainfull dame,
> With publique plaints of his conceived flame.
> Then poures he forth in patched *Sonettings*
> His love, his lust, and loathsome flatterings.

Yet Hall exempts Spenser and Sidney from his criticism, and underneath the iconoclasm is the Puritanism of the man who would end as Bishop of Norfolk. We have seen the same phenomenon with Donne's satires. The same combination of iconoclasm and conservatism energizes Hall's; the same point can be made for Marston or Guilpin. The satirist is a 'satyr', abusive, rough yet self-conscious in his rhetorical skills; yet he has half an eye on accommodating the institutions he rejects. In short, the contradictions of the satires of the 1590s have socio-cultural not simply rhetorical origins. The satirist argues that his aim is to speak the truth and yet he continually draws attention to his own prowess and superiority:

> The Satyre onely and Epigramatist
> (Concise Epigrame, and sharpe Satyrist)
> Keepe diet from this surfet of excesse,
> Tempring themselves from such licenciousness.
> The bitter censures of their Critticke spleenes,
> Are Antidotes to perilentiall sinnes.[2]

The satirist is rhetorician and moralist, at once self-effacing and egocentric. The verse satires of Hall, Marston, Donne, Guilpin, and others represent the taste of highly educated, ambitious yet cynical young men-on-the-make, eager to become part of what they are excluded from – an increasingly narrow and paranoid ruling class. Theirs is the same virulence and intellectual wavering Shakespeare so brilliantly exploits in *Hamlet* and *Troilus and Cressida*, where a tired and yet still powerful public discourse is at once called into question by new and disturbing experiences and yet remains residually strong enough to overcome any challenge to its authority. Shakespeare's so-called 'problem' plays have often been linked to personal crises, as have Marston's, Donne's, and Hall's satires. But such crises, however real and powerful, are not merely personal. They are simultaneously private and public, as if in the powerful collective representation of order – or the continuing desire for what was represented as 'order' as opposed to 'disorder' – and in the growing uneasiness between real and apparent power, as well as in the increasingly intensely experienced pressures of different social relationships, the old languages, and with them the old poetry, were no longer adequate. It is in the crises – the discontinuities, the silences, and repressions – of such a period that we can sense, better than the men and women of the time, the growing points of history. Raymond Williams writes of the way in what we call avant-garde literature, the cultural practices which are reaching beyond the residual, are never fully realized in textual form, in language, because while they might be apprehended in practice, they cannot be put into words – for there are as yet no words for them.

Our reading of the poetry of the late sixteenth century is, therefore, inevitably affected by our knowledge of what came through in subsequent history. The shadow of the Civil War, the failed Revolution of the mid seventeenth century, and the Restoration of the monarchy, cast their shadows not only forward, but backward. To write history is to realize how the future in a real sense determines the past. 'Determines' is perhaps too strong a word, unless we use it in the same sense Williams argues for, the application of pressures or the recognition of limits. Perhaps 'opens up' is more appropriate, since a vital part of writing an account of a period of our cultural history is to question the seemingly most assuredly given aspects of that history – the cultural artefacts themselves. Here I approach a probably controversial part of this final chapter. Surely, it might be argued, regardless of how interpretations may differ, we *know* what poetry the poets between Dunbar and Donne produced; we may change our ways of reading it, and occasionally discover in manuscript new poems or even, rarely, a whole new poet's work, but the masterpieces – the poetry of Wyatt, Sidney, Donne, Shakespeare – are known and unassailable. Perhaps it is so, although the history of taste and criticism does not bear such confidence out. In Palgrave's *Treasury*, where is the place of Greville? Or Donne? It took twentieth-century critics and readers, with changing questions and interests, to read *their* poetry back into the accepted account of the period. But even if such matters can be shown to be determined by taste or (more accurately) ideological appropriation, none the less there has in recent years been developing an awareness that the whole notion of a received canon of poetry from our past is suspect, that the received, seemingly stable, monuments of our literary history are present for us only because of a ruthless and continuing struggle to *make* them present. It is not a question of saying, to adapt a phrase of Stanley Fish, there is 'no text in this class', but that we create what we call the canon.

   The historical production of the poetry we have considered in this study is material, complex, yet if not objectively explicable, certainly able to be discussed and theorized. But the significance of any text is not inherent only in its original production: it is generated by criticism, by use in educational institutions, by appropriation into courses and literary histories and made to serve different ideological and political purposes. As Eagleton puts it, the 'unquestioned "great tradition" . . . has to be recognized as . . . fashioned by particular people for particular reasons at a certain time'. And it is always a highly selective process. Behind the writings of the canon lie the repressed or vanished carcasses of other writings. If all writing is the product of socio-cultural struggle, where are the adversaries that were rejected and defeated? Some, it is true, have survived; others lie buried by the triumphant texts of the dominant canon. As Fredric Jameson argues,

> since by definition the cultural monuments that have survived
> tend necessarily to perpetuate only a single voice . . . the voice of
> a hegemonic class, they cannot properly be assigned their
> relational place in a dialogical system without the restoration or
> artificial reconstruction of the voice to which they were initially
> opposed, a voice for the most part stifled and reduced to silence,
> marginalised, its own utterances scattered to the winds, or
> reappropriated in their turn by the hegemonic culture.[3]

And so how do we discover such voices? Where is the underground counter-culture, the Elizabethan samizdat? I want to mention two such areas. The first is what we might loosely call 'popular culture', specifically the poetry written or, in most cases handed down, by oral transmission outside the dominant court culture and assimilated in large part by it in the form of ballads, songs, low-life characters in drama, jokes, bawdy or low life stories. Some can be found in the drama: the interaction of theatre and social rituals has been carefully reassembled by the work of such critics as C. L. Barber and Robert Weimann, and by the discussion of the gradual suppression of carnivalesque elements of the Middle Ages by Mikhail Bachtin.[4] The success of the Renaissance authorities' repression of popular opposition, much scatological or expressed in folk customs and rituals, can even be seen in the poetry. Much of the oppositional poetry is lost; some was collected and somewhat gentrified in the eighteenth century by Bishop Percy and others, and thus incorporated and assimilated into the dominant canon. As Tom Scott comments on the popular poetry of late medieval Scotland, where much of the most powerful of this material flourished most vigorously, 'behind, under, around and through the art-poetry of court and cloister',[5] it lurked and was passed down, usually orally, among clans and families, embodying the repressed or puzzled inarticulate emotions and yearnings of the dispossessed, and serving (as Falstaff does in Shakespeare's *Henry IV* plays) to remind us of the energies that were lost and destroyed in the ruthless struggles of the period. It turns up, less in the poetry than in the drama, that most dialogic of all Elizabethan forms, to disrupt and challenge the apparently unquestioned dominance of other culturally hegemonous forms of discourse – as the world of Falstaff challenges that of the royal Court, Autolycus the Court of Sicily, or Caliban the power of Prospero. It is usually neutralized, tamed, and resides as a reminder of how energetic counter-dominant cultural modes can be both appropriated and yet remain dormant, waiting for later readers and social formations to tease them into new life.

We can see something of how the canon was established by glancing back once again at Puttenham's disapproval of Skelton's metrics and political sympathies. As Anthony Edwards notes, Skelton 'was the first English writer whose works excited interest across a wide social spectrum during his own lifetime',[6] but by the end of the century, Skelton was being scorned for his condescending to write in the common style instead of the golden, harmonious concord of the courtly maker. The low popular culture with which Skelton was identified is closely associated with the oral tradition of folk wisdom and anti-aristocratic complaint and with the anarchic melancholy of the ballad. At least in the written records, it becomes less and less central to the dominant culture of the sixteenth century as the Court gradually exercises its hegemony.

We often (as in the case of the Walsingham ballad, mentioned or used by such poets as Robert Sidney, Ralegh, and Shakespeare) have to reconstruct this increasingly marginalized folk-poetry by means of collections put together between the late seventeenth to nineteenth centuries in England or, slightly earlier, from the collections of work from Scotland where the popular tradition resisted assimilation more strongly largely because, as we have seen, of the virtual disappearance of the Court from Scotland in 1603. Ballads, broadsides, versified Robin Hood tales and folk-poetry are permitted to become the material of comedy, anti-masque, or incidental effects in the public theatre, but they are largely excluded from the canon of polite verse. Significantly, such material rarely appears in the pastoral where, one might have thought, the Court's taste should be closest to the material practices of the society. But the pastoral in the sixteenth century is primarily the preserve of the urban, sophisticated courtly aspirant, 'the product', Louis Montrose notes, 'of a handful of ambitious young men who came to social and political maturity in the later 1570s and 1580s'.[7]

In short, to trace the disappearance, marginalization, or assimilation of popular poetry through the sixteenth century is another means by which we see the development of the Court's hegemony. A process of active struggle is going on behind and through the establishing of a poetic canon by marginalization, incorporation, and repression. Such a process shows how a culture imposes its dominance and reduces the texts of any potential counter-culture to symbols, fragments, and so-called subliterature. In the drama of the time, something similar happens, as state control, by censorship and bureaucracy, increases – first over the traditional religious drama, and then over the closely regulated secular plays, which were encouraged strongly to reflect the Tudor regime's view of cosmic and centralized national order. Like the poetry, Elizabethan and (increasingly) Jacobean drama became not the glorious manifestation of a whole national culture but part of an institutionalized plan to use the apparatuses of society to, once again, make 'art a work of state'. The Puritans' abolition of the public theatre in 1642 cannot be totally explained in terms of religious iconoclasm; it represents the calculated assertion of counter-dominant political and cultural forces. Like poetry, the drama had become an instrument of state policy.

My second example is taken from the poetry written by women in the period. Joan Gadol has queried whether the model of Renaissance history we have inherited from Burckhardt actually fits women's (as opposed to men's) history, arguing that there was no renaissance for women at the time.[8] The women poets of the sixteenth century whose writings have come down to us are fixed, no less than Astrophil's Stella, within a discourse they did not invent and could not control. When permitted to write, they were largely confined to religious writing or to translation, and acknowledged their boldness in the unusual intensity with which they use the traditional humility topos to apologize for entering a male domain. We have looked at how the age's most significant woman writer, Mary Sidney, Countess of Pembroke, wrote as the *ephebe* of her brother, translating works according to his ideals, promoting and publishing his work. What stands out in her work, and in other women poets, including the Queen herself, and Aemilia Lanyer (a candidate for Shakespeare's Dark Lady), is that they are given roles very strictly within a structure of discourse that creates them as subjects and denies them any owned language. A very condition of their permission to write is the acceptance of constraints which deny them authentic speech. Repression, that is to say, is not only located within social systems, but very specifically in language, which provided the women poets only gaps, silences, the role of the other, within male discourse. 'The relations of power and perhaps among the most hidden things in the social body', writes Foucault, and it is in language, or more revealingly, the gaps and silences in language, that the operations of power can be seen most clearly.[9]

We can perhaps put it this way: what is the status of woman within the dominant vocabulary, syntax, rhetoric, of Renaissance poetry? How in its absences, in the ways the texts are not only silent but are actually unable to speak, does the poetry written by women call attention to gender-specific items? The seemingly replete words are men's, creating and manipulating the woman as object or, where she is permitted speech, controlling her as subject; otherwise she is relegated to the aporias of the text. In 1630, as Bob Hodge and David Aers point out, the courtesy writer Robert Cleaver voiced his culture's subjection of women's language: 'as the echo answereth but one word for many, which are spoken to her; so a woman's answer should be in a word'.[10] The language of the Petrarchan sonnet sequence passed for public language but was in fact the creation of the male-dominated Court. Even when, as in Elizabethan England, the highest rung of that system was occupied by a woman, the language of the court poet was that of a discourse that elevated the woman only to subjugate her, and imprisoned her in her apparent autonomy. It is always true that to enter history an oppressed or underprivileged class can speak only through the dominant discourse and disrupt only by its negation or subdued silences – and it is in such silence that women finally do speak.

Let me illustrate these rather cryptic theoretical assertions by glancing at another of the Sidney poets, Robert's daughter, Lady Mary Wroth. Her *Pamphilia to Amphilanthus*, a collection of Petrarchan sonnets appended to her Arcadian romance *Urania* (published in 1620 but probably written much earlier and probably just within the purview of this study) is purportedly written by her long-suffering heroine to her fickle male lover. Lady Wroth had great difficulty in having her work accepted. Poetry is an art 'rare in women', says a character in the romance. Lord Denny, a courtier who believed himself to be satirized in her work, wrote scathingly that she should 'leave idle books alone for wise and worthyer women have written none'. He further wrote to her

to 'repent you of so many ill spent yeares of so vaine a booke and . . .
redeeme the tym with writing as large a volume of amarous toyes that at
the last you may followe the rare, and pious example of your vertuous
and learned Aunt, who translated so many godly books and expecially
the holly psalmes of David'.[11] The ideology is clear: what emerges is the
way language and literary form, not simply dominant ideas, are its
vehicle. Erotic–political romance and Petrarchan love poetry are, in
court circles, part of the dominant literary discursive structures; books
of piety and devotion only are permissible for women.

When we turn to the poems, we find that like the romance itself, they
are dominated by betrayal, deception, broken promises, and erotic
frustration: we are in the familiar Petrarchan world of plaint and paradox, sophisticated but generalized emotion, rhetorical smoothness
occasionally counterpointed by the mild disruption of question,
ejaculation, despair, or joy. We can, once again, explain away her poetry
empirically as a minor, belated, variant of Petrarchan love poetry,
pointing out that Mary Wroth writes in the shadow of both her uncle's
Astrophil and Stella and her father's poems. But we might ask the further
questions: what difference does the author's *gender* make to her
sequence? Or is she rendered so controlled a subject that we hear the
dominant discourse, speaking without interruption, through her?
Wroth is writing within a genre entirely structured by male categories –
by the distancing of the erotic by logic, by the fixing of the female as a
body which is the subject of power, requiring her passivity as the object
of anguish or manipulation. Do we see any signs at all of what is
increasingly seen today as the psychic distortion and alienation that
occurs when a woman writer represses her gender-specific desires to
write?

We do, I think, see something of the sort in a process of displacement
by which the age's dominant discourse controlled Wroth when we see
the central means by which poetry was determined and deciphered – the
Court. In both *Urania* and *Pamphilia* there emerges a deep disillusion
with court civilization that is unusual for its wholesale and helpless
passivity, reminiscent of the ultimate helplessness of the central female
characters in Webster's court tragedies. Often it emerges in the commonplace *otium* of the pastoral desire to escape from the Court to the
country, but inevitably the country too is fundamentally deceptive. The
all-encompassing melancholy of Wroth's poems seems to grow from
wider cultural disillusion than the Petrarchan convention affords. In her
poems, the woman is happiest alone, even in her abandonment; love's
only constancy is its changeableness, which is presented not as a
theological or psychological observation, but growing from love's
location within discourse as activity for men, a passivity for women.
Whereas a courtier-lover, like the fickle Amphilanthus, has the

autonomy of constant adventure, martial, erotic, and linguistic, Pamphilia must wait, abandoned and insecure, the more threatened the more she is faithful. She is, as one poem puts it, 'married to sorrow', bound in her passive helplessness. Whenever she acts or speaks she is, in a word that recurs through both the romance and the poetry, 'molested'.

Part of the frustration that emerges from *Pamphilia to Amphilanthus* may be read, therefore, as a frustration at the subjection to a language which emphasizes the woman's role as empty, passive, helpless, and yet which insists that Lady Wroth, as a woman and a woman in the Court, write within linguistic and social structures that do not permit her to transcend that role. The Platonic–Petrarchan metaphors which dominate the sequence at once create a place within the discourse of love and exclude her from the production of authentic speech. Pamphilia projects herself only as an absence awaiting Amphilanthus's presence – as lack, incompleteness, and finally, as silence, waiting to be completed. She transfers her alienation upon the object that is afforded her by her society's seemingly public discourse – the Court. Indeed, she can speak only with the language of the alien and oppressor, and her speech is unusually charged with rejection and frustration that go beyond the courtly Petrarchan situation, but which cannot name the cause or the solution of its fragmentation.

As we have seen in Chapters 3 and 4, one distinctive note that erupts through most Renaissance poetry, men's and women's, is the fragile anxiety of the individual speaking voice, struggling to find within the inherited discourse a space for the increasing self-consciousness of ego-psychology. Petrarchan poetry is part of the age's will, to quote Foucault, to hear the others speak the truth of his sex'. But, in this case, what about the truth of *her* sex? Is there any sense of the truth of woman's sexuality becoming part of the discourse in the poetry of the period? As we sense the gaps and frustrations in Wroth's jagged, disruptive text, can we sense the silent inexpressibility of woman's sexuality, never put into words since there are, as yet, no words for it? The logic of love poetry in the Renaissance is that of the gaze, the discrimination of form, and the rendering open and passive of the beautiful object – the woman perceived as territory. Within such a language situation, the woman can speak only as a blank space, a hole in discourse, or (as a passive recipient of the male organ of speech/sex) within man's language. We must wait for a later age to see the development of a discourse adequate to women's sexuality and women's poetry.

Conclusions

The final chapter in a study like this should properly not just sum up but point forward to the work being done on bringing the poetry of the sixteenth century alive for us. The poetry of Shakespeare, Donne, Spenser, Sidney, and other Elizabethans is so central to what is conceived of as our cultural heritage that to insist (as I have) on the disruptive nature of textuality, the gaps of discourse as well as its plenitude, to demystify and deconstruct, to look more closely at fragmentation and silence than what has appeared to us as replete presence, may all suggest a monstrous perversion of the historian's role and the critic's responsibility. What supports me in the task is the inherently collaborative nature of reading and writing history. I refer not only to the many scholars and critics who are carrying on the same work today, but to the critical community which has made up this poetry's history, its common readers: Sidney's friends, Dryden and Johnson, Coleridge, Browning, Eliot, all the well-remembered and forgotten common readers of Wyatt's 'They Flee from Me', Shakespeare's 'Let Me Not to the Marriage of True Minds', or Donne's 'For God's Sake, Hold your Tongue and Let Me Love'. All of us have reinscribed the poems of the sixteenth century in our own lives and our own languages; throughout their history, their words have struggled to be heard through our appropriations of them. Literary history is not the careful preservation of a fixed canon, nor the humble prostration before the fixed stars of an unalterable past. It is the perpetual struggle to write ourselves into our own history, and to do so in the company of as many of those who have struggled before us.

This study is offered therefore as one such re-enactment of a most fascinating and demanding part of our cultural past. Our history is, as Alan Sinfield has insisted, both alien to us, and yet inescapably ours.[12] Every aspect of the past that has made us exists as a judgement upon what we have made of it. Sixteenth-century poetry is not, or should not be seen as, an arcane or antiquarian world of 'treasures' into which we can escape: to read and study poetry, to 'delight' in it, in Sidney's terms, is to become aware of how 'worldly' it is. At the end of Shakespeare's *The Tempest*, Prospero, the poet–magician–scientist–politician, steps out of the play and addresses the audience, asking them (in a moving version of an old trope) for applause. But he also asks for something more difficult. He acknowledges that the play the audience has just witnessed will be 'confined', trapped, nullified, unless its impact is taken out of the theatre, into the lives as well as the words, of its audience. How they will do that is not up to the actor who speaks; nor is it up to the dramatist who wrote his lines. It is up to the members of the audience themselves, to break the confines of the theatre, of art, of literature, and to into the world, to become themselves, in Edward Said's phrase, 'worldly'. We must learn that literature, and in particular poetry, are not separate from the rest of the world around and within us. We are spoken by, given language by, our past as well as our present, and that language is at its most powerful in poets like those studied in this book. That is why we read and reread the poetry of the sixteenth century – that we may know, and use, its power.

Notes

1. Francis Barker, 'The Tremulous Private Body', in *1642: Literature and Power in the Seventeenth Century* (Colchester, 1981), pp. 1–10 (p. 2).

2. Joseph Hall, *Collected Poems*, edited by Arnold Davenport (Liverpool, 1969), p. 18.

3. Terry Eagleton, *Literary Theory: An Introduction* (Oxford, 1983), p. 11; Fredric Jameson, *The Political Unconscious* (Princeton, 1980), p. 85.

4. See Mikhail Bachtin, *Rabelais and his World*, translated by Helen Iswolsky (Cambridge, Mass., 1968); C. L. Barber, *Shakespeare's Festive Comedy* (Princeton, 1959); Robert Weimann, *Shakespeare and the Popular Tradition in the Theatre* (Baltimore, 1978).

5. *Late Medieval Scots Poetry*, edited by Tom Scott (London, 1967), p. 32.

6. *Skelton: The Critical Heritage*, edited by Anthony S. G. Edwards (London, 1982), p. 59.

7. Louis A. Montrose, 'Of Gentlemen and Shepherds: The Politics of Elizabethan Pastoral Form', *ELH*, 50 (1983), 415–60 (p. 433).

8. Joan Gadol, 'Notes on Women in the Renaissance and Renaissance Historiography', in *Conceptual Frameworks for Studying Women's History*, edited by Marylin Arthur *et al.* (Lawrence, 1975), pp. 4–7.

9. Michel Foucault, 'The History of Sexuality: Interview', *Oxford Literary Review*, 4, no. 2 (1980), 3–14 (pp. 10–11).

10. Robert Cleaver, *A Godly Form of Household Government* (London, 1630), p. 3.

11. *Pamphilia to Amphilanthus*, edited by Gary F. Waller (Salzburg, 1977), p. 13. Quotations from Lady Wroth's poetry are taken from *The Poems of Lady Mary Wroth*, edited by Josephine A. Roberts (Baton Rouge, 1983). For an extension of the argument here, see the essays in *Silent But for the Word*, edited by Margaret Hannay (Kent, 1985).

12. Alan Sinfield, 'Against Appropriation', *Essays in Criticism*, 31, no. 3 (July 1981), 181–95 (p. 182).

Chronology

Note: One problem of establishing a chronology for poetry of this period is that most of the poetry written was not published, or often not for many years. Dating of poems and poets' work is often, therefore, very difficult. Dates in this chronology are necessarily more approximate when they refer to writing (w.) than the date of publication (p.).

DATE	WORKS OF POETRY	OTHER WORKS	HISTORICAL/CULTURAL EVENTS
1460			James II of Scotland killed at Roxburgh; accession of James III
1461			Henry VI of England deposed; Edward IV ascends throne
1462	Henryson *Fables* (w.) *Testiment of Cresseid* about now		
1470		Malory *Morte D'Arthur* (w.)	Henry VI (deposed 1461) restored as King of England (–1471); Edward IV deposed
1471			Henry VI murdered in Tower; Edward IV becomes King of England again (reigned previously 1461–70)
1474		Caxton *Recuyelle of the Histories of Troye* (w.) – first book printed in English	

DATE	WORKS OF POETRY	OTHER WORKS	HISTORICAL/CULTURAL EVENTS
1475	*Cockelbie's Sow* (w.) (appears in Bannatyne Manuscript, 1568)		
1476			Establishment of printing press in England by Caxton
1477	Dunbar writing about now	*Dictes and Sayings of the Philosophers* (p.) – first dated book printed in England	
1478	Chaucer *The Canterbury Tales* (p.)		
1481		Caxton *Godeffroy of Boloyne* (tr.) *Mirror of the World* (tr.)	
1483		Caxton *The Golden Legend* (tr.)	Edward IV dies; his 12-year-old son succeeds as Edward V; Richard Duke of Gloucester seizes power, becomes Richard III Herald's College founded
1484		Caxton *Book of the Knight of La Tour-Landry* (tr.)	
1485		Malory *Morte D'Arthur* (p.)	Battle of Bosworth Field; end of the War of the Roses; Henry Tudor marries Elizabeth (daughter of Edward IV of York) and so unites houses of Lancaster and York; ascends throne as Henry VII

DATE	WORKS OF POETRY	OTHER WORKS	HISTORICAL/CULTURAL EVENTS
1486		Medwall *Fulgens and Lucrece* (p.)	Diaz circumnavigates the Cape
1488		Caxton *The Royal Book* (tr.)	James III of Scotland murdered; accession of James IV
1490			The Oxford Humanist Reformers (Linacre, Grocyn, Colet, Erasmus, More) active (−1520)
1492			Columbus commissioned by Isabella of Castile, voyages to the New World
1494	Lydgate *Fall of Princes* (w.) (p. with and as an addition to the suppressed first edition of *A Mirror for Magistrates*, 1555)		
1496	Douglas writing		
1497			Cabot reaches America
1498	Skelton *The Bowge of Court* (w.)		
1500		Erasmus *Adages* (p.) *Everyman*	
1501	Douglas *Pallace of Honour* (w.) (p. London c.1553, Edinburgh 1579)	Sannazaro *Arcadia* (p.)	

DATE	WORKS OF POETRY	OTHER WORKS	HISTORICAL/CULTURAL EVENTS
1503	Dunbar *Thistle and the Rose* (w.)	Erasmus *Enchiridion* (p.)	Michelangelo active
1504	Skelton *Philip Sparrow* (w.) Hawes *Exemple of Vertu* (w.) (p. 1509)		Colet Dean of St Paul's Raphael active
1505			Christ's College, Cambridge founded
1506	Dunbar *Lament for the Makaris* (w.)		Ariosto begins writing *Orlando Furioso*
1509	Barclay *Ship of Fools* (p.) Hawes *The Pastyme of Pleasure* (p.)	Erasmus *Moriae Encomium* (w.)	Accession of Henry VIII and his marriage to Catherine of Aragon Brasenose College, Oxford founded
1510			Colet founds St Paul's School
1511			Henry joins the Holy League Erasmus becomes Reader in Greek at Cambridge
1512	Douglas *Eneados* (w.) – translation of *Aeneid* (p.1553)		
1513		Machiavelli *Il Principe* (w., p. 1532; English tr. 1640)	James IV of Scotland killed; accession of James V
1514	Barclay *Eclogues*, I–III (w.)		

DATE	WORKS OF POETRY	OTHER WORKS	HISTORICAL/CULTURAL EVENTS
1515			Wolsey becomes cardinal
1516	Ariosto *Orlando Furioso* (p.); 2nd edition 1521; final edition 1532	More *Utopia* (p.)	Mary, later Queen of England, daughter of Henry VIII and Catherine of Aragon, born Titian active
1517			Luther's Wittenberg Theses
1519			Cortés invades Mexico Magellan begins voyage around the world
1520			Field of the Cloth of Gold
1521	Skelton *Speake Parot* *Colin Clout* (w.)	Henry VIII *A Defence of the Seven Sacraments* (p.)	Diet of Worms
1522	Skelton *Why Come Ye Not to Court* (w.)		
1523	Barclay *The Mirror of Good Manners* (p.)		Pope Clement VII accedes
1525		Tyndale *New Testament* printed at Worms – first English translation of any part of the Bible	

DATE	WORKS OF POETRY	OTHER WORKS	HISTORICAL/CULTURAL EVENTS
1528	Lindsay *The Dreme* (p.)	Castiglione *Il Libro del Cortegiano* (p.); 1st English tr. by Hoby, 1561	
1529	Lindsay *Complaint* (w.)		The Reformation Parliament
1531		Elyot *Book of the Governor* (p.)	
1532		Rabelais *Pantagruel* (p.)	Henry divorces Catherine of Aragon
1533	Wyatt writing first satires about now		Cranmer becomes Archbishop of Canterbury; Henry excommunicated; marries Anne Boleyn; Elizabeth born; separation of English Church from Rome
1534		Rabelais *Gargantua* (p.)	Act of Supremacy; Henry VIII Head of Church of England
1535		Coverdale, first complete English Bible	More and Fisher executed
1536		Calvin *Institutes of the Christian Religion* (p.); 1st English tr. by Norton, 1561	Anne Boleyn's miscarriage and execution; Henry VIII marries Jane Seymour
1537		Cranmer *Institution of a Christian Man* (p.)	Jane Seymour dies giving birth to Edward (later King)

DATE	WORKS OF POETRY	OTHER WORKS	HISTORICAL/CULTURAL EVENTS
1538		Elyot *Dictionarie* (p.)	James V of Scotland marries Marie de Guise
1539		The Great Bible (p.)	Greater Abbeys suppressed
1540	Wyatt *Defence* (w.)	Lindsay *Satire of the Three Estates* performed (p. 1602)	Fall and execution of Cromwell. Henry marries Anne of Cleves; marriage annulled; marries Catherine Howard
1542		Hall *Chronicle* (p.)	Catherine Howard executed
1543		Copernicus *De Revolutionibus* (p.)	Mary Queen of Scots betrothed to the Dauphin; goes to France. Henry marries Catherine Parr
1545		Henry VIII *Primer* (p.)	Council of Trent opens
1546			Christ Church, Oxford founded; Trinity College, Cambridge, founded
1547			Henry VIII dies; Edward VI succeeds. Execution of Surrey
1548	Sternhold *Certain Psalms* (p.)	*The Book of Common Prayer* (largely work of Cranmer). Hall *Union of . . . York and Lancaster* (p.)	

DATE	WORKS OF POETRY	OTHER WORKS	HISTORICAL/CULTURAL EVENTS
1549	Wyatt *Certain Psalms drawn into English Meter* (p.)	Du Bellay *Défence et Illustration de la langue française* (p.)	
1552		*Second English Prayer Book*: considerable doctrinal changes	
1553	Lindsay *A Dialogue between Experience and a Courtier of the Miserable Estate of the World* (p.)	Wilson *The Art of Rhetoric* (p.)	Edward VI dies; Mary accedes
1554	Lindsay *The Monarchie* (p.)		Execution of Lady Jane Grey Marriage of Mary to Philip of Spain; England reconciled with Rome but Mary retains title of Supreme Head
1555	Abortive first attempt to print *A Mirror for Magistrates;* two variant title pages and one leaf of text extant	Heywood *Two Hundred Epigrams* (p.)	Persecution of Protestants in England: Latimer and Ridley burnt at the stake; Cranmer burnt
1557	Tottel's *Miscellany* (p.)		Stationers' Company incorporated
1558		Marguerite De Navarre *Heptameron* (p.)	Loss of Calais to France; Mary dies; Elizabeth I accedes
1559	Baldwin *A Mirror for Magistrates* (full edition) (p.)	Foxe *Actes and Monuments* (p. in Latin; 1st edition tr. 1563)	Pope Pius IV succeeds; Matthew Parker Archbishop of Canterbury Acts of Uniformity

DATE	WORKS OF POETRY	OTHER WORKS	HISTORICAL/CULTURAL EVENTS
1560		Geneva Bible (tr.)	
1561	Robinson, tr. of More *Utopia* (p.) Stowe edition of Chaucer (p.)	Googe, tr. of Palingenius *Zodiake of Life* Hoby *The Courtier* (p.); tr. of Castiglione	
1562	Sternhold, Hopkins, Norton, and others *The Whole Book of Metrical Psalms* (p.)	Jewel *Apologia pro Ecclesia Anglicana* (p.)	
1563	Googe *Eclogues, Epitaphs and Sonnets* (p.) Sackville *Induction* to portion of 1563 edition of *A Mirror for Magistrates*		
1565	Golding, tr. of Ovid *Metamorphoses*, i–iv (p.)		
1566	Painter *Palace of Pleasure* (p.)		
1567	Drant, tr. of Horace *Art of Poetry, Epistles, Satires* (p.) Turberville *Epitaphs, Epigrams, Songs and Sonnets* (p.)		Revolt of the Netherlands
1568	Bannatyne Manuscript compiled		English College at Douai founded

DATE	WORKS OF POETRY	OTHER WORKS	HISTORICAL/CULTURAL EVENTS
1569	Spenser *The Visions of Bellay* *The Visions of Petrarch* (p.)		
1570		Ascham *Scholemaster* (p.) Foxe *Ecclesiastical History* (p.)	Pope Pius V excommunicates and announces deposition of Elizabeth I
1571	Third edition of *A Mirror for Magistrates* (p.)		
1572			Pope Gregory XIII accedes Massacre of St Bartholomew
1573	Du Bartas *Judith* (p.) Gascoigne *A Hundred Sundry Flowers* *The Adventures of Master F.J.* (p.) (prose romance, includes, poetry) Tasso *Aminta* (p.)	Cartwright *Reply to an Answer* (p.)	
1575	Breton *A Small Handful of Fragrant Flowers* (p.) Churchyard *The First Part of Churchyard's Chippes* (p.) Gascoigne *The Poesies of Gascoigne* (p.) Ronsard *Sonnets Pour Hélène* (p.) Tasso *Gerusalemme Liberata* (p.)	Laneham *A Letter* (p.)	

DATE	WORKS OF POETRY	OTHER WORKS	HISTORICAL/CULTURAL EVENTS
1576	Edwards (ed.) *Paradise of Dainty Devices* (p.) Gascoigne *Princely Pleasure of . . . Kenilworth* *The Steele Glas* (p.)		The Theatre in London built
1577		Peacham *Garden of Eloquence* (p.) Gascoigne *Glass of Government* (p.)	Drake begins voyage around the world
1578	Du Bartas *Sepmaines* (p.)	Lyly *Euphues, the Anatomy of Wit* (p.)	Mary Sidney marries William Herbert, Earl of Pembroke
1579	Churchyard *General Rehearsal of Wars* (p.) Spenser *Shepheardes Calender* (p.)	Gosson *School of Abuse* North, tr. of Plutarch *Lives of the Noble Grecians* and *Romans*	Pope Gregory XIII sets up Jesuit College in Rome; sends missions to England
1580	Sidney *Astrophil and Stella* (w.; p. 1591)	Harvey *Three Proper Letters* *Two other Letters* (p.) Lyly *Euphues and his England* (p.) Sidney *Defence of Poesie* (w.; p. 1595) *Arcadia* begun (p. 1590)	
1581	Howell *Howell his Devices* (p.)	Mulcaster *Positions* (p.) Pettie, tr. of Guazzo *Civil Conversation*	French marriage crisis

DATE	WORKS OF POETRY	OTHER WORKS	HISTORICAL/CULTURAL EVENTS
1582	Ralegh's poems written (–1592) and circulated at Court Watson *Hecatompathia* (p.) Whitestone *Heptameron of Civil Discorses (Aurelia)* (p.)		Bruno in England
1583			Whitgift Archbishop of Canterbury
1584		Bruno *Cena delle Cinere* *De La Causa* *De L'infinito* (p.) Peele *Arraignment of Paris* acted (p.) Scott *Discovery of Witchcraft* (p.)	Ralegh founds first English colony in Virginia; failure of the colony Cambridge University press founded
1585	Bruno *Eroici Furori* (p.)		
1586	Warner *Albion's England*, I–IV (p.)	Knox *The History of Reformation of Religion Within the Realm of Scotland* (p.) Kyd *Spanish Tragedy* acted? Pettie, tr. of Guazzo *Civil Conversation* (p.) Webbe *Discourse of English Poetry* (p.) Whetstone *English Mirror* (p.)	Sir Philip Sidney dies of wounds in Battle of Zutphen; Robert Sidney becomes Govenor of Flushing Trial of Mary, Queen of Scots James VI signs Treaty of Berwick with Elizabeth I

DATE	WORKS OF POETRY	OTHER WORKS	HISTORICAL/CULTURAL EVENTS
1587	Fraunce, tr. of Watson *Amyntas* (p.) Monteverdi first book of madrigals	Day, tr. of Longus *Daphnis and Chloe* (p.) Golding and Sidney, tr. of Du Plessis Mornay *Of the Trueness of the Christian Religion* (p.) Marlowe *Tamburlaine*, Pts I and II acted	The Pope proclaims a crusade against England Execution of Mary, Queen of Scots
1588	Byrd *Psalms, Sonnets and Songs* (p.)	Fraunce *Arcadian Rhetoric* (p.)	The Spanish Armada defeated
1589		Nashe *Anatomy of Absurdity* (p.) Puttenham *Arte of English Poesie* (p.) *The Marprelate Tracts* (p.)	
1590	Spenser *The Faerie Queene*, I–III (p.) Watson *First Set of Madrigals Englished* (p.) Monteverdi second book of madrigals (p.)	Guarini *Pastor Fido* (p.) Lodge *Rosalynde (p.)* Marlowe *Tamburlaine the Great* (w.) Shakespeare *The Comedy of Errors* (w.) Sidney *Arcadia*, revised edition (p.)	

DATE	WORKS OF POETRY	OTHER WORKS	HISTORICAL/CULTURAL EVENTS
1591	Breton *Briton's Bower of Delights* (p.) Fraunce *Countess of Pembroke's Emanuel* (p.) Harington, tr. of Ariosto *Orlando Furioso* (w. 1506–16) Sidney, Sir Philip *Astrophil and Stella* (p.) Southwell *Mary Magdelene's Tears* (p.) Spenser *Complaints Daphnaida* (p.)	Greene *Notable Discovery of Couzenage* Ralegh *A Report about the Flight of the Isles of Azores*	Trinity College, Dublin, founded Ralegh imprisoned and released
1592	Breton *Pilgrimage to Paradise* *The Countess of Pembrokes Passion* (p.) Constable *Diana* (p.) Daniel *Delia . . . with the Complaint of Rosamund* (p.) Harvey *Four Letters and Certain Sonnets* (p.) Sylvester, 1st instalment of tr. of Du Bartas *Sepmaines* Warner *Albion's England,* I–VIII (p.)	Marlowe *Edward II* acted? Nashe *Pierce Penniless* (p.) Shakespeare *Richard III* (w.)	Essex recalled to Court by Elizabeth Rose Theatre opened

DATE	WORKS OF POETRY	OTHER WORKS	HISTORICAL/CULTURAL EVENTS
1593	Barnes *Parthenophil and Parthenophe* Drayton *Idea* *The Shepherds' Garland* (p.) Marlowe *Hero and Leander* (entered in Stationer's Register) Shakespeare *Venus and Adonis* *Phoenix Nest* (w.)	Harvey *Pierce's Supererogation* (p.) Nashe *Christ's Tears Over Jerusalem* (p.)	Theatres closed by the plague
1594	Barnfield *The Affectionate Shepherd* (p.) Constable *Diana Augmented* (p.) Daniel *Delia* *Rosamond augmented* *Cleopatra* (p.) Davies *Orchestra* (w.) Drayton *Idea's Mirror* (p.) Shakespeare *The Rape of Lucrece* (p.)	Hooker *Ecclesiastical Polity*, I–IV (p.) Kyd *Spanish Tragedy* (p.) Shakespeare *Titus Andronicus* *The Taming of the Shrew* *Two Gentlemen of Verona* *Love's Labour's Lost* (w.) Tasso *Discorsi del Poema Eroica* (p.)	Beginning of a period of bad harvests in England Swan Theatre built (–1596)

DATE	WORKS OF POETRY	OTHER WORKS	HISTORICAL/CULTURAL EVENTS
1595	Barnes *A Divine Century of Spiritual Sonnets* (p.)	Ford *Ornatus and Artesia* (p.)	Execution of Southwell Unsuccessful voyage of Drake and Hawkins to the West Indies and deaths of both
	Barnfield *Cynthia with Certain Sonnets* (p.)	Montaigne *Essais* (final ed. p.)	
	Breton *Mary Magdalen's Love* (p.)	Shakespeare *A Mid-Summer Night's Dream* (w.)	
	Campion *Poemata* (p.)	Sidney *Apology for Poetry (Defence of Poesie* p.; w. 1580)	
	Chapman *Ovid's Banquet of Sense* (p.)		
	Donne's early poetry circulating in MS		
	Drayton *Endimion and Phoebe* (p.)		
	Shakespeare's sonnets (w.?– 1599)		
	Southwell *Saint Peter's Complaint* (w.)		
	Spenser *Amoretti Epithalamion Colin Clouts Come Home Again* (p.)		
1596	Davies, Sir John *Orchestra* (p.)	Deloney *John Winchcomb (Jack of Newbury*, entered in Stationer's Register)	Essex storms Cadiz
	Harington *Metamorphosis of Ajax* (p.)	Nashe *Have With You To Saffron Walden* (p.)	
	Smith *Chloris* (p.)	Ralegh *Discovery of Guiana* (p.)	
	Spenser *The Faerie Queene*, IV–VI, and new edition of I–III (p.)	Shakespeare *Romeo and Juliet The Merchant of Venice* (w.)	

DATE	WORKS OF POETRY	OTHER WORKS	HISTORICAL/CULTURAL EVENTS
1597	Dowland *First Book of Songs* (p.) Drayton *England's Heroical Epistles* (p.) Montgomerie *The Cherrie and the Slaye* (p.)	Chapman *Humorous Day's Mirth* acted? James I *Demonology* (p.) Shakespeare *Henry IV*, 1, 2 *Henry V* *Merry Wives of Windsor* (–1600) (w.)	Philip's second Armada dispersed by bad weather
1598	Chapman-Marlowe *Hero and Leander* (p.) Hall *Virgidemiarum* IV–VI (p.) Marston *Scourge of Villany* (p.)	Jonson *Every Man in his Humour* (p.) Shakespeare *Much Ado about Nothing* (w.) Young, tr. of Montemayo *Diana* (p.) Meres *Palladis Tamia Wit's Treasury* (p.)	
1599	Daniel *Poetical Essays* (including *Civil Wars*, I–V) *Musophilus* (p.) Marston *Scourge of Villainy Corrected with New Satires* (p.) *The Passionate Pilgrim* (p.)	James I *Basilikon Doron* (p.) Shakespeare *As You Like it* *Julius Caesar* (w.)	Essex rebellion Globe Theatre built for Shakespeare's company
1600	Bodenham (ed.) *England's Helicon* (p.) Dowland *Second Book of Songs* (p.) Davies *All Ovids Elegies: Three Books* (p.)	Jonson *Cynthia's Revels* acted Fairfax, tr. of Tasso *Godfrey of Bouloigne* Gilbert *De Magnete* (p.) Shakespeare *Hamlet* (w.)	Bruno burnt at Rome Fortune Theatre opened

DATE	WORKS OF POETRY	OTHER WORKS	HISTORICAL/CULTURAL EVENTS
1601	Campion *A Book of Airs* (p.) Shakespeare *The Phoenix and the Turtle* (p.)	Shakespeare *Twelfth Night* *Troilus and Cressida* (w.)	East India Company founded
1602	*A Poetical Rhapsody* (p.)	Campion *Observations on the Art of English Poesie* (p.) Shakespeare *All's Well That Ends Well* (w.)	Bodleian Library, Oxford founded
1603	John Davies of Hereford *Microcosmos* (p.)	Daniel *Defence of Ryme* (p.) James I *The True Law of Free Monarchies* (p.)	Elizabeth I dies; James I (James VI of Scotland) accedes

General Bibliographies

Note: Place of publication is London unless otherwise stated.

(i) Approach and methodology

Sixteenth-century poetry and Renaissance studies generally have been well served by some energetic scholarship this century and, in the late 1970s and 1980s, by the great advances in literary theory. Since about 1977, we have seen the development of a 'new' or 'revisionist' literary history of the whole Renaissance period, represented by such critics and scholars as Alan Sinfield, Jonathan Dollimore, Jonathan Goldberg, Stephen Greenblatt, Louis A. Montrose, as well as the present study. As Annabel Patterson, another of the revisionist scholars has put it, 'We have here evidence of a revolution in critical thinking.' We are, she says, 'now more likely to talk of "culture" than of "literature" and it may eventually produce a new aesthetics in which problems of value in the arts can be grounded in a network of social, economic, political and linguistic practices' ('Talking about Power', *John Donne Journal*, 2, no. 2 (1983), 91–106 (p. 92)). Contemporary readers should benefit greatly from the enthusiasm and inconoclasm of this new movement which draws insights into the study of literature from philosophy, anthropology, sociology, linguistics, and from a variety of philosophical positions – Marxism, Deconstruction, and from post-Structuralism generally. The result of this heterogeneous new movement should be to make the reading of sixteenth-century poetry most exciting.

At the same time, the tradition of sound scholarship, in the editing of texts and the patient investigation of historical context, has continued. It may be best represented by the *Spenser Encyclopedia* (General Editor A. C. Hamilton) which has drawn on a great variety of viewpoints and which is useful far beyond its immediate focus on Spenser and his works.

To trace something of the way the new approach combines traditional historical scholarship, close attention to the texts we have inherited from the period, along with the newer focus on such matters as power, discourse, 'author', 'reader', and suchlike, readers are directed to Chapter 1 of this study. For more detailed discussion, two articles by the author might be further consulted. They are 'Author, Text, Reading, Ideology: Towards a Revisionist Literary History of the Renaissance', *Dalhousie Review*, 61 (1981), 405–25, and 'Deconstruction and Renaissance Literature', *Assays*, 2 (1982), 69–94, both of which extend the argument in Chapter 1. There is a succinct description of the new movement's British and American manifestations, with some fine distinctions between the two, in Jonathan Dollimore's review of Goldberg's *James I and the Politics of Literature*, in *Criticism*, 26 (1984), 83–86.

For deeper investigations into the methodology employed in this study, a prime text is Michel Foucault, *The Order of Things* (English trans. New York, 1970); and Pierre Macherey, *A Theory of Literary Production*, translated by Geoffrey Wall (1978), which is one of the most important treatments in recent years of the notions of absence and repression in texts. Raymond Williams's writings are also relevant. See especially *Marxism and Literature* (Oxford, 1977) which is an unusually flexible account of his topic; or *Problems in Materialism and Culture* (1982); and a moving account of two great keywords in our cultural history. *The Country and the City* (1973). The last-named is especially relevant for this period in its treatment of Sidney and country houses. Also relevant for methodological considerations are the increasingly in-fluential works of Bachtin and Kristeva. See for instance Kristeva's *Desire in Language*, translated by Thomas Gora *et al.* (Oxford, 1980) which is especially stimulating for its accounts of the interconnections of language and desire. Lacanian considerations are also to the forefront in Rosalind Coward and John Ellis's *Language and Materialism* (1977), which is especially good for its clear discussion of the notion so central to sixteenth-century poetry, the 'self'. Very lively is Bernard Sharratt's *Reading Relations* (1982), which although not specifically on this period, has an excellent account of 'suture' in Donne.

The interaction of 'literary' with 'social' text in the period is a strong emphasis in recent work, and characterized by an avoidance of the older 'background'–'text' dichotomy. The opening chapters of Fredric Jameson's *The Political Unconscious* (Princeton, 1980) are especially relevant, notwithstanding what some reviewers have seen as their neo-Hegelian brand of Marxism. Terry Eagleton's recent criticism is also relevant. His *Literary Theory* (Oxford, 1983) is a superb and very lively introduction to the whole subject of recent approaches to literature, and his *Criticism and Ideology* (1976) and *Walter Benjamin or Towards a Revolutionary Criticism* (1981) are stimulating (if occasionally a little tactless) for their discussions of critical practice. The Benjamin book is very useful for its 'little history of Rhetoric'. Tony Bennett's *Formalism and Marxism* (1979) is a lively account of the interaction of formalist and historicist criticism. Readers of Renaissance literature will benefit especially from the last few chapters. Behind many of these studies is the ubiquitous figure of Louis Althusser. The essay on 'Ideological State Apparatuses' in *Lenin and Philosophy and other Essays*, translated by Ben Brewster (New York, 1972) is particularly important.

Students will, of course, have come across the approaches represented above in their reading of other periods. Among the many useful accounts of the paradigm shift in criticism since the late 1960s perhaps the most useful is Frank Lentricchia's *After the New Criticism* (Chicago, 1980); Eagleton's *Literary Theory*, mentioned above, should also be consulted. For an important theoretical work on literary history in general, see H. R. Jauss, *Toward an Aesthetic of Reception*, translated by Timothy Bakhti (Minneapolis, 1982). Useful anthologies include Robert Young, ed., *Untying the Text* (1981) in which the essays by Roland Barthes on 'Theory of the Text' and by Michel Foucault on 'The Order of Discourse' are of first importance; and *Modern Literary Theory*, edited by Ann Jefferson and David Robey (1982). The thinker whose work should be given particular mention here is Roland Barthes, whose emphasis on the peculiar pleasure of textuality in *The Pleasure of the Text*, translated by Richard Miller (New York, 1975) has great relevance to the texts treated by this book.

(ii) General background studies (historical and cultural)

Coming directly to the sixteenth century and the Renaissance period generally, the classic study against which all subsequent scholarship has argued, usually in admiration, has been Jacob Burckhardt's *The Civilization of the Renaissance in Italy*, translated by S. G. C. Middlemore, 2 vols (New York, 1958). Of the older historicist accounts of this century, E. M. W. Tillyard's *Elizabethan World Picture* (1943) is outdated and simplistic. It is mentioned only because it resides on the bookshelves (and book lists) of many university teachers. Much more useful older studies are L. C. Knights's *Drama and Society in the Age of Jonson* (1937) and John Buxton's attractive, if slightly idealizing, picture of the period in *Elizabethan Taste* (1963). A corrective to Tillyard and to the dominant aristocratic view of the period is the important exercise in the new social history, Carlo Ginzburg's *The Cheese and the Worms*, translated by John and Anne Tedeschi (Baltimore, 1980), which provides a startling account of the 'world-view' of an ordinary Renaissance man. Guy Fitch Lytle and Stephen Orgel, eds., *Patronage in the Renaissance* (Princeton, 1981) contains a number of essays on a topic long dominated by unexamined commonplaces. A. B. Ferguson's *Clio Unbound: Perception of the Social and Cultural Past in Renaissance England* (Durham, North Carolina, 1979) is a reliable study of the period's discovery of history.

Admirably robust – oversimplified but delightful reading – are A. L. Rowse's *The Elizabethan Renaissance: The Life of Society* (1971) and *The Elizabethan Renaissance: The Cultural Achievement* (1972). More substantial historical studies are Lawrence Stone's classic and much debated *The Crisis of the Aristocracy 1558–1640* (Oxford, 1965), and Perez Zagorin's *The Court and the Country* (1970). For a discussion of the arts in the Court in the period, *Splendour at Court*, by Roy Strong (1973) is also a useful corrective to older views, as is Thomas Greene's fine discussion of the Renaissance humanists' discovery of the irrecoverability of the past in their idea of history in *The Light in Troy: Imitation and Discovery in Renaissance Poetry* (New Haven, 1982).

For introductions to recent work on the Renaissance in which the new 'revisionist' approaches are explicitly discussed, see the following: Michael McCanles, 'The Authentic Discourse of the Renaissance', *Diacritics* (March 1980), 77–87, and Jonathan Goldberg, 'The Politics of Renaissance Literature: A Review Essay', *ELH*, 49 (1982), 514–42. Goldberg's longer study, *James I and the Politics of Literature* (Baltimore, 1983) contains seminal readings of literary and cultural interaction, and is especially relevant for Spenser, Donne, and Shakespeare. It is one of the most important manifestations of the new movement, along with Stephen Greenblatt's *Renaissance Self-Fashioning: From More to Shakespeare* (Chicago, 1980), an important pioneering work on the relations of discourse to power. See also Greenblatt's 'Invisible Bullets: Renaissance Authority and its Subversion', *Glyph 8: Johns Hopkins Textual Studies* (Baltimore, 1981), 40–61. Two important studies, using insights from modern linguistics as well as anthropology and philosophy, are *Literature, Language and Society in England 1580–1680* by David Aers, Bob Hodge, and Gunther Kress (Dublin, 1981), and Frank Whigham's *Ambition and Privilege: The Social Tropes of Elizabethan Courtesy Theory* (Los Angeles, 1984).

There are many general studies of the poetry. Maurice Evans's *English Poetry in the Sixteenth Century* (1955) is still a useful, compact summary. Fred Inglis's *The Elizabethan Poets* (1970) is stimulating but rather rigid (see also his *English Poetry 1550–1660* (1965)). In *Transformations in the Renaissance English Lyric* (Ithaca, 1979), Jerome Mazzaro argues for a movement from musical to philosophical lyrics occuring over the century, while Douglas L. Peterson's *The English Lyric from Wyatt to Donne* (Princeton, 1967) concentrates on the so-called 'plain style' tradition. J. W. Lever's study, *The Elizabethan Love Sonnet* (second edition, 1968) argues for a very popular viewpoint, the distinctive moralization of Petrarch by the Elizabethan poets.

Petrarchanism itself is excellently treated in Leonard Forster's *The Icy Fire* (Cambridge, 1969). An important article on the organization of sonnet collections is '"Love's Sweetest part, variety"; Petrarch and the Curious Frame of the Renaissance Sonnet Sequence', *Ren. and Ref.*, 11 (1975), 14–23. The same author's study of Petrarch and Petrarchanism is eagerly awaited. Another important study of the sonnet sequence which deserves to be widely read is Ann Rosalind Jones's unpublished doctoral dissertation (Cornell, 1976), 'The Lyric Sequence: Poetic Performance as Plot'. An important book dealing with the adaptation of Petrarchan and other courtly modes in the English Court is John Stevens's study, *Music and Poetry in the Early Tudor*

Court (1961). It is richly suggestive, beautifully written and presented. Stevens's more recent views on Elizabethan poetry are briefly but highly suggestively put in *The Old Sound and the New* (Cambridge, 1982) which deals with the century's metrical revolution. A pioneering study, applying post-Structuralist analysis to the language of Petrarchanism, is Eugene Vance's 'Loves Concordance: The Poetics of Desire and the Joy of the Text', *Diacritics*, 5 (1975), 40–52; another suggestive article on the subject is William J. Kennedy's 'Petrarchan Audiences and Print Technology', *JMRS*, 14 (1984), 1–20.

(iii) General studies of literatures

When readers turn to literary history and criticism, it is often difficult to distinguish purely 'literary' accounts from those discussed under section (ii) above. One of the marks of the most important recent work in the period is a stress on the indissolubility of the codes of literary and other cultural texts. But works that focus on the literature rather than the politics or philosophy are listed here, including anthologies and collections of criticism. A useful collection of primary sources in the criticism of the period is J. W. H. Atkins's *English Literary Criticism: The Renaissance* (1962). The standard collection, *Elizabethan Critical Essays*, edited by G. Gregory Smith, 2 vols (1904) is still very useful. Of the many surveys of the period's literature in general, readers might consult (with care) the revised edition of the Pelican *The Age of Shakespeare*, edited by Boris Ford (Harmondsworth, 1955; revised edition 1982). The emphasis remains astringently Leavisite but includes new essays, on Sidney and Spenser, by J. C. A. Rathmell and W. W. Robson respectively, which (in the former case at least) change the direction very slightly. C. S. Lewis's magisterial, lively, prejudiced (depending on one's taste) study in the Oxford History series, *English Literature in the Sixteenth Century Excluding Drama* (1954) is still remarkably fresh as well as thorough. Although a little dull, Gregory Krantzmann's *Anglo-Scottish Literary Relations 1430–1550* (Cambridge, 1980), is an indispensable survey of a neglected subject. Other specialized studies of the period's literature include the following. The older richly detailed historicism is represented ably by S. K. Heninger, Jr in *The Cosmological Glass: Renaissance Diagrams of the Universe* (San Marino, 1974) which traces the presence of both classical and medieval elements in the philosophical and poetical ideas that inform the period's literature. By contrast, more briefly, Alan Sinfield's *Literature in Protestant England 1580–1660* (Brighton, 1983) represents the newer trend. Sinfield's study is both methodologically rich, provocative, and so far the best and most lively account of the impact of religious ideas on the period's literature. It might be read alongside another suggestive and rigorous study, *Radical Tragedy*, by Jonathan Dollimore (1983) which deals with the period's drama. Sinfield and Dollimore represent the best recent English criticism in the period; their work connects (and in some respects can be interestingly contrasted) with some recent American work, notably by Goldberg, Whigham, already noted, and by Louis A. Montrose, who has produced an important series of essays on the interaction of literary forms and socio-cultural production. See for instance 'Celebration and Insinuation: Sir Philip Sidney and the Motives of Elizabethan Courtship', *Ren. Drama*, n.s. 8 (1977), 3–35; or 'Of Gentlemen and Shepherds: The Politics of Elizabethan Pastoral Form', *ELH*, 50 (1983), 415–20.

  Secondary studies of the period's criticism which deserve special notice are Lawrence Manley's *Convention 1500–1750* (Cambridge, Mass., 1980) which is provocative although never quite living up to its Foucaultian premises, and Robert L.

Montgomery's *The Reader's Eye: Studies in Didactic Literary Theory from Dante to Tasso* (Berkeley, 1979). Marion Trousdale's *Shakespeare and the Rhetoricians* (1982) is a careful application of recent theories of language to a topic long dominated by anti-quarianism, while Frank Whigham's article in *PMLA*, 76 (1980), 864–82, 'The Rhetoric of Elizabethan Suitor's Letters', is similarly ground-breaking. Howard C. Cole's *A Quest of Inquirie: Some Contexts of Tudor Literature* (Indianapolis, 1973) discusses literary theory along with much else that is relevant in a rambling, chatty, and very suggestive study. Perhaps the best brief introduction to Elizabethan poetic theory is Earl Miner's 'Assaying the Golden World of English Renaissance Poetrics', *Centrum*, 4 (1976), 5–20.

(iv) Studies and anthologies of poetry

When we turn specifically to poetry, there are many useful anthologies for readers to browse in, in addition to scholarly editions or selections of particular poets. Norman Ault's *Elizabethan Lyrics from the Original Texts* (New York, 1969) is an old favourite, organized chronologically; Nigel Alexander's edition, *Elizabethan Narrative Verse* (1968), is useful, as is Elizabeth S. Dunno's *Elizabethan Minor Epics* (1963). Richard Sylvester's *Anthology of Sixteenth-Century Verse* (Garden City, 1974) concentrates on the major poets; while John Williams's edition, *English Renaissance Poetry* (Garden City, 1963) is more idiosyncratic in its preference for plain-style poets. More specialized is H. E. Rollins's standard edition of *Tottel's Miscellany (1557–67)*, 2 vols (Cambridge, Mass., 1965). Scottish verse is conveniently collected in Joan Hughes and W. S. Ramson, eds., *The Poetry of the Stewart Court* (Canberra, 1983), a valuable collection of poetry from the Bannatyne Manuscript, although with a somewhat pedestrian introduction. John MacQueen's *Ballatis of Luve* (Edinburgh, 1979) is a brief collection, a delightful assemblage of love songs.

Other specialized studies of poetry worth pursuing include Richard Helgerson's two studies, *The Elizabethan Prodigals* (Berkeley, 1976) on the 'new generation' of late Elizabethan writers, and *Self-Crowned Laureates: Spenser, Jonson, Milton and the Literary System* (Berkeley, 1983) which discusses the vocationalism of late Elizabethan poetry. For the increasingly important topic of women writers, see the collection of essays edited by Margaret Hannay, *Silent But for the Word* (Kent, 1984) which includes essays by Diane Bornstein, Mary E. Lamb, Barbara Lewalski, Gary Waller, and others. E. W. Pomeroy studies *The Elizabethan Miscellanies: Their Development and Conventions* in a useful if rather superficial survey (Berkeley, 1973). A major study of poetry in the Court is David Javitch's *Poetry and Courtliness in Renaissance England* (Princeton, 1978). Javitch was the first to show in detail the overlap between the courtly life and its poetic. See also his 'The Impure Motives of Elizabethan Poetry', *Genre*, 15 (1982), 225–38. The political dimension of the sonnets is dealt with in an important article by Arthur F. Marotti, 'Love is not Love': Elizabethan Sonnet Sequence and the Social Order', *ELH*, 49 (1982), 396–428. Charles Altieri's 'Rhetoric, Rhetoricity and the Sonnet as Performance', *Tennessee Studies in Literature*, 25 (1980), 1–23, is an intriguing reading of the sonnet's concern with its audience.

Other specialized studies include the following. While Sinfield's study of Protestantism and literature (noted above) is more stimulating, John N. King's *English Reformation Literature: The Tudor Origins of the Protestant Tradition* (Princeton, 1982) is a solidly researched compilation of material from the neglected Protestant poets of the mid-century period. Derek Attridge's *Well-Weighed Syllables: Elizabethan Verse in Classical Metres* (Cambridge, 1974) is likely long to be the standard work on an obscure topic. A more general study by Antony Easthope, *Poetry as Discourse* (1983) is important as an account of the pentameter as an hegemonous cultural form with deep implications for this period.

Individual Authors

Notes on biography, major works, and criticism

ALEXANDER, Sir William, Earl of Stirling (1567–1640), Scottish poet and statesman who came to England in 1603 with James I and VI after a distinguished career as a poet and courtier in the Scottish Court. Author of four verse tragedies written 1603–07, the *Monarchicke Tragedies*, and poems including sonnets published in *Aurora* (1604). He had been one of King James's poetical protégés in the Scottish Court, and although his literary career went well beyond the sixteenth century (he lived, indeed, nearly until the start of the Civil War), his poetical style in the new century remained Elizabethan rather than Jacobean. His work was influenced by his contacts with the later phase of the Sidney Circle, and *Aurora* is a rather feeble late manifestation of the Sidneian mode. The verse tragedies attracted the attention of the admirers of the Countess of Pembroke's attempts to encourage Senecan verse tragedy.

> Kastner, L. E. and Charlton, H. B., eds, *The Poetical Works* (Edinburgh, 1921–29). (The standard edition).

> See: Waller, G. F., 'Sir William Alexander and Renaissance Court Culture', *Aevum*, 51 (1977), 505–15. (Widens the discussion to consider the disintegration of Scottish court culture.)

BARCLAY, Alexander (1457?–1552), courtier, monk, poet. Probably born in Scotland, educated in England, France, and Italy, and became a religious. His best-known work is a moralistic adaptation of a German original, *The Ship of Fools* (1509).

> *Certayne Egloges* (reprinted New York, 1967).

BARNES, Barnabe (*c.* 1569–1609), poet, educated at Oxford, though left without a degree. Volunteer in the expedition led by the Earl of Essex to Dieppe to assist Henry IV of France, 1591. His poetry drew heavily on French originals, mediating the Petrarchan tradition from continental rather than English models. He also dabbled in religious sonnets. See *Divine Century of Spiritual Sonnets* (1595). Frequently ridiculed for the quaintness and preciousness of his conceits, notably by Nashe and Campion.

> Doyno, Victor A., ed., *Parthenophil and Parthenophe, 1593* (1971). (A critical edition of Barnes's main Petrarchan collection.)

> See: Blank, Philip E., Jr, *Lyric Forms in the Sonnet Sequences of Barnabe Barnes* (The Hague, 1974).

BARNFIELD, Richard (1574–1626), country gentleman and poet. He was educated at Oxford, taking his B.A. in 1592, and went to London to seek for court preferment. Before he was twenty-five, he had published three collections of sonnets, *The Affectionate Shepherd* (1594) which was dedicated to Lady Penelope Rich; *Cynthia* (1595); and *The Encomion of Lady Pecunia* (1598). He sought the friendship and patronage of other authors and noblemen, including the Sidneys.

Summers, M., ed., *Poems* (1936). (A collected edition.)

See: Morris, Harry, *Richard Barnfield, Colin's Child* (Tampa, 1963). (An overview.)

BRETON, Nicholas (1545?–1627?), an enormously prolific and popular poet. He was the son of a prosperous London trader, and (after his father's death) stepson of the poet George Gascoigne. Probably educated at Oxford, he started publishing poetry in the late 1570s, but his main burst of writing seems to have been under the aegis of the Countess of Pembroke for whom he wrote lyrics, religious allegory, and dialogues. She is the subject of some fulsome praise in the dedications to *Pilgrimage to Paradise* (1592) which is subtitled *Joined with the Countess of Pembrokes Love, The Countess of Pembrokes Passion* (?1592), *Auspicante Jehova, Maries Exercise* (1596), and *A Divine* Poem (1601). His other sixteenth-century verse includes *A Small Handful of Fragrant Flowers* (1575) and *Britton's Bowre of Delights* (1591, 1597). He wrote mainly in pastoral and devotional modes, continuing later in his life to echo the musicality and courtly poetry of the Sidneys.

Grosart, Alexander B., ed., *The Works in Verse and Prose* (1879; reprinted, Hildesheim, 1969). (A collected edition.)
Robertson, Jean, ed., *Poems* (not hitherto reprinted) (Liverpool, 1967). (Contains a useful introduction.)

CAMPION, Thomas (1567–1620), court poet and musician. Student at Peterhouse (1581–84), Gray's Inn, and also studied medicine in Europe. He wrote poetry as a student and some of his poems appeared in the unauthorized edition of Sidney's *Astrophil and Stella* (1591). In 1595, he published a volume of Latin epigrams, and his best-known work, for which he wrote the lyrics and most of the music, was a *Book of Airs* (1601). His prose treatise, *Observations on the Art of English Poesy* (1602) included a controversial defence of quantitative verse in opposition to Samuel Daniel's views. In the Court of James VI Campion wrote airs, music, masques, and is one of the most distinguished practitioners of the mixed art of music and poetry.

Davis, Walter R., ed., *Works* (1969). (The standard edition.)
Hart, J., ed., *Observations in the Art of English Poesie* (1969). (A modern reprint.)
Observations in The Art of English Poetry (Cheadle, 1976). (Contains selection of poems.)

See: Kastendieck, M. M., *Thomas Campion, England's Musical Poet* (New York, 1938; reprinted 1963).
Lowbury, Edward, Salter, Timothy, and Young, Alison, *Thomas Campion: Poet, Composer, Physician* (1970). (The standard biography.)
Eldredge, M. T., *Thomas Campion: His Poetry, and Music, 1567–1620* (New York, 1971).
Bryan, Margaret, R., 'Recent Studies in Campion', *ELR*, 4 (1974), 404–11. (A useful survey of modern criticism).
Doughtie, Edward, 'Sibling Rivalry: Music vs. Poetry in Campion and

Others', *Criticism*, 20 (1978), 1–16. (Raises the most interesting question in considering Campion's work.)

CHAPMAN, George (1559?–1634), poet, soldier, writer, translator. He was born in Hertfordshire, and may have studied at Oxford, despite his claim that he was self-taught. He travelled in Europe and may have served in the Low Countries War. He was associated with a number of intellectually avant-garde groups, and his friends included Christopher Marlowe. Among his patrons were the Earl of Essex, Prince Henry, and King James's favourite, the Earl of Somerset. He became one of the major dramatists of the Jacobean period, with poetry playing a relatively minor part of his literary career.

> Bartlett, P. B., ed., *Poems* (New York, 1941). (Standard edition.)
> Zocca, L. R., ed., *Elizabethan Narrative Poetry* (New Brunswick, 1950).

See: Lord, G. de F., *Homeric Renaissance: The 'Odyssey' of George Chapman* (New Haven, 1950). (A study of Chapman's translation of Homer.)
> MacLure, Miller, *George Chapman, A Critical Study* (1960). (An overview.)
> Spivack, Charlotte, *George Chapman* (New York, 1967). (A basic introduction.)
> Waddington, Raymond F., *The Mind's Empire: Myth and Form in George Chapman's Narrative Poems* (1969). (Concentrates on interests in mythology.)

CHURCHYARD, Thomas (1520?–1604), poet, soldier, minor courtier and poetic hack. He may have started his 'literary' career in the reign of Henry VIII, and published poems and prose until the reign of James I. His poetical style remained the clumsy, repetitive, thumping lines of the worst of the 1540s and 1550s. He contributed poems to many miscellanies and his best work is probably the story of *Shore's Wife* which was added to the 1563 edition of *A Mirror for Magistrates*. His poetry includes *The Firste Parts of Churchyeards Chippes* (1575). Modern criticism is mainly confined to brief remarks, usually derisive. There is perhaps a case for a modern selection and introduction.

CONSTABLE, Henry (1562–1613), born into Warwickshire gentry, educated at Cambridge; became a Catholic and spent much of his time in Europe. Like Marlowe, was possibly a spy, even a double spy, for both the English and French governments, and was in touch with King James before he became King of England. Many of his poems circulated in manuscript or were published in miscellanies or other poets' collections. His religious sonnets, with their strong Catholic sentiments, were unpublished until the nineteenth century. His major collection of sonnets was *Diana* (1592, 1594).

> Grundy, Joan, ed., *The Poems of Henry Constable* (Liverpool, 1960). (A modern edition, with a useful introduction.)

CROWLEY, Robert (1518?–88), protestant printer, propagandist, and poet. An early Puritan leader whose verses were part of his propagandist campaign for the new ideas. He published the first printed edition, modernized and annotated, of Langland's *Piers Plowman*, seeing it unambiguously as hostile to Catholicism. His own poetry adapted traditional popular devotional and satiric styles to Protestant theology, and he was one of the earliest versifiers of the Psalms.

> *The Psalter of David newly translated into English* (1549). (Psalm translation; not reprinted.)

See: Freer, Coburn, *Music for a King* (Baltimore, 1972). (Contains some brief references in Ch. 1.)

King, John N., *English Reformation Literature: The Tudor Origins of the Protestant Tradition* (Princeton, 1982). (Ch. 7 has a detailed discussion.)

DANIEL, Samuel (1562–1619), poet, courtier, diplomat, translator, teacher. He was born in Taunton, educated at Oxford. A typical professional writer of the period: his father and brother were both musicians and he spent some time at Court. He acted as a tutor and was employed by various aristocratic figures, including the Countess of Pembroke, and held minor court offices through such patronage. Under James I, he was employed to write court entertainments and masques. His poetry includes both sonnets, especially *Delia* (1592 and many other revised editions), and longer poetry, including the national epic, *The Civil Wars* (1595). His prose work includes *The Defense of Rhyme* (1603), in which he courteously opposed the Countess of Pembroke's and Campion's championing of quantitative verse.

> Grosart, A. B., ed., *Complete Works* (5 vols, 1885–96; reprinted New York, 1963). (Long the standard edition.)
> Himelick, R., ed., *Musophilus* (West Lafayette, 1965). (Edition of Daniel's minor epic.)
> Michel, L., ed., *Civil Wars* (New Haven, 1958). (Modern edition of the long epic.)
> Sprague, A. C., ed., *Poems and A Defense of Ryme* (Chicago, 1905). (A useful collection for modern readers.)

See: Rees, Joan, *Samuel Daniel* (Liverpool, 1964). (A useful, well-organized introduction.)

Seronsy, Cecil, *Samuel Daniel* (New York, 1967). (Overview.)

Hulse, S. Clarke, Samuel Daniel: The Poet as Literary Historian', *SEL*, 19 (1979), 55–69. (Daniel's interest in history.)

Rist, M. S., A Frame of Words: On the Craftsmanship of Samuel Daniel', *ES*, 60 (1979), 122–37.

DAVIES, Sir John (1509–1626), born in Wiltshire, educated at Oxford, then like so many other aspiring courtiers, at the Middle Temple. He became a courtier, poet, and under James I held a number of posts in Ireland including Solicitor-General and Speaker of the Parliament. 'Orchestra', his best-known poem, was published in 1596. He wrote epigrams, poetical praises of the Queen, and satires. Like Greville's or Chapman's his work tends to be serious and philosophical. *Nosce Teipsum*, like Greville's long poetical treatises, remains an interesting guide to some of the commonplace philosophical ideas of the late Renaissance.

> Grosart, A. B., ed., *Works* (2 vols, 1876).
> Tillyard, E. M. W., ed., *Orchestra* (1945).

See: Sanderson, J. L., *Sir John Davies* (Boston, 1975). (A useful introduction.)

DEVEREUX, Robert, Earl of Essex (1566–1601), nobleman, courtier, favourite of Elizabeth, husband of Sir Philip Sidney's widow Frances Walsingham, and incidental poet. One of the most brilliant figures in the Court, he gained increasing power over the ageing Elizabeth in the late 1580s and 1590s, until he was sent to Ireland, in part because he was becoming politically embarrassing and too obviously ambitious. His return in 1599 may have been designed to effect a coup, but he was not supported widely, was arrested and executed in 1601, along with many of his supporters. Like most other highly placed courtiers, he played, danced, and wrote incidental poems, many of which turn up in miscellanies and notebooks.

> May, Stephen, ed., 'The Poems of Edward de Vere, Seventeenth Earl of Oxford and of Robert Devereux Second Earl of Essex', *SP*, 77, no. 5 (1980), 5–132. (A fine modern edition.)

DONNE, John (1571/72–1631), clergyman, politician, poet, Donne's career began with a reputation as a fashionable young libertine with great political ambition and ended with him as Dean of St Paul's. Born into a Catholic family, he was educated at Oxford, Cambridge, and Lincoln's Inn though, because of his religion, he never took a degree. He drew himself carefully up the political ladder in the 1590s, was one of the most brilliant and fashionable young aspiring men about Court and became an MP in 1600. His elopement with his employer's niece meant the end of his public career and he languished unhappily for a few years until he gradually found employment under James I as a religious propagandist. Realizing he would find high office only as a clergyman, he was ordained in 1614 and thereafter developed into one of the Church of England's most brilliant preachers and divines. Late in his life he acquired a reputation for eccentricity and miserliness but continued to be highly regarded as a churchman. The poetry he wrote in the sixteenth century includes satires, elegies, and the famous *Songs and Sonets* which were among the most admired poems of the last decade of the century, and well beyond. Donne's reputation grew enormously in the first half of this century and he remains perhaps the most accessible poet of the period for our time.

> Grierson, H. J. C., ed., *The Poetry of John Donne* (1912). (Still the most reliable edition, preferable textually to the Gardner edition of *Songs and Sonnets.)*
>
> Gardner, Helen, ed., *The Elegies and the Songs and Sonnets* (Oxford, 1965). (See also, for Donne's later poems, *The Divine Poems*, Oxford, 1952.)
>
> Milgate, Michael, ed., *Satires, Epigrams and Verse Letters* (Oxford, 1967). (Standard edition of the Satires.)
>
> Smith, A. J., ed., *The English Poems of John Donne* (Harmondsworth, 1971). (A useful reader's edition with the *Songs and Sonets* alphabetically organized.)
>
> Smith, A. J., *Donne: Songs and Sonnets* (1964). (An introductory reading.)

See:
> Empson, William, 'Donne in the New Edition', *CQ*, 8 (1966), 255–80. (Controversial, lively; see also 'Donne the Space Man', *KR* (1957), 337–99.)
>
> Bald, R. C., *John Donne: A Life* (1970). (The standard biography.)
>
> Sanders, Wilbur, *John Donne's Poetry* (Cambridge, 1971). (Still the most stimulating study; see also the review by Peter Dane in *AUMLA*, 37 (1972), 83–84.)
>
> Everett, Barbara, *Donne as a London Poet* (1972). (Focuses on Donne's peculiarly brittle urban sensibility.)
>
> Aers, David and Kress, Gunther, '"Darke Texts Need Notes": Versions of Self in Donne's Verse Epistles', *Literature and History*, 8 (1978), 138–58. (A fine stylistic and semiotic study.)

Carey, John, *John Donne: Life, Mind and Art* (1981). (Argues for religious anxieties as a source for many of Donne's characteristics.)

Marotti, Arthur, 'John Donne and the Rewards of Patronage', in Orgel, Stephen and Fitch Lytle, Guy, eds, *Patronage in the Renaissance* (Princeton, 1982). (Pioneering essay on the political connections, relating Donne to contemporary cultural practices.)

Rajan, Tilottama, '"Nothing Sooner Broke": Donne's Songs and Sonnets as Self-Consuming Artifacts', *ELH*, 49 (1982), 809–28. (Moderate and stimulating deconstructive treatment.)

John Donne Journal (North Carolina State University, 1982–   ). (A journal which promises to be useful.)

DOUGLAS, Gavin (1474?–1522), Scottish poet, cleric, translator. Aristocratic background, and one of the leading writers of the Scots tradition in the Renaissance, especially known for his translation of Virgil's *Aeneid*. Educated at St Andrews and possibly in Paris, he took clerical orders and enjoyed court patronage all his life, rising to be Bishop of Dunkeld (1515).

Small, S., ed., *The Poetical Works of Gavin Douglas* (4 vols. Edinburgh, 1974).

Bawcutt, Priscilla J., ed., *The Shorter Poems of Gavin Douglas* (Edinburgh, 1967). (Useful introductory edition.)

Coldwell, Davis F. C., ed., *Selections from Gavin Douglas* (Oxford, 1964). (A brief selection.)

DRAYTON, Michael (1563–1631), writer, dramatist, friend of Shakespeare and Jonson. Born in Warwick into the gentry, attached to Sir Henry Goodyere's household and dedicated his idealistic *Idea* sonnets to Goodyere's daughter Ann. In the sixteenth century his poetry includes the sonnets in *Idea* (1593), and longer poems in *Ideas Mirror* (1594). He also wrote in the epic vein, in *Englands Heroical Epistle* (1597 and many subsequent editions).

Buxton, John, ed., *Poems* (1953). (A useful collection in The Muses Library Series.)

See: Hardin, Richard F., *Michael Drayton and the Passing of Elizabethan England* (1961). (Deals with the nostalgia for the Golden Age of Elizabeth.)

Newdigate, Bernard H., *Michael Drayton and his Circle* (1961). (Literary friendships.)

Berthelot, Joseph A., *Michael Drayton* (New York, 1967). (A useful brief overview.)

Wrestling, Louise H., *The Evolution of Michael Drayton's Idea* (Salzburg, 1974). (An account of the revision of *Idea*.)

Johnson, Paula, 'Michael Drayton, Prophet without Audience', *SLit I*, no. II (1978), 44–55. (Nostalgia, isolation, moral concerns.)

DUNBAR, William (1460?–1520?), Scottish poet and courtier. Educated at the University of St Andrews, and active at the Court of James IV of Scotland. His varied career as a poet grew directly out of his association with the Court; his poetry is arguably the best produced in Scotland between Henryson and Alexander Scott.

Kinsley, James, ed., *The Poems of William Dunbar* (Oxford, 1979). (A useful introductory edition.)

See: Scott, Tom, *Dunbar: A Critical Exposition of the Poems* (Edinburgh, 1960). (A fine study focusing on the socio-cultural milieu.)

DYER, Sir Edward (1543–1607), courtier, diplomat, and poet, knighted in 1596. Had been educated at Oxford, and had grown up with Sidney and Greville, and was part of their group, sometimes referred to as the 'Areopagus', in the late 1570s and shortly thereafter. But he was never as prominent a figure as they, either as a courtier or poet. His poetry circulated at Court, but remained uncollected, even though it appears frequently in miscellanies and is referred to often in incidental references. His most famous lyric, 'My Mind to Me a Kingdom Is', is frequently anthologized.

ELIZABETH I (1533–1603), Queen of England (1558–1603), daughter of Henry VIII and Ann Boleyn, she came to the throne strongly supported by Protestants; by personal force and political cunning, held together the warring factions of the age. She wrote verse occasionally, but it was never published or collected in her lifetime, although her learning was frequently mentioned, for example, by Puttenham who speaks of how her 'noble muse easily surmounteth all the rest that have written before her time or since'.

> Bradner, Lester, ed., *Poems of Elizabeth I* (Providence, 1964).

FOWLER, William (1560–1612), Scottish poet, attended St Leonard's College and St Andrews; and worked as a Protestant spy. Studied civil law in Paris. None of his poetry was published in his lifetime, but it included a collection of seventy-two sonnets, *The Tarantula of Love*, and a rather wordy and jumbled translation of Petrarch's *Trionfi*. He became a Protestant clergyman, came south with King James and helped in the preparation of the King's political treatise, *Basilikon Doron*.

> Meikle, H. W., ed., *Works* (Edinburgh, 1914).

See: Jack, R. D. S., 'William Fowler and Italian Literature', *MLR*, 65 (1970), 481–92. (Continental influences on the Scottish Renaissance.)

FRAUNCE, Abraham (1557–1633), schoolmaster, historian, translator, minor poet. Protégé of the Countess of Pembroke, a member of her Wilton House Circle, and constant praiser of her bounty and talent. He was one of the most assiduous practitioners of hexameter verse, arguing for and exemplifying the adaption of classical metre into English.

> Snare, Gerald, ed., *The Third Part of the Countess of Pembroke's Ivychurch* (Northridge, 1975). (Classical affinities, mythology.)

See: Attridge, Derek, *Well-Weighed Syllables* (Cambridge, 1974). (A judicious account which sees Fraunce as the best practitioner of classical metres.)

GASCOIGNE, George (1542?–77), soldier, courtier, poet, fiction writer. Born into Bedfordshire gentry, educated at Cambridge and Gray's Inn. Became courtier and MP for Bedford, but to escape being prosecuted for debt, fled to the Low Countries and became a soldier. One of the earliest professional writers in England. In the last thirty years or so, has become increasingly seen as the most interesting English poet between Wyatt and Sidney, as well as the most coherent literary theorist in England before Sidney.

> Cunliffe, J. W., ed., *Complete Works*, (2 vols, Cambridge, 1907–10).
> Prouty, C. T., *A Hundreth Sundrie Flowers* (Columbia, Missouri, 1942). (Gascoigne's most important poems; see also the edition by B. M. Ward and R. L. Miller (Port Washington, New York, 1975.)
> *Notes of Instruction in English Verse*, reprinted in G. Gregory Smith, ed., *Elizabethan Critical Essays* (Oxford, 1904–6).

The Steele Glas and the Complaint of Phylomene, A critical edition, (Salzburg, 1975).

See: Johnson, Ronald C., *George Gascoigne* (New York, 1972). (A useful introduction in the Twayne Series.)
Mills, Jerry L., 'Recent Studies in Gascoigne', *ELR*, 3 (1973), 322–26. (An account of recent criticism.)

GOOGE (or GOUGE), Barnabe (1540–94), kinsman of Sir William Cecil, educated at Oxford and Cambridge. Primarily a translator or adaptor of the classics, Googe translated moral and religious works as part of the Protestant progaganda movement of the 1560s and 1570s. His *Eclogues* (1563) are the product of a bright student of poetry, and are among the earliest example of pastoral eclogues in English. Like other mid-century poets, his work is conventional, alliterative, mainly written in fourteeners.

Stephens, Frank, ed., *Selected Poems of Barnabe Googe* (Denver, 1981). (A useful selection.)

See: Sheidley, William E., *Barnabe Googe* (Boston, 1981). (A Twayne survey.) A study by Judith Kennedy is in preparation.

GREVILLE, Fulke, Lord Brooke (1554–1628), poet, statesman, landowner, friend of Sir Philip Sidney. Born in Warwickshire; educated at Shrewsbury with Sidney, and at Cambridge. Went to Court with Sidney in 1577, and remained closely associated with the Sidneys during his early career, an account of which he gave in a revealing *Life* of Sidney, written about 1610 as he looked back from what he saw as the less illuminated days of the Jacobean Court, but not published until 1652. Greville served in many political positions, including a period as Lord Chancellor under James, and was one of the longest surviving public servants of the period. He was a generous patron of writers, but was himself quite reticent about his own poetry – except for the series of verse treatises and other public poems. His most significant work – one of the major collections of poetry in the period – was *Caelica*, a kind of poetic diary, written in quasi-Petrarchan manner, over perhaps forty years. He died in 1628 from a wound inflicted by a servant who believed he had been cut out of Greville's will.

Grosart, A. B., ed., *Works* (4 vols, 1870).
Bullough, Geoffrey, ed., *The Poems and Dramas* (2 vols, Edinburgh, 1983). (The standard edition along with the next item.)
Wilkes, G. A., ed., *The Remains* (1965). (Completes the standard edition.)
Gunn, Thomas, ed., *Selected Poems of Fulke Greville* (1968). (A stimulating selection, superbly introduced.)
Smith, N. C., ed., *Life of Sidney* (Oxford, 1907). (The only accessible edition, although textually unsound, soon to be superseded by John Goews's Clarendon edition).

See: Rebholz, Ronald, *The Life of Fulke Greville* (Oxford, 1971). (A first-rate study.)
Rees, Joan, *Fulke Greville, Lord Brooke* (1971). (A useful overview.)
Waswo, Richard, *The Fatal Mirror: Themes and Techniques in the Poetry of Fulke Greville* (Charlottesville, 1972). (A close reading of the poems.)
Waller, G. F., 'Fulke Greville's Struggle with Calvinism', *SN*, 44 (1972), 295–314. (Theological interests.)
Warkentin, Germaine, 'Greville's *Caelica* and the Fullness of Time', *English Studies in Canada*, 6 (1980), 398–408. (Thematic study.)

HALL, Joseph (1574–1656), clergyman, satirist, poet. Born at Ashby de la Zouch and
educated at Emmanuel College, Cambridge. He had Puritan affinities, and
though his early literary career made him known as a satirist in verse and prose,
he was intent on a clerical career and proceeded to a B.D. (1603) and then D.D.
(1612). He later became Bishop of Norwich. His theological works, published
from 1605 on, were mainly polemical, continuing the wit and learning with
which he packs his satires. *Virgidemiarum* (1957) was a landmark in the satiric
revival of the 1590s. In it he claimed to be the first English satirist.

> Davenport, A., ed., *Poems* (Liverpool, 1949). (Standard edition.)

> See: Huntley, Frank, L., *Bishop Joseph Hall, 1574 – 1656: A Bibliographical
> and Critical Study*. (Cambridge, 1979). (Thorough, scholarly.)
> McCabe, Richard A., *Joseph Hall, A Study in Satire and Meditation*
> (Oxford, 1982). (Satire, religious ideas.)
> Cortell, Ronald J., 'Joseph Hall and Protestant Meditation,' *TSLL*, 20
> (1978), 367–85. (Relates Hall to the Protestant devotional tradition.)

HAWES, Stephen (1475?–1523), courtier, poet in Henry VII's reign. Educated at
Oxford, travelled on the continent, served as diplomat and civil servant. His
poetry includes long allegorical and moral works, including *The Pastyme of
Pleasure* (1509?).

> Spang, Frank J., ed., *The Works of Stephen Hawes* (Delmar, 1975).
> Gluck, Florence W., and Morgan, Alice B., eds., *The Minor Poetry of
> Stephen Hawes* (1974).

> See: Edwards, A. S. G., *Stephen Hawes* (Boston, 1982). (An unusually good
> Twayne survey.)

HENRYSON, Robert (1429?–1508?), Scottish poet, lawyer, notary and
schoolmaster, and one of the most important medieval poets of Europe. The
Scottish equivalent (and in some few ways superior) to Chaucer, Henryson's
poetry marks the high point of the early Scottish Renaissance. Information on
his life is limited, but he probably studied in Paris and seems to have been a
teacher at Dunfermline Abbey. His poetry blends a traditional medievalism, a
Chaucerian and urbane humour, fluent narrative control and rhetorical
vivacity, with a sharp and often tragic moralism. His major works (although a
little outside the period covered by this study, they are none the less a mark of
the richness of the late medieval Scots tradition as opposed to the English) are:
The Moral Fabillis, which reworks the old Aesopian material, the magnificent
and sombre *Testament of Cresseid*, which extends and deepens Chaucer's great
poem, and *Orpheus and Erudices*, another moral reworking of classical
mythology.

> Elliott, Charles, ed., *Robert Henryson: Poems* (Oxford, 1974).
> Wood, G. Harvey, ed., *Poems and Fables* (Edinburgh, 1958).

> See: MacQueen, John, *Robert Henryson* (Oxford, 1967). (Still the standard
> study.)
> Jamieson, I. W. A., 'Henryson's Fabillis: An Essay towards a
> Reevaluation', *Words*, 2 (1968), 20–31.
> Kindrick, Robert L., *Robert Henryson* (Boston, 1979). (A Twayne
> survey which needs to be complemented by MacQueen.)
> MacDiarmid, Matthew P., *Robert Henryson* (Edinburgh, 1981).
> (Detailed, commonsensical, a little too patriotic.)

HOWELL, Thomas (fl. 1568–81), his life is obscure, but he was attached to the Earl of Salisbury and the Countess of Pembroke. *Devices* (1581) was written at Wilton and dedicated to her. He seems to have been at Wilton during the time Sidney was working on the *Arcadia*, since there are references to it in one of his poems.

> Grosart, A. B., ed., *The Poems of Thomas Howell* (1879).

JAMES VI and I (1566–1625), King of Scotland (1567–1625) and of England (1603–25). Among James's many works are political and theological writings including *Basilikon Doron* (1599) and *A Counterblast to Tobacco* (1604). He supported poetry generously, seeing poets as part of the necessary entourage of a learned and cultured monarch. He created an important group, the 'Castalian' poets, in Scotland, and in England supported, among others, Jonson and Donne.

> *The Essays of a Prentise on the Divine Art of Poesie* (reprinted Edinburgh 1955).

See: Akrigg, G. P. V., 'The Literary Achievements of King James I', *UTQ*, 44 (1975), 115–29.
Jack, Ronald D., 'James VI and Renaissance Poetic Theory', *English*, 16 (1967), 208–11.

LINDSAY, Sir David (1490?–1555), Scottish courtier and poet. Born into a prosperous family, and may have attended St Andrews. By 1511, he was at the Court of James IV and closely associated with the King. Under James V, too, he was a courtier and diplomat. He wrote medieval dream allegories like *The Dreme* (1528) and a large amount of public poetry, including *An Pleasant Satyre of the Thrie Estaitis* (1540), *The Monarchie* (1554), and the *History of Squire Meldrum* (1582).

> Small, J. and Hall, F., eds, *Works* (New York, 1969).

See: Clewitt, Richard M., Jr, 'Rhetorical Strategy and Structure in Three of Sir David Lindsay's Poems', *SEL*, 16 (1976), 3–14.

MARLOWE, Christopher (1564–93), a major dramatist as well as a poet. He was the son of a prosperous Canterbury shoemaker, attended Corpus Christi, Cambridge, and probably became a member of Walsingham's secret service, spying for England on the continent. On his return to London, he worked for the Earl of Nottingham's theatrical Company in the late 1580s. He was killed in a tavern brawl, possibly at the instigation of the government. His best-known poems are *Hero and Leander* (1598) which was completed by Chapman, and 'The Passionate Shepherd to his Love' which has a companion piece by Ralegh.

> Orgel, Stephen, ed., *The Complete Poems and Translations of Christopher Marlowe* (Harmondsworth, 1971). (The best modern edition.)

See: Bush, Douglas, *Mythology and the Renaissance Tradition in English Poetry* (revised edition New York, 1963).
Post, Jonathan F. S., 'Recent Studies in Marlowe (1968–1976)', *RES*, 29 (1978), 36–61. (A useful survey.)
Drew, Cynthia, 'Hero and Leander: A Male Perspective on Female Sexuality', *Journal of Women's Studies in Literature*, 1 (1979), 273–85.

MARSTON, John (1575–1634), one of the bright young satirists of the 1590s who, like Hall, later became a clergyman. Born in Oxfordshire, he was the son of a lawyer, attended Brasenose, Oxford, and the Middle Temple. His *Pygmalions Image* (1598) was a fashionable piece of erotic verse in the vein of *Hero and*

Leander and *Venus and Adonis*. He published satires, which were banned in 1599 along with satiric writings by others. He became a dramatist, collaborating with Dekker and others, quarrelling and later reconciled with Jonson. In 1609 he was ordained, and became a country parson in Hampshire. His most important poems are the satires which, along with Hall's and Donne's, are the high point of the fashion in the 1590s. His major collections are *The Metamorphosis of Pygmalions Image* (1598), and *The Scourge of Villaine* (1598).

> Davenport, Arnold, ed., *Poems* (Liverpool, 1961).

See: Ingram, R. W., *John Marston* (Boston, 1978). (The Twayne survey.)
       McGrath, Lynnette, 'John Marston's Mismanaged Irony: The Poetic
       Satires', *TSLL*, 18 (1976), 393–408.

MONTGOMERIE, Alexander (1545?–98), Scottish courtier and poet who was active in James VI's Court in Scotland among the Castalian poets. He had Catholic sympathies and was banished from Scotland; he probably died abroad. His poetry combines religious allegory and complex lyrical grace.

> Shire, Helena M., ed., *Songs and Poems* (Edinburgh, 1960).

See: Jack, Ronald D. S., 'The Lyrics of Alexander Montgomerie', *RES*, n.s. 20
       (1969), 168–81.

MORE, Sir Thomas (1478–1535), courtier, humanist, statesman and (to Catholics) martyr and saint. His greatest contribution to literature is *Utopia* (1516). His poetry plays a small but interesting part in his life and works, his best work being a collection of Latin epigrams and some English poems. They will be adequately edited in the forthcoming Yale edition of his complete works.

> Campbell, W. E., ed., *The English Works of Sir Thomas More* (2 vols, 1931).

See: Willow, Mary Edith, *An Analysis of the English Poems of St Thomas More*
       (Nieuwkoop, 1974).

RALEGH, Sir Walter (1552?–1618), courtier, explorer, statesman, philosopher, historian, poet – a man of many roles and parts. Born into Devonshire gentry, his rough provincial speech and striking manners were legendary. By the mid 1570s he was a great favourite of the Queen's at Court and seemingly inseparable from her. He led expeditions to Virginia and Guiana, and dominated the Court until he was found to have married one of Elizabeth's ladies-in-waiting without the Queen's consent. He was imprisoned and though eventually released, never regained his status. With James taking the throne, he was tried for alleged conspiracy, imprisoned in the Tower for over ten years and then released for a last expedition to South America, after the failure of which he was executed. His major work is the encyclopaedic, sombre *History of the World*. His poems were written incidentally, occasionally copied into miscellanies, but never published. The standard editions of his poems are unreliable and we await an adequate edition.

> *Works* (8 vols, 1829; reprinted New York, 1962).
> Latham, Agnes, ed., *Selected Prose and Poetry* (1965).
> *The Poetry of Sir Walter Ralegh* (1960). (The Muses Library edition.)
> Oakeshott, Walter F., *The Queen and the Poet*(1960). (Entertaining but
>   suspect).
> Ruddick, Michael, 'The Poems of Sir Walter Ralegh: An Edition'
>   (unpublished doctoral dissertation, Chicago, 1970). The best discussion of
>   the canon.

See: Greenblatt, Stephen, *Sir Walter Ralegh: The Renaissance Man and His Roles*
(New Haven, 1973). (A pioneering study of Raleigh's shifting 'selves'.)
Tennenhouse, Leonard, 'Sir Walter Ralegh and the Literature of Clientage',
in *Patronage in the Renaissance*, ed. by Stephen Orgel and Guy Fitch Lytle
(Princeton, 1981), pp. 235–58.
Waller, Gary F., 'Sir Walter Ralegh', in *Critical Essays on Poetry*, ed. by F.
Magill (Pasadena, 1982), pp. 2301–9.

SACKVILLE, Thomas, Earl of Dorset (1536–1608), aristocratic family; educated at both
Oxford and Cambridge and later Chancellor of both. Attended the Inner Temple
and became a leading courtier and statesman of the early part of Elizabeth's reign,
serving eventually as Lord Treasurer. About 1561 he wrote, along with Thomas
Norton, the play *Gorboduc*, the first blank verse tragedy in English. He collaborated
with William Baldwin and others to produce *A Mirror for Magistrates* (1563 and
subsequent editions), a collection of verse stories of prominent monarchs and
statesmen. Sackville's Induction and the accousnt of the tragedy of Henry, Duke of
Buckingham are probably the best parts of the work.

Campbell, Lily B., ed., *The Mirror for Magistrates* (Cambridge, 1946; New
York, 1960).

See: Berlin, N., *Thomas Sackville* (New York, 1976). (A survey.)

SCOTT, Alexander (?1525–?1584), perhaps the most interesting poet of the mid–century
period in Scotland, whose work circulated widely at the Scottish Court and was
collected in the Bannatyne Manuscript. Scott is the best Scottish poet of the period
after Dunbar.

MacQueen, John, ed., *Ballattis of Luve* (Edinburgh, 1970); *Alexander Scott
and Scottish Court Poetry of the Middle Sixteenth Century* (1968).

SHAKESPEARE, William (1654–1616), dramatist. Born at Stratford-upon-Avon to a
prosperous yeoman family, probably educated at Stratford Grammar School. In
London in the late 1580s, working for various theatre companies, especially the
King's Men. After a successful theatrical career, retired to Stratford 1611. His
poems were probably all written early in his career.

Booth, Stephen, ed., *Shakespeare's Sonnets* (1979). (The best modern
edition.)
Prince, F. T., ed., *William Shakespeare: The Poems* (1963).

See: Knights, L. C., *Explorations* (Harmondsworth, 1964). (Reprints an earlier
Scrutiny article on Time in the Sonnets.)
Winny, James, *The Master-Mistress: A Study of Shakespeare's Sonnets* (1968).
Martin, Philip, *Shakespeare's Sonnets: Self, Love, and Art* (1972).
Melchiori, Giorgio, *Shakespeare's Dramatic Meditations* (1976). (Statistical
and philosophical analysis of great suggestiveness.)
Waller, Gary F., 'William Shakespeare', *Critical Essays on Poetry*, ed. by F.
Magill (Pasadena, 1982), pp. 2209–38.

SHEPHERD, Luke (fl. 1548–54), a shadowy, mid-century Protestant propagandist poet,
whose works in Latin and English include a number of popular religious satires in
the mode of Skelton, e.g. *Jon Bon and Mast Person* (1548) and *The Upcheringe of the
Messe* (1548?).

King, John N., *English Reformation Literature* (Princeton, 1982). (Has a useful
discussion.)

SIDNEY, Mary, Countess of Pembroke (1564–1621), sister of Sir Philip Sidney, to whose ideals she devoted most of her adult life. Born at Penshurst Place, she was educated at home, and became one of the most learned ladies of the age. She married William Herbert, Earl of Pembroke, set up what one of her followers termed a 'little court' at Wilton House, and became one of the most widely praised patrons of the age and, as well, a fine poet in her own right. Her major works include a translation of Petrarch's *Trionfo della Morte*, a verse translation of Garnier's play *Marc-Antoine*, and other works.

> Rathmell, J. C. A., ed., *The Psalms of Sir Philip Sidney and the Countess of Pembroke* (New York, 1963).
>
> Waller, G. F., ed., *The Triumph of Death and Other Unpublished and Uncollected Poems* (Salzburg, 1977).

See: Waller, G. F., *Mary Sidney, Countess of Pembroke* (Salzburg, 1979). (A biographical and critical study.)

> Roberts, Josephine A. 'Mary Sidney, Countess of Pembroke', *ELR*, (1985), 426–39. (A valuable, detailed annotated bibliography).
>
> *Sidney Newsletter* (Waterloo, Ontario 1980–83; Guelph, Ontario, 1983–   ).

SIDNEY, Sir Philip (1562–86), Elizabethan England's most celebrated courtier and poet whose death in 1586 created a legend even more powerful than his actual literary achievement. Born at Penshurst Place, he was educated at Shrewsbury and Oxford, went on a triumphant tour of Europe where he was befriended by monarchs, statesmen, and literary figures. He returned to the English Court where he allied himself to the Earl of Leicester's Protestant faction and never quite gained the influence with the Queen he desired. Sent to the Low Countries as Governor of Flushing, he was mortally wounded in battle, and given a hero's funeral, mourned by friends and enemies alike. *Astrophil and Stella* (1581–82) is the first major Petrarchan collection in English; his treatise, *The Defence* (in one version called the *Apology*) is the first major treatment of poetry in English in the period, and his *Arcadia*, a long prose romance written first for his sister and then revised, is the most important prose fiction in English before Richardson. None of his work was published in his lifetime, though it circulated widely at Court and among the members of his Circle, which included Greville, his sister Mary, brother Robert, Dyer, and others.

> Ringler, William A., Jr, ed., *The Poems of Sir Philip Sidney* (Oxford, 1962). (A landmark edition.)
>
> Duncan-Jones, Katherine, and van Dorsten, Jan., eds, *Miscellaneous Prose of Sir Philip Sidney* (Oxford, 1973). (Contains the *Defence* and other works.) The letters will appear edited by Charles Levy and Roger Kuin.
>
> Kimbrough, Robert, ed., *Prose and Poetry* (revised edition 1982). (A useful selection.)

See: Kalstone, David, *Sidney's Poetry: Contexts and Interpretations* (Cambridge, Mass., 1965). (Close analysis.)

> Levao, Ronald, 'Sidney's "Feigned Apology"', *PMLA*, 94 (1979), 223–33. (A stimulating reading of the rhetoric of the *Defence*.)
>
> McCoy, Richard C., *Sir Philip Sidney: Rebellion in Arcadia* (New Brunswick, 1979). (An exciting reading of the cultural politics of Sidney's career.)
>
> Hamilton, A. C., *Sir Philip Sidney* (Cambridge, 1980). (The best modern overview.)
>
> Sinfield, Alan, 'Sidney and Astrophil', *'SEL'*, 20 (1980), 25–41.

Sessons, William A., ed., *New Readings of Sidney: Experiment and Tradition*, in *Studies in the Literary Imagination*, 15 (1982). (Includes essays by Jane Hedley, G. F. Waller, Annabel Patterson, and Germaine Warkentin.)

Waller, G. F., 'Sir Philip Sidney', in *Critical Essays on Poetry*, ed. by F. Magill (Pasadena, 1982), pp. 2570–81.

Sidney Newsletter (Waterloo, Ontario, 1980–83; Guelph, Ontario, 1983–   ).

Jones, Ann and Stallybrass, Peter, 'The Politics of *Astrophil and Stella*', *SEL*, 24 (1984), 53–68. (A brilliant essay, on the interaction of literary and cultural codes.)

Waller, Gary F. and Moore, Michael D., eds., *Sir Philip Sidney and the Interpretation of Renaissance Culture* (1984). (Includes essays by Maurice Evans, S. K. Heninger Jr, Marion Campbell, Jacqueline Miller, Germaine Warkentin and Jon Quitslund. A collection of both traditional and revisionist views.)

Fienberg, Nona, 'The Emergence of Stella in *Astrophil and Stella*,' *SEL*, 25 (1985), 5–19. (Feminist reading).

Wayne, Don E., *Penshurst: The Semiotics of Place and the Poetics of History* (Madison, 1984). (An intriguing analysis of Jonson's poem on Penshurst and the Sidney family).

SIDNEY, Sir Robert, Lord de Isle (1563–1626), younger brother of Philip and Mary. His career existed under the shadow of his brother whom he succeeded as Governor of Flushing. Returning to the Elizabethan Court in the mid 1590s he enjoyed a moderately successful public career but most of his commitment went to his estate at Penshurst Place, which is celebrated in Ben Jonson's 'To Penshurst'. Sidney was not widely known as a poet until the 1970s when his poetry was first identified by P. J. Croft.

Croft, P. J., ed., *The Poems of Robert Sidney: Edited from the poet's autograph notebook* (Oxford, 1984). (A fine edition, not very imaginative in its critical perspective).

Duncan-Jones, Katherine, ed., 'The Poems of Sir Robert Sidney', *English*, no. 136 (1981), 3–72. (But see Deborah K. Wright, 'Modern-Spelling text of Robert Sidney's Poems Proves Disappointing', *SNew*, 3, no. 1 (1982), 12–16.)

See: Croft, P. J., *Autograph Poetry in the English Language* (Oxford, 1973), vol. 1. (Contains reproduction and discussion of one of the poems.)

Hay, Millicent V., *The Life of Robert Sidney, Earl of Leicester (1563–1626)* (Washington, 1985). (A rather pedestrian account).

'"The Sad Pilgrim": The Poetry of Sir Robert Sidney,' *Dalhousie Review*, 55 (1975–76), 689–705.

Waller, Gary F., '"My Wants and your Perfections": Elizabethan England's Newest Poet', *Ariel*, 8 (1977), 3–14.

Wright, Deborah K., The Poetry of Robert Sidney: A Critical Study of his Autograph Manuscript' (unpublished dissertation, Miami University of Ohio, 1980).

Waller, Gary F., 'Sir Robert Sidney', in *Critical Essays on Poetry*, ed. by F. Magill (Pasadena, 1982), pp. 2582–89.

Sidney Newsletter (Waterloo, Ontario, 1980–83; Guelph, Ontario, 1983–   ).

SKELTON, John (1460?–1529), priest, courtier, and the most striking poet of the early sixteenth century in England. Educated at Oxford and Cambridge, and attached to the household of Henry VII and later Henry VIII, he became rector of Diss, Norfolk, but spent most of his time at Court. His verse is largely

satiric and popular: in particular he attacked Cardinal Wolsey, formerly a
patron, and he had to take sanctuary with the Abbot of Westminster until his
death just before Wolsey's fall from power in 1529. His poetry was denigrated
by most late Elizabethan courtly commentators who found it rough in manner
and uncourtly in sentiment.

> Kinsman, Robert S., ed., *Poems* (Oxford, 1969).

> See: Fish, Stanley, *John Skelton's Poetry* (New Haven, 1965).
> Edwards, A. S. G., ed., *Skelton: The Critical Heritage* (1981). (An
> account of criticism since Skelton's time.)

SMITH, William (1546?–??), little is known of his life: he was one of the many
Petrarchan poets flourishing in the 1590s, and may have had or wanted some
attachment to the Countess of Pembroke's household.

> Sasek, L. A., ed., *The Poetry of William Smith* (Baton Rouge, 1970). (A
> useful edition.)

> See: Van den Berg, Kent T., 'An Elizabethan Allegory of Time by William
> Smith', *ELR*, 6 (1976), 40–59.

SPENSER, Edmund (1552–99) the sixteenth century's most outstanding public poet,
whose *The Faerie Queene* made great claims for both English epic poetry and
the Elizabethan regime. Born in London and educated at Merchant Taylors'
School and Cambridge. As early as the late 1560s, in fact, he was writing
poetry, and by 1579 published the *Shepheardes Calender*, which was a milestone
in the history of English poetry. He was employed by the Earl of Leicester and
so came into contact with Sidney and his Circle. He went to Ireland in 1580,
remaining there in various public posts until the year before his death, but had
frequent contacts with the Court, notably in 1590, when he visited to oversee
the publication of the first three books of his epic. Greatly disillusioned by the
atmosphere at Court and especially by the treatment of his friend and patron
Sir Walter Ralegh, the last books of the poem became less celebratory. But he
remained a faithful servant of the regime: the Queen granted him a life pension
in 1591, he advocated increased pressure upon the Irish in *A View of the Present
State of Ireland*, and finally he was forced to flee Ireland under the threat of a
rising under the Earl of Tyrone. He returned to England in 1598 where he died
a month later.

There is a huge literature on Spenser; its monumentality is summed up by the
new *Spenser Encyclopedia*, ed. by A. C. Hamilton *et al.* (Toronto, 1986), in
which the many (and varied) modern schools of criticism are represented. But
until very recently, most scholarship and criticism on *The Faerie Queene* in
particular has taken the poem very much at its face value. Goldberg's book (see
below) marked the start of a new phase of criticism.

> Greenlaw, E. *et al.*, eds, *Works*, Variorum Edition (10 vols, Baltimore
> 1932–58; reprinted 1966).
> Smith, J. C., and De Selincourt, E., eds, *Poetical Works* (3 vols,
> Oxford, 1909–10).
> Hamilton, A. C., ed., *The Faerie Queene* (1977). (The Longman
> Annotated Poets edition; the best annotated modern edition.)
> Roche, Thomas P. Jr, ed., *The Faerie Queene* (New Haven, 1981). (Also
> a useful edition.)

> See: Lewis, C. S., *The Allegory of Love* (Oxford, 1936). (A classic study.)

Hieatt, A. Kent, *Short Times Endless Monument: The Symbolism of the Numbers in Spenser's Epithalamion* (New York, 1960). (Numerological reading of one of Spenser's more charming poems.)

Fowler, A. D. S., *Spenser and the Numbers of Time* (1964). (A numerological analysis, but see W. Nelson in *RenQ*, 18 (1965).)

Roche, Thomas P. Jr, *The Kindly Flame – A Study of the Third and Fourth Book of Spenser's Faerie Queene*, (Princeton, 1964).

Cheney, Donald, *Spenser's Image of Nature: Wild Man and Shepherd in the 'Faerie Queene'* (New Haven, 1966).

Fowler, Alastair, ed., *Spenser's Images of Life* (Cambridge, 1967). (C.S. Lewis's Cambridge Lectures; a delightful introduction.)

Williams, Arnold, *Flower on a Lowly Stalk: The Faerie Queene VI* (East Lansing, 1967).

Alpers, Paul J., *The Poetry of the Faerie Queene* (Princeton, 1967). (A New Critical reading.)

Sale, Roger, *Reading Spenser* (New York, 1968). (Still one of the best introductions.)

Evans, Maurice, *Spenser's Anatomy of Heroism* (Cambridge, 1970). (Puritan elements in the epic.)

Freeman, Rosemary, *The Faerie Queene: A Companion for Readers* (1970). (An overview.)

Tonkin, Humphrey, *Spenser's Curious Pastoral: Book Six of the Faerie Queene* (Oxford, 1972).

Parker, Patricia A., *Inescapable Romance* (Princeton, 1979). (Rigorous neo-formalist reading of romance.)

Quilligan, Maureen, *The Language of Allegory* (Ithaca, 1979). (Fine linguistically sophisticated approach to allegory.)

Goldberg, Jonathan, *Endlesse Worke: Spenser and the Structures of Discourse* (Baltimore, 1981). (An important landmark in Spenser criticism: the first deconstructive reading.) See also the 'new historical' Spenser chapter in Goldberg's *James I and the Politics of Literature* (Baltimore, 1983).

There is no collection of recent essays on Spenser equivalent in importance to the Sessions and Waller/Moore volumes on Sidney; older collections of essays include A. C. Hamilton, ed., *Essential Articles for the Study of Edmund Spenser* (Hamden, 1972). See also the *Spenser Newsletter* (1968–   ) (an invaluable publication, now published at Albany, New York).

SURREY, Henry Howard, Earl of (1517?–47), aristocrat, soldier, courtier, poet. Educated amidst the early Tudor humanists and learned in classical and modern languages. In 1546, was convicted for treason and executed in 1547. Had acquired a reputation for a quarrelsome, arrogant but magnificent figure as a courtier. His poetry, which includes some of the earliest Petrarchan verse in England, was not published in his lifetime, but appeared in Tottel's *Miscellany* (1557), along with those of Wyatt and others. In the sixteenth century, Surrey's poems were generally praised above Wyatt's probably because he was an aristocrat but, although still acknowledged for its technical pioneering, it has not continued to have such a high reputation. There is as yet no satisfactory complete modern study; William A. Sessions's Twayne volume is forthcoming.

Jones, Emrys, ed., *Poems* (Oxford, 1964).

See: Davis, Walter R., 'Contexts in Surrey's Poetry', *ELR*, 4 (1974), 40–55.
Tromly, Frederic B., 'Surrey's Fidelity to Wyatt in "Wyatt Resteth Here"', *SP*, 77 (1980), 376–87.

TURBERVILLE, George (1540?–1610), educated at New College and The Inns of Court, and became courtier and diplomat. In 1568 went to Russia, and some of his poems deal with what he saw there. Most of his verse is lugubrious, moralizing, and sing-song. There are some translations of Ovid and Mantuan which are reasonably competent and he followed in Googe's footsteps by writing eclogues.

> Sheidley, William A., *George Turberville* (New York, 1981). (A Twayne survey.)

VERE, Edward de, Earl of Oxford (1550–1604), related to Surrey and to Arthur Golding. Oxford was a favourite of the Queen's, and a rival to Ralegh. Vain, handsome, and irresponsible, he adopted many Italianate customs into England, and yet was generous patron of writers and the theatre. He quarrelled publicly with Sidney, and with other rivals for the Queen's affections. He sat on the panel of noble judges who condemned Essex in 1601. He was only an occasional poet, whose work circulated in manuscript, and was never collected until long after his death.

> May, Stephen, ed., 'The Poems of Edward de Vere, Seventeenth Earl of Oxford and of Robert Devereux Second Earl of Essex', *SP*, 77, no. 5 (1980), 5–132. (A fine edition.)

WATSON, Thomas (1555–92), probably educated at Oxford, and a prolific translator from Latin and Italian. One of the earliest published Petrarchan collections, his *Passionate Century of Love*, helped bring Petrarch into wider circulation in England.

> Heninger, S. K. Jr, ed., *Passionate Century of Love* (Gainesville, 1964).

WYATT, Sir Thomas (1503–42), courtier, diplomat and probably one of Queen Anne Boleyn's lovers. His poems, along with some by Surrey, Vaux and others, first appeared in Tottel's *Miscellany* (1557) and constitute the first substantial body of poetry in English of real importance between Chaucer and Sidney. Wyatt's reputation has increased enormously since his death, in the twentieth century in particular. His work is often seen as anticipating the seemingly realistic tones of Greville or Donne later in the century. He crammed an enormous amount into his thirty-nine years. He was born in Kent, educated at St John's Cambridge, and became a seasoned diplomat before he was twenty-five. Marshall of Calais 1528–32, knighted in 1536, imprisoned under suspicion of treason in 1536, but released, a pattern that was repeated in 1541. In 1542, he fell ill while on a diplomatic mission and died. His poetry brought the power of Petrarchan love poetry into English for the first time. He visited Italy in 1527, and his poems were widely circulated at Court. Some appeared in *The Court of Venus* (1540), but most waited until Tottel's *Miscellany*.

> Daalder, Joost. ed., *Collected Poems* (1974).
> Rebholtz, Richard, ed., *Collected Poems* (1978).

See:
> Southall, Raymond, *The Courtly Maker: An Essay on the Poetry of Wyatt and his Contemporaries* (1954). (Excellent on court background.)
> Thompson, Patricia, *Sir Thomas Wyatt and his Background* (1964). (Old-fashioned but still useful.)
> Freedman, Donald M., 'The Mind in the Room: Wyatt's "They Flee From Me"'. *SEL*, 7 (1967), 1–13.
> Leonard, Nancy S., 'The Speaker in Wyatt's Lyric Poetry', *HLQ*, 41 (1977), 1–8.
> Kamholtz, Jonathan Z., 'Thomas Wyatt's Poetry: The Politics of Love', *Criticism*, 20 (1978), 349–65.
> Greenblatt, Stephen, *Renaissance Self-Fashioning* (Chicago, 1980). (Important revisionist study.)

Index